MAKING THE SCENE:
YORKVILLE AND HIP TORONTO IN THE 1960S

Making the Scene is a history of 1960s Yorkville, Toronto's counter-cultural mecca. It narrates the hip Village's development from its early coffee-house days, when folksingers such as Neil Young and Joni Mitchell flocked to the scene, to its tumultuous, drug-fuelled final months. A flashpoint for hip youth, politicians, parents, and journalists alike, Yorkville was also a battleground over identity, territory, and power. Stuart Henderson explores how this neighbourhood came to be regarded as an alternative space both as a geographic area and as a symbol of hip Toronto in the cultural imagination.

Through recently unearthed documents and underground press coverage, Henderson pays special attention to voices that typically aren't heard in the story of Yorkville – including those of women, working-class youth, business owners, and municipal authorities. Through a local history, *Making the Scene* offers new, exciting ways to think about the phenomenon of counterculture and urban manifestations of a hip identity as they have emerged in cities across North America and beyond.

STUART HENDERSON is a SSHRC postdoctoral fellow in the Department of History at York University.

STUART HENDERSON

Making the Scene
Yorkville and Hip Toronto
in the 1960s

UNIVERSITY OF TORONTO PRESS
Toronto Buffalo London

© University of Toronto Press Incorporated 2011
Toronto Buffalo London
www.utppublishing.com
Printed in Canada

ISBN 978-1-4426-4152-5 (cloth)
ISBN 978-1-4426-1071-2 (paper)

Printed on acid-free, 100% post-consumer recycled paper
with vegetable-based inks.

Library and Archives Canada Cataloguing in Publication

Henderson, Stuart Robert, 1977–
Making the scene : Yorkville and hip Toronto in the 1960s / Stuart Henderson.

Includes bibliographical references and index.
ISBN 978-1-4426-4152-5 (bound). – ISBN 978-1-4426-1071-2 (pbk.)

1. Yorkville (Toronto, Ont.) – Social conditions – 20th century.
2. Counterculture – Ontario – Yorkville (Toronto) – History – 20th century.
3. Toronto (Ont.) – Social conditions – 20th century.   4. Counterculture –
Ontario – Toronto – History – 20th century.   I. Title.

FC3097.52.H45 2011   971.3'541   C2011-900845-9

This book has been published with the help of a grant from the Canadian
Federation for the Humanities and Social Sciences, through the Aid to
Scholarly Publications Program, using funds provided by the Social
Sciences and Humanities Research Council of Canada.

University of Toronto Press acknowledges the financial assistance to its
publishing program of the Canada Council for the Arts and the
Ontario Arts Council.

 Canada Council   Conseil des Arts    ONTARIO ARTS COUNCIL
for the Arts   du Canada   CONSEIL DES ARTS DE L'ONTARIO

University of Toronto Press acknowledges the financial support of
the Government of Canada through the Canada Book Fund for its
publishing activities.

Yorkville has become not so much a district in Toronto as a word in Toronto's argot. It has only to be uttered. It requires no adjectives, no expanded narration to conjure all sorts of repugnant images in the public mind.

– Michael Valpy, *Globe and Mail*, 16 December 1968

And we rejected the values of the mainstream society. We wanted it to be an alternative way of living and so on: a counterculture, if you want to call it that. We were against the mainstream culture, fair enough; but, we believed in peace and love and understanding, essentially.

– David DePoe, 2005

If you seek authenticity for authenticity's sake, you are no longer authentic.

– Jean-Paul Sartre, 1947–8

Contents

PART FOUR
Hold It, It's Gone, 1968–70

Illustrations follow page 148

Acknowledgments

Making the Scene began as a PhD dissertation at Queen's University and owes much to the collaborative efforts of my supervisors, Karen Dubinsky and Ian McKay. Their guidance and wisdom no doubt saved me from myself on more than one occasion. I have been extremely fortunate to have such helpful, brilliant, and amiable supervisors – my thanks and, as always, my great admiration are theirs to share.

An earlier form of this book was read by Alice Echols, Barrington Walker, Kip Pegley, and Caroline-Isabelle Caron, each of whom offered a wealth of advice and criticisms which helped me to lift my analysis out of the murk. Thanks to Bob Shenton for working tirelessly to find me funding when I was contemplating dropping out of my PhD program. Thanks also to Suzanne Morton, my wonderful MA supervisor, who introduced me to an array of ideas and approaches, most of which are on display in this book in one form or another. And, finally, thanks to Michael Cross, my undergraduate supervisor, who once encouraged a young, unsure hippie kid to write freely, but with purpose. No way I'd still be here if it hadn't been for him.

My clever, insightful, and inspirational colleagues in the Canadian Historical Association have helped me immeasurably to find my voice and to settle down into life as a wandering academic. This is a bigger deal than I had ever expected it would be: having good and supportive friends when you need them is as vital at work as it is at play. Alison Norman, Sean Mills, Cara Spittal, Robin Grazely, Julie Johnson, Ryan Edwardson, Matthew McKean, and Bruce Douville helped make grad school and the weird post-grad-school years both fun and intellectually invigorating. Thanks also to Craig Heron, Marcel Martel, Franca Iacovetta, Ken Cruikshank, Viv Nelles, Kevin Brushett, and Bryan Palmer, all of whom have offered helpful advice, critiques, and support along the way. We are immensely lucky to have so many wonderful people in our little corner of the world.

This project was funded by fellowships, scholarships, and post-doctoral grants, without which none of this would have been possible. Thanks to the Queen's University School of Graduate Studies, the Ontario Graduate Scholarship (OGS) program, the Social Sciences and Humanities Research Council (SSHRC), and the L.R. Wilson Institute for Canadian History at McMaster University.

I offer my gratitude to my interview subjects for their always friendly agreements to work with me towards presenting a fuller picture of the Toronto of their youth. I hope I have done well by their memories. Thanks to Jim Felstiner, Gale Marion Jones, Paul Ferri, and Peter Evans for offering me access to a bunch of material from their private collections. Thanks also to the Harshman Foundation for their generous gift of some two hundred pages of correspondence and inter-office memoranda pertaining to the summer of 1966 in the Village – this material would have been otherwise unavailable.

Thanks to the anonymous readers at the University of Toronto Press, whose sage critiques helped me to bring this thing home, and to UTP's Wayne Herrington and to Curtis Fahey for their editorial guidance. My deepest appreciation goes out to my editor at UTP, Len Husband, who must be commended for two reasons: 1) he is an island of kindness and support in an often frustrating process, and 2) he has *great* taste in rock'n'roll. And a special thank you to my buddy Greg Albisser for contributing the map of Yorkville.

Finally, thanks to my parents, Gordon and Pam, my sisters, Kate and Liz, and all of my extended family and friends, who have helped to build in me the kind of insane self-confidence required to write a five-hundred-page manuscript. I love you all.

Making the Scene is dedicated, with love love love, to Sarah and Angus.

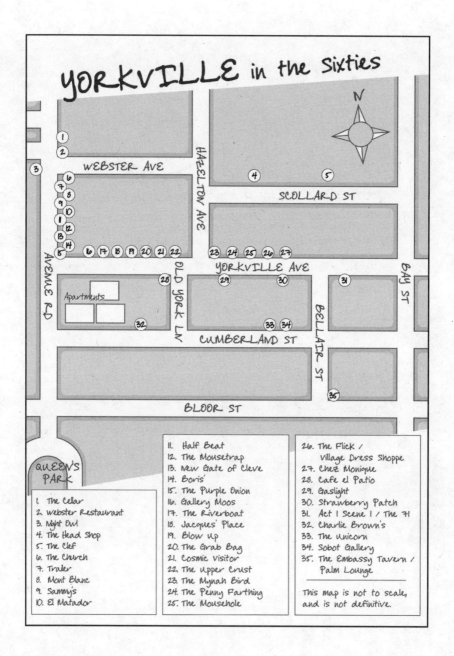

YORKVILLE in the Sixties

WEBSTER AVE

HAZELTON AVE

SCOLLARD ST

YORKVILLE AVE

OLD YORK LN

BELLAIR ST

BAY ST

AVENUE RD

Apartments

CUMBERLAND ST

BLOOR ST

QUEEN'S PARK

1. The Cellar
2. Webster Restaurant
3. Night Owl
4. The Head Shop
5. The Clef
6. The Church
7. Trailer
8. Mont Blanc
9. Sammy's
10. El Matador

11. Half Beat
12. The Mousetrap
13. New Gate of Cleve
14. Boris'
15. The Purple Onion
16. Gallery Moos
17. The Riverboat
18. Jacques' Place
19. Blow Up
20. The Grab Bag
21. Cosmic Visitor
22. The Upper Crust
23. The Mynah Bird
24. The Penny Farthing
25. The Mousehole

26. The Flick /
    Village Dress Shoppe
27. Chez Monique
28. Cafe el Patio
29. Gaslight
30. Strawberry Patch
31. Act 1 Scene 1 / The 71
32. Charlie Brown's
33. The Unicorn
34. Sobot Gallery
35. The Embassy Tavern /
    Palm Lounge

This map is not to scale, and is not definitive.

PART ONE

Setting the Scene, to 1963

1

Remaking the Scene

And those who are beautiful –
oh, who can retain them?

– Rainer Maria Rilke[1]

There was a time when I thought that 'hippies' were the coolest people on earth, and I fully intended to become one when I grew up.[2]

I was, let's say, eight years old. I had been, ever since I was in the cradle, exposed to the music of my parents' generation, the 1960s rock'n'roll that had redefined what teenage life could sound like, had opened up new dimensions of sound and fury, had played soundtrack to countless back-seat fumblings, had fuelled the dreams and desires of a generation. Bored, even at that age, by the overwhelmingly synthetic music that poured over the airwaves in the mid-1980s, I was entranced by what I heard coming through my old man's speakers. The Beatles, the Rolling Stones, the Kinks, the Grateful Dead, Neil Young, Fairport Convention. There are photos of a toddler version of myself, long curls of blond hair falling across my face, standing on tiptoes trying to turn up the volume on our comically ancient Hi-Fi.[3]

My generation, then, or at least my demographic, was brought up by baby boomers. We were raised by the richest cohort in the history of the world, in the most affluent surroundings imaginable and amid the most highly developed technologies of comfort and convenience that had ever been devised. We had nothing to worry about, nothing about which to complain. Our parents loved us, gave us Big Wheels and He-Man toys, let us stay up to watch *Family Ties* and, if they were liberal enough, *Cheers*. We went to schools that had been redefined by our parents' generation – redefined by an influx of so many children into the system that it had seemed that schools were being built faster than homes by the mid-1960s.

In Toronto, where I grew up, and where this story takes place, the baby boomers were in control by the mid-1980s. Already homeowners in their early thirties, they were having second and third kids, tinkering with cars, and mowing lawns just as their folks did. And they were wealthy too. In curious, distorted ways, my demographic – white, Anglo-Saxon, suburban North Toronto wide-eyed kids – reflects its parents' demographic as though through the fun-house mirror. Maybe that's why it was so easy for me, and for so many of my friends, to identify with their time, with the concerns of their teenage years, with their music, literature, ideologies, refusals, dreams. Or, perhaps, as Freud suggested, my own 'archaic heritage … includes not only dispositions, but also ideational contents, *memory traces* of the experiences of former generations.'[4]

Either way, by the time we were teenagers, my friends and I were long-haired, tie-dye-wearing, neo-hippie kids. We smoked grass and tried LSD, some of us even eschewing liquor for drugs not simply because it was more expensive and harder to get (the usual reasons why teens use drugs instead of alcohol) but because we felt booze to be a downer when compared to the transformative powers of dope. We deeply envied what we heard about 'free love,' although we largely failed to implement any aspect of this titillating, but ultimately terrifying, sexual ethic.

If we were lucky, we went to Grateful Dead concerts and saw something of a revival (or persistence) of the 1960s that we were so dejected to have missed. Some of us spoke in hushed tones about the transformative power of such music – the Dead, Phish, the Band, and the Allman Brothers were perennial favourites – about the way that the right guitar solo heard under the right psychedelic conditions could literally *change* us, rearrange our mentality, bring us third-eye insight. Sure, most of us didn't care one way or the other about stuff like this – we just wanted to get lit up, listen to good tunes, hang around with our friends, maybe try to get laid. But isn't that high school all over? What else do North Americans do at that age if not experiment with drugs, sex, music, identity?

The difference was that some of us, and perhaps me especially, were actively trying to re-create a scene over which we all knew we had no real purchase. This was our parents' generation, the mythic 1960s, and we, wishing we could have been there, tried to recuperate something of it every weekend when we blasted Credence Clearwater Revival and ate 'magic' mushrooms, throwing the frisbee around in the sun in our Guatemalan skirts and patchouli oil.

And so we grew up, and most of us 'grew out of it.' We became doctors, lawyers, accountants, and, some of us, perpetual university students. We all, by the old logic, rapidly and effectively 'sold out' to the system, to *the Man*. No matter how much we had talked about rejecting money, business suits, and consumerism when we were seventeen, virtually all of us had immersed ourselves in such waters by the time we reached the age of twenty-five. A combination of cynicism, 'sensibleness,' and disillusionment conspired to relieve us of our collective dreams of living in some new and different, better world. Instead, we wound up inheriting the very world we had initially refused as corrupt, immoral, insane. We had become enamoured of various aspects of the 'real world' (pay cheques, security, the stuff behind the counter at Future Shop), and the ease with which we had fallen into the flow of 'straight society' exposed a truth that we had been unable, and certainly unwilling, to recognize only years before: we had *always* been mainstream.

Our little attempted 'counterculture' was as illusory as every counterculture has always been. That is, put simply, counterculture is best defined not as an alternate system of social interactions and ideologies existing *outside* the expected, dominant culture but rather as the shifting sets of responses, refusals, and acceptances performed by actors in the cultural process. In other words: a hippie does not, never can, exist wholly outside his or her cultural context.

In his or her rejection of this dominant culture, the hippie is in fact operating from within, *not without*, the same culture – he or she, however accidentally, is serving a necessary and by no means aberrant purpose in their refusal of dominant cultural ideology. They are part of the constant call-and-response between dominant powers and ideologies and subaltern powers and ideologies that characterizes what Antonio Gramsci has termed the hegemonic process, the process through which dominant classes seek to retain their dominance.[5] Understood this way, the hippies and their ilk cannot be said to have 'sold out,' or failed, or otherwise shirked their responsibilities by shifting out of the so-called counterculture into the dominant culture by the end of the 1960s. For they had always been a part of something much greater than the simple 'us versus them' relationship that was so commonly articulated by authority figures, parents, politicos, and hippies alike.

What we usually refer to as 'the system,' or 'society,' or even 'the way it is' is by no means pre-determined or inevitable, but it *is* persistent and all-encompassing. One cannot be said to live *outside* the system just because one smokes crack or regularly engages in group sex, as countercultural as those activities may appear. Rather, such activities must be understood to be, to have been, to *always be* part of a wider hegemonic process, the process in which we all play a part. No one is outside this set of relationships, and no activity, no matter how countercultural it may appear, can be said to have taken place outside the wide confines of hegemony.

When I embarked on this project, such ideas were rather fresh in my mind. Why is it, I wondered, that the 1960s generation, and its attendant association with the counterculture which, in so many ways, endeavoured to shake up the status quo, had become the parents of the 1980s, a group of folks who looked nothing like the hirsute, 'beautiful people' they supposedly were as teenagers? How did they become this group of concerned citizens against whom my friends and I felt so compelled to rebel?[6]

And so I, a grown-up second-generation hippie kid, undertook, at the age of twenty-six, a study of the most famous hippie centre in Canada: Toronto's Yorkville district. It was a perfect metaphor for all of this stuff, I decided, not only because it was where bohemian youth *were*, and then suddenly *weren't* (a narrative line that indicates to many the ultimate insubstantiality of hip ideologies and lifestyles), but also because the Yorkville district, for anyone of my generation, is about as far removed as can be from what we understand to be bohemian. Since the early 1970s, and ever more so today, Yorkville has been known to all who have visited its thin streets as the Rolls-Royce of Toronto neighbourhoods. Flashy, absurdly wealthy, home to martini bars and salons and overpriced restaurants, Yorkville is defined by the kinds of joints where conspicuous people wear three-hundred-dollar sunglasses inside at midnight during the Toronto International Film Festival, hoping to be mistaken for a movie star. It's all like some kind of stage, a place where people go to 'see and be seen.' How could this have been Canada's 'hippie ghetto'?

But what if Yorkville was *never* merely a 'hippie ghetto'? What if our memory of this place has become obscured, corrupted, transfigured by years and nostalgia? As I wrote these pages, I tried always to bear in mind something Neil Young wrote in 1974, in a long elegiac song about his years playing folk music in Yorkville coffee houses while looking for a record deal. 'Oh Isabella, proud Isabella,' he sang, substituting the name of a nearby street for the name of the district he was lamenting, 'They tore you down, and ploughed you under / But you were only real with your makeup on / How could I see you, and stay too long?'[7] Only real with her make-up on: What if the very reality of Yorkville was in its facade, its illusions of authenticity, of difference, and, when this facade was no longer needed, its unreality, its desperate *plasticity* was left exposed?

People, in the idiom of the 1960s hip culture, used to use the expression 'making the scene' to refer to being someplace, as though it were the people, not the structure, that constituted the scenery in any given location. (*We made the scene last night around ten o'clock, she made the scene a few hours later*, and so on.) But there is an attractive connotation here, perhaps hidden under layers and decades of underuse, which suggests that the hip folks recognized the power of *presence* in creating meaning in any particular locus. The same way that an actor on a sparse, even empty stage can make the scene around her seem to respond to *her*, and not the other way around, I like to think that the phrase 'making the scene' can refer to the way that we, as human actors, do much the same thing to our own surroundings. And so 'making the scene' in Yorkville was what everyone was up to, and all the time, as the place was up for grabs, as it became a battleground over identity, meaning, and power. In effect, the politicians, hippies, journalists, bikers, 'greasers,' 'speed freaks,' shopowners, and 'teenyboppers' alike were all active participants, all performers, in the continuous making and remaking of the Yorkville scene throughout the 1960s, as each tried to imbue the stage with their own (contrastable, but often overlapping) meanings.

Yet, in the end, one particular set of meanings survived where others bled away. Neil Young, revisiting Yorkville in 1974, would have seen his old stomping grounds utterly remade. New houses, shopping centres, and a massive, imposing hotel would be hastily constructed following the demise of Yorkville's hip era in 1970. Most significantly, Young would have found the old coffee houses to be disappearing and the rock'n'roll clubs fading away. Yorkville was a land changed: its hip youth culture seemingly erased, eradicated, obliterated. A scene remade.

Yorkville as a Contested Space

Yorkville sits in the geographic centre of Metropolitan Toronto. Like a belly button, it is a natural point of intersection. And during the 1960s it was a key centre for budding Canadian youth cultures as curious young people congregated in and around the district, enjoying the live music and theatre in its mushrooming coffee houses, the nearby low-rent housing in overcrowded Victorian walk-ups, and its perceived saturation with anti-establishmentarian energy. For a period of roughly ten years, Yorkville served as a crossroads for Toronto's youth, as a venue for experimentation with alternative lifestyles and beliefs, and as an apparent refuge from the dominant culture and the stifling expectations it had placed upon them. Indeed, by 1964 most young Torontonians (and many young Canadians) likely knew that excitement and Yorkville went together as fingers interlaced.[8] By 1970, however, most would have known that the excitement had fled, and it was time to look elsewhere.

Making the Scene encounters Yorkville as a contested space, a literal and metaphorical site in which a wide variety of conflicts closely identified with the 1960s were played out. Though a local history, this book contends that hip Yorkville was reflective of much wider cultural debates and conflicts in the period. Indeed, to study the 1960s is to study the emergence of 'youth' as a category of great political significance on a global scale. All over the world in those years, people under the age of twenty-five stood under the hot soft lights at centre stage. As so many young people came forward, often angry, alienated, spouting varying degrees (versions) of revolutionary rhetoric, media, politicians, and academics swarmed them in recognition of the mighty potential inherent in such a phenomenon. Fears, anxieties, and concerns swirled around nascent youth cultures – those articulations of resistance that have retrospectively come to be collected, somewhat arbitrarily, under the umbrella of *counterculture*.[9]

In North America and Western Europe, anxiety over the Cold War with the Soviet bloc was exaggerated by this sudden surge of interest among youth in such subversive ideologies as pacifism, civil disobedience, and even (most distressing of all) revolution. In North America, especially, post-war affluence had led to a paradoxical condition of alienation and resistance to materialism among many university-aged young people. Fomented in the civil rights and nuclear disarmament drives of the late 1950s and early 1960s, a New Left arose on many college campuses, cohering around a politics of authenticity. By 1963, the Students for a Democratic Society (SDS) (in the United States) and the Student Union for Peace Action (SUPA) (in Canada) were emerging as a veritable political force and (most significantly) as touchstones for young people searching for a voice.

Meanwhile, alongside this more overtly political phenomenon, there developed a much more accessible culture of refusal among youth of the same (or similar) demographic. Inspired by a romance with Beat abandon, artistry, and hedonism, and infused with a belief in the authenticity of life on the margins, a significant minority of white, middle-class teenagers and twenty-somethings began to turn away (to widely varying degrees) from the materialism and conformity of the suburban imaginary of their youth. Seeking out an authentic experience after growing up in the cookie-cutter post-war suburbs, in what was widely acknowledged (even among their parents and authorities) to be a falsified version of reality, the most comfortable generation in the history of the world began to look uncomfortably to the world they would inherit.[10]

But how, indeed *where* to find authenticity amid all of this phoniness? In major (U.S.) cities such as New York and San Francisco, reasonably well-established bohemian centres were available, offering their curious tourists and neophytes a taste of that genuine experience (whatever that might have meant). Before long, the world would hear of Haight-Ashbury, the intersection of the hip universe by 1965 and the primary destination for what were being referred to (with much concern) as 'alienated' or 'drop-out' youth. But what is often forgotten is that there were bohemian centres in just about every major city in North America by the mid-1960s, some big, some small. The phenomenon of what would come to be called the counterculture was by no means an isolated Haight Street phenomenon. Vancouver, Austin, Milwaukee, Chicago, Montreal, Detroit, Boston, and Winnipeg (for example) all had bohemian scenes. In Canada, no scene grew to match the proportions (real or mythical) of Toronto's Yorkville. A budding multicultural metropolis, straddling a staid, puritanical past and a complex, immigration-fuelled future, Toronto would play reluctant host to what was widely perceived to be the centre of the Canadian hip world in the 1960s.

Making the Scene explores manifestations of 1960s youth culture using the crossroads of Yorkville as a way in, a means to get at the otherwise sprawling history such an undertaking implies. The lines intersecting in Yorkville represent diverse practices, institutions, and ideologies appearing elsewhere which, inevitably, collided with the concentrated community therein. This book emphasizes the view of Yorkville as a vital Canadian space in which such practices, institutions, and ideologies came into contact. However, one of its primary concerns is interrogating the variety of competing heuristics which defined discourse on Yorkville throughout the period. Such contending visions of the essential identity and meaning of Yorkville ultimately helped to shape and develop the characters, narratives, and events that converged in what was popularly referred to as the Village.[11]

The early Yorkville scene is often remembered (by both its observers and its participants) as a happy, even idyllic neighbourhood peopled by artists and musicians, whose calm was shattered by relentless police incursions, 'teenybopper' infestation, evil amphetamines, and unabated coercive municipal pressure. As the early 1960s became the late 1960s – a paradigm shift frequently characterized as a swing from innocence to violence, idealism to nihilism – Yorkville moved beyond its role as a mere nuisance in the public imagination. When City Controller (and former Toronto Maple Leaf) Syl Apps famously decried Yorkville as 'a festering sore in the middle of the city' in 1967, the new era was beginning in earnest.[12] By the end of that year, Yorkville was increasingly characterized by violence, drug abuse, addiction, and homelessness. One year hence, most of the early waves of hip youth had turned away from their former haunts – 'the true hippies' had left, according to Yorkville denizen and media firebrand David DePoe.[13]

But who were the *true hippies*? They were white. They were young. They were male. They were middle class, (sub)urban, and heterosexual – that is, according to media constructions of Yorkville (both those projected from without *and within* the Village community). In reality, of course, the scene was far more diverse than this expectation allows; besides, the boundaries surrounding these expected categories (especially 'white,' 'middle class,' and 'male') were being renegotiated at precisely this historical moment in significant ways. During the immediate post-war years, Canada, and especially Toronto, became home to vast numbers of immigrants, an influx that led to the flaring of anxiety over cultural degeneration among established, privileged Canadians. As Franca Iacovetta has demonstrated, the inclusion of southern and eastern Europeans (not to mention African, Asian, and Caribbean peoples) in post-war Canada was hardly a smooth and casual process. With a famously conservative Toronto experiencing the twin demographic shifts of post-war suburbanization (the process that saw large numbers of white, Anglo-Torontonians moving out of the downtown core) and post-war immigration (the process that saw the downtown core broadly repopulated by non-Anglos), apprehension over the rapidly changing face of the city was commonplace. As we shall see, such apprehension found a public forum in the debates over emerging youth cultures as they played out on the Yorkville stage. On the one hand, these debates explored public concern over the newfound presence of immigrant-reared (read: un-Canadian) youth in Toronto; on the other hand, these debates reflected fear and confusion surrounding what was perceived to be a collapse of suburban, middle-class youth identity (as expressed through drug use, alternative sex practices, and asceticism, among other performances). Consequently, we must recognize that strong undercurrents of race and class anxiety flowed through Yorkville in these years, and through both the expressions and the recognitions of Village identity performances. This book, then, interrogates those expressions and recognitions, offering space to consider the roles of women, working-class youth, political activists, homosexuals, rural transplants, and ethnic and racial identities in the Village scene. Throughout, in an effort to make more inclusive my discussion of what was never merely a 'hippie ghetto,' the assumptions of so many observers aside, I have chosen to employ the umbrella term 'Villager' to refer to the young people who made the scene in Yorkville. Villagers were working class, they were middle class, they were men, they were women, they were comprised of no one homogeneous racial background, and they demonstrated no one ideological, aesthetic, or spiritual point of view.

That said, we *will* encounter a set of four principle identity categories (hippies, greasers, bikers, 'weekenders') that became the dominant ethnographic understanding of Village youth culture. They appear in media coverage, in recent interviews, in contemporaneous studies, and in subsequent histories of the scene. I have approached these identity categories with caution – in general, one must approach *all* identity categories with scepticism – but I do not reject them entirely. In the weird cosmos that was the Village scene, figuratively cut off from the wider cityscape as it was, these identity categories *did* form their own distinct constellations. Indeed, it is clear that the press, the municipal authorities, and the Villagers alike generally relied upon these categories to make sense of the identity politics in the district. And, while many Villagers may have made no conscious effort to align themselves with any particular performative category when they approached the Village, the availability of these categories in the public imagination allowed for their easy assimilation into the framework. Performance, identification, and conformity all intermingle in this process; because

Villagers were aware that these categories existed (and they did exist, in various forms, from as early as 1963), they were inescapable. Presence in Yorkville might have made you a Villager, but your identity performance as a Villager was inevitably interpreted through the prism of these four categories of Village identity.

Because the category 'hippie' was usually taken to be comprised of white, male, heterosexual, middle-class youth, it commanded the lion's share of attention. The roles of bikers, shopkeepers, working-class youth, virtually all women, and any other non-hippies in the district were generally reduced to perfunctory, even elliptical, roles. A key aim of this book is, then, to destabilize this arrangement. For example, women generally appeared in media accounts of the day as liberated sexual beings, victims of violence, or as powerless hangers-on; and indeed, in the tradition of paternalist concern for the essential purity of femininity, narratives of sexual violence, exploitation, and defilement dominated media and municipal accounts of hip female identity in the Village in the 1960s. Yet these caricatures are hardly sufficient – other roles were available to the thousands of young women who made the Yorkville scene. While the reality of sexual exploitation and violence cannot be discounted, it must not be accepted as the defining feature of female identity in Yorkville. For their part, bikers – that is, members of local motorcycle clubs – about whom it remains difficult to gather information owing to a combination of their own relentless secrecy and the paucity of academic attention directed at them, will not be footnoted as simply an 'ever-present threat' against which 'peaceable hippies' can be defined. Indeed, an often free alliance was enjoyed between bikers and other Villagers. Much the same can be said for the so-called greasers, the generally working-class and immigrant-reared youth in the scene, whose roles in the construction and trajectory of Yorkville as a youth centre were central and pervasive, their exclusion from the 'hippie' mantle notwithstanding.

In short, *Making the Scene* explores the mutable identity performances on display in the Village scene, and interrogates the discursive contexts through which they arise.[14] It will not accept the expectation that a middle-class man occupied the centre of the Yorkville scene, or that he was the pin around which the hip world revolved. Indeed, much of what this project is about is the pulling of that pin. This book contends that Yorkville played host to a diverse and ever-changing, vibrant but highly unstable culture of youth cultures – the *scene* – and that it was an intersection point for a wider swath of young people than is generally remembered.[15]

Similarities between Yorkville and key hip scenes in New York and San Francisco are many and varied, and were frequently called upon in the period by observers.[16] In their respective geographies, these sites are both similar and dissimilar: while all three radiate out from a symbolic centre (Yorkville Ave, Washington Square Park, the intersection at Haight St and Ashbury Ave), they grew out of rather different circumstances.[17] For instance, while Yorkville is very close to Rosedale, one of Toronto's wealthiest neighbourhoods, the Haight grew up on the edge of the Fillmore, a poor and largely black district.[18] And, since Greenwich Village had been a centre for alternative lifestyles and bohemianism for decades prior to the 1960s, it bears little functional resemblance to the sudden emergence of other scenes.[19]

Culturally, these so-called hippie ghettos tended to share some common features. Drug use (especially of marijuana, psychedelics, and amphetamines), a general loosening of restrictions on sexual relationships, a high concentration of artists and writers, and a broad aesthetic of colourful, antiquated dress, beards, and long hair were all shared characteristics of the scenes of the mid- to late 1960s.[20] Also, Greenwich Village, the Haight, and Yorkville each produced some of the best-known and most enduring musicians of the period: Bob Dylan, Joan Baez, Richie Havens, the Lovin' Spoonful (Greenwich Village), the Grateful Dead, Janis Joplin, Sly and the Family Stone, Jefferson Airplane (the Haight), Neil Young, Joni Mitchell, Gordon Lightfoot, Steppenwolf, Bruce Cockburn (Yorkville).[21] But these similarities aside, each neighbourhood must be studied in its own particular context – Yorkville's destiny was as much shaped by Toronto and Canada in the 1960s as the Haight was by San Francisco and the United States in the era of Vietnam and the civil rights movement. They were both hubs of their own contexts, both similar and distinct.

The Politics of Hip Identity

The term 'hip,' although not a little amorphous itself, transcends too-narrow identity categories to become a more general, umbrella term for particular forms of popular dissent. As a term, it is *politicized*, without being overtly *political*; and, as an expression contemporary to the 1960s, it is both historically appropriate and theoretically useful for this discussion. Indeed *hip*, unlike the fraught and, finally, ill-defined *counterculture*, is open to the vicissitudes of youth cultural rebellion in the 1960s without forcing an excessively rigid set of defining characteristics around them. I have, as much as possible, stuck to this term below in an effort to move us away from a strict one-versus-other interpretation of the Yorkville scene.

Calling something, someone, *hip* is somewhat like employing the word *cool*; it is black American argot co-opted by a white youth culture seeking to establish an alternative lingo. Among the world's most multifarious terms, *hip* holds a rich, if muddy, etymological history, with some experts tracing it back to a root word in a pre-contact language. In this view, unlike related words like *interesting* (from the Latin *inter*: 'it concerns' + *esse*, 'to be') or the slang term *awesome* (from Old Norse *agi*, 'to be feared'), *hip* was not born of a connection to European ancestry. Rather, like *jive* and *dig*, *hip* likely has its origins in the Wolof language and culture of western Africa.[22] The Wolof *hepi* means *to see*, while its corollary *hipi* means *to open one's eyes* – thus, hipness probably refers, in its original and purest definition, to an ability to understand, to be aware, to be enlightened.[23] According to this theory, the closely related words *dega* (to understand) and *jevi* (to lie or disparage) survived as *dig* and *jive* with rather precisely the same meanings in American slang.[24]

Emerging in the twentieth century alongside the post-Reconstruction ascendancy of black American culture, terms such as these gained wider comprehensibility and enjoyed more exposure until they, like other varied aspects of African American culture, entered the mainstream. By the 1950s, they were simply accepted slang for that elusive identity embodied by black jazz musicians, white Beats, and those few young people Norman Mailer would eventually refer to as 'White Negroes' in a much-maligned but prescient 1957 article on what he called the 'Hipster.'[25] Into the 1960s, then, the term 'hip' had developed from an African word to a form of black slang, to a code for white youth enamoured of black culture, to one of the few words that came close to describing accurately the various social rebellions undertaken by young people in the 1960s.[26] To be hip, to strive towards open-eyed awareness, in the authenticity-starved world of post-war suburban alienation, was to be *alive*. It was life through refusal, life born of rebellion against conformity and the system so deftly exposed in William Whyte's 1956 book *Organization Man*.[27]

But, vitally, unlike the term 'hippie,' which carried clear connotations of aesthetic, attitude, and identity, hipness was conferred in wildly different ways and was accessible to most anyone through a variety of identity performances: anyone was a possible candidate for hipness. It must be said, however, that the difference between being a possible candidate and being an authentically hip subject was significant (if only spectrally defined), and the mutable dialectic between supposedly authentic hipsters and their inauthentic pretenders seemed part of the game. As jazz great Julian 'Cannonball' Adderley once (sort of) explained: 'You get a lot of people who are *supposed* to be hip, you know, and they *act* like they're supposed to be hip, which makes a big difference … Hipness is not a state of mind; it's a fact of life. You see what I mean? You don't *decide* you're hip, it just happens that way.'[28] Whether one's hipness appeared to be innate or not, its outward expression was always a performance of some kind – it may have been learned, practised, and/or spontaneous, but it was a *performance* of hip. As a result, identity categories in the Village were ill-defined, often contradictory, and, when reduced, usually illusory. Just like the scene, identity was there to be made, unmade, remade.

A Foreign Country Taken over by Teenagers

The mid-1960s saw a re-evaluation of the very conception of youth.[29] As one observer has argued, 'no longer simply an age category, youth became a metaphor, an attitude toward life, a state of mind that even adults could access.'[30] Of course, this argument that sympathetic adults could be hip too only went so far – the don't-trust-anyone-over-thirty ideology was developed alongside this new valuation of youth culture. Most often, the distrust of the over-thirties was more than a straightforward expression of baby boomer camaraderie. Rather, it was a politicization of 'youth' as a force for good in society. Or, as one observer put it, 'throughout the west it is the young who find themselves cast as the only effective radical opposition within their societies.'[31] The old, went this line of argument, were corrupt, conformist, racist, sexist, violent, boring, lonely, unhappy.[32] They were the perpetuators of every problem from civil rights to militarism to imperialism; if they were the reason social progress had stalled, then an embrace of youthfulness as a political framework would push the boat back on course. And since, in the period, 'marginality was the key to radical agency,' the project was to rearticulate youth as a site of oppression.[33]

Initially, the idea of youth as a metaphor for living otherwise carried little of the darkness that it would eventually accumulate. Youth was attendant in the (newly developed) mini-skirt, Beatlemania, the fashions of swinging London, the chrome-bright memory of JFK, and the excitement of the latest dance craze. As word spread, painting Yorkville as a midtown district seemingly geared for such emerging trends, the first whisper of curious youth began to drift down towards the Village. And, of course, as more teens arrived to see what there was to be seen, the description of Yorkville as a youth centre became ever more apt. By 1965, an article in the *Globe and Mail*'s Women's section cautioned its readers that 'if you were born before 1935, the sea of mohair sweaters, swinging hair and tennis sneakers may make you feel chillingly old.'[34]

The baby boom, the effects of which are sundry and pervasive, must be understood both as the catalyst for and as the exaggeration of youth cultural dissent in the 1960s.[35] The basic impact of the baby boom was the massive, full-scale societal, cultural, and political shift towards accommodating young people. One rather obvious reason for the disproportionate amount of attention placed on the children of the 1960s is that there were simply *so many* of them: in any given year through the late 1940s and early 1950s, one in five Canadian women between the ages of twenty and twenty-five gave birth. From 300,000 babies born in 1945, the figure jumped to 400,000 by 1952, and the rate remained above 400,000 babies born per year for fourteen years.[36] This demographic shift – often illustrated by the colourful 'pig in a python' image – precipitated an institutional crisis. There were so many babies in the same or similar demographic that, as they grow up, huge new facilities had to be established in order to accommodate them, such as primary, junior, and high schools and, of course, universities. As the first baby-boom-era youth came of age in the early 1960s, a shockwave rippled through Canadian institutions, forcing them to adapt or be crushed.

The blinding fear developing among Dr Spock-reading parents, schoolteachers, city controllers, and the like was that, without the proper institutions in place, Canadian society could break down. The stakes were clearly high – in the five years between 1963 and 1968, university enrolment would increase as much as it had in the previous fifty. Across the country, governments scrambled to open up new universities: Trent, Brock, York, Lethbridge, Simon Fraser, Calgary, Regina, Sir George Williams, and Waterloo universities all date from the baby boom period.

Perhaps this is why, in many ways, Yorkville was itself cast as a kind of youth institution. As was the case with the two major North American countercultural centres in San Francisco and New York, a trickle of curious youth in the early 1960s turned into a torrent. And it was in this surge, inevitably comprised of a wide swath of youth from all over Toronto, Canada, and the United States, that Yorkville was caught. Its very existence as a district became the subject of frenzied debate, its essential character as an appendage of greater Toronto evaluated, explored, decried. 'The City didn't like Yorkville because the City was full of old white men,' explains Martin Barber, a Villager and former *Telegram* reporter. 'But not liberal white men either: the kind of boring provincial farts who in those days ran small cities and small towns ... They were absolutely against youth! And especially this kind of youth who stood up to them and said, *hey, we want to do* ... They were terrified that things would happen that they would have no control over.'[37] However abstract, the idea of Yorkville as a famous place to perform *youth* tended to underscore the script and reify the boundaries surrounding the Village.

As a geographic location, Yorkville was thus metaphorically cut off, recast as a strange land, an unstable and increasingly immoral zone of decadent self-absorption and vice. As a business district, it was teetering on the precipice, apparently about to fall, its impending economic doom blamed on the Villagers. As a metaphor for a Canadian failure to control an increasingly inscrutable generation, it was potent, vivid, and fearsome. Here was an impromptu institution: a pseudo-college for the disenchanted, the thrill-seeking, the alienated, the stoned.

Significant work over the past two decades by historians and urban geographers has deepened our understanding of such transgressive spaces within cities. Judith Walkowitz's and Seth Koven's respective monographs on London's Whitechapel district, that infamous incarnation of Victorian England's moral degradation, have established that the London of the late nineteenth century was, at least figuratively, a 'bifurcated cityscape' which seemed to protect class identity by placing geographic boundaries along class lines.[38] This separation between the middle (and upper) classes and the 'other' side of the city promoted the idea of tourism within the wider cityscape. The frequent middle-class expeditions into lower-class districts (such as Whitechapel, with its wide variety of illicit and vice-indulging activities) emphasized a subject/object relationship between the voyeur and the studied. In other words, this bifurcation 'reinforced an imaginative distance between investigators and their subjects, a distance that many urban explorers felt nonetheless compelled to transgress.'[39]

The motives of these nineteenth-century slummers were very similar to those of many of their Toronto counterparts some eighty years later: curiosity, moral outrage, and pursuit of wicked, enthralling vice.[40]

The way Yorkville was discursively constructed as a site marked by illness, decay, and danger shares much with the way racialized spaces in Canada have been cast as places apart. Kay Anderson's seminal work on Vancouver, for example, demonstrates that its Chinatown was understood to be a malignancy, or a tumour, that could be dealt with only through 'surgery.'[41] As Jennifer J. Nelson has elucidated in her recent study of Halifax's Africville, the discursive construction of the 'infected slum' grounded much of the discussion about eradicating the community. Indeed, her book serves as a thorough interrogation of the idea of a separate zone within the wider cityscape, and of the various ways spaces 'influence how their occupants know themselves, and how they are known by outsiders.'[42] While her primary concern is race and racism, Nelson's insights into the functions of different spaces are easily applied to the idea of a Yorkville defined by an opaque foreignness.

In these diverse cases, then, space, class, foreignness, and race operate in interwoven, inseparable ways.[43] Widespread sexual deviance (including promiscuity, prostitution, and homosexuality) and illicit activities (including drug use, gambling, and drunkenness) were generally cited as the worst results of allowing Chinatown, Africville, Whitechapel, *and* Yorkville to be shaped by the hands of an unchecked and morally bankrupt culture.[44] And, while there was no one 'Jack the Ripper' to terrorize the Yorkville denizens, the ever-present threats of hippie sex fiends and biker gangs preying on poor, out-of-pocket girls emphasized an atmosphere of pervasive sexual violence and moral depravity which did not go unnoticed by either media observers or city officials.[45]

From the moment a place is set apart as separate, as somehow distinct, it becomes a de facto foreign territory. At the most basic level, the casting of Yorkville as a *village*, while tied to an historical reality (Yorkville *was* a village until it was annexed by the city in 1883), served to establish the district as a zone of local-foreignness, at once present and removed from the local and the foreign contexts. As Jacques Derrida has observed, only once a thing is named, is bounded through language and common sense, is it rendered comprehensible.[46] This thing can now be characterized (as 'thing'), its meaning(s) debated, evaluated, (mis)understood.[47] In terms of geography, such a process is doubly important, because oftentimes we are speaking in the abstract when we discuss place – we may have never been there, and are never going to go, but because it is named, we are able to develop the sense that it *is*. And so we develop mental maps, onto which we can project our understandings of these places. As geographer Peter Jackson has argued, such 'maps of meaning' are 'ideological instruments in the sense that they project a preferred reading of the material world, with prevailing social relations mirrored in the depiction of physical space.'[48] Or, as sociologist Henri Lefebvre has concluded, '[space] is a product literally filled with ideologies.'[49]

Because Yorkville was understood as a space in which both subversion and dissent flourished, the map of meaning through which the area was read by most observers was reflective of this common sense. In other words, hegemonic distrust and fear of cultural and social dissent fostered a common-sense treatment of Yorkville as a distinct, local-foreign land – a view that served both as a warning to some to stay away, and, crucially, as an invitation to the curious to come and partake. This process, in turn, helped to inculcate the characterization of the Yorkville youth cultures as somehow unfathomable, alien, dangerous: hence the need for a framework that allowed Yorkville to be foreign even while it was situated in the local context.

But, as this metaphorical community was established in the public imagination, it was simultaneously reinforced by the imaginative marginality performed by Villagers, a process that reflects a lengthy history of living otherwise through cultural appropriation and performance. As Mary Gluck has so carefully argued in her work on European bohemianism in the nineteenth century, early Romanticists 'performed their identities through outrageous gestures, eccentric clothes, and subversive lifestyles that came to be associated with a distinctive phenomenon.' In their case, they chose 'to enact their opposition to bourgeois modernity through the literal embodiment of medieval, and more generally exotic, characters.'[50] Nan Enstad, in her excellent study of working women in turn-of-the-century New York, demonstrated that 'by appropriating and exaggerating the accoutrements of ladyhood, working women invested the category of lady with great imaginative value, implicitly challenging dominant meanings and filling the category with their own flamboyant practices ... Like gay men in drag, working-class ladies seemed more absorbed in the element of *display* than in verisimilitude.'[51] What we are seeing in Yorkville (and throughout the counterculture) is much the same process. Young people, invited to engage with what they had been taught was *their* place, *their* community, couldn't help but pick up on the politicization of youth linked to this development. If young people (as with any subjects who might be identified as a group) are localized, and their activities categorized, their identity is then politicized as different, foreign, deviant, even when this identity is mere window dressing. For some, this suggests the ultimate insubstantiality of the hip rebellion; as Frank Musgrove concluded in 1974, 'the Counterculture is a revolt of the unoppressed.'[52]

But as Michael Valpy puts it: 'There was that sense that young people weren't just young people, but were the *enemy* of established society. And vice versa ... There was just simply this feeling, and it was quite pervasive among the editors at the *Globe*, that you know, that young people were a *mistake* somehow.'[53] If, by the mid-1960s, 'youth' was widely appreciated to be an ethic, an act, not so much about age as it was about spirit, then youth, like Yorkville, was accessible to all – that is, if you were up to the performance.[54] Considered in this way, the battle for Yorkville was as much about a battle for the physical space *Yorkville* as it was about the meaning of that space. Could Yorkville be liberated from its overlords?

By the mid-1960s, the political dimensions of youth were – following black writers such as Eldridge Cleaver and Frantz Fanon – often being expressed in terms of a Third World-ism, as if youth were an identity (even a race) in need of liberation from the repressive colonizing 'establishment.' David DePoe, for example, referred to plans to evict Villagers in 1967 as a 'final solution'; and a 1968 front page for *Satyrday* (a Village newspaper) proclaimed the 'New Anti-Semitism ... Destroy the Hippies!'[55] For his part, Cleaver, future minister of information for the Black Panthers, read this developing current of imagined marginality among white middle-class youth as a potential boon to the liberation of the human spirit. 'The characteristics of the white rebels which most alarm their elders – the long hair, the new dances, their love for Negro music, their use of marijuana, their mystical attitude toward sex – are all tools of their rebellion,' he observed. Citing hip touchstone Jack Kerouac and his infamous romanticization of the authenticity of black culture – specifically this famous passage from *On the Road*: 'At lilac evening I walked with every muscle aching among the lights of 27th and Welton in the Denver colored section, wishing I were a Negro, feeling that the best the white world had offered was not enough ecstasy for me, not enough life, joy, kicks, darkness, music, not enough night' – Cleaver was encouraged by the desire, however misinformed, on the part of white youth to emulate blackness.[56] 'They have turned these tools against the totalitarian fabric of American society,' he declared, 'and they mean to change it.'[57]

Significantly, Toronto's growing black communities (fed by increased immigration from the West Indies, Africa, and the United States) did not have much beyond a figurative influence on the development of the Yorkville scene. While a scattering of black people certainly visited and took part in Yorkville – famously, as in the cases of Lonnie Johnson and Ricky Mathews, as Village-based musicians – few recall the scene as incorporating a significant black presence. In fact, as the movement towards black self-empowerment and social justice burgeoned in the mid- to late 1960s in Toronto, so did a general disinterest in the Yorkville scene among its activists. 'They were privileged white youth in Yorkville,' recalls Dudley Laws, a key black power activist after 1965. 'There was not much reason for us to go down [there] … There was no connection between the black community as such and Yorkville.'[58] In the general absence of people of colour to confuse the issue, the white, middle-class youth in the Village were able to construct their own subjectivity in the vein of a solidarity with a black community about which, in reality, they were unacquainted.

Consider this exchange, the centrepiece of one of the National Film Board's two documentaries on the Yorkville scene in 1967. On a moving bus, a Villager interviews an older man, the picture of establishment in his dark suit. The young man complains to his interviewee that local politician Allan Lamport refuses to really listen to the needs of the Villagers. And so, he wonders aloud, to the obvious shock of his interviewee:

Young: What would any minority, what would the negroes in the States do, when people refuse to take their ills seriously?
Old: You wanna talk about the negroes in the States, or about the boys up here?
Young: They're both the same thing![59]

By the late 1960s, many otherwise privileged young people were no longer so sure that they did not constitute some kind of embattled minority, akin to revolutionary blocs around the world.[60] As the expected core of the Village scene (and thus the voices most loudly heard), white, male, middle-class, suburban youth aimed to 'grant themselves a greater imaginative role' as marginalized subjects; in turn, this appropriation of a certain Third World status promoted the notion of Yorkville as a politicized space.[61]

The Question of 'The Counterculture'

Hunter S. Thompson, writing in 1971, already considered the counterculture – and especially his experiences in the San Francisco scene – to be *historic*. This, he argued, was true in at least two senses of the word: on the one hand, it was historic because it had already slipped into the past (a telling point considering the period on discussion had ended no more than a couple of years before his writing). On the other hand, it was historic because, to so many people who had lived it directly, those years seemed imbued with significance. The problem was, he concluded, that no one will ever know what that significance was. 'Even without being sure of "history,"' Thompson mused, 'it seems entirely reasonable to think that every now and then the energy of a whole generation comes to a head in a long fine flash, for reasons that nobody really understands at the time – and which never explain, in retrospect, what actually happened.'[62] For Thompson, as for many others who came of age in hip scenes around North America in the mid- to late 1960s, that 'long fine flash' looked increasingly blurry, unformed, and incoherent in hindsight. Such dreamy retellings of the value of the historical moment underline both the significance and the complexity of the counterculture. One detailed history of the Haight-Ashbury district concludes with a discussion of precisely this interpretive problem, entitled, evocatively, 'What *Was* That?'[63]

Theodore Roszak, follower of Herbert Marcuse (then a key influence on many New Left intellectuals), is generally credited with coining the term *counterculture* in 1967–8, although he avoided offering a concise definition of his new category.[64] What he did, however, was demonstrate the theoretical connection between bohemianism and politics: both hippies and activists were responding to the same thing, he argued, albeit in different ways. The counterculture, ran his argument, was a wide category comprised of rebellious youth cultures united in their mutual revulsion for the *technocracy*.[65] This technocracy (loosely defined as the hegemony of 'experts' and 'specialists' over liberal-capitalist society) had stifled creativity, had promoted malaise and existential dread, and had, in the most radical sense, actually *inspired* the counterculture. At times prescient, at others obtuse, his book was devoured by university students and New Left activists excited to have found their own Marcuse: a Marcuse who spoke specifically about *them*.

Roszak's obvious disdain for corporate America, and his equally apparent delight over the ascension of what he saw as a revolutionary class which he hoped would tear down the technocracy, caused more than a minor stir in the academy.[66] But, since his book was published at the tail end of the 1960s, amid the waning days of the Haight-Ashbury and Greenwich Village and Yorkville scenes, not to mention the catastrophic implosion of the Students for a Democratic Society and the Student Union for Peace Action, his influence didn't have very long legs.

In the immediate term, however, his view was widely taken up by the sociologists and cultural theorists across North America who followed in his wake and developed the idea of counterculture in mainstream society. Much of this wave of studies (from the period 1968–74) adopted the term at face value, assuming that it had some stable meaning, often treating it as a monolith. 'Counterculture,' then, was generally understood to be any rejection of white, middle-class, corporatist society by drug-using, rock'n'roll-listening, probably white, middle-class youth. This vast framework persists today.[67]

All of Yorkville's Villagers were, if only momentarily, living otherwise from the mainstream of society. The participants in the scene were all countercultural insomuch as they refused to engage (for however long) with aspects of the common sense of their society. Their performances of identity undermined, stretched, and (if only mildly in most cases) subverted the ideologies that informed the general common sense. And yet, as sustained media exposure constructed them as dangerous 'others,' their numbers swelled as so many from the mainstream began to identify with their darkly attractive ideologies and behaviours. Simultaneously, through repetitive (and oversimplified) media frames, the mainstream against which they were set apart began to reincorporate a basic, homogenized version of the counterculture, effectively limiting its counter-hegemonic capacity (and reinforcing its spectacular value). As the counterculture expanded, it was simultaneously diffused – while the mainstream was enriched by the incorporation of so much contrary ideology, the counterculture itself (in the popular forms that it took in the mid- to late 1960s) was refigured. But it never went away.

At any given moment, hegemonic culture comprises views on normality and deviation, order and havoc, propriety and indecency, sexuality, gender, and race, and all of the major categories of activity and identity that concern the general public.[68] Indeed, as Raymond Williams has claimed, this is what constitutes 'a sense of reality for most people in the society, a sense of absolute experienced reality beyond which it is very difficult for most members of the society to move, in most areas of their lives.'[69] But, because Yorkville offered precisely an 'area of life' in which people might explore another 'sense of reality,' the Village was perceived as a danger by those in authority. Yorkville was widely understood to constitute a threat to the established order, and to the common sense of an affluent post-war society, through its inhabitants' apparent rejection of many of the basic tenets of the real. The 'free love,' drug use, asceticism, poverty, and outlandish aesthetics associated with most Villagers were all factors in a central refusal of a hegemonic version of reality. Moreover, the preoccupation of many Villagers' with psychedelic drugs geared more towards introspection than social lubrication (LSD, certainly, but perhaps marijuana as well) stands as a key reflection of this wilful rejection of external reality.[70]

We can account for the rise of dissent embodied in the Yorkville scene if we accept that, while hegemonic ideology constitutes a part of what (most) everyone does and thinks of as normal behaviour, 'people only partially and unevenly accept the hegemonic terms; they stretch, dispute, and sometimes struggle to transform the hegemonic ideology.'[71] Indeed, the contents of hegemony are always in flux, always prone to modification, mutation, transformation. This is not at all to say that dissent cannot or does not exist – let me be clear that I am arguing quite the contrary position – but rather that its manifestation is in proportion to (and always interconnected with) the success of current hegemonic ideology. Villagers were all responding to certain key deficiencies in dominant ideologies as they saw, lived, and experienced them, and making a scene in which they hoped to be able to live otherwise.

Methods and Sources

Making the Scene relies on a range of materials, from films to monographs, from interviews with former Villagers to unpublished papers and letters, from official reports to unofficial documents, and from underground newspapers to a variety of mass-media sources. The main source that I have mined is the rich catalogue of weekly (at times near-daily) coverage of Yorkville found in the three local newspapers, the *Toronto Telegram*, the *Globe and Mail*, and the *Toronto Daily Star*. In the case of the former, I have sought out and read articles rather at random, considering the major statements made by the outlet but not engaging in any precise survey of its offerings. However, in the case of the latter two papers, I have examined virtually every single entry on Yorkville in the period 1958–72, a reading list of well over 6,000 articles, reports, and mentions.[72]

This book explores the idea that Yorkville was, prior to the transfiguring influence of sustained media exposure (so, before 1965), a markedly different animal from the one that would become infamous by the late 1960s. Therefore, it treats media influence as a key factor both in the construction of Yorkville as a spectacle (a construction that invited and supported the massive influx of transient youth in the mid- to late 1960s) and in the mobilization of the forces of municipal authority against it. As the idea of Village identity penetrated the general common sense, dominant ideology shifted towards a grudging (halting) acceptance of its value, perhaps even its necessity, at the very time when the Village scene was disintegrating, its power diminishing. In this way, the influence of the Villagers was enormous, reaching far beyond the boundaries of the tiny neighbourhood. The media concentration that turned the nation's attention to Yorkville (simultaneously driving out the first wave of hip youth while advertising it to a younger, more transient cohort) went a long way towards introducing the alternative versions of reality celebrated and lived by the Villagers to the wider public. In exposing the Yorkville scene to the mainstream, media allowed the voices, practices, and modes of dissent therein a forum in which to propagate their spectacular performances of reality.

To be clear, the intention is not to *indict* media for their role as catalyst in the destruction of hip Yorkville. Because media construct events and frame them (i.e., situate them, impose order upon them) not from scratch but out of ideologies interconnected with the general common sense of the society in which they are based, *Making the Scene* investigates their function in debates over the meanings of the district and its habitués. Media had power, to be sure, but they were not alone in this regard. And they were never monolithic in their responses. Indeed, some of Yorkville's best defenders were full-time and frequent writers at the *Globe and Mail*, the *Toronto Daily Star*, and the *Toronto Telegram*. But the net effect of all of this reportage – and the oversimplified oppositional frame into which it was so often squeezed – was that Yorkville was then known, and has since been misremembered, as a reasonably uncomplicated space in which the central actors were hippies and everyone else comprised their collective adversary, the establishment.

While the study of contemporaneous media debates and report-age offers one set of pratfalls and interpretive dilemmas, memory, the other major source employed in this book, offers another. The guiding rule in my decision-making process over which interviews could be included in this book (and which could not) was that I was not going to seek out the sensational where I might be better served recognizing the ordinary. In total, I have interviewed twenty-eight subjects; this is a small number and no doubt could have been twenty times larger. A great many people – tens of thousands, probably – passed through Yorkville in the 1960s. All have stories, many of them surely fascinating, funny, frightening, sincere. But it would be impossible to cata-logue even a fifth of them, or to provide the kind of context and depth of field necessary to situate even a tenth of *that* fraction. Because this book was never designed as a strictly defined oral history of Yorkville, but rather as a multidisciplinary treatment of the space, I confined myself to this manageable number of interviews. I have sought out some major figures from the period – David DePoe, Clayton Ruby, Gopala Alampur, Mike Waage, Bill Clement, June Callwood, Michael Valpy, Marilyn Brooks – and some of the supporting cast of Villagers who have come to me upon learning of my project. I have avoided tracking down famous musicians (partly because their stories have been amply told in Nicholas Jennings's fascinating study of that aspect of the Village, and partly because the music scene and the street scene were not always connected).[73] I have also attempted to leave out or downplay any self-aggrandizing and any unhelpful invective (especially that directed at people unable to defend themselves). I told each of my interview subjects at the outset that I had no interest in 'scooping' – instead, the intention was to develop a fuller, clearer pic-ture of the Village scene.[74]

It should be noted that the practice of oral history has faced persist-ent attacks from critics uncomfortable with the subjective (and muta-ble) nature of memory.[75] Australian historian Patrick O'Farrell spoke for many when he penned a damning (and much referenced) attack in the late 1970s, complaining that such an approach was liable to push the serious business of history into 'the world of images, selective memory, later overlays and utter subjectivity.' His concern that this approach to the past will lead us 'not into history, but into myth' remains a legiti-mate (though deeply Eurocentric[76]) worry.[77] Nevertheless, while we must acknowledge that memory is a difficult animal – hard to corral and harder still to tame – we must also see that it would be foolhardy to refuse to speak to those people who directly experienced the events at issue. Consequently, I have tried to accommodate both sides of this argument, recognizing the legitimacy of both positions. Throughout this book, for example, I have tended to favour contemporaneous, eyewitness media reports of particular details of events over recollections of such events by my interview subjects. *Making the Scene* has followed the general line that memory is by no means trustworthy in any absolute sense but, rather, that it constitutes a text, another source that we must read and interpret just as we would any piece of written or recorded evidence.[78]

Of Time and Narrative: The Organization of *Making the Scene*

At the root of so many retrospective analyses of the 1960s, especially those concerning culture and youth, is the assumption that one can divide the decade into good and bad periods. American commentator Todd Gitlin, to cite a famous example, reduced 'The Sixties' to the 'Years of Hope' and the 'Days of Rage' in the title of his memoir-cum-history of the decade.[79] This persistent framework sets up two main, and not unrelated, stumbling blocks which cannot but affect our interrogation: on the one hand, if we accept this position, then we are left with the demonizing of the late 1960s, the period about which we have the richest and deepest cultural memory, not to mention the widest breadth of surviving visual/audio/textual materials. We risk turning this period against itself, becoming party to the alarming scheme – which has been gaining cultural currency in the past two decades under the ever-increasing social-conservative and neo-liberal stranglehold on American spin politics and some news media – to cast this era as evil, as shameful, blaming it for every uncomfortable development in the Western world since 1970.[80]

The impetus behind spiralling divorce rates, the legalization of abortion, the liberalization of pornography, the widespread abuse of drugs, and the ascendancy of affirmative action and political correctness has been variously determined to have been born alongside that baby at muddy Woodstock, in the fading months of 1969. As Kobena Mercer notes, this 'ideological onslaught against the myth of the "swinging sixties" has been a key theme of neo-liberal hegemony both in Britain and the United States: neo-conservatism hegemonizes our ability to imagine the future by identifying its adversaries with the past.'[81] In other words, this persistence in viewing the late 1960s as a period of unremitting darkness, of failure, of the waning of whatever was beautiful and dynamic about the preceding years, helps to further reactionary and repressive neo-liberal and social-conservative agendas.[82]

Of course, at the same time, what this framework does for the 'good' period is just as regrettable. Because it has become commonplace to treat the late 1960s as a convoluted, swirling, dissonant period, the complexities of the early 1960s are often left underdeveloped. What's worse, the period is habitually romanticized as some prelapsarian age of innocence and idealism, a time when real social change seemed possible, before the crushing disillusionment swept through, washing away the virtue, the beauty, the *value* of what had come before. And so, while it would be patently ahistorical to refuse this framework entirely – the influx of drugs, violence, anti-intellectualism, and commercialism really *did* change the nature of North American youth cultures in the late 1960s – it is also plainly dangerous to infer too much from it, or to fail to notice the subtle ways it serves to oversimplify key issues.

Such concerns underwrite the chronological format of *Making the Scene*. This book is divided into four parts defined by temporal boundaries which are each further subdivided into thematically coherent chapters, themselves comprised of a series of focused examinations of key events, concerns, sites. But, as Paul Ricoeur famously theorized (following Aristotle), 'to make up a plot is already to make the intelligible spring from the accidental, the universal from the singular, the necessary or probable from the episodic.'[83] The danger, then, of imposing a narrative structure on any given area of historical inquiry (or 'time frame') is that in so doing we impose a 'plot' on what musician Jerry Garcia once poetically referred to as 'the plain old chaos of undifferentiated weirdness.'[84] But because Yorkville *wasn't*, then *was*, then again *wasn't* a hotly contested site for youth cultural rebellion and congregation, there is indeed a rise-and-fall framework within which I have chosen to operate. However, in an effort to avoid a too-straightforward narrative treatment of the scene (a format that can also have the effect of silencing events, actors, and issues which appear to be peripheral to the adopted plot line), this book explores Yorkville thematically *within* each temporally defined section.

Following this introductory chapter, chapter 2 of Part One details the ascension of the Village onto the cultural radar as it moved from an unassuming ethnic enclave to a lively bohemian haunt. This chapter offers examinations of the folk music clubs, gay dance parties, working-class-youth hangouts, existentialist Beats, and artsy 'Happenings,' demonstrating that their emergence was deeply connected with the local immigrant community in these years, promoting a multihued and stimulating centre in what many perceived to be an otherwise grey Toronto.

Part Two (chapters 3 and 4) looks into what are widely considered to have been the peak years of the Village scene, 1964–6. These chapters detail the nearly simultaneous discovery of the Village by mass media, local teenagers, and the wider university-aged community. With the scene expanding every weekend, Yorkville went from being a mere cultural curiosity, an enclave defined by Euro-chic shopping by day and bohemians by night, to a thronging, intensely crowded party zone. Meanwhile, a triune formula of the Village identity performance – sex, drugs, and rock'n'roll – came to the fore as permissive attitudes towards sexuality became a defining feature of the Village after 1965, drugs were increasingly ubiquitous, and clubs moved to accommodate new electric trends in popular music.

Part Three (chapters 5 and 6) is focused on 1967, certainly the noisiest, and arguably the watershed, year in Yorkville's 1960s. Defined by an ever-expanding population of runaways, drop-outs, activists, drug users, emerging rock'n'roll superstars, bikers, and peace-and-lovers, Yorkville's 'Summer of Love' was fractious, exciting, and often dramatic. This was the year Yorkville became unavoidably politicized, a self-conscious cultural battleground over which various factions clamoured for control, arguing over the elusive mantle of authentic Village identity. As national media outlets provided saturation coverage, as spokesman David DePoe and other local leaders were famously maligned and even arrested, as the National Film Board of Canada and the Company of Young Canadians (both publicly funded and federally regulated) became involved in scandals related to the district, as biker clubs moved freely among the crowds, and as crime, addiction, and disease began to tiptoe around the darker corners of the Village, thousands upon thousands of curious teens and twenty-somethings crossed the country to join the party, to play at Yorkville identity, and to make the scene.

Part Four (chapters 7 and 8) explores hip Yorkville's unhurried, but by now inexorable, sunset. As undercover police officers, drug merchants, sexual predators, and paranoid drug addicts pervaded the scene, the generally peaceable climate of 1965 had all but disappeared. In its wake remained younger pretenders to the style, a few latecomers who had finally decided to join in the fun, and a general belief that the whole Yorkville thing had been played out. By the end of 1969, as some believed that a humanitarian crisis in Yorkville (characterized by violence, addiction, and diseases of the mind and body) had taken hold, the curtains began to close on the Village stage. Developers moved in, buying up the cheap properties and vowing to eradicate the remaining youngsters.[85] By the mid-1970s, Yorkville would re-emerge as Toronto's premier boutique district, a haven for the upper crust, the disco-chic, for permed hair and polyester flash; a scene remade.

2

Getting to Yorkville

The condition of freedom to choose and to act in unique and unpredictable ways was accompanied by a sense of urgency and anxiety; in one common form, conventional or predictable or 'programmed' choices and acts are failures of existence, which implies taking responsibility for one's own life, with no possible certainty of any known outcome in the terms of some known scheme.

– Raymond Williams[1]

The story of how Yorkville came to be a youth centre is bound up with the story of an emerging cosmopolitan city. Toronto, even as late as 1965, had rarely been accused of being an exciting place. In fact, 'Toronto the Good' was much more often criticized for its sober, sleepy character than for any dangerous, subversive underbelly. Big-city issues such as crime, unemployment, homelessness, narcotics dealing, addiction, and prostitution all played roles in the Toronto of the day, but they held nowhere near the same mythic associations with Toronto's reputation as they did in Chicago, New York, or even Montreal.

More important, Toronto was popularly believed to be a deeply puritanical place. Budd Sugarman, a vivacious young entrepreneur who opened a pioneering interior decorating business on Cumberland St in a rundown house in 1948, puts it succinctly: 'When I arrived in Toronto, I asked people "Where is the cultural centre of Toronto." People said: "There *isn't* any."'[2] To many Canadians (and Montrealers especially), Toronto's reputation for culture was summed up in an old saw, much repeated in the post-war years, that told of a lottery offering as its first prize a week's vacation in Toronto. Second prize? Two weeks.[3]

A combination of cultural segregation due to widespread suburbani-

zation and a famously dogged determination to adhere to a traditionalist ethic helped Toronto to slip into a bit of a cultural slumber by the
1950s. Moreover, although it was a huge city (by Canadian standards,
at least), Toronto had remained remarkably homogeneous right into the
1950s. In 1951 the majority of people who lived in Toronto were still
ethnically British (73 per cent), religiously Protestant (72 per cent), and
Canadian-born (69 per cent). Part of the reason for this was the persistence of federal immigration restrictions, some of which would be
liberalized in the coming years.[4] By 1971, with the population sitting
at 2,583,925, the combined number of British and Irish was 1,478,910,
or down to 57 per cent of the total (and this number includes many
Catholics, of course).[5]

If, as John LeLand has so persuasively argued, there can be no 'hip'
without the abrasive friction caused by racial and ethnic intermingling
in an urban environment, Toronto didn't seem to have much claim to
the title.[6] Unlike such ur-hip centres as New York or San Francisco or
New Orleans, Toronto's ethnic mix was hardly sufficient to provide
the proper environment for the process of cultural sharing, appropriation, and bastardization that constructs hipness. Indeed, people from
recent enemy countries such as Germany and Italy were permitted to
immigrate to Canada again only after 1950; and the policy that forbade
visible minorities and the impoverished from Africa, Asia, and other
predominantly Third World regions was not re-evaluated until the
1960s.[7]

In the 1950s, then, most of the immigrants who *did* help to enliven
the city tended to be European. Following the war in Europe, many
displaced and impoverished Europeans (many of them doubly displaced following Soviet revolutions in their eastern European home-
lands) turned to Canada for a new start. Following years of post-war
suburbanization projects that drew many Torontonians from the core of
the city farther north, east, and west, Toronto's relatively empty inner-
city Victorian and Edwardian houses became home to such European
transplants.[8] With their arrival came a new era in Toronto's history, and
the beginning of its flirtation with hip culture.[9]

This chapter explores associations between Yorkville and bohemianism into the early 1960s. The advent of the popular awareness that
Yorkville was the spot to find Toronto's hip scene dates from around
this time, as does the beginning of the massive influx of people curious to partake in whatever such a scene had to offer. Beat poets, folksingers, artists, and entrepreneurs all formed a nucleus of Villagers in

the early 1960s, coming together in a shared desire to create spaces in which they might live differently, reason otherwise, and uncover the authentic life that had eluded them elsewhere. Getting to Yorkville was a fairly straightforward process; but now that they were there, what would they do?

From Gerrard St to Yorkville

The area immediately to the south, southeast, and southwest of Yorkville, a series of thin streets full of nineteenth-century row houses, was an ideal spot for new Torontonians to set up their first Canadian digs. And, alongside their colonization of the area in the late 1940s and throughout the 1950s, came the establishment of distinctly European enterprises. Among these, the European coffee house was perhaps the most surprising to Torontonians. For many cynical Toronto students and artists, perhaps equally enamoured of Henry Miller, Jean-Paul Sartre, and Gregory Corso, the coffee house suggested a Euro-bohemian hangout unlike any previously known to the city. According to ballet dancer Clifford Collier, such tastes of Euro flavour were a revelation. 'I mean there were *never* coffee houses in Toronto! The closest thing we had to anything fancy was Diana Sweets. There were two of them, really tea shops, where ladies went and had sandwiches and sweets. *That* was the closest Toronto had to a coffee house! And ... because of the Europeans coming into Toronto after the war, here were coffee houses.'[10]

A small hip scene grew up in the mid-1950s around Gerrard St, just over a kilometre south of Yorkville, and was often referred to as 'Greenwich Village' by Torontonians in these years. In fact, much like its American forebear, the Gerrard Village 'was a place of small galleries, framing shops, and coffee houses,' writes David Burnett, 'which began to attract devotees of *avant-garde* jazz, art, poetry, and drama.'[11] (Avrom Isaacs even opened a *Greenwich* Gallery in 1955.) In such a setting, European owners and their clientele would mix with curious teens and twenty-somethings from around the city – it was through this alchemy, a fruitful combination of Euro émigrés, Beat youth, aspiring poets, musicians, artists, and students, all breathing the air of *difference*, that the soon-to-emerge Yorkville scene found its genesis.

The Gerrard Village was gradually removed in the mid- to late 1950s as part of a municipal development scheme which made room for an expanding Toronto General Hospital.[12] In the ensuing months, many of the erstwhile Gerrard Villagers moved a few blocks north. Hand-made jewellers John and Nancy Pocock, for example, were among the first to make the move to Yorkville, in 1956. Their daughter, Judy, recalls that this decision was taken by many artists from the Gerrard St scene: 'Their next door neighbour Albert Frank (who was an artist) moved to Hazelton. There were always rumours that they were going to tear down the old Village, so my parents decided they would move to Hazelton [too].'[13]

From the turn of the century to the 1950s, Yorkville had remained almost entirely residential.[14] In 1945, for example, only seven small businesses operated out of the neighbourhood, including two groceries (one on Scollard and one on Yorkville) and a Chinese-owned laundry.[15] Until the mid-1950s, 'for the most part the houses were not subdivided into apartments or rooms for rent.' According to a 1967 York University BA honours thesis detailing Yorkville's growth before 1950: 'Only two buildings on Yorkville Avenue had been converted into boarding houses for girls' while 'the rest were occupied by families, two-thirds as tenants and the rest as owners.'[16] However, the number of young children declined throughout this period, and the residential population became predominantly elderly. At the same time, the quality of housing deteriorated until, in the words of one long-time resident, it was merely a 'slum.'[17] 'It was skuzzy,' recalls Judy Pocock, who grew up right in the heart of Yorkville. 'Toronto is a changed city. It was much poorer. [Because of suburbanization,] middle-class people kind of left, and then it was mostly working class and immigrants, and the artistic community.'[18]

In fact, in 1944 the City of Toronto had designated Yorkville (which then included the as yet underdeveloped stretch of Bloor St to the south) as one of the three residential areas most in need of municipal attention. By 1954, as Bloor St was being developed into a commercial strip in anticipation of the coming subway line, Cumberland St had became home to an overflow of boutiques and other endeavours. In the late 1950s, Yorkville may have still been in a state of disrepair, full of crumbling Victorian houses, but, of course, it was also situated in an undeniably desirable location: not quite downtown, adjacent to the largest student body in Canada, steps away from the busy Yonge St bars and theatres, and on the doorstep of a developing middle-class North Toronto.

Perhaps the very first entrepreneur to take full advantage of this underexplored locale was Mary Millichamp. In late 1947 Millichamp (of a wealthy family, owners of Canada's largest manufacturers of glass display cases) took over one of the dilapidated houses on Yorkville Ave and began to refashion it into a 'charming and expensive restaurant with city-wide appeal.'[19] She was widely credited with being, along with Budd Sugarman, the pioneer entrepreneur in the district, and her gutsy efforts – her friends strongly discouraged her plan, assuring her that the moneyed classes would 'never patronize anything "on that street"' – were well noted by others who saw the potential for growth in the district.[20] As Judy Pocock puts it, 'when we moved onto Hazelton [in 1956], it was still very working class. There basically wasn't anything going on. I mean, there was Mary Millichamp's on Yorkville, but [otherwise] it was a very ordinary working-class street.'[21]

Upon Millichamp's death in 1962, one obituary stated that 'when a resident [in Richmond Hill] she lived with her close friend and business associate [Pansy Reamsbottom] on Centre Street West.' According to Harold Averill, archivist at the Canadian Lesbian and Gay Archives, such vague information was regularly used in the early 1960s to describe the passing of middle- and upper-class Torontonians known to be involved in same-sex partnerships.[22] One wonders whether Millichamp, an upper-class woman in an era in which same-sex activity and identity were pilloried, may have been drawn to Yorkville in those early days by its *déclassé* associations. Since Yorkville was very much a non-issue in the late 1940s and into the 1950s, Millichamp may have felt that she could hide her sexual identity to a certain extent by moving into an unexpected milieu. Regardless, Millichamp's restaurant on Yorkville Ave was unquestionably a ground-breaking venture; that very space soon became home to the Gaslight, one of the most successful of the early 1960s café/restaurant ventures. Indeed, the Gaslight made $450,000 on food and drink alone in 1961.[23]

By the mid-1950s, a pair of antique shops, two interior-decorating establishments, and 'several professional offices of the architectural and engineering type' had opened in the neighbourhood, furthering the trend away from residential land use in the district.[24] The year 1957 saw the opening of Old York Lane, a pedestrian walkway containing around ten storefronts, linking Yorkville Ave with Cumberland. Three years later, Lothian Mews was opened on the south side of Cumberland, at Belair, an innovative shopping complex and garden court boasting a pedestrian path from Bloor St through to Cumberland. By 1961 'forty-five new businesses had located in Yorkville [since 1945] … bringing the total of non-residential uses in the area to fifty-three.'[25] But the real shift was in the types of businesses taking up in the district – in 1961 these included 'six interior decorators, three dress designers and several millineries, photography studios, art galleries, antique shops [and] hair stylists.'[26]

While Yorkville developed into a commercial centre, its population continued to age, to move away, and generally to decrease in number. Those who remained tended to be more transient, and the percentage of home ownership continued to diminish. Less than 35 per cent of the people living on Cumberland in 1956 were still there in 1961; that same year saw only 26 per cent of the Yorkville Ave residents and a mere 13 per cent of those on Cumberland owning their own homes.[27] Their empty apartments were increasingly being rented to frugal students, young married couples, and others looking to take advantage of this inexpensive, but central, location. However, the conditions inside many of the apartments was, even in 1960, pretty grim. Myrna Wood, who moved to Yorkville in 1960, describes a typical apartment on Cumberland: 'In the very early beginnings of the counterculture, when it was sort of an embryo in Toronto, perhaps, I lived on Cumberland St, before there was a *Yorkville* ... This was literally a *garret*, you know? In one of these big narrow old houses that were all connected on Cumberland St. My husband and I rented the top room – it was really just a *room*, with a little small room off the back, which had a hotplate – that was our stove! ... And you looked out the front window and the whole backside of Bloor St was a construction site for the Bloor subway.'[28] The construction of the Bloor subway line – Bay St station would open in 1966, although the work was largely completed by 1963 – would see all of the houses on the south side of Cumberland demolished. For the better part of the next five years, this short section of Cumberland would be the subject of significant debate as a proposal to build a seven-level parking garage made its way through the approval process. It was finally quashed in 1968, owing to hefty agitation from hip youth and supporters of Yorkville's quaint atmosphere. An innovative concrete park was eventually decided upon as the best way to use the space.

The rapid development of Yorkville from a low-rent residential zone into a shopping, restaurant, and boutique centre was helped along by wider trends in development taking place throughout the city's core. Toronto was in one of its most active development periods, as a new city hall, a two-line subway system, and various suburban initiatives were undertaken to modernize the city.[29] With the establishment of increasingly vast banks, department stores, and malls on downtown streets, valuable real estate was gobbled up and many small storefronts closed down. Re-establishing on smaller but still nearby streets, such as Cumberland and Yorkville, made eminent sense. And, as luxury shops migrated to the area, so did their clientele. Often flanking such stores, restaurants and specialty coffee houses were established in old homes by clever businessfolk who planned to take advantage of enervated shoppers.

Now that Yorkville had begun to play host to some fashionable clothing stores and restaurants, the still inexpensive flats above these establishments became more attractive to young people in a variety of occupations. Living alongside immigrant entrepreneurs and recently uprooted former denizens of the Gerrard St Village, these young artists, students, and professionals found themselves in a rapidly intensifying site of difference.[30] By late 1960, trendy new coffee houses (like the Purple Onion, the Half Beat, and the 71 Coffee House) had begun to open up. A still small and discrete group of writers, musicians, actors, and hangers-on found in the burgeoning coffee-house trend in Yorkville a kind of community of clubhouses, some offering outdoor patios and, eventually, stages for the fledgling folk musicians among their ranks. And so this growing group of disconnected and diffuse hip youth comprised the first wave of 1960s Yorkville. 'We started the whole thing,' boasts coffee-house entrepreneur Miguel Maropakis.[31]

In the early 1960s, the relationships between young residents with diverse social lives and schedules were rarely friction-free. Myrna Wood, although a young woman, did not count herself among the young people who were filling the neighbouring flats: 'The house next to us, I mean there was just this one wall between our bed and the other place. So weekend nights it filled up totally with some kind of band, and we couldn't sleep at all. God knows what kind of band it was, but it was LOUD! There were I-don't-know-how-many-people packed in there. And this was up on the third floor, or whatever. Anyway, I complained, but the super said well, "I don't even know who owns the building!" So I immediately went out and phoned another apartment. That was the last I had to do with that street until later.'[32] This process, which saw Wood move from the Village to make way for perhaps an aspiring folksinger or poet to move into her apartment, was well under way by the early 1960s. Music was getting louder, parties rowdier, and the stamp of youth culture on Yorkville ever more pronounced.

More open to gay men (and, to a lesser degree, lesbians) among their ranks – the centrality of homosexuality to much Beat artistry being dif-

ficult to misconstrue – the Village community offered something of a
haven for young people whose sexual identities set them apart in other
public contexts.[33] In this setting, among people dressed all in black,
some even affecting berets, beards, or close-cropped Jean Seberg-esque
hairstyles, some practising libertine sexuality, some taking drugs, and
some even reading Marx, Marcuse, and Lenin, queer youth might have
been comforted to realize that they were not the only 'deviant' identity subgroup in the scene. These were the older brothers and sisters
to the hippies of the late 1960s, a group that helped to set the stage, to
establish the district as home to the hip elsewhere, a refuge from the
boredom of everywhere, and an escape from the existential nowhere.

Here it was, perhaps: cafés, romantic poverty, artists, and musicians
mingling together, looking for sex and inspiration in the blue-smoke
closeness of a cavernous coffee house. In the tradition of Byron, Shel-
ley, Baudelaire, Jack Reed, Emma Goldman, Gertrude Stein, Ernest
Hemingway, Henry Miller, and more recent heroes like William Bur-
roughs, Jack Kerouac, and Allen Ginsberg, Toronto's young bohemian
crowd disassociated themselves from wider society, reinventing (redis-
covering) their own identities, artistic and otherwise, as around them
the world carried on obsessing over such 'necessities' as tailfins and
salad cream. In Yorkville, it was somehow decided (if only telepathi-
cally), this counterculture would take its stand: the existential alienation and all-consuming false consciousness of the suburban imaginary
found there its salve, even its escape hatch. By 1961, according to
early Village folksinger Ian Tyson, coffee houses were 'sprouting like
mushrooms' in Yorkville and were filled with his new audience: hip,
chain-smoking, refuse-nik youth, dressed all in black.[34] Yorkville was
suddenly, vibrantly, happening.

All around them, in some ways even mirroring the vicissitudes of
their identity transformations, Yorkville's identity as a shopping centre underwent a series of startling changes. Throughout the 1960s, the
turnover rate among businesses in the Village was extraordinary. A
1967 survey of commerce in the district found that none of the coffee
houses opened in the early 1960s remained in existence, while the longest running (the Penny Farthing) was merely three years old. 'The life
span of most,' the survey concluded, 'has been two years or less.' But
this high turnover did little to stem the influx of prospective coffee-
house owners who felt their business plan to be stronger than their contemporaries – between 1960 and 1965, when the number of Yorkville
coffee houses peaked at twenty-two, businesses were constantly chang-

ing hands as too many cafés fought for too few customers, especially during the slow winter months. The 1965 peak of twenty-two coffee houses shrank to fourteen by the end of 1966 – a perhaps more manageable number for such a small district.[35]

The first coffee houses to open had been the Purple Onion, the 71, and the Half Beat, back in 1960 and 1961.[36] Such places would serve expensive, exotic coffees (espressos, cappuccinos, and lattés were new to the scene) and light food such as sandwiches and cakes. They were sparsely decorated, often to the point of it being an artistic conceit. One café-goer recalls that '[places] would get travel posters and make wallpaper out of them, so to speak. Just to give some colour, but with no expense. Once you went inside, it was "used" furniture. In fact, what I remember about the Penny Farthing was that probably its most expensive thing was the bloody penny farthing [bicycle] that they had sitting on the roof!'[37] *Maclean's* reporter Mackenzie Porter artfully described the Purple Onion as 'a Victorian parlour that was blown up by a gas explosion during a whist drive,' where 'the customers sit at rickety card tables and look at the remains of a fretwork-fronted upright piano, fragments of bombazine sofas and aspidistra pots, fractured specimens of spelterware and bits of stuffed birds.'[38]

In the early days, little in the way of entertainment was provided at such establishments; generally, people would come to them following the hockey game, the late movie, or last call at the bars on Yonge St. 'Toronto, particularly, had hardly any places that were licensed,' recalls former Villager Judy Perly. 'You didn't have places to go out to, or a pub culture, or even cafés and licensed restaurants. [Whereas] the whole Yorkville scene was not licensed, it was all coffee!'[39] Besides, the drinking age was still twenty-one in Ontario, and the bar scene tended to be farther downtown and generally attracted older men who would stop in after work. 'They put all the liquor licences in one area,' emphasizes downtown musician Ronnie Hawkins. 'You couldn't get booze anywhere else. All of the people getting out of work from Eaton's and Simpson's would stop by for a drink and sometimes stay over.'[40] Generally quiet, subdued environments, the Village coffee houses tended to be full of people in their early to mid-twenties playing chess, reading, and talking into the wee hours, with almost no alcohol. Some hosted poetry readings, some local musicians, but most steered clear of paid entertainers for financial reasons.

According to Village observer Barbara Key, 'the Purple Onion was the first to let folk singers, poets and satirists perform [for] free, but gradually in the following years more coffee houses opened and all began hiring entertainers, either local folk singers and jazz musicians or in some cases well known American performers.' By 1964, the shift was complete, and 'almost all the coffee houses depended for their existence on their folk singing entertainers rather than on simply serving refreshments.'[41] It was not until the spring of 1965 – when the popular coffee house Jacques's Place revamped its format to become a rock'n'roll club – that folk music was supplanted as Yorkville's dominant entertainment draw for young people.

As rock'n'roll bands moved into Yorkville from the raucous bars on Yonge St (such as the Le Coq D'Or, the Upstairs, the Zanzibar, and the Famous Door), more and more teenagers came to hear the kind of music that had only recently become radio-friendly. Key explains that 'this [music] appealed more to the teenagers than to the people in their twenties and thirties who up until this time had formed the largest proportion of the clientele.'[42] Folk music expert and former Village regular Judy Perly has tried to pin down that appeal. 'Folk music. That was a culture of people writing songs that had some *meaning*. It was coming out of black music, so it was authentic. People started writing songs; well, *Dylan* started writing songs about social protest. Ian and Sylvia too. But, there was far, far less music then than there is now! Some people of my generation have sat across from me and said: there's been no good music made since the Sixties. But, it was so *relevant* then, and it was so focused, so the [folk musicians] who were there were getting so much attention.'[43] The allure of folk music was often found in its apparent working- and black-underclass-borne authenticity.[44] In a world of pop superficiality and a widely articulated existential yearning for the real, genuine human experience, folk music offered a white entrée into that elusive space beyond alienated identity performance. The advent of rock'n'roll, then, does not just denote a swing in musical tastes and trend patterns, it also bespeaks a shift in the appreciation of the authentic potential of white, middle-class youth. If early 1960s authenticity was to be found in the radical refusal of middle-class whiteness, by the mid-1960s white, middle-class youth had found their own version of authentic experience and performance in the burgeoning psychedelic scene. And so Yorkville was again reimagined as its participants responded to these seismic changes.

As this entertainment transformation was taking place, Yorkville was simultaneously emerging as a shopping destination, the site of expensive clothing stores, gift boutiques, hair salons, a hat shop, and a variety of galleries specializing in imported art and jewellery that operated alongside the coffee houses and discos. In less than a decade, Yorkville had been transformed from a working-class enclave to an increasingly sophisticated centre for the so-called carriage trade.[45] By 1967, very few of the houses left on Yorkville and Cumberland were being used exclusively as residences; most Yorkville residents lived in apartments above or below such establishments, or on Hazelton and Scollard streets, which had seen considerably less commercial development.[46] Since these boutiques and galleries operated out of the main floor of what had been residences until only recently, they tended to be quite small – most occupying only one or two rooms – and somewhat informal. Such shops were designed for browsing as much as buying.[47]

What was referred to as the carriage trade was really a euphemism for upper-class female shopping. The predominance of expensive gown shops and artisans' boutiques in the Village throughout the 1960s suggests that many of the people frequenting the district would have been counted among the more wealthy women in the city and beyond. For example, Yorkville, by 1967, was home to Helmar of London (a dress-designing salon boasting a selection of imported fabrics and nine in-house seamstresses, offering gowns for between $100 and $1,000); Pot Pourri (a similar, but somewhat less dear, dress-designing salon); the Recamier Boutique (the owner of which travelled to Europe twice each year to buy new gowns); along with a number of 'sportswear, hats, furs, and wig boutiques as well as several *haute couture* salons for styling hair, [all of which] cater[ed] to the female customer.'[48] Moreover, bath boutiques, candle shops, and stores devoted to imported merchandise and curios from India, Persia, and Japan helped fill out the short blocks.[49]

Throughout the 1960s, Yorkville housed a series of art galleries and showrooms that often exhibited the cutting edge in Canadian, American, and European art. Although not strictly speaking a part of Yorkville, the nearby Isaacs Gallery was certainly the most famous of the local spots. However, Avrom Isaacs was hardly alone in his efforts to further the development of a modern art scene in Yorkville and Toronto. In 1966 the Sobot Gallery at 128 Cumberland held a successful exhibition of graphics by Pablo Picasso, Henri Matisse, Georges Braque, Marc Chagall, and Joán Miro, the largest showing of international artists ever held in a Canadian commercial gallery, at which – *maddeningly* – none of the pieces sold for more than $800![50] Others, including Tysegen Gallery (on Scollard), Gallery Moos (138 Yorkville), Gallery Pascal (104

Yorkville), and the Monyo Art Gallery (84 Yorkville), offered a wide range of modern and local painting, pottery, sculpture, and simple drawings. According to Stephan Sobot, proprietor of the Sobot Gallery, Yorkville played an important role in the development of Toronto into a global (which is to say a less old-Canadian) city. 'We have here a unique area which has contributed to the beauty – in term [sic] of character – of this country ... As a growing metropolis, Toronto is developing certain eccentricities: we are in the wonderfully eccentric area. You can enjoy a range of pleasantly different characteristics in the variety of shops and restaurants.' The new-Canadianness of the district was, to Sobot (and presumably to others as well), its very charm. 'This is truly,' Sobot proclaimed, 'a little bit of Europe.'[51]

In other words, throughout the 1960s, Yorkville was virtually at all times home to decidedly upper-crust shops and boutiques, galleries, and salons. It was, in fact, among the most expensive places *in the country* in which to shop for clothing. While noise and indecorous young people *did* pour out of coffee houses and, later, discothèques, much of this took place at night, long after these upscale shops had shut down for the evening. In my interviews, former Village residents tended to bristle at the suggestion that Yorkville was some kind of slum in the early 1960s ('Oh No! Oh gosh no! I was there, and it wasn't like that *at all!*'[52]). Rather, it was a symbiotic combination of cheap housing and ambitious, upscale boutiques, an intermingling of bohemian poverty and Euro-chic. Indeed, while Yorkville Ave developed into the famous Village scene, Cumberland remained tied to the fashion industry in a more overt way. 'Yorkville the *street* is a lot different from Cumberland the *street*,' stresses fashion maven Marilyn Brooks. 'The drugs and the music and the coffee houses were on Yorkville. And I was on Cumberland, which was more of a watered down Bloor St ... I think you'd have to say that Cumberland was a little more elegant than get-down-and-get-dirty, which was more Yorkville.'[53]

In the early 1960s, the European flavour was unmistakably leading the charge; at first, according to Myrna Wood, the people filling the coffee houses hardly mattered to most observers of the scene:

You see, even the opening of the early coffee houses didn't mean anything. Yorkville was [filled with] cheap, old houses, kind of run down, and what have you. But the first floor of my house, and of most of them, was an attempt towards high-end fashion ... The building I lived in was owned by a Hungarian. There was this community of European people like him.

He was a landowner that ran from the Hungarian Revolution! He had a lot of paintings and big old guild frames and stuff like that. Velvet smoking jackets! ... To the extent that Yorkville meant anything at all, that was the future that they wanted it to become.[54]

The future was to be built with the kind of money carried on the back of European style, flavour, and accents. But, attracted to the district by that very same Euro-style, the new residents would complicate this trajectory, at least for a time.

Ultimately, the picture of Yorkville that one gets from studying its commercial make-up is of a district in which shrewd immigrants, high-minded artists, and moneyed-class propriety ruled the scene. By 1964, it had ceased to be residential in any meaningful way – for it was now the domain of landlords and their increasingly overcrowded (and decrepit) rooms – and had become home to a growing number of expensive, classy businesses and galleries. Property values had risen impressively since 1957; the same house on Yorkville that was listed at $48,000 in January 1965 had been listed at $23,000 eight years previously. Ginger Eisen, owner of a bathroom fixture 'salon,' commented in early 1965 that, 'sitting at my window on a good day you can probably see every Rolls-Royce in Toronto stopping somewhere on [Yorkville Ave].'[55]

Beats, Art, and the Allure of Mourning

Charles Reich, in a much-discussed 1970 book, emphasized the emancipatory politics of 1960s youth. '[The counterculture] promises a higher reason,' he reckoned, 'a more human community, and a new and liberated individual. Its ultimate creation will be a new and enduring wholeness and beauty – a renewed relationship of man to himself, to other men, to society, to nature, and to the land.'[56] For Reich, the counterculture represented a struggle for an *authentic* identity, an ideal of true humanity. Such a sentiment was indeed often anticipated in the early 1960s, rooted in the hyper-individualism of Beat novels and poetry and later finding its contemporary articulations in the lyrics of folk songs and psychedelic rock and in the various assertions and editorials in underground newspapers.

The key to understanding the development of youth unrest in the 1960s – and for a start at answering the big questions of *what was it?* and *why did it arise?* – can be found in the linked themes of alienation, authenticity, and existentialism. Alienation, in a Marxian sense, refers to the feeling of disconnection between a subject and her 'true' self, or her human nature (*Gattungswesen*).[57] This is an absolutely central term – Doug Rossinow notes that 'possibly no word was used more frequently in discussions of political discontent in the United States during the [1960s].'[58] Alienation, related to Emile Durkheim's notion of the *anomie*, is balanced against its implied binary opposite, authenticity.[59] In short, a subject's struggle to overcome alienation from his human nature constitutes his search for authenticity, for a truer experience of the self. The existentialist approach to such a theory, repeatedly explored by Simone de Beauvoir and Jean-Paul Sartre in the decades prior to the 1960s, applies these terms to a belief that the universe is meaningless.[60] In such a context, man's alienation stems as much from his inability to know himself as it does from his incapability of understanding his place in the universe. To escape this alienation – which is to be understood as the ultimate goal of life in the absence of external meaning – is to seek authenticity. In a basic sense, to live by convention (that is, to conform, or to 'go with the flow,' especially if you do so out of fear or anxiety) is *inauthentic* insomuch as it melts individuality into community, linking the self to a hegemonic cultural process. To live authentically is to find a way in which to live life on your own terms, but only so long as you are doing it for yourself, and not for others.[61]

Most Villagers, in all of their various incarnations, would grapple with these themes in some way. The Beat-influenced bohemians who spent their evenings at the First Floor Club (a jazz and sometimes folk joint on Asquith Ave) spoke of 'false values and phony ideals' when asked what it was they meant to escape;[62] the hippies of the mid-1960s concurred, railing against 'fake' or 'plastic' Villagers who were merely following, rather than *being*; by the late 1960s, bikers were venerated by many other Villagers for their supposed authenticity, their radical commitment to wish-fulfilment; and both women and men who refused to engage with the supposedly liberating ethic of free love were criticized for their alienation from their bodies. As Doug Rossinow has argued (using an alternative term for the counterculture), 'like the new left, freaks believed in the power of transgression, of crossing boundaries. Like the new left, they felt they lived in a society of alienation, and they searched, above all, for authenticity.'[63]

There are a variety of competing theories as to what promoted such a widespread phenomenon of alienated (especially middle-class) youth in post-war North America. In Leerom Medovoi's impressive analysis, post-war suburbanization is explored as 'a primary Cold War ideological apparatus' which promoted the rise of rebellious teens.[64] Because 'the suburbs were widely seen as a space of assimilation into a white, middle-class consumer ethos that would alleviate social conflict,' in other words, because they would promote a kind of anesthetizing effect on its inhabitants, a certain anxiety took hold over the impact this might have on young people born into such a structure.[65] In the suburbs – spaces closely associated with women and children in public discourse – would people become soft, feminized, incapable of individual thought?[66] In the mid-1960s, Canadian sociologist S.D. Clark looked back to the suburbs in the 1950s as places where 'families turned in towards themselves … [this was] not a society in which people were alert to the important issues of the world.'[67]

In a Cold War climate of concern over totalitarianism and social control, this cookie-cutter suburban conformism was cause for alarm. As a result, the figure of the rebel teenager – the subject of much debate and consideration in the 1950s – became a terribly complex site of competing political concerns. 'Lurking as a continual risk for the teenager,' Medovoi continues, 'was the lure of juvenile delinquency, the Scylla which adults needed to weigh against the Charybdis of incipient authoritarianism resulting from excessive adult control.'[68] Into the 1960s, then, the idea of youth rebellion was tied (at least in part) to a refusal of the dehumanizing effects of the suburbs on white, middle-class North Americans. And, since Toronto was immersed in its own period of protracted suburbanization, and continuing debates over the conformity this implied, Medovoi's analysis fits our purposes nicely.[69]

Emerging out of a period of affluence and relative safety – the 1950s led to the shadow of the Bomb but did not live directly under it – young people of diverse backgrounds and demographics came to similar conclusions about the state of the world and of their place relative to it. 'We are people of this generation,' began a famous 1962 student position paper, 'bred in at least modest comfort, housed now in universities, looking uncomfortably to the world we inherit.'[70] For many students both in the United States and in Canada, this sentiment seemed on target – in most retrospective views of the formation of New Left movements on campuses around North America, the Port Huron Statement (named for the town at which the paper was first presented) is treated as a significant moment.[71]

What theorist Herbert Marcuse would dub the 'Great Refusal' – the striving for liberation from the conformism and alienation fostered by the affluent society – was taken up by many young people in the early

1960s as a political project.[72] While student groups more actively pursued this goal through political agitation, writing, and demonstration, many individuals chose to act out their versions of this rebellion against affluence through a great cultural refusal. Following the Beats, a growing number of teenagers and university students by the early 1960s were engaging with a politics of authenticity through the adoption of unconventional aesthetics, practices, and behaviours. Performances of bohemia, widely believed to have been precursors to this contemporary pursuit of the authentic, became visible and even pronounced in some urban centres across North America. Yorkville, by 1960, can be counted among these.

Throughout this history of Yorkville and its Villagers, we will repeatedly come across young people whose articulations of rebellion against contemporary society correspond with these interrelated themes of alienation and authenticity and an existential approach to both. However, it is only in the rarest case in which a Villager employed these specific terms, or couched their feelings in such rhetoric. Rather, words like 'phony,' 'plastic,' and 'commercialized' abound – with each of these terms related to a central anxiety over the phenomenon of tourism which would take hold in the Village after 1964. The pursuit of living otherwise, as it was variously explored in the Village, often stemmed from a desire for authentic life and experience – but it was frustrated by the persistent feeling that whatever Yorkville meant to represent was being co-opted, faked, performed by poseurs and pretenders.[73]

In early March 1959, *Toronto Daily Star* reporter Lotta Dempsey published a pioneering two-part column on 'Toronto's Beatnik Cult.' Her exposé, as it were, stands as one of the only first-hand examinations of Toronto's pre-Yorkville hip scene, and as such it demands some close attention. Dempsey was clearly overwhelmed by what she found in the unnamed hangouts in which she gathered her information, and her reaction is reflected in prose that is both purple and theatrical. But her ear for dialogue is what pushes her work beyond mere sensationalism: 'Legs melted under, soundless and boneless. Long sweatered arms knitted into the body. He was a charcoal shadow, caught against the glare of the studio lights. "What are Beatniks about?" he repeated … Let's say it's more like we've resigned. Resigned from the race … We've withdrawn, that's all. Withdrawn from a contemporary world of false values and phony ideals.'[74] Dempsey, who within a year would found the Voice of Women, an upper-middle-class second-wave feminist and peace organization, was intrigued by such a refusal of hegemonic expectation, principles, and common sense.[75] Her examination of Toronto's Beat scene was, she admitted, motivated by her fascination with the famous American Beat generation, to whom she had been paying attention for some time. 'I had listened attentively to Beat generation telecasts, plays, movies, and broadcasts,' she explained, exposing her mediated version of the Beats. 'But had the cult really reached [Toronto]?'

The young people she interviewed seemed proof that yes, indeed, the Beat 'cult' existed in urban Canada too. But were the Canadian Beats mere copies of the American characters they had seen on television? Was this an authentic Beat culture? Dempsey's subjects seemed to her to be too automatic in their responses, their phrases too pat, their sentiments somehow familiar. After one young man told her that Beats dressed in black because 'we are in mourning for our lives,' Dempsey's scepticism overflowed. 'This sounded suspiciously like a quote – and they use many, with or without credit. For instance, asked for the nub of Beat philosophy, one said glibly, "it's being at the bottom of your personality and looking up." "Yes," I said. "I heard that broadcast, too."'[76]

Toronto's Beats, like their Villager progeny, were profoundly influenced by hip fashions, aesthetics, and ideology from south of the border. The mere fact that Dempsey's article seems an introduction to Toronto's Beat scene is enough to suggest a time lag here – the United States had been wrestling with Beat youth for at least five years by 1959, and had certainly moved beyond such 'do-we-have-Beatniks-too?' journalistic efforts. But the volatility of hip lies in the paradox that it is as much about following as it is about leading. The call-and-response between hip and square is the dialectic that maintains the passageway of hip through history. There would be no hip without co-optation, no cool without imitators.[77]

By 11 June 1960, at least some Torontonians knew they were being had when Susan Kastner, a twenty-year-old from the toney Forest Hill neighbourhood, rented herself out as a Beatnik for hire.[78] Such schemes (as much about critiquing the public fascination with Beats as a pseudo-anthropological identity category as they were about cynical co-optation) were not uncommon in the United States in the late 1950s, and offer a complicated set of interpretive possibilities.[79] Their apparent sundering of the counter-hegemonic qualities of Beat authenticity in an embrace of capitalism and material gain leaves them open to heavy criticism, yet their acknowledgment of the performative aspects of the 'Beatnik' reminds us of the difficulty inherent in any discussion of authenticity and essentialism when it comes to identity.

Beat identity, knotty and defiant of simple definition, must be understood as the dominant influence on what would come to be known as
the hippie identity.[80] However, any overemphasis on the sway that Beat
Toronto enjoyed in its immediate time period (say, 1957–62) would be
foolish. At their height, Toronto Beats were but a tiny manifestation of a
multitude of emerging youth identities; they were among the most fascinating to observers, perhaps, but were not yet the vanguard of some
new cultural groundswell. Their greatest immediate contribution, and
the contribution with which this book is most concerned, was their propensity for new, exciting, and otherwise under-appreciated innovations
in the world of art, film, music, and literature. Their experimentalism
contributed to an atmosphere, in those few establishments that catered
to their ilk, of spontaneity and cacophonous energy.

Ian Tyson, among the very earliest (and soon to be the most famous)
folksingers in the Yorkville coffee-house scene, was heavily influenced
by the American Beats and tended to run with other such aficionados
once he arrived in Toronto in 1958. He had made the trip from Vancouver alone, thumbing rides and hopping buses across the country,
chasing dreamy visions of Sal Paradise, Carl Solomon, Hart Kennedy,
and all of those 'angel-headed hipsters' of Beat fame.[81] Toronto's scene,
bolstered by the arrival of such excited, talented, and Beat-influenced
artists, developed slowly, at first, but surely. By the early 1960s, the
kinds of scenes that Kerouac and Ginsberg had envisioned, depicted,
and detailed in their work were being re-created, lovingly and with
great respect, by their Canadian cousins. The early draw to Yorkville
was, fittingly given the artistic and poetic tendencies of the Beats, felt
most keenly by aspiring artists, musicians, and writers. David DePoe
recalls that it was a poet who first alerted him to the scene. 'When I
first started to go there in '63 it was very Beat, basically. Sort of like:
you go there and you listen to poetry, music, and y'know. That year I
had a friend who was a poet in residence at University of Toronto and
together we started going to Yorkville, to this coffee house where a poet
could just get up and read something and then somebody would sing
a couple of songs.'[82]

The early Village coffee-house scene, exemplified by such key establishments as the Village Corner (an L-shaped folk club on Avenue
Road), the First Floor Club, the Half Beat, the 71 Club, and the Clef
Club (an underground Yorkville Ave haunt boasting the stage on which
a young Sylvia Fricker [later Tyson] played her first Toronto gig), was
comprised of just the kinds of artsy young people that had blown open

the San Francisco-area scene some years earlier. As venerable jazz joints like the House of Hamburg (which had played host to luminaries like Miles Davis and Cannonball Adderley in the 1950s) looked to local acts like Ed Bickert and Moe Kauffman, Village clubs began to book folk musicians as their hip entertainment. Typical of these establishments was the Village Corner, in journalist Nicholas Jennings's words, a 'Hipster's Heaven: a smoky room with dark blue walls and a large mural of black slaves being unshackled.'[83] Amid the stirring of support for a swelling civil rights movement in the United States, such a gesture of solidarity was both overtly symbolic and implicitly performative; a white-owned club that (almost always) featured white performers and catered to a nearly exclusively white clientele suggesting a common need for freedom from bondage. The literal freeing of the black slaves is invoked as a reflection of the figurative enslavement of white, middle-class youth; the dominating image of the slave losing his chains, the definitive model of authenticity achieved, was there not so much for admiration as for *identification.*

When it opened on St Nicholas St in 1960, the Bohemian Embassy seemed like a bridge between the gloaming Gerrard St scene and embryonic Yorkville. Famous for its wildly eclectic entertainment, the Embassy promoted local talent of all kinds, from folksingers to comedians, writers to painters. Toronto's strong stable of poets were encouraged to use the Embassy's stage to try out new material, and Margaret Atwood, Milton Acorn, Earle Birney, and Gwendolyn MacEwen all made that heady scene. Atwood's biographer Rosemary Sullivan paints a charming picture: 'The Bohemian Embassy was up two flights of narrow, bannisterless steps, on the second floor, a barn of a room with walls painted black ... There were little tables, covered with red-checked tablecloths and candles stuck in Chianti bottles, and chairs for about 120 people, with a stage at the back and a sound system of sorts. The washroom was a cubicle that opened directly onto the main room. It had no lock, and you had to learn to pee with one hand on the door if you weren't to find yourself, pants down, staring into the audience under the glare of the naked bulb swinging above your head.' Of those who would make the legendary scene, Atwood recalled that they represented the swath of Torontonians who looked for escape from 'the lumpen bourgeoisie and the shackles of respectable wage-earning.'[84]

It was in that diversity, the shifting sands of artistry and performance, that lay the charm and function of a smoky room such as the Embassy. The sublime cacophony of contrasting, even clashing voices was absolutely central to the bohemian aesthetic by the early 1960s. Immediacy, authenticity, and trickster ingenuity were all rolled together in such a haphazard flow. It was all about the NOW. 'We had the Bohemian Embassy,' recalls Marilyn Brooks, whose Gerrard St fashion outlet moved up to Cumberland St in the early 1960s, becoming the ever-popular Unicorn. 'The first time I went there – I'm from Detroit, Michigan – it was like *woooooah*, this is hot! You walked up the steps and you got stamped and then you sat there and you got your coffee – I mean, it wasn't a bottle of white wine, it was coffee after coffee. And somebody would read poetry against St Nicholas Street ... and I thought, wow, this is *it*, you know?'[85]

If the 1960s was, as a recent survey of post-war Canadian art has declared, 'a decade unabashedly focused on the present,' the influence of the American Beats had as much to do with this obsession with the 'now' as did the atom bomb.[86] The self-centredness usually ascribed to the baby boom generation, the dawning of philosophical and artistic movements in structuralism and postmodernism (which both, to varying degrees, destabilized historical perspective in their pursuits), and the sudden, rapid-fire shifts in cultural perspectives and common-sense ideological positions all fit hand in glove with such a view of the period. Here were a few years under the influence of the immediate, and a brief period in which conservatism and classicism were largely pushed aside by cultural industries in pursuit of the ever elusive zeitgeist: the impulsive, the instantaneous, the unanticipated.

At a time when the international art world was rocked by what appeared to be radical refusals of convention, of modernism, and, most overtly, of idealism, and the resurgence and/or development of such deconstructionist enterprises as neo-Dadaism, Pop, and Abstract Art, critics and artists alike struggled to express the acceleration and contradiction of the decade through increasingly unpredictable messages. As the boundaries of the category 'youth' broadened under the conditions of social experimentation and counter-hegemonic ideologies in the 1960s, so did the boundaries of the category 'art'; for the expression of the dissonance and volatility of youth culture (and its post-war corollary, counterculture) could be served only through new and radical aesthetics. The Toronto Beat scene, enticed by the prospect of engaging with something novel, something indefinite, something that celebrated the existential unknown, latched onto this movement, peopling its shows, galleries, and Happenings.[87]

Such expected late-1960s countercultural activities as drug use, free sex, and social protest and dissent were already active pursuits in Toronto by the late 1950s. Moreover, new methods and ideas about representation helped to engender a sense of renaissance in the scene, which in turn invited Beat interest and participation. The key factors that can be associated with the change of course taken by many artists in the period include: a widespread refusal of artistic convention, formalism, and the influence of the Western aesthetic canon; a tendency towards fusion and eclecticism; the integration of new media into the process; and overtly political, even activist, messages and meanings.[88]

In Toronto, as it was in artistic centres all over the Western world, the neo-Dada movement (heavily influenced by New York-based Marcel Duchamp's formidable body of work) rocked the art scene in the very early 1960s.[89] A couple of years prior to the psychedelic revolution that would forever change popular music, a similar sort of revolution was transforming the landscape of aesthetics and design. New techniques, especially assemblage and collage and the use of weird, counter-intuitive materials, were suddenly taken up by a wave of artists increasingly ready to throw off what many saw as the bankrupt framework of formalism. With great gusto, Toronto artist Graham Coughtry voiced the frustration shared by many of his colleagues with the Group of Seven-dominated Canadian art mould: 'Every damn tree in the country has been painted,' he joked.[90] Even as conservatives loudly failed to understand such developments – Toronto mayor Nathan Phillips had publicly denounced a Painters Eleven exhibition in 1956, complaining that 'these pictures are something I wouldn't want my children to see'[91] – the undeniable draw of the avant-garde was electrifying Toronto's expanding ranks of rebellious artists, attracting some surprising new aficionados.[92] One young man who would eventually join a biker gang remembers being attracted to Yorkville in those years by the revolutionary Village artistry. 'So I went through the Village scene, with my sisters, for something to do,' he explains. 'The art galleries interested us, especially the small ones. We had friends that were in the gallery world; two ladies I knew then started a gallery in Yorkville.'[93]

While there was no real art hub in Canada in the 1960s, Toronto (in semi-partnership with London, Ontario) represented a key site for the exhibition and production of progressive art. At the centre of this neo-Dada scene, Toronto's Isaacs Gallery (which moved to the edge of Yorkville, at 832 Yonge St, in 1961) played host to work by virtually every experimental Canadian artist in the 1960s, including such luminaries as Michael Snow, Greg Curnoe, and Joyce Wieland.[94] However, in the spirit of expanded visions of the boundaries of 'art,' Avrom Isaacs's groundbreaking gallery wasn't solely confined to painting and sculpture, but included exhibitions of experimental film, free jazz music, modern dance, and poetry.[95] Judy Pocock recalls that the poetry readings at the Isaacs were 'quite the going concern. My dad got involved in organizing those poetry meetings. And I remember Gwendolyn MacEwen, I remember Milton Acorn [reading]. So those would be your bohemians. They brought all kinds of these well-known Beat poets up. I remember LeRoi Jones (who is now Amiri Baraka) came, and Greg Corso, I think. There were a number of people.'[96] For a time, the Isaacs Gallery even doubled as a publishing house for such underground poets; in an innovative endeavour, their verses would be paired with the work of local painters in illustrated volumes.[97]

The marriage between folk music and art in early 1960s Yorkville was a significant factor in the development of coffee houses as sites for bohemian community building. While some curious youth may have come for the music, perhaps some would have stayed for the art (or vice versa); thus, for example, as Ian Tyson or Malka Marom performed onstage at the Cellar, the walls might have been hung with the latest from local artists, just as young and hip. In some cases, neighbourhood art galleries formed associations with coffee houses in order to doubly promote their creations. The Half Beat entered into a partnership with the Here and Now Gallery in the early 1960s, developing a successful formula for others to follow.[98] Still, some artists refused to hang their work in the coffee houses, complaining that they rarely sold.[99]

Of course, there were always exceptions to this rule. The venerable Bohemian Embassy and the less venerable Chenel coffee house both planned regular exhibitions in the early 1960s, attracting buyers as well as aficionados. Such shows could make for fairly lucrative business for the right artist, at the right time. For example, a nineteen-year-old Ontario College of Art student named Zigy Blazejy sold seven avant-garde paintings at his November 1962 opening at the Bohemian Embassy.[100] But, in keeping with the eclecticism of the early 1960s Village scene, coffee houses celebrated and sold whatever they chose, regardless of aesthetic or other value. Confounding expectations was part of the fun, part of the excitement behind the scene – agreement was a kind of stultification of thought. And so the modes ranged from the surreal (favoured by the Bohemian Embassy) all the way to the realist (often hung on the brick walls of the 71 Club and the Cellar). But, more often than not, contrasting modes would hang together, side by side, taunting the purists.

A cousin to Beat experiments in uniting disparate forms of art into messy harmony, Dada-inspired mixed-media spectacles called Happenings were becoming increasingly popular with artists and consumers alike.[101] Often held in galleries such as the Isaacs, but just as often in apartments, lofts, and coffee houses in and around Yorkville, Happenings were designed around neo-Dadaist preoccupations with juxtaposition, theatre/reality, and disorder. As a contemporary art critic explained, 'the vital aspect at least in the happenings was that there were few guidelines, no style, no measure beyond the act and the spirit of the act.'[102] A transparent attempt to refigure the expected manner (grave and conventional as it is) of viewing art in silent, empty, cold galleries, and museums, Happenings were designed to err on the side of chaos.

Toronto's first documented Happening took place in 1959 in local artist Dennis Burton's studio on Huntley St.[103] From this first event, interest in the Happening blossomed, and it became a popular local activity. Participants (for this is what they were called – they were not consumers, but collaborators in the very art which they had come to experience) crowded together in cramped rooms, overwhelmed by noise, by visual stimuli.[104] Susan Sontag's vivid description of a 1962 New York Happening helps to get at the kind of experience one might undergo at one of these events. 'To describe a Happening for those who have not seen one means dwelling on what happenings are not,' she begins, in her famously contrary manner. 'They don't take place on a stage conventionally understood, but in a dense object-clogged setting which may be made, assembled, or found, or all three. In this setting a number of participants, not actors, perform movements and handle objects antiphonally and in concert to the accompaniment (sometimes) of words, wordless sounds, music, flashing lights, and odors. The Happening has no plot, though it is an action, or rather a series of actions and events. It also shuns continuous rational discourse.'[105] Toronto author Michael Kirby concurs. A Happening, in his view, was 'a piece of art that does not focus on an object, but on an event. The artist begins with a plan of action in which the public is brought into an active relationship with the art event. The action does not take place in the closed environment of a gallery but rather in various public places of a city, where the artist breaks in suddenly with his performance.'[106]

At the root of all of this, of course, is performance. Happenings –

designed as they were around a recognition and celebration of the performative aspects of identity – relied on the participation of their audience. The collaboration involved a kind of agreement, an unspoken desire to play at weird, to engage with others in a highly theatrical manner, to accept that, within the parameters of the Happening, one's identity was always in flux, at risk, contested ground. Gender, race, sexual orientation, age, sanity, all of these and more could be treated as mutable in the Happening environment. The attraction for Beat youth, a group that might be defined through a common refusal of liberal-capitalist identity expectations, lay precisely in the wholeness of the rejection of normality. In a Happening, one could lose oneself, at least in theory, and explore that loss for what it was: a fleeting, but no-less ecstatic, *freedom*.[107]

Marijuana: Exhibit A

In mid-summer 1961, before many Torontonians had likely even heard of Yorkville, this still quiet site for after-dark bohemianism was abruptly thrust into a media spotlight. Caught holding a 'drinking party' at their private house at 71 Yorkville Ave (at which they had allegedly sold liquor and 'permitted drunkenness'), thirty-year-old Werner Graeber and his wife, Eva, were brought up on charges.[108] The twenty-two other (mostly younger) people busted at their party by the Morality Squad were charged as 'found-ins' and brought down to the Don Jail for a night of interrogation, physical abuse, and confinement in a cold jail cell.[109] In Pierre Berton's succinct words (written a year later, once the ensuing court proceedings had finally concluded): 'They bundled the lot up and sent them to the Don Jail ... where each was stripped, showered, deloused and given an intimate physical examination. Later, in court, all the charges, which were based on scanty evidence, were thrown out.'[110]

This apparent police brutality was both roundly and directly condemned by many media sources and municipal authorities.[111] In fact, the fallout from the 'Yorkville Row' included a systematic review and change of police arrest procedure, not to mention a formal investigation of the modus operandi at the Don Jail.[112] Moreover, the public outrage over a group of young people being physically assaulted by a boorish police squad was compelling enough to force the mayor to speak out against his own police force in severe tones. '[Such raids] bring disrepute to the police force,' complained Phillips. 'There's something wrong with this system.' In a move that seems highly unlikely today in our 'just a few bad apples' climate of buck passing, Phillips actually adopted the position that the problem was institutional, not exceptional. 'I don't think the men have been properly instructed,' he concluded. 'Somebody fell down on the job; there's got to be a change.'[113]

And yet, barely two months later, much of this anti-police sentiment – or, at least, this benefit of the doubt offered to the young found-ins – was turned on its ear. In a subsequent raid on the Graebers' house (now a legitimate place of business following a successful application to turn 71 Yorkville Ave into one of the original local coffee houses, the 71 Club[114]), the Morality Squad came up with 'four marijuana cigarets [sic].' Public sentiment, which had largely been behind Graeber and his unfortunate friends in the two months between the first and second raids, shifted dramatically in the wake of this new charge.

Marijuana was still mostly an unknown proposition in Toronto – pot was a forbidden whisper, a spectre haunting back alleys and ethnic ghettos, a fog hanging in the stifling air of some beatnik jazz club like George's Spaghetti House.[115] In fact, Canada had good reason to consider itself marijuana-free: the number of convictions (national) for marijuana possession had dropped from an all-time high of twenty-two cases in 1959 to a mere seventeen by the end of 1961.[116] Drug use as an issue hardly surfaces in media reports on Yorkville in the years prior to 1965 – if one were to judge by newspaper articles alone, narcotics would appear to have been an acknowledged, but rarely central, focus of concern. So the idea in 1961 that Yorkville could contain such a rare and menacing substance, and that Graeber's coffee house could have been operating as a sort of speakeasy for 'hop heads,' was deeply troubling.[117]

Troubling, but also humiliating. For many (such as Berton) who had supported Graeber and his companions in the face of the initial raid, this revelation came as a slap in the face. Public sentiment pulled a wild about-face. As Berton complained later: 'The reaction of some of my readers to this startling criminal [narcotic] charge was predictable, though a little saddening. I received many letters and phone calls, which said, in effect: *You see, the police were right all the time and you were wrong … They should have jailed the lot and thrown the key away.*'[118] But Berton, unable to comment on a case as it was before the courts, had been forced to hold his tongue.

There can be little doubt that Graeber was the victim of a corrupt police action. Faced with the embarrassment stemming from the overzealous (and illegal) raid of mid-summer, and continued rebuke and public outcry over the subsequent cavity searches of people against whom all charges were later dropped, it seems likely that some police officers were looking to mend their reputations. And so it appears that, in a gambit still regularly performed by those very few crooked cops unable (or unwilling) to do the work necessary to make the case against their suspects, they planted evidence.

The circumstances surrounding the detection of the four joints in the Graebers' coffee house were (and remain) sketchy – when Graeber was acquitted in April 1962, it was largely because of the lack of an unambiguous police narrative. It was never made clear just how the joints (which were hidden in odd, unlikely places) were discovered. One joint – the one around which much of the trial revolved – seemed to simply *fall* out of nowhere as a policeman opened a locked door (with Graeber's consent). In fact, Graeber's largely conciliatory efforts throughout the raid never appeared to have been those of a guilty man.[119]

Because Graeber had, ever since opening his house to the public as a business, suspected at least one of his patrons to be an undercover policeman, the raid was entirely expected. Not only that, but Graeber (and others) testified that, for some two and a half hours prior to the raid, they watched a dozen police officers gather in an adjacent parking lot to survey the 71 Club in preparation for the action. If they had wanted to dispose of the evidence, certainly they had ample time to do so. Moreover, once the raid had begun, Graeber was quoted as offering to let the policemen 'tear the place apart' if they wished.[120] He even helped them to open unlocked doors (which they were preparing to knock down). Once the marijuana was found, and Graeber was incarcerated, he disregarded the advice of his counsel and underwent both a voluntary lie-detector test and a psychiatric interview while under the influence of sodium amytal, a kind of 'truth serum.' He passed both examinations.[121]

In the end, it was not Graeber's conciliatory efforts that saved him but rather a bit of evidence that demonstrated that none of the joints were uncovered in private sections of his house. All of the marijuana was found in public areas, where it could not be definitively established to whom it belonged. The solitary joint which was thought to have been found inside a locked room (the one that had fallen as if from thin air) looked to be the only one that could put Graeber away. But a last-minute argument that the door frame leading *into* this room was wide enough on top to stash a cigarette demonstrated that the joint might have been on the public side of the door to begin with.[122]

Consequently, Pierre Berton pushed his readers to demand: 'How *did* those reefers get in that Yorkville coffee house?' And, more to the point, 'how did the Toronto police learn of the presence of these cigarets [sic]?'[123] Neither question was ever answered. But the stage was set for a conflict that would persist – like a tear across worn fabric, expanding, ever widening – throughout the decade. Still a few years before Yorkville would become a centre for widespread youth activity, here was an episode that appeared to establish all of the elements of the subsequent narrative. The major players now seemed to be in place: a hip culture that saw itself as persecuted, misunderstood by the wider society, and subject to violent, degrading coercion by the police; a municipal authority aghast at the presence of a deviant subculture so near the heart of Toronto; a police force that found itself torn between both sides, with the twin ghouls of drugs and vice their chief concerns; a public prone to a certain degree of hysteria over its young people; and a media whose reportage, varied and complicated, would play a most significant, if perplexing, role.

Sophistication versus Bohemia: Towards a Village of Yorkville Association

Perhaps as a result of the liberal dose of embarrassment that followed the Graeber incident, for the following two years Yorkville was allowed to develop without much in the way of media or municipal attention. Few articles on the Village found their way into the major newspapers, and those that did invariably detailed the art, fashion, or coiffure one might discover in the upscale shopping district. There was little indication (beyond the rare mention of the coffee-house scene) that the Village was anything but a jewel in Toronto's crown.

This was a period of intense growth for Yorkville's carriage trade, and the moment when its reputation for upscale couture was first solidified in the popular perception. An exotic cheese shop, a series of abstract art galleries, and a variety of fashion outlets and hair salons moved in before the end of 1963, all with a share in the idea of Yorkville as a zone of difference, a 'little bit of Europe.'[124] A scan of the advertising for the new storefronts suggests that Yorkville was to be understood as an exciting upscale cultural experience. Of the hair salon Club Coiffure, the *Globe and Mail*'s Mary Walpole wrote (in her affected prose): 'You only need to stroll up Old York Lane a bit ... that fascinating brick paved walk between Cumberland and Yorkville ... to discover Club

Coiffure.'[125] Her language is instructive: she is at once advertising a new venue for haute couture while reminding her readers that the goal of a visit to Yorkville is exploration and *discovery*. Can a brick walkway (uncovered by mural, design, or other artifice) be 'fascinating'? Sure it can: if it is among the only ones in the city. In a Toronto devoid of otherwise classy urbane enclaves, exploring Yorkville's faux-European cobblestone footpaths and discovering a chic boutique or hair salon is a distinctly exciting, attractive experience.

Alongside such attempts to establish Yorkville as an exotic local get-away, a quiet but concerted effort was made by local businesses and residents to keep their Village free and clear of negative (read: youth) connotation. What was at stake for them was the fear that, if Yorkville were to become a bona fide bohemian centre, their interests would suffer. This conflict, frequently reduced by observers, participants, and commentators to the uneasy either/or of sophistication/bohemia – *as if the two categories were mutually exclusive!* – played out between 1961 and 1965 in a variety of ways. This struggle over the identity of the Village, especially in the *Toronto Daily Star* and the *Globe and Mail*, became the central frame through which Yorkville was presented by media sources. In these early years, before the youth culture had really taken hold in the district, the media representations of the Village already tended towards this divisive notion that there were two factions at play, each vying for the right to call Yorkville *theirs*. On the one hand, the Village was claimed by the sophisticated carriage-trade merchants and (to a lesser extent) the long-time residents, and, on the other, it was becoming home to a new, amorphous, and indistinct bohemian youth contingent. Such media frames emphasized the suspense created by such unlikely factions facing off: Who will come out on top? What, indeed *who*, will the Village look like when the smoke clears?[126]

The early 1960s, then, saw Yorkville rise to a new position of prominence as a 'destination.' Yet it is striking how often in these years Yorkville was introduced geographically at the outset of articles detailing its charms. Even as late as 1962, merchants were still describing their Yorkville Ave locations as 'just two short blocks above Bloor Street.'[127] It had not yet achieved a stand-alone *Yorkville-refers-to-this* distinction and definition. It was still an unknown proposition: to some, just another series of streets; to others, a Village in the heart of the city.[128]

This vision of Yorkville as 'the Village' was crucial to its growth as an idea, a destination, and a scene. In most cases, Yorkville Ave was its synecdochical conduit; if it happened on Yorkville Ave, it was a Vil-

lage event. But this was not always so. For instance, a 1961 article by
Pierre Berton (who clearly had his eye on the Village, and was always,
in his way, hip) made the case that, after three years of development,
Cumberland St had become 'slightly gayer and wackier than Yorkville
St. [sic].' It was colour and design that Berton emphasized most strenuously – 'lilac hues' were everywhere, and the exotic seemed to furnish
the otherwise staid scenery. 'The area lends itself to the decorative,' he
wrote, referring now to the Village scene more generally. 'Modern art,
baroque statuary Chinese jade, espresso coffee, spring hats, black lamp-
posts, boutiques, antiques and Yoga' characterized what was, to Berton,
a neighbourhood with more of Paris in it than Hogtown. Already, however, shades of the ensuing crises over ownership of the Village were
falling on the discussion. One of Berton's interviewees complained of
'*very* expensive' real estate; a young Budd Sugarman (who upon his
recent death would be remembered as the unofficial mayor of Yorkville
for his myriad contributions to the scene) complained that the street
might already be 'doomed by soaring taxes and astronomical rents.'[129]

But it wasn't just taxes and rents that concerned Yorkville's homeowners and merchants. In the blue TV light of the post-war era, as University of Toronto professor and intellectual-landmark-to-be Marshall
McLuhan was busily pointing out, cultural acceleration was the order
of the day, and many were finding the changes too abrupt, too total-
izing, too severe. Character and identity were at stake here; if Toronto
continued on this path (in areas both cultural and physical), who would
recognize it in a few short years? Or more to the point: Was the old
Toronto so bad anyway? Why kill it off?

In what was dubbed 'The Battle to Save Toronto's Past' by the *Toronto
Daily Star*, the first 'front' was Yorkville. A year and a half on from the
Graebers' initial bust, after almost five years of sustained development
on the part of merchants and gallery owners, and with new after-hours
clubs and coffee houses opening in every vacant storefront, basement,
and rentable space, Yorkville appeared to have reached a fight or flight
moment. Homeowners (especially those on the older end of the age
spectrum) were concerned by the sudden shift in the character of their
neighbourhood; merchants were frustrated by an influx of youthful
energy and nightly noise; and venture capitalists were standing on the
sidelines, waiting for the area to be completely rezoned in their favour,
opening up the district to bulldozers, 'wide-open' commercialization,
and the wrecking ball of progress.

In the first official showdown of this 'battle,' a meeting of Village property owners in February 1963 exposed a rift between the residents and the merchants, categories that also divided the old from the new. Called by long-time resident Mary Cassidy (whose anti-carriage-trade vision of Yorkville set the tone), the meeting brought together some 180 people, including observers from the Toronto Planning Board. Opinions were divided, but the key issue was character. Whose Yorkville *was* this? 'Working widows and old-age pensioners,' whose numbers were dwindling, were singled out as the victims of Yorkville's rapid development since the emphasis on attracting wealthy customers alienated those unable to afford their wares. 'Let's look after the people in our own district – not after those people on Bloor St.,' complained a Hazelton Ave resident. But this argument failed to move the younger, capital-minded merchants who saw in Yorkville a venue for excitement, growth, and prosperity. 'This business about lavender and old lace is all right,' offered one such merchant, summarizing the feelings of many, 'but you can't have an old village in the centre of the city.' For his part, Alistair Crerar, director of the long-term division of the Planning Board, fell clearly on the side of the boutique merchants, declaring that 'we think [the Village carriage trade] is desirable, pleasant and unique in Toronto, possibly in Canada.'[130]

Following the restless meeting, a loose association of Yorkville businesses and residents came together under the umbrella concern of 'protection' for the Yorkville that they knew and loved. Comprised of interested parties from the immediate Yorkville area (including Budd Sugarman, John and Nancy Pocock, and John and Marilyn McHugh), the Village of Yorkville Association (VYA), as it came to be called, was designed as a political bulwark against any possible rezoning and development of their territory. As the *Globe and Mail* reported of its first official meeting, the VYA was most concerned with the 'preservation and development' of this 'colourful district.' The initial meetings of the association were focused largely on keeping parking lots and bulldozers out of the area, arresting the automobile traffic as much as possible, and preserving the essential character of the buildings themselves. In fact, the group's main foes in this endeavour were pro-business factions from the surrounding area such as the Yonge-Bay-Bloor Businessmen's Association, which aimed to have Yorkville largely razed to make room for high-rises.

This conflict had mainly played itself out by early June 1963, a few short months after the VYA was formed. In front of one of the largest crowds ever gathered for such an event, the Toronto Buildings and

Development Committee came down on the side of the VYA over the pro-business fractions. 'Acting on the recommendations of the Toronto Planning Board,' reported the *Globe* the next morning, 'the committee resisted pressures for zoning changes to permit a substantially greater commercial development than is now allowed.'[131] However, soon after this first series of meetings, the association would find itself much more concerned with internal battles than these external encroachments.[132] After some initial victories against big business and parking-lot schemes in the spring of 1963, the VYA's stated mandate began to shift. No longer simply designed to protect the interests of Yorkville residents and businesses from corporate intrusion, the VYA now emphasized its goal to underline *sophistication* and diminish *bohemian* influences in the Village. It was believed that the very character of Yorkville was in jeopardy.

The Mousetrap: Gay and Lesbian Yorkville, 1957–61

Crucial to Yorkville's attractiveness to gay and lesbian youth in these years was the relative quietude of the scene, which meant that a degree of anonymity could be maintained. In an era when Toronto was only barely moving along the road towards respect and acceptance of gay and lesbian identities, and when media-driven sensationalism was by no means an unlikely prospect should a subversive enclave be uncovered, the opportunity to perform gay and lesbian identities within a multifaceted public context was surely enticing.

Intermingling with a relatively safe alternative community, gays and lesbians found in the early Yorkville scene a kind of security in numbers, and a degree of non-gay acceptance and respect (even admiration and veneration) unlikely elsewhere in Toronto. According to Clifford Collier, a fixture in the Village in the late 1950s and early 1960s, being 'out' within the coffee-house scene 'was never a problem – you went in and they had flamboyant people and all the rest of it, and no one seemed to have any problem with it.' Collier explains this exceptional scenario in terms of capital and pragmatism. 'I think the coffee houses at that time were trying to make a go,' he explained, 'so they weren't going to turn away *anybody* who was a paying customer.'[133]

For a period of roughly three years, the centre of gay Yorkville was a tiny unheated room off the back of the Greek-owned Avenue Rd coffee house La Coterie.[134] Run by a recent immigrant named Bob Stavros, La Coterie was quintessential Yorkville Euro-chic. More into jazz than folk music, Stavros endeavoured to attract the crowds by booking jazz acts into the small back room behind the somewhat elaborately decorated (by Village standards) main space. However, the room proved too small for full jazz outfits, and Stavros was left with a record player and an empty, but charmingly antiquated, space. 'This little back room was very, very rustic,' recalls Collier. 'Barn board, covered walls, little tables *yay* big so you could just hold a coffee cup, and benches all around the walls, with some little stools.'[135] The space also had its own entrance around back, and its own porch overlooking a parking lot.

Stavros decided that, since the back room boasted a decor so radically different from the posh front space, it could become a separate café. Stavros approached Collier, who had been working at La Coterie for a few months, and complained about his lack of success at filling the small space. 'And I said, well, I knew it could work if he was willing to accept the [gay] crowd. And I don't know whether it was because he was young, or whether it was because he was Greek, but he said ok, let's give it a try.'[136] Collier's view was that, given the scarcity of hip gay spaces in the city, filling the room with the gay community would never be a problem. Stavros agreed, and the Mousetrap coffee house was born.

Collier, who went on to manage the Mousetrap for about three years, recently explained the significance of this space to Toronto's young gays and lesbians: 'Other than our club, I can't think of any [gay coffee houses]. No one would have been turned away from any of the [Yorkville] clubs because you were obviously gay or lesbian. I mean, there was that kind of fluidity. But none of these coffee houses would have said they were *gay* coffee houses. I can tell you that right now. Even La Coterie. Although [Stavros] obviously got gay people going. When we opened up the Mousetrap, which was *aimed* at the gay crowd, that was to my knowledge the first activity. Otherwise, you were dealing with the bars downtown.'[137] The downtown bars, while vibrant and exciting places for the same-sex communities, were inaccessible to younger lesbians and gays. The drinking age was still twenty-one, and, especially for a community subject to police shenanigans, this law was often very strictly followed. A gay bar was one thing, but a gay bar that served underage youth? Not for long.[138]

The Mousetrap was surprisingly accessible, and refused to allow issues of gender separation or other such political subjects to corrupt the scene. Collier describes the coffee house as a truly pioneering venture; as he demonstrates, the key draw of the Mousetrap was its offer of a space in which younger and older gays and lesbians (and straights as well) could connect, share conversations, and dance to jazz music: 'And so the guys came up, well, kids, they were every age ... which was good in that respect. There were males and females – we never had a problem with it being segregated. The bars were segregated, you see. And the beer houses. The women all hung around a place down around Dundas and Elizabeth St called the Continental, where the drag queens might go, but you only rarely got other gay guys going there.'[139] The Mousetrap, unable to serve liquor, was thus saved from a variety of otherwise persistent barriers between men and women, not to mention younger lesbians and gay teens and their older friends and lovers. 'So it took off. We started when the weather got reasonable – it had to be reasonable because there was no heat!'[140]

Perhaps the greatest legacy of the Mousetrap was its introduction of all-ages queer-friendly afternoon and evening dances in 1959. Such tea dances (as they were known)[141] became enormously popular, with line-ups stretching down the alleyway behind Avenue Rd.[142] Collier's brainchild, the tea dances were an innovation to pick up slack business on Sundays. Tickets were sold during the week, ensuring that, if nobody showed, money would still be pocketed. But people did indeed come. Collier remembers the crowds fondly. 'I liked that we had some real regulars, I mean they came early and reserved their place, and a great percentage of people just [showed up]. And the more people heard about it, the more crowded it got.'[143] While Happenings and civil rights-infused folk performances dominated most Village coffee houses, the tea dances became a parallel celebration of difference, identity, and community.

A gay coffee house was, it seems, not the source of much consternation from the police, the neighbours, or the straight crowd. Collier describes Toronto's bohemian scene in the late 1950s and early 1960s as being an especially safe one, and that gays and lesbians who mixed within it were usually left alone by would-be adversaries: 'You were circumspect, and you didn't sort of hit people in the face with it the way a lot of these kids do now. But at the same time, I never found the problems. We don't remember a lot of gay bashing in those days. There was that *fluidity*, you went in and out. Maybe it was because we stuck with the music crowd, a crowd that was already a subculture. They were more interested in your being interested in what *they* were interested in, than your differences.' One positive result of the heavy influence of the American Beats on the Toronto bohemian scene was that hip and gay were not necessarily thought to be irreconcilable categories. Leading American Beats (most notably Allen Ginsberg) were famously out, and homosexual imagery figured heavily in virtually all key Beat texts – indeed, Jack Kerouak's celebrated *On the Road* can be read as an epic of closeted longing.[144]

While many readers of such texts no doubt missed (or simply blocked out) the homosexual undercurrents – although can one imagine reading Ginsberg's epic *Howl*, with its imagery of men who had 'let themselves be fucked in the ass by saintly motorcyclists, and screamed with joy,' with a blind eye? – it was hardly unknown that, among the Beats, a certain measure of gayness was part of the package.[145] As such, the hip coffee-house crowd was much more readily accepting of gays (and, to a lesser extent, lesbians, who were not much glorified in Beat texts) than was the wider society, and gay and lesbian youth were often among the crowds at the Bohemian Embassy, the Gaslight, or the Penny Farthing, right into the mid-1960s. In an illuminating recollection, Marilyn Brooks paints her first visit to the Mousetrap as a kind of entrée into the hip scene. 'In 1961 when I arrived [from Detroit] a person took me to this coffee house on Avenue Rd. I think gay people were ... they might have been gay but they didn't *say* they were gay. It was more hidden ... I thought it was so incredible! I thought I was such a hippie [sic]! Marty took me there, my first assistant, and I thought: *this is it!* And it *was*.'[146] However, with the advent of the hippies, a scene in which gayness lost its cachet of cool (despite lingering respect and admiration for the Beats), Yorkville would lose much of its former appeal to the community.

Besides, La Coterie (and the Mousetrap) had closed by 1963, and a variety of new gay dance clubs had opened down the Strip, on Yonge St, making Yorkville unnecessary for the gay and lesbian community. Such new clubs took up the same tack as had Collier and Stavros a few years previously: they offered dancing, community, and safer gay spaces, but no alcohol.[147] Collier is quick to reject the notion that hip youth had begun to make things uncomfortable in Yorkville for the gay and lesbian crowd: 'More [gay] spaces drew them away. We weren't driven out, shall we say. Let's put it this way: I think it was just a change in circumstances.'[148] But within a couple years it wouldn't be a question of gay Toronto intermingling with the Yorkville hip scene. When asked if he recalled there being much of a gay presence in Yorkville, Collier laughed. 'I don't remember *anybody* crossing over. It was seen as a straight phenomenon.'[149]

The Ramsden Park Gang and the Church Drop-In Centre

Just up the street from La Coterie and the Mousetrap, at the corner of Webster and Avenue Rd, south of Davenport (and so just within the confines of the Yorkville district), sat St Paul's Avenue Road United Church.[150] And, in its basement, lay a room which for the next eight years would be known as a Village safe house: a place of refuge, a warm and friendly space in which one could duck the rain, meet up with friends, or perhaps even dance.

The centre was overseen by the Reverend James E. Smith – 'Smitty' to the youths he worked tirelessly to protect. Smith had moved to Toronto in 1957 to work for the Ecumenical Council as director of Christian education for Metropolitan Toronto. Early upon arriving, he and his colleagues, working as they were on problems of youth deviance and delinquency, were approached by the Reverend Stewart Crysdale. As Smith recalled in 1972, 'it seems fortunate and providential now that our office was moved to St Paul's Avenue Road United Church ... It also seems providential that Stewart should have introduced us to the gang members who came to his church for sanctuary.'[151] For it was Crysdale who had, since the late 1950s, worked to provide relief and shelter for the Ramsden Park gang, a group of street-smart working-class youth (referred to as 'greasers' by nearly everyone) from the neighbourhoods surrounding his church. And, by the early 1960s, he was getting ready to pass along the reins.

The key characteristics of the greaser in these years – according to the impressions and assumptions of observers of their dress and behaviour – were a working-class background, a taste for alcohol, reasonably uniform clothing, and (for boys) short, greased hair. Jim Felstiner, a youth worker who was employed at a Settlement House a kilometre south of Yorkville, described the greaser look as he recalled it: 'They had their collars up and they walked with a swagger ... We used the word *culture*, street culture. America had street gangs, Toronto did not at that point. My kids [at the Settlement House] used a lot of grease on their hair, and their hair was terribly important. Their hair and their trousers. They all wore bell bottoms that were *this* wide [fifteen inches, approximately] and they were split here with some silver chains dangling. That was the best.'[152] James Smith, recalling the young greasers whom he got to know, offered a similar (but not identical) impression: 'The boys wore expensive tailor-made trousers, always black, tapered legs and a knife-edge press. One wrinkle in the straight drop to the shoe could bring a chorus of criticism and another trip to the tailor. Banker's shoes went with the trousers and they were always shined to perfection. They wore a crispy conservative shirt with cuffs folded just above the wrists and they never wore a tie ... It was customary to wear a light raincoat, always black, rarely buttoned, and never removed for fear of a rip-off.' To this detailed description, Smith adds one more telling piece of colourful evidence. The other reason the greasers never removed their raincoats was also practical, if slightly more ominous. 'If a member never had to look for his coat,' Smith explained, 'he could always make for another exit if the boys in blue appeared with a warrant.'[153]

What is unspoken in these descriptions is that race and ethnicity were just as central to greaser identity as were their working-class backgrounds. The very idea of this term as a marker of identity carries associations with rampant anxieties in post-war Toronto over expanding ranks of immigrant families and their progeny. Indeed, the term was initially coined (and gained wide use) in the mid-nineteenth century amid concerns over expanding Mexican labour populations in the American southwest.[154] From there, the term migrated through North America, eventually becoming a generalized name for Latinos, southern Europeans, and, eventually, eastern Europeans (that is, for everyone not explicitly associated with northern European ancestry).[155]

In Toronto, by the mid-1950s, the term was being used more specifically to denote recent immigrant (male) youth of a certain deportment. As Franca Iacovetta has demonstrated, Toronto's expanding post-war immigrant population constituted a site for a series of complicated, competing debates over urban identity, politics, normality, and even childrearing. The designation of greaser youth as Other is tied up with the more general, and pervasive, concerns articulated throughout the 1950s over the un-Canadian ways in which recent immigrants took to raising their (now Canadian) children. Anxiety over this new, large cohort of young people emerging from a foreign upbringing into Canadian society was rampant: What would this group do to 'traditional' Canadian society? What would the attenuation of white, Anglo-Protestant hegemony do to Canadian society? Complicating such concerns were concurrent preoccupations with the juvenile delinquent (JD) during the 1950s, a legal category masquerading as a psychological condition. The expected JD was the child of more grievously delinquent parents – as Iacovetta puts it so succinctly, 'the main problem, it was said, was the [immigrant] parents, who had particularly "backward" marriages and parenting methods.'[156]

This appropriation of the derogatory term 'greaser' by a segment of working-class immigrant youth suggests an exercise in reclaiming – they were called 'greasers' by everyone, it seems, including themselves. For a community of young people coalescing around their shared status (and angst) as working-class, immigrant youth in a city and country shaken by the birth pangs of a nascent multiculturalism, greaser identity afforded a means to express frustration with the dominant order. In their way, greasers (especially into the early 1960s) were expressing their twin desires to 'fit into' and to 'tear down' the society and structures around them. As Felstiner's and Smith's reflective descriptions of their clothing and gait suggest, the apparent paradox of a community of 'rowdies' and car thieves who were deathly afraid of not looking 'sharp' and 'clean' is tied to this equally paradoxical identity puzzle. As Gopala Alampur would later conclude (based on his studies of the Village scene in 1967–8), greasers desperately wanted to transcend their class status, but they repeatedly followed illicit paths in their efforts to do it. 'Their economic aspirations are middle-class,' wrote Alampur, 'but their methods come from the underworld.'[157]

Young women don't fit the mould for the archetypal greaser aesthetic – in most discussions of Toronto street youth in the early 1960s, women are rarely described, seeming to achieve their status by virtue of their association with greaser boys. But this does not mean that girls were left out of discussions over the 'clash of cultures' associated with immigrant youth; it was just that, while the concerns over boys tended towards their flirtations with anti-social behaviour and crime, with young women the potential transgressions were always sexual. Prostitution was the elephant in the room whenever such issues arose – and social expectations that immigrant girls were more sexually aggressive than 'Canadian' girls lay behind much of the thinking on the subject.[158] Greaser women, then, were not only in social but *moral* danger. Moreover, while the greaser boys were playing at rebellious toughness and pulling petty crimes – both the kinds of performances of rebel identity that could usually be shrugged off later in life – teenage women who were hanging with these boys were faced with the possibility of life-long consequences like motherhood. According to Felstiner:

Greaser girls: their crimes were drinking, getting pregnant, and getting married. Or sleeping around, getting laid. There were no girls in that neighbourhood [Queen and Spadina] of real aggression as you have today. Girls always hung out in groups, they were always in groups, you know, clusters. That was the word we used, *clusters*. But there were none that lasted. Times were very different. Their trouble was they got ... too much was revolving around sex. And getting married too early ... five of my sixteen [male] kids got married during the last two years of my project. The eldest being eighteen, the youngest being sixteen. And they married girls their own age.[159]

Single parenthood, hasty and unhygienic abortions, and emotional turmoil often overcame young women playing at greaser identity in the early 1960s, underlining the centrality of sexual transgression in female performances of rebel identity in these years.

Felstiner, who would go on to become a juvenile court judge by the late 1960s (a bench from which he would meet many Villagers as they were paraded in front of him on vagrancy and drugs charges), maintains that the greaser aesthetic and behaviour was all about imitation of a rebel archetype that was born of the 1950s, and was, essentially, harmless to anyone but themselves: 'They were imitating the eighteen-year-olds who were imitating the twenty-two-year-olds, the guys who may have been into some sidelines. They [the twenty-two-year-olds] were in and out of jail, but ... Look, this was the time when people stole *cars*. They didn't rob people, they didn't shoot people; they stole *cars*. They broke and entered a lot of places; they stole and they fenced cigarettes – twenty cartons, mind you, not 2,000 or 20,000 from a truck! They'd fence twenty cartons of cigarettes, and so forth ... It seemed serious in those days, but it was petty, compared to today!'[160]

In the years before drugs took hold, before middle-class youth began to gravitate towards their own versions of the rebel archetype, these working-class youth, who were proud of the 'greaser' label derisively applied to them by others, commanded their little corners of the city. And one of these corners was right there amid the Beat-fused jazz-high hipsters hanging around the Yorkville coffee-house scene.

Smith's lengthy description of his experiences with the Ramsden Park gang who hung around the Drop-In Centre stands as among our most detailed records of this greaser scene. His approach to the gang (written from the distance of some ten years) emphasizes their ornery nature and his own role as missionary among them. He tended to characterize the gang through its practices, its likes and dislikes, and its relationship to the law, referring to a group of individuals as though they thought, acted, and lived as one.

He details the exclusivity of the gang (underscoring its territoriality and distrust of outsiders) and provides a vague but effective outline of gender dynamics within the group. 'The girls played their role in a subtle way. They were subjugated and slapped around by their current swain, but in an underhanded way they could put the men at each other's throats.' Smith's sense that the girls had a kind of mystifying, but muscular, power over their boys is interesting in the context of the casual remark that the boys very likely would beat and abuse them. (It's also worth noting that he refers to the males as 'men' and the females as 'girls,' perhaps suggesting his own take on gender and power?) But violence and influence were clearly the best ways Smith knew to approach the dynamic. 'The [girls] were influence peddlers who could watch cruelty with delight if things were going their way. When the occasion arose they could dress like queens and usually got what they wanted.'[161]

This was, then, a dangerous but sensible community in Smith's view: the rules were clear (once one became accustomed to them), and, although all were touched by the creeping threat of violence, it was unlikely for the cruelty to arise randomly. There were rules, and if broken, there were consequences. However, Smith was sure to add a brief footnote to this discussion of gender relations, elucidating the traditional formula for sexual behaviour espoused by this Ramsden Park gang: 'Homosexuals and lesbians who tried to crash the club did so with great peril to themselves.'[162] Unlike their hipster neighbours around the corner, these young people hewed close to the dominant line with regard to heteronormativity.

Curiously, Crysdale's ministerial efforts (as a traditional labour-oriented social gospeller[163]) to work with this group in the 1950s were widely disparaged in the wider community: 'Stewart [Crysdale] befriended them when they were *persona non grata* everywhere and the victims of police harassment ... In those days the Social Planning Council's pundits were listening to ... the restaurant owners who wanted teenagers' allowances ringing their cash registers, but none of their nonsense. When churchmen and social workers talked of Drop-in Centres there was always a hue and cry from this heap of Urias [sic]. Even the churches were too scared to offer the use of their premises. Nevertheless, the Greaser Gang came to the church and Crysdale took them in.'[164] Crysdale, ministering to what he saw as a troubled youth group in need of some spiritual guidance, tried a variety of methods to demonstrate to his charges that the world was bigger than just the streets of Toronto. He would take the gang up north to his summer cottage, finding that when they were removed from their element these once street-savvy youths were reduced to terrified and needy campers.[165] (Later, after Smith had taken the reins, the gang was organized into a series of sporting teams and enrolled in the Protestant Youth Council's leagues around the city – in hockey and softball, the St Paul's teams dominated even the well-established (and better-funded) middle-class North Toronto clubs like Fairlawn and St Clements.[166])

But, by the early 1960s, the kids hanging around at the Drop-In Centre had become a headache for local police and residents. Crysdale, recognizing that poor leadership was at the root of their criminal activities, called for an election to reorganize the structure of this 'gang.' The unfortunate result saw the previously unified group descend into factionalized camps, splitting over who would become their next leader. Smith claims that Crysdale 'never knew how close the factions came to violence but he sensed enough danger to disband the club.'[167]

So, when Smith came on the scene in the early 1960s, it was in the context of the reorganization of the Ramsden Park gang and the early days of the Community Services Organization (CSO) providing oversight of the Drop-In Centre.[168] Certain of the leaders had recently been banned, and as a result the gang had been shrunk down to a more manageable size. Still, Smith reports that, even under this new leadership, the gang 'preyed on [local school] Jesse Ketchum's drop-outs who were leaving school at fifteen' and involving them in substantial crimes such as 'thefts, rollings, muggings, and joy riding (car theft).'[169]

Although redesigned and somewhat more manageable for the ministers, the gang kept up with their criminal activities. Smith relied on the Reverend Phil Karpetz, a Drop-In Centre staffer and former trainer for the McMaster football team, to restrain rowdy underage drinkers or break up brawls in the basement of his church. Karpetz must have made quite an impression – Smith claims that 'underage drunks who were violent the night before often came back to repair the damage. The slogan became "equal work for equal damage." Often as many as ten boys were busy at carpentry at any one time and the girls painted the walls over and over again.'[170] According to David DePoe, Smith set himself up as a great and sympathetic friend to his charges, despite their problems: 'He had compassion for those ... kids who were maybe getting themselves into a bit of trouble. Greasers, as everybody called them. They would be working-class kids who wore black leather jackets or Elvis Presley haircuts or whatever.[171] Some even had a tattoo or two. It was a class thing – even in high school it was a class thing; not that I understood that when I was there.'[172] Smith's background as a prairie Baptist – a position that had taken him to some fairly troubled areas of urban Canada in the early years of his ministry – surely prepared him in some ways for the tough kids he was to encounter at the church. As Drop-In Centre volunteer Mike Waage explained of his old boss: 'He started working for the United Church maybe at First United at Hastings and Main here [in Vancouver] before he went to Toronto. So he was used to some pretty rough stuff. He wasn't as unrealistic or silly as one might suppose sometimes.'[173] Although the church, as a public space, signified a conformity and moral hierarchy perhaps out of sync with the gang's particular style of rebellion, it had become a necessary space for gang activity and identity. Messes were cleaned up, respect was paid.

The church basement may have operated as an unlikely refuge from the pressures of street life, but the Drop-In Centre was, for many of its frequenters, simply a great place to party. Smith recalls that on any given night as many as 150 kids could be found 'rocking and rolling in the basement.'[174] Formalized weekend dances were part of the schedule, as the latest records or 1050 CHUM (Toronto's only rock radio station) would keep the room buzzing. In yet another significant divergence between this working-class youth identity and the gathering bohemian scene around the corner, while the artsy Villagers were enamoured of folk music and the sonic experimentation of free jazz, these greasers were among those holding to the rock'n'roll line in the years prior to Beatlemania.

By 1964, according to Smith, 'almost all of the gang members had settled down [and] many of them were married and raising their own children.'[175] In a show of thanks and respect for all that had been offered them through the efforts of the centre, many of these couples chose to be wed at St Paul's, and were more than likely to bring their children back to be baptized as well. In their stead the Drop-In Centre became a hangout for their younger, bolder, but apparently less troubled siblings. According to Smith, who proudly claimed to have succeeded in 'cultivating' them, the 'young fry' were 'a new breed who did not fall into the depths of juvenile delinquency.'[176] These new greasers began to look more like their contemporaries around the corner in the Village, but Smith is quick to draw a line between the two apparently different groups. The new greasers 'grew long hair but they did not join the hippies,'[177] he maintains, reifying the boundaries separating what was supposed to be a middle-class identity (hippie) and the working-class greasers. Still, his writing betrays a confusion regarding this distinction between the groups; 'they were a strange combination of Greaser and Hippy [sic],' he somewhat awkwardly concludes.[178]

Although this new generation would prove much less adaptable to the church than their older siblings, friends, and cousins, these new kids still wanted to be a part of a viable scene. They had noticed Yorkville in around 1964, moving through the district and alerting media to the possibility of class disturbances in the Village. Municipal authorities, until now generally accepting of Yorkville's draw to young people, soon awoke to the possibility of 'toughs' and 'rowdies' colonizing the district. Media sources, sniffing out the suspicion of conflict, probably violent, between the 'beatnik' youth and their working-class, leather-jacket-wearing counterparts, began to pay attention. The battle for Yorkville was no longer simply about merchants versus bohemians, or old versus young. While these greasers may have initially refused the drugs, folk music, and world views of their Villager counterparts, they *did* agree with them that they needed a space to explore new currents of youth identity and activity. By the spring of 1964, Yorkville seemed to everyone the best place to find it.

PART TWO

Performing Yorkville, 1964–6

3

Riots, Religion, and Rock'n'Roll

'I wish to denounce my Canadian citizenship,' bellowed a red-faced Andrew Mikolasch at an unmoved, 'unperturbed' magistrate upon being found guilty of disturbing the peace. Mikolasch, a thirty-one-year-old Hungarian-born artist – and editor of the *Yorkville Yawn* underground paper – who had been living in Canada for nearly sixteen years, then pulled out his citizenship card and tore it up, letting the pieces fall to the floor of the courtroom. Storming out of the building, Mikolasch was heard to holler 'God save the Queen from her representatives!'

Histrionics notwithstanding, it isn't difficult to sympathize with Mikolasch's position. He had just been handed a guilty verdict, and the attendant $50 fine or ten days in prison, for causing a disturbance by sitting on a patio and sketching 'Yorkville scenes' for passers-by. It seems that, while he perched at his easel on an early July evening in 1965, he attracted a number of onlookers hoping to see him at work. At one point, a constable of the Toronto Police – whose Yorkville detail had been expanding in recent weeks – asked Mikolasch to 'move along' because he was attracting a crowd and 'blocking the flow of traffic.' Or was it because he had an unruly beard and affected a hip attitude?[1]

Because Mikolasch had both the permission of the owner of the café on whose patio he had set up his gear, and a permit allowing him to sell his sketches in public, he resisted this request to move along because, basically, he was trying to make some money, and these onlookers were potential customers. When he was further pressed by the police officer to leave the scene, he responded by calling Constable Archibald King a 'useless bastard.' Mikolasch was quickly handcuffed, arrested, and taken into custody.[2]

Mikolasch's case speaks volumes about the climate of Yorkville in the summer of 1965, following months of protracted conflict over the 'ownership' of the district.[3] The patchily bearded Mikolasch was a representative – albeit an older-than-average, foreign-born representative – of the fraction of Yorkville that had increasingly come to see the Village as its own: the post-Beat, hip youth who were spending ever more of their time there. Nevertheless, there was a mounting ambivalence on the part of the municipal authorities, the local shopowners and residents, various media observers, and the shoppers who still frequented the district over allowing hip youth the rights to this claim.

As Toronto's press became aware of the significance of Yorkville as a disputed territory in the first half of the 1960s, it emphasized the conflicts between fractions with claims to the area, frequently couching descriptions in the language of ownership. *Whose Yorkville is this, anyway?* seems to have been the underlying question. As this story demonstrates, Mikolasch thought it was his.[4] So, possibly, did the folks out on the sidewalk watching him at work. So did the municipal authorities, whose police representative was acting on their express wishes to keep Yorkville 'sophisticated' and to curb 'bohemianism.' So did the working-class youth, variously dubbed 'greasers,' 'rowdies,' or 'toughs' by municipal authorities and in media reports, whose numbers in the Village were expanding in these years. And, finally, so did the shopowners and residents, whose new lobby group, the Village of Yorkville Association, was explicitly designed to keep out the rowdies and keep in the 'charm.'

This was still Yorkville as anybody's land, still up for grabs. The stakes were clearly defined: someone was going to own this place when the deal was done. Who would come out on top? This chapter is designed around the competing heuristics at work throughout this period, heuristics that reduced Yorkville variously to a hip sanctuary, a troubled but ascendant boutique district, the site of a violent turf war, a rock'n'roll hub, and, most remarkably, a 'foreign country … taken over by teenagers' right in the centre of English Canada's most populous city.[5]

The Village Is a Riot!: The Yorkville Festival and Its Aftermath

By early 1964, the Village of Yorkville Association was growing adept at petitioning the City of Toronto. Protect Yorkville from unnecessary development, it argued, and a little bit of colour will be preserved in an otherwise monochromatic Toronto. Its initial successes had prevented any zoning changes in the district which would affect the 'character' of the Village, even though this 'character' was never very well defined, just loudly trumpeted. But, by the end of 1963, it was felt that the sophisticated spirit of the Village was being threatened by a fascination with youthful bohemianism. According to a former Village resident, that fascination translated into a whole lot of young people arriving in the Village without much of a plan on what to do next: 'So, you would have all kinds of people on the street, just walking around. Walking around, talking, meeting. There weren't a whole lot of bars, and young people couldn't get into bars. So there were the coffee houses that didn't have [liquor] licences. And it just somehow became: *So, what do you want to do tonight? I dunno, let's go down to Yorkville.*'[6] The fear that Yorkville would slip into a kind of teenagers' paradise undoubtedly kept many merchants awake at nights, perhaps even in drafty apartments above their storefronts, as they listened to the ominous rumble of motorcycles, the hoots and hollers of drunken university students, or the off-key warble of some moon-eyed folksinger, wondering bitterly how it had come to this. And so the decision was taken to advertise Yorkville to standoffish Toronto consumers as *anything but* the haven of disaffected teens. A festival would be held, over three warm days in May 1964, designed to reinvigorate the failing reputation of the district and to promote its continued and stated role as a centre for sophisticated boutiques, expensive shops, and quirky cafés. But what if the kids refused to allow the festival its moment in the sun? A considerable risk, to be sure, but one that, it was agreed, must be run.

The Yorkville Festival opened quietly, with most observers pleased to see little in the way of disturbance in the Village. After a minor scuffle had broken out the previous Saturday night (in which the unfortunate Werner Graeber, by now among the elite coffee-house owners, had had his leg broken), tensions were riding high over the possibility of violence at the week-long event. Still, the festival's opening night, Thursday, 14 May 1964, was virtually devoid of excitement. 'At nightfall, the joint came alive,' allowed the *Toronto Daily Star*, if only 'in a sort of moribund way.' But 'business was brisk,' despite a heavy police presence. In his snapshot descriptions of the scene, the *Star*'s Gerry Barker paints a rather wan landscape, tempered by the occasional splash of red: Graeber (referred to as the 'Coffee House Kaiser') makes the scene, cast and all, holding court at his newly opened Zee Spot; abstract photographers sell their work on street corners while flamenco guitarists perform their music underground in cafés; sketch artists stand on the sidewalk in front of the Penny Farthing letting fly with their curious brand of caricature. In fact, the festival was going so quietly that the *Globe and Mail*, usually quick to advertise such celebrations of high-brow arts (there were opera performances, folk dances, and other such entertainments also planned as part of the weekend program), failed to notice it in the paper's Friday section on things to do for the weekend.[7] The *Star* happily concluded that, on that first night, the 'anticipated crowds were elsewhere.' Indeed, descriptions of what crowd there *was* emphasized the absence of the expected Yorkville scene: its throng of young people. 'The narrow sidewalks were packed with police, a few clergymen, more police,' joked the article. Moreover, even though the one-way street had been temporarily converted to a two-way thoroughfare, few traffic issues were noted.[8] All in all, it was a great night for the VYA and its effort to curtail Yorkville's regrettable reputation as a haven for teenagers.

The following evening would not go quite so well. Young people, many of them high-school teens taking advantage of a Friday night, filled the street looking for something to do. In anticipation of violence and rioting (word of a planned 'raid' by fifteen hundred crazed kids had been leaked anonymously from the University of Toronto campus, according to media reports), police presence was elevated to the point of absurdity. No fewer than thirteen uniformed police officers, three paddy wagons, and untold numbers of plainclothesmen descended on the tiny stretch of road. The stage was set for confrontation, and confrontation was what they got. Of a sort, anyway. As Friday evening gave way to Friday night, noise complaints compelled police to shut down guitar playing and singing in the streets, leaving many revellers unsure of where to go, or what to do. So they hung around. Before long, hundreds of people were blocking traffic and making noise, which created a confusing situation for the policemen. Unsure of how to respond to the horde, the officers allowed them to congregate unmolested, seemingly hopeful that if they waited long enough the kids would get bored and go home. Still, as they held back, tensions mounted – when was this 'raid' to begin? What would it look like? Until an unnamed coffee-house owner took it upon himself to clear the milling crowds in front of his establishment by opening a hose on them, it appears that, for a while, the police remained on the periphery of the scene. In the end, however, four young people were taken into custody, pushed into paddy wagons, and hauled off to jail, while the rest of the crowd was forcibly removed from the streets by the uniformed officers. By 1:30

a.m., the Village was empty and quiet; with only four arrested, and no injuries reported, a potential disaster had been averted, but it didn't matter.

Saturday's *Toronto Daily Star* jumped at the chance to report on the 'riot' that would have broken out had police not been there to haul the young offenders off to jail. Although the *Star*'s reportage appears to carry an undertone of disgust at the overbearing police response, the main thrust of the coverage is the effectiveness of the 'no-nonsense lesson' they had delivered to the kids.[9] But, judging by the available evidence, this was no youthful insurrection. Tellingly, the *Globe and Mail* at first neglected to notice the 'riot,' just as it had failed to mark the festival itself. It was simply not a big enough deal to report in the national paper. Judy Pocock, who both lived right in the middle of the scene and was herself a teenager at the time, doesn't even remember anything like that having taken place.[10] When we look at the situation – underwritten by a general fear and distrust of the young people in the district on the part of police, compounded by the ambiguous, but compelling rumour of a planned 'raid' on the festival – we see little to suggest that any violent outrage took place. Rather, it would seem that the young people were up to their usual tricks, filling the streets in their numbers, frustrating drivers, annoying unhappy residents trying to sleep, and scaring merchants, until the police decided that enough was enough and shut them down. In light of the fact that no charges were filed against anyone for anything worse than 'creating a disturbance' – no resisting arrest, no assault, no destruction of property – we are left with the conclusion that the famous Yorkville Festival riots (to which many subsequent attacks on the deterioration of the district refer) were about as momentous as a passing subway train, and over just as quickly.

Another seminal instance in the development of the impression of Yorkville as a volatile youth centre was a well-reported incident in October 1964 which saw a 'near-riot' (now apparently the accepted term for young people gathered into a swelling crowd) develop out of a massive sing-song.[11] Loud and disruptive enough that the police were forced to break it up, the 400-person-strong group of singers responded to the sudden police surge by turning into a disordered mob. Suddenly difficult to contain, the singers' energy exploded through the Village, and the police found themselves forced to make arrests to try to quell the crisis that they had created by refusing to allow the singalong to come to an organic conclusion. Citing this incident, as well as one from the previous week in which a Thornhill youth removed his shoes and blocked traffic on Yorkville Ave, Toronto police announced plans to 'close in' on the Village in the following weeks.[12] Emphasizing the potential for a youth riot as the real impetus behind the action, local media generally praised the decision. This media frame, establishing Yorkville as a potential site of irrational masses of young people, is perhaps the most significant of all the advertisements offered to teenage Torontonians that Yorkville was a fun place to check out. But, as a metaphor for a general mainstream concern over an emerging youth culture, it is illustrative. The pervasive fear felt by many parents of baby boomers, as they looked uneasily at the teens they had carried into the new world of the 1960s, must have been intensified by the oft-repeated fact that there were more of these young people than there ever had been before, in the *history of the world*. And so any incident that exaggerated their power-in-numbers seems to have been sobering. Their potential to swarm, to mass together in violent, irrational surges of adolescent abandon – while rarely ever realized in Yorkville, even in the more volatile later 1960s – underscores the hyperbolic coverage of both of the 'riots' discussed above.

What Will They Ban Next?: Legislating Youth out of the Village

As early as January 1965, Yorkville had already played out its hip period in the eyes of at least some observers – a telling *Star* article from early that year claimed that it had already become 'Squaresville' as it drifted towards the upscale and rejected its bohemian colonists.[13] Moreover, the early associations with coffee-house bohemia were disappearing from Yorkville, only to be replaced by younger, more raucous, volatile, and apparently less artsy connotations.[14] By the end of the year, the gathering dawn of a youth crisis had finally bled over the horizon: gangs of toughs had begun to appear in the area, some of them gunning their motorcycles up and down the streets; drugs were appearing with greater frequency; and it seemed that, while street fighting and sexual violence were up in the district, calm and bohemian style appeared to be on their way down. Worst of all, more and more young people were arriving with each passing weekend, while fewer and fewer merchants felt safe in their investment in a district that was apparently under siege. No group was more active in endeavouring to slow this slide into associations with violence and danger than the VYA.

Considering the events of the previous May, the VYA was decidedly apprehensive about restaging the action. Only a year later, the general memory of the festival was that, although it *had* helped to engender the impression that Yorkville was an exotic, exciting place in an otherwise pallid Toronto, it had also wound up attracting a great deal of negative attention. A widespread assumption was that the influx of toughs – not to mention the throng of suburban beatniks – was a direct result of the heavily advertised event (and the excitement of the much-discussed 'riot').[15] More than ever, the sense that Yorkville was a divided territory, contested by two principal factions of merchant/resident (old) and Villager (young), highlighted the discourse. The VYA finally announced in early May that the festival would be cancelled for the year, citing the potential for violence as the key concern behind the decision. Stephan Sobot, gallery owner and president of the festival committee, summarized the situation to the *Globe and Mail*. 'The one we had last year attracted a group of people who created a great deal of noise and damage. We thought we had better let the memory of that fade before starting again.'[16]

The association between the Village and riotous youth underwrote the discussion during the spring of 1965. On 9 April, for example, some '2,000 young men and women jammed Yorkville Ave between Bay Street and Avenue Road,' blocking traffic and transforming the street into a roiling dancehall. Few of these revellers seemed to have come to the district for the coffee – it was the *scene* they were after. According to some, this was evidence of a growing discordance between the coffee houses and the street parties. Bryan Walker, employee at the popular Penny Farthing, complained that 'tonight [9 April] they scared a lot of the public away … The people who listen to our folk music and jazz are not the hoodlums who take part in street riots.'[17] Reducing the conflict to a distinction between troublemaking 'hoodlums' and bohemian aesthetes, Walker was iterating a newly dominant discourse surrounding Village youth factionalism.

A month later a headline in the *Globe and Mail* would simplify Yorkville to the shorthand of 'Twanging Guitars, Tepid Cappuccino and Police,' hardly the three things the VYA wanted to see defining its district.[18] This sensationalist article emphasized an interview with a 'once-a-week shaver' who offhandedly reported that 'they tell me it's really cool in Yorkville. Riots and all. I wish a riot would start.'[19] Apparently, simply avoiding the festival hadn't been a strong enough message against the relationship between Yorkville and youth agitation. Besides, the gesture hadn't done anything to slow the influx of these so-called toughs who now congregated in the streets. And so, in late May, residents and merchants took a decisive step, petitioning the Building and Development Committee with a motion to prohibit any new coffee houses from opening in the Yorkville area.[20]

The motion, put forward in an explicit effort to stop 'gangs of teenagers' from turning 'the area into a powder keg,' was passed with only two members opposed. Among the evidence presented to the committee was the testimony given by a Yorkville hairdresser, whose description of biker activity painted a frightful picture: 'The other night a gang of nine toughs all dressed alike rode their motorcycles abreast down Yorkville, gunning them and holding up traffic. They seemed to be saying: "here we are, what are you going to do about it?"'[21] Alderman David Rotenberg, who presented the motion, explained that his intention was not to put the twenty or so coffee houses already operating in Yorkville out of business, but rather to block the twelve pending applications already before the Metro Toronto Licensing Commission. But, if it was these toughs that had caused all of the problems, why were the 'coffee house set,' the people supposedly listening to the jazz and folk music in the Penny Farthing while the 'riot' went down, being driven out of the Village too? John and Marilyn McHugh, who had been running coffee houses in Yorkville since the early 1960s, were incredulous of claims that the espresso crowd was to blame for the commotion. 'The discos attract the kids because they can't serve liquor,' McHugh explained. 'It's the people over 20 who actually go into coffee houses and order. The kids wander aimlessly around ... The last straw ... was the introduction of rock'n'roll [at the discos].'[22] On the other hand, according to a local boutique owner, the last straw might have been media exposure of the district. 'Shirley-Anne Heit ... says that every newspaper that recounts trouble on Yorkville "is like an ad for every punk in town to come down here."'[23]

James Cooper's *Globe and Mail* editorial took the decision to ban coffee houses to task for its inherent short-sightedness and its failure to understand the root of the issue. 'If Toronto City Council changes its zoning bylaws to prohibit the opening of more coffee houses in the Yorkville area,' Cooper complained, 'it will achieve nothing more useful than a curb on the sale of espresso.'[24] His liberal view was that 'delinquency' will not be curbed by 'keep-off-the-grass' by-laws, and that the development of proper youth programs was a better way to impose order on this apparent chaos. In response to all of this, Controller William Dennison (not yet mayor), along with aldermen Charles Caccia, Michael Grayson, and Hugh Bruce, toured Yorkville on a busy

Saturday evening on what would undoubtedly today be referred to as a
'fact-finding mission.' Although they failed to locate any real evidence
of violence or vandalism – it was a relatively quiet weekend for arrests
and activity – they emerged from their trip with four different opinions
on what needed to be done, all orbiting around the central notion that
Yorkville must continue to be a 'high class store and boutique area.' In
fact, this description (offered by Mayor Phillip Givens, who did not
go on the tour) appeared to infuse each councillor's interpretations
of the issues at stake. Whereas two of them took to the idea that the
coffee houses were at fault for promoting youth idleness and unruly
late-night crowds on summer weekends, the other two placed this fault
squarely on the shoulders of the bikers and motorists in general. Dennison – in a move that would come back to haunt him less than two
years hence – suggested that a traffic ban on the weekends would do
the trick. No cars, no cruising, no noise, and, most important, no motorcycles. Following the current view that 'boys in black leather jackets
… looking almost ritualistically tough' were 'the symbol of worry and
uncertainty' in Yorkville, Hugh Bruce agreed with Dennison.[25] Using
more deliberate language, Bruce argued for an outright ban on motorcycles themselves: 'Motorcyclists don't go where their machines cannot
be seen,' he explained.[26]

Bikers, many of them attached to clubs centred in the east and west
ends of the city, had recently taken to cruising the Village streets with
the swarm of cars, playing along in the parade of weird that comprised
the Yorkville Saturday night. Former biker 'Wild Bill' recalls that the
Yorkville thing appealed to bikers in the same way it did everyone else,
at least at first. 'The bikers came into Yorkville just as somewhere to
hang out. Because there were discos, coffee houses; [later] a couple of
members of the Vags [Vagabonds biker gang] had a home they owned
[nearby].'[27] Fun, identity performance, and the convenience of familiar
places to hang out, meet people, find a good party – the scene offered
many of the same things to biker clubs that it did to young suburbanites or inner-city youth interested in playing at hip. 'Wild Bill' jokes that
it was the bikers themselves who invented the Village scene, since they
constituted such a primary attraction after 1964. 'We got into the Village
scene because we were moving out of [Gerrard St] because we were
getting too popular. College kids used to follow us *wherever* we went!'[28]

But what of the supposed conflict, the fighting between the 'coffee
house set' and 'toughs' in these years? Though it is clear that all appreciated the class-based distinctions between them, few of my interview

subjects recollect violence as being a major issue between different identity groups in the Village. Unquestionably, these class-based distinctions were part of a process of identification – many people came to Yorkville attentive to which performance would most readily reflect their class and ethnic backgrounds. In a telling example, a Villager (variously labelled by his interviewer as a greaser and a biker, a reflection of the mutability of Village identity) suggested that his reasons for joining a biker club in the mid-1960s had been influenced by his alienation from white, middle-class society. 'I was antisocial at that time,' he explained. 'People made jokes about me, called me a D.P. (displaced person). I had just come to Canada. I couldn't speak English well and people made fun of me.'[29]

For his part, 'Wild Bill' emphasizes that, while there *was* considerable class friction between Villagers, violence wasn't a part of the scene in the mid-1960s: 'A lot of the conflicts between the hippies and the bikers were the attitude of ... Look, any situation where you get upper middle-class kids, half of them are wannabes. They weren't even hippies. Hippies were the guys like me! *They* all came from upper middle-class families, and that was the *whole* hippie scene. Three-quarters of the hippies were rich kids, over-rich kids that were able to afford [it].' In the most likely scenario, such class conflict undergirded most of the contact between working-class Villagers and their counterparts from suburban Toronto, but not all. It was but a symptom of a more reflexive identity condition – in their different uniforms, these young people exaggerated their differences, accentuated their dissimilarities, and tried, in their respective ways, to be *cool*. Yorkville was their stage, and their performance was to make the scene. And, anyway, they were all in it together – by the end of the month, they were all to be tarred with the same brush. Whatever racial, ethnic, and class-based anxieties were at work in the vicissitudes of concern over the youth cultures inhabiting the Yorkville scene, the key category, and the one that subsumed all others when it came down to the telling of it, was youth. Ultimately, although the Village scene was performed in different ways by these participants, and although these performances were connected to thorny identity issues, such concerns melted away in dominant, reductionist accounts of the Village as a 'foreign country taken over by teenagers.'

By late June, spurred by a nightmarish story recounted to the City Council by Helen Johnson (a vociferous local alderman), the decision to run young people out of Yorkville became official public policy. The tale of a pool of blood found on a resident's porch after yet another Village brawl was enough to push the council to draft a by-law banning motorcycles from dusk to dawn in Yorkville. It also moved the council to look into forcing businesses to close at 1 a.m. rather than 3 a.m., and to uphold the plan to refuse to license new coffee houses. The following day, in another critical editorial punchily entitled 'What Will They Ban Next?' James Cooper argued that 'a dramatic and exceedingly exaggerated tale of the horrors of juvenile lawlessness in Yorkville's few square blocks of shops and coffee houses' should not have been enough to scare the council into banning motorcycles. Rather, he suggested that motorcyclists were being singled out as the group responsible for everything – scapegoating in the absence of any real substantiation of this position. 'There is no evidence that teen-age violence and vandalism ride only on the seats of motorcycles,' he maintained. 'Nor is there one thread of evidence to suggest that the coffee houses that City Hall would restrict are the incubators of any of Yorkville's trouble.' In his view, the only way to quell youth conflict in Yorkville was to add more police to the mix (a position forwarded by some coffee-house owners and employees as well).[30]

On 9 June, fifteen coffee-house proprietors petitioned city hall suggesting that the youth rowdiness that was being blamed on their establishments was little more than politically motivated nonsense. According to the *Globe and Mail*, these coffee-house owners 'said complaints of teenage rowdiness are just a cover-up for the real issue': 'They charged that the boutique owners are losing money and have made the coffee houses their scapegoats – blaming them for scaring away carriage trade patrons. They said civic authorities, in turn, have deliberately tormented them with daily visits from fire department and health inspectors, who used to come once every two months before the complaints were lodged two weeks ago.'[31] The owners pressed the point that reports of youth rowdiness were 'grossly exaggerated,' and that the real issue was the fact that the city was siding with the boutiques without considering how important the coffee houses had become to the tourist-enticing image of the district. 'The boutiques,' they argued, 'have followed the coffee houses into the district and depend on the atmosphere they have created.'[32] Furthermore, some claimed, the city's emphasis on all this phoney violence was doomed to backfire. Harry Finegold suggested that this had already begun to happen: 'With all this publicity ... our image is taking a terrible beating. It is being made to look as if it is a crime to come down here. It's getting to the point where people are ashamed of being seen here.'[33] Bernie Fiedler, proprietor of the popular

Riverboat coffee house, agreed with his competitor but charged that the problem was really just the number of teenagers, and suggested that a curfew on people under the age of eighteen might be the best solution.[34] Ultimately, the conflict fizzled when, in early June, the Metro Toronto Licensing Commission simply disregarded the municipal requests to refuse new coffee-house licences. Three new licences were granted, and the commission gave frank notice to the City Council that it was not prepared to invoke Yorkville exceptionalism merely based on their rec-ommendation to do so.[35]

This episode, heavily covered by media sources, served, like the festival in 1964, to inculcate and exaggerate the characterization of Yorkville as a disputed terrain. But, perhaps more significantly, it loud-ly proclaimed Yorkville as an *important* place: something worth paying attention to was afoot in this little area; and it was something even the mayor was interested in checking out for himself. The day after the coffee-house fracas had played out, Scott Young, a popular columnist for the *Globe and Mail* (and father to local folksinger Neil), admonished Mayor Phillip Givens for failing to speak up in support of Yorkville at the City Council meetings. Young had seen the mayor and his wife 'making the scene in style' the previous Friday evening, even attending a concert by local band the Dirty Shames with prominent friends Pierre and Janet Berton. 'Monday in City Council when his colleagues were seeking ways to prevent more coffee houses from opening in Yorkville, he said not a word ... Why the silence?' Young demanded. 'Maybe I should have spoken in Council,' came Givens's unsatisfying reply. 'But with the kind of public atmosphere there was ... well I found it difficult in face of all those massive allegations to do other than sit back and let the Aldermen, who after all should know their own ward, tell what it was all about.'[36]

If the mayor and his friends could tour the district on a Friday evening, how dangerous could it really be? How prone to violence and depravity, how demonstrably in need of increased municipal pressure and scrutiny, of official sanction? It seems clear that the real issue at stake here, as was well pointed out by the coffee-house owners, was the municipal endeavour to redirect development (and public expec-tations) of Yorkville away from youth and towards upscale shopping. And all of this stress on malevolent working-class toughs appears to have been part of a design to root out the burgeoning scene by forcing it under an umbrella category of 'unruly youth.' However, each effort towards this end, from the noisy cancelling of the festival through the attempted coffee-house and motorcycle bans, served to advertise to young people that there was a place in Toronto that held some deep, if still amorphous, attraction.

There is an irony here, creeping around the corners of this narrative. Although anxiety over violence in Yorkville in the spring of 1965 relied upon specious claims and exaggeration, within months there was considerable evidence that such a condition was now *in fact* developing in the district. These advertisements for a violent Yorkville (wearing the garments of admonition and warning) filled newspapers throughout that spring, leading to the first sign of weapons in the scene and the first sign of factionalized street fights. Less than a month after the debates over the coffee-house ban, a nineteen-year-old from Etobicoke 'accidentally bumped into a group of youths' on Yorkville Ave. These 'youths' followed him and his friend to the corner of Cumberland and Belair where they got into a brawl. When the fight was over, the nineteen-year-old had been stabbed three times in the chest, and once in the abdomen. Though he would survive his wounds, Yorkville wouldn't survive their significance. Violence had come to the Village, but only after everyone had been told it was already there.[37]

The Shape of Things to Come: The Advent of the 'Toronto Sound'

Murray McLauchlan, who would soon emerge as one of Canada's foremost folksingers, remembers the Village in 1964–5 as 'still a pleasant, relaxed place on a sunny afternoon.'[38] Judy Perly (today among Toronto's greatest benefactors of independent folk musicians) recalls that the reason it was so pleasant was that Yorkville was still mainly interested in acoustic music until the mid-1960s. Perhaps because she has spent the past twenty-five years running the Free Times Café (possibly the most accessible stage for neophyte folkies in Toronto), what stands out in her recollection is the novelty of the Village and its astonishing success at supporting a lot of pop-chart-unfriendly music.[39] 'Then, because folk music was big, and people were particularly into folk music, [my older sister] would influence me to go to places like the Riverboat ... Don't forget, there wasn't that much happening in Toronto [in those days]. Yorkville was where it was happening. It wasn't happening in fifty different places like it is now. So they would have a cover charge for the music, which was high in comparison to today's prices, but then it was a new thing so people were willing to pay for it.'[40]

For many, folk music seemed to channel the frustrations and the anger of the civil rights struggles in the United States, even while it connected to the bohemian intellectualism of the post-Beat scene. Many of my interview subjects recalled their music fandom starting with folk music before sliding into folk-rock and psychedelic rock'n'roll as the decade (and the trends) progressed. But it always began with folk music. For example, David DePoe's account of his first exposure to the Village music scene reads like the prototypical folk-music-inspired 1960s awakening.

> When I got to the University of Toronto [in 1963], Bill [Cameron, then an aspiring journalist] brought me to his room and he played me Bob Dylan. I had never heard Bob Dylan, had never even heard *of* Bob Dylan or anything, and so I started listening to all this music: the Dylan, the Joan Baez, all the folksingers of the times. And I started hanging out in Yorkville where there was this early folk music scene. I heard Gordon Lightfoot, started going to the Riverboat and saw [American blues artists] Muddy Waters, Sonny Terry and Brownie McGhee, and all these black musicians. And soon I got in with some people who decided they wanted to form an organization called the Student Union for Peace Action.[41]

Like some fantasy born of the lonesome highway mind of Greil Marcus, yet another narrative of 1960s participation is here funnelled through the apocalyptic power of Bob Dylan's music.[42]

The same people who were drawn to Yorkville after hearing those records may have been among those who were shocked and dismayed (or elated and thrilled) by Dylan's fabled shift away from the folk-music idiom in favour of rock'n'roll.[43] Suffice it to say that the transition from folk music to rock'n'roll in the Village can be tied to the more general transition between these two genres commonly associated with Dylan's about-face. As Perly reminds us, until about the end of 1965, folk music really *was* the Village sound, while the adjacent Yonge St 'Strip' was Toronto's rock'n'roll scene. This series of bars about one kilometre south of Yorkville had offered amplified country music and live bands to the rock'n'roll crowd from the mid-1950s on. In stark contrast to the expected Gerrard and Yorkville scenes, Ronnie Hawkins and the Hawks, the top draw on the Strip, typically played to crowds of teenagers and 'rounders,' a now dated term for criminals. 'They must've idolized Al Capone, or something,' Hawkins told Nicholas Jennings, 'because they all had names like Squeaker, Dukie, and Basher.'[44] Such characters were fairly unlikely to attend, say, a poetry reading.

Even if Hawkins and his crowd didn't care one way or the other about the artsy heaviness up in Yorkville, his extraordinary band was creating a space for hip youth with a rock'n'roll sensibility. A still astoundingly young Robbie Robertson, the Hawks' minimalist lead guitarist, was attracting an army of devotees, come to worship at his altar every Friday night. 'His disciples dressed like him,' John Kay (later the lead vocalist for Sparrow and Steppenwolf) recalled. '[They] played blond Fender Telecasters like him, and emulated his stinging staccato lead-guitar style.'[45] In Robertson's work, in the sublime three-part harmonies of Rick Danko, Richard Manuel, and Levon Helm, and in the spectral excursions of organist Garth Hudson, these young music fans were hearing something that seemed hip in ways that neither the predictable radio programming nor the darkened coffee houses up the street could approach.[46] 'Ronnie Hawkins did a lot for the music scene,' explains Kelly Jay, later the lead singer of Crowbar. 'He let everybody know that the clock was running and that nobody would get any better unless they practiced. He made sure we knew that we wouldn't get anywhere by sitting around drinking and smoking pot.'[47] Following Dylan's turn, and the advent of the 'British Invasion' (the term for the raft of popular English pop groups who began to dominate the North American charts after 1963), the Strip and the Village were on a collision course. The budding draw of rock'n'roll music began to cause problems for many of the folk acts in the Village; as their audiences grew less and less interested in acoustic music and ever more drawn to electricity, some former folkies turned to embrace the new form.[48] Perhaps the most famous example of this trend can be found in the account of a scruffy, singular musician who had arrived from Winnipeg in early 1965: Neil Young.

A rock'n'roll musician as a teenager, Young had come to Yorkville with a mind to score folk gigs at the various clubs. At first, he recalls, 'I didn't see much folk-rock in Toronto. It was either folk or rock.'[49] The division was clear, and Yorkville seemed to offer space only for the mellower sound. 'The Yorkville scene,' muses Young. 'I'd never seen anything like it. Music was everywhere. Two years before the Summer of Love. It was like this big deal. Toronto in '65 [...] The Riverboat was an upscale thing – people who played there were really making a living. There was the New Gate of Cleve, which was just down the street – that's where I saw Lonnie Johnson. And I think I saw Pete Seeger there, too, and Sonny Terry and Brownie McGhee.'[50] Living wherever he could (even though his father, Toronto journalist Scott Young, had a house in nearby Rosedale), Young fell into the scene, lifting boxes at a Coles bookstore and trying to get started as a musician.

One of his friends at the time was Village maven Vicky Taylor, a resident folksinger at the Mousehole. Taylor's $90-a-month apartment above the Night Owl on Avenue Rd was 'a communal home to many starving musicians,' according to Young's biographer Jimmy McDonough. 'Neil Young, Joni Mitchell, John Kay of Steppenwolf (known then as the Sparrow), David Rea and Craig Allen all passed through Vicky's apartment, sleeping on the floor, jamming with other musicians and subsisting on a no-budget concoction Taylor whipped up called "guck." "I was kinda like the mother hen," said Taylor.'[51] Taylor was famous in the scene for her magnum opus, a twenty-verse dynamo entitled 'The Pill,' a confessional about her battles with depression and pharmaceuticals. Not coincidentally, her apartment was known to be a good place to score prescription drugs when other supplies got scarce. But 'pharmies' weren't the only thing that got her and her flatmates going that year. 'A friend of ours came back from Israel with a four-dollar Hershey bar of hash in her brassiere,' recalls Taylor's on-and-off roommate Craig Allen. 'And we proceeded to clean it up. We lost three months with that brick of hash.'[52]

By the end of 1965, Young watched as joints like the El Patio and the Mynah Bird began to move beyond the acoustic-only bill, experimenting with allowing local garage rockers to tear up the air in the diminutive venues. Bands like the Paupers (who, following the addition of vocalist and songwriter Adam Mitchell, were moving beyond their early, Mersey-clone incarnation), A Passing Fancy, Little Caesar and the Consoles, and the Ugly Ducklings were getting their respective acts together, and delighting their crowds of caffeine- and pot-fuelled Villagers with blues-based rock'n'roll. Young, having never done terribly well as a folkie in the intense Yorkville environment – he once complained that it 'was a very humbling experience for me and I just couldn't get anything going' – liked what he heard, and saw an opportunity.[53] Popping amyl nitrate pills for energy, Young and some friends (many of them also transplants from Winnipeg) practised at every opportunity, eventually forming a series of bands (the Mynah Birds most significant among them) and rocking the Village for a brief but legendary period.[54]

In general, the early 1960s connections between folk music, Yorkville, and New Left groups were much stronger than the later connections between rock'n'roll, the Village, and the Movement, a reality that helps to explain the general exodus of politicos from the Village stage after the rock'n'roll turn. Students and activists in the Village scene as it developed through 1964 and into 1965 often saw folk music and politics as inextricably connected, while rock'n'roll rarely carried such connotations.[55] Jazz and folk (both idioms that included blues music under their wide umbrellas) were seen as authentic expressions, heartfelt and sincere, whereas rock'n'roll was commercial, and thus fallen. No angel-headed hipster was going to try to make it on the pop charts, at least not without taking a lot of sass for her efforts.[56] Typically, Village folk-singers proselytized on diverse political issues including the U.S. civil rights debacles and the horrors of nuclear war (Village singer Bonnie Dobson's haunting 'Morning Dew' comes to mind), concerning themselves with the same issues as were their political counterparts at the University of Toronto.[57] Buffy Sainte-Marie, one of the more successful folksingers of the 1960s, was profoundly influenced by the politicized atmosphere in Village coffee houses. 'It was all talk, talk, talk and listen, listen, listen,' she explained to Nicholas Jennings. 'It was really about exchanging ideas. People participated in what was going on on-stage, not clapping or singalong stuff so much as talking about what an artist's set was all about. That led to a lot of original thinking.'[58] Such original thinking led to her scribbling down her most famous song while between sets at the Purple Onion. Her 'Universal Soldier,' with its provocatively general finger-pointing and sincere anti-war message – *And he's fighting for Canada, he's fighting for France, he's fighting for the USA/ And he's fighting for the Russians, and he's fighting for Japan, and he thinks we'll put an end to war this way* – perfectly encapsulates the relationship between the folk idiom and the political awakening of many young people in the early 1960s.[59]

Many in the Village scene in the mid-1960s felt that sharing, camaraderie, and collaboration were paramount to their survival. Indigence was expected, so a certain kind of openness was the rule. If you were demonstrably part of the community and you needed a place to crash, couldn't afford a meal, or wanted to see a show but didn't have the 'scratch,' you would be looked after. In a gesture of openness and communitarianism, when touring musicians passed through Toronto to play for Villagers, they also spent time in their living rooms, slept on their couches, and shared stories, world views, and experiences. Consider this anecdote, offered by David DePoe:

So I was singing at the open stage at the Riverboat and stuff, and I was totally into the music scene and everything, and I was supporting myself. I drove a cab for a living, and hung out at Yorkville when my shift was over. That was the summer of '65 and through the fall and winter of '66 … We lived in the basement [of a building on the outskirts of the Village], and we hung out at Yorkville a lot, smoked a lot of dope and, you know? Missis- sippi John Hurt slept on our couch once! I was totally into it! He showed me how to play 'Candyman' on my guitar. And Bernie Fiedler, who ran the Riverboat, he used to let me in the back door quite a lot. Because once I got well-known in Yorkville, he'd just say: *Come and hear these guys …*[60]

To be able to circumvent the steep cover at the Riverboat (by then the premier folk club in the Village) by virtue of his already commanding Villager status must have been a chest-puffer. But DePoe has an even better story that grew out of his connection to the folk scene, the coffee- house owners, and the community of couch surfers.

Phil Ochs was writing the song 'Changes' when he came to Toronto. There's stories, like he was over at Peter Gzowski's place on Toronto island working on it, and then he went over to Gordon Lightfoot's house and was working on it some more. Anyway, our guest room was upstairs and he came down one night and he said: *Ok David, I think I've got this song, let me sing it for you.* And I said to him: *You know, that one line there doesn't scan. How about this?* So he scratched it out, wrote it in, what I suggested to him, and then he ran over to the Riverboat and sang it whole, for the first time.[61] Yeah, *Phil.* I kept in touch with him for about two years after that until he went into his depression.[62]

The story stands, if nothing else, as an example of the kind of close-knit community of Villagers fostered by the concentration of activities in the district.[63]

Not only did established musicians, writers, and performers gravi- tate to the Village, but Yorkville also offered exposure for novices too. Most other stages in Toronto in the 1960s were bound by union regu- lations which forbade them from hiring non-union musicians. How- ever, spots like John and Marilyn McHugh's Penny Farthing were able to offer up their basement stage to beginners – for the McHughs (and music fans in general), this was to be a fruitful move. While upstairs audiences thrilled to blues greats like Lonnie Johnson or Brownie McGhee (the blues being the McHughs' preferred genre), non-union singer-songwriters such as Joni Mitchell found their legs on the downstairs stage.[64] The Penny Farthing, boasting an outdoor patio (offering unparalleled sightseeing opportunities) and the Village's only semi-public swimming pool, wasn't just a draw for aspiring folkies. By 1964, its bikini-clad waitresses (their pool-ready attire wasn't required but certainly wasn't discouraged) had helped to inspire an atmosphere of hip decadence under the groovily absurd Penny Farthing bicycle hanging by the bar.[65]

The Riverboat, perhaps Yorkville's most enduring symbol (it remained open until June 1978), became the premier folk club in the Village almost immediately after it opened in December 1964. Bernie Fiedler, a former salesman who had been turned onto the Village coffee-house scene by none other than Werner Graeber the previous year, had started out at the Mousehole with his wife, Patti, in October 1963. The Mousehole was charming and decidedly hip but seated only sixty people at its Yorkville Ave space; Fiedler knew he had to expand his operation, and, judging by the crowds he got virtually every night, this was to be no fool's errand.[66] The Riverboat, seating almost 120, still managed to feel intimate and cozy; by all accounts, it was an ideal folk venue.[67] Perhaps that's how it was able to attract all the right acts. 'For me,' recalls Gordon Lightfoot, who enjoyed a lengthy engagement at the newly opened club, 'the Riverboat was my first taste of the big time. It was very dark and had a wonderful ambiance. And, it really did give you the idea that you were on some sort of *boat*.'[68] Within months of opening, superstars Simon and Garfunkel would play a legendary show on the Fiedlers' stage. After that, the training wheels were surely off. As Village folkie Brent Titcomb (whose band Three's a Crowd often played its stage) put it: 'Yorkville was really the epicentre of the whole music scene in Canada … and the Riverboat was its most prestigious venue.'[69]

As Nicholas Jennings so effectively demonstrates in *Before the Gold Rush*, his irresistible study of 'the Dawn of the Toronto Sound,' Yorkville's music scene was fascinatingly diverse and exciting by mid-1965. 'There was literally something for everyone,' he recalled.

The traditional jazz of Jim McHarg and his Metro Stompers at the Penny Farthing, the delicate ballads of Joni Mitchell at the New Gate of Cleve, the bluesy folk of John Kay at the Half Beat and the stirring songs of Lightfoot at the Riverboat. Meanwhile, the new pop sound had infiltrated Yorkville, with go-go dancers at the Mynah Bird and British-influenced bands everywhere: The Ugly Ducklings at Charlie Brown's, Jack London and the Sparrows at Café El Patio and Dee and the Yeomen at the Night Owl. Even the venerable Purple Onion had switched from folk to feature the blues-rock sounds of Luke and the Apostles. The close proximity of all the venues meant that club hoppers could easily catch up to a dozen different acts a night. It also meant that musicians could readily check out what others were playing.[70]

You could even hear David Clayton-Thomas, the tough-as-sinew blues singer (who would soon lead his Bossmen to a Canadian hit single with 'Brainwashed'), holding court all night long on the steps of St Paul's Church. Such variety breeds innovation. Yorkville Ave had become a kaleidoscopic mixture of ideas, sounds, talent, and hack artistry, all of which (when combined with the latest in psychedelic drugs) promoted creativity, competition, and, frequently, brilliance.[71]

Joining the Strip to the Village in a more formalized way, new clubs offered much the same entertainment as their Yonge St competitors with the added cachet of being situated right in the midst of the (supposedly) riot-friendly Yorkville scene. The marriage of rock'n'roll clubs and milling crowds of teenagers finally pushed aside the expectation that Yorkville's youth scene was all about bohemian artistry and folk music. While the Purple Onion and the Penny Farthing still booked major American folk acts like Phil Ochs and John Hammond, Jr alongside popular folkies and local jug bands like the Dirty Shames and the Colonials, new rock joints like the Embassy Club, the Brave New World, and the Mynah Bird were booking the Hawks, Robbie Lane and the Disciples, David Clayton-Thomas and the Shays, and the Paupers. Among the elite rock'n'roll groups after 1965 were the bluesy, proto-psychedelic Luke and the Apostles, the exciting Motown-meets-Midtown sound of Neil Young and Rick James's Mynah Birds (which, boasting a black American draft dodger as a frontman, was among the very few integrated bands in all of rock'n'roll music at the time), and erstwhile Rolling Stones clones the Ugly Ducklings. Each of these bands tends to represent something of the range of the Yorkville music scene: its progressive, experimental tendencies (Luke and the Apostles), its surprising ability to bring future stars together (the Mynah Birds), and its often derivative spirit giving way to playful tribute (the Ugly Ducklings).

There can be no denying the intense appeal of Yorkville as a musical centre par excellence, a veritable magnet for aspiring rockstars, and a breeding ground for a few of the most commercially and critically successful songwriters Canada has ever produced. In many ways, it was the *entire* industry in those years – as Village songwriter, booking agent, and manager Colleen Riley puts it (perhaps overzealously): 'The heavy concentration of clubs in Yorkville meant one could simply walk down the street and meet, at one time or another, nearly everyone in the music industry, from artists to managers to booking agents to record company executives to promotion people. Deals were done,' she maintains, 'from a sighting and a wave.'[72]

Gender, Sex, and Village Identity

Sex and gender played interweaving, intriguing roles in the performance of Village life. A growing obsession with Yorkville as a zone of hedonistic, liberated sexuality overcame many observers and participants alike as they tended to equate the Village with such activity nearly as readily as with drug use. For many, adopting the ethic of liberated sexuality constituted a certain refusal of middle-class values and hegemonic ideology, a rejection of the staid sexual politics of their parents' generation. Since many young people grew up with the famous 'wholesomeness' of television programming in the 1950s – on *I Love Lucy*, married couple Lucy and Desi Arnaz slept in different beds, for example – simply enjoying a furtive grope before marriage may have seemed revolutionary to some.[73]

The uneven distribution of sexual freedom and the negative consequences and connotations associated with freer sexuality (especially as played out within this tiny community) demonstrates the serious limitations of the free-love ethic in the period.[74] Many young people, and most of them young women, found that too often what masqueraded as a liberated sexuality was something rather less beautiful – it was sex for money, for drugs, for food, for a place to crash; it was a pernicious, quietly effective STD, stealing your fertility before you discovered its presence; it was a smooth-talking stranger who brought you home to his gang of friends for a lopsided orgy; it was yet another 'village pregnancy,' a highly unwanted, terminally uncool, and tremendously unwelcome situation. It was by no means always like this; many women found sex in the Village to be a healthy, attractive, and ultimately safe experience. Yet some, it must be said, did not.

In mid-August 1966 the Mynah Bird took a stab at answering a central question: How does one exploit liberated sexuality, the Village rock'n'roll scene, *and* the public fascination with hippies all at once? This coffee house had always relied on male voyeurism to sell itself to the general public – Rosemary Sullivan recalls the spectacle of 'girls in fishnet stockings, fringed mini-skirts, and shimmering white boots … dancing in cages at the second-floor window' – and frequently boasted in advertisements about the physical features of its female staff.[75] ('Where else can you watch the Mynah Bird Girls?' read one such ad, setting up the relationship between the dancers, the young waitresses, who were expected to wear a pseudo-uniform of bikini tops and mini-skirts, and their male customers.) Still, in an atmosphere of 'liberated' sexuality, the performance of female nudity and sexual power had taken on a certain political significance for at least some of the women who chose to work at the Mynah Bird. In response to condescending suggestions that she was a victim of the male gaze, one dancer declared to the *Toronto Telegram*: 'A-go-go dancing signifies to me woman's final break from man.'[76] Looking back, feminist writer Susan Swann recalls that she had seen those dancers as representing an exciting new space for the female sexual performance, 'somewhere between the wholesome bounce of a cheerleader and the allure of a stripper.'[77] Building on this reputation (and such support from within the community), the new initiative was that those famous go-go dancers were to be complemented, at least on some occasions, by topless dancers.[78]

Colin Kerr, the club's twenty-nine-year-old proprietor, was well known in the Village as an untamable schemer. ('He was out of his mind,' offered sometime Mynah Bird bassist Bruce Palmer.) As band manager to the Rick (James) Matthews-fronted Mynah Birds, he had gone to bizarre lengths to create publicity and buzz for his charges, once hiring a throng of young women to chase the band through Eaton's Department Store. As a coffee-house owner, his antics were no less ribald. By the late 1960s, his coffee house would boast X-rated film screenings and day-glo nude body painting. To top it all off (or perhaps to offset the gender imbalance he had established with bikini-clad women out front), he employed a nude male chef for a time.[79]

In the weeks prior to the public event, which was to be held on 12 August, a Friday night, the police were informed of the impending show – indeed, they were even invited to a Thursday night preview – but they refused to attend, claiming that they did not want to play 'censor.' Inspector William Pilkington of the Morality Squad explained that, since the Thursday night performance was basically a private demonstration intended for the police and reporters, it was unnecessary for him and his colleagues to attend. However, 'if such an exhibition is put before the public,' he warned, 'then the necessary investigation will be made.'[80] Reporters, though, were more than happy to make the scene, to bear witness, as it were, to the migration of topless dancing from established (if furtive and generally illegal) burlesque and strip joints on nearby Yonge St to the Village. Prepared for what was expected to be a new kind of topless performance – new because it was to be a hip version of burlesque, fuelled by the liberated sexuality of the youth culture, carried on the electric waves of über-cool rock'n'roll music – reporters from various media outlets filled the small club, awaiting the arrival of Toronto's first bohemian nude show.

Kerr, for his part, played up the ambiguity surrounding the performance. He refused to say just who would be dancing, except to offer that she was a 'local girl' who had been 'recommended' by various Villagers. She was '21 years old,' 'of Swedish extraction,' and, oddly enough, would wear a mask. The mask, in fact, had as much to do with theatrical intentions ('we're selling mystery,' Kerr explained) as it did with Kerr's somewhat paradoxical ambivalence over displaying a semi-naked woman in front of an audience. Whether motivated by a certain respect for the female body or, more likely, by a fear of being prosecuted for lewdness, Kerr would also use a dry-ice smoke machine, iron bars, and a black light to 'further screen the dancer' from the audience. The young proprietor tried to underline to the press that his intentions were not purely sexist and exploitative: 'I can't even say what her measurements are,' Kerr explained, adding: 'I think this whole business of measurements is terribly crude anyway.'[81]

The Buñuelian scene that ensued on that Thursday evening is the stuff of legend. After hours of waiting for the show to begin, for the one paid dancer of the night to step onstage and perform, the throng of reporters and onlookers got something rather unexpected instead. It seems that the smoke machine, chugging away to provide the necessary ambiance for the gyrations of Yorkville's first stripper, went berserk. Choking, coughing, and gasping for air, the press representatives scrambled to escape the venue, pouring out into the street as an exhaust of oily smoke billowed from the broken contraption. Apparently, the only non-reporter allowed in the room that night was Miguel Maropakis, who laughs at the memory: 'The first show they had there was a woman, an ex-girlfriend of mine. And they had all the *Telegram* and the *Star* and everybody [there]! But you couldn't see! You couldn't see anything because there was so much [dry] ice! I was the only outsider allowed there because she was my girlfriend. [Kerr] was crazy, just trying to make a buck.'[82]

Such gauche attempts at co-optation were the exception, not the norm, in the Village. However, an uncomfortable power dynamic remained at work in the relationship between women and what was repeatedly constructed as a male-centred counterculture.[83] Trina Robbins, a San Francisco-based writer, speaks for many in summarizing her recollections of the expected role for women in the wider hip scene: 'The ideal chick just had a good time. Whatever he did, she went along with it. If he moved in, you took care of him, but you got nothing in return. If he wanted to dump you, it was, "Well, babe, the road calls."'[84] Myrna Wood, one of the 'founding mothers' (as she referred to herself) of the Toronto (and Canadian) women's liberation movement, recalled the tenor of those years with some frustration. In her mind, the trajectory of hip in the scene was about the saving of white, middle-class males from the pervasive feminization of their identity category. To be hip was to transcend Canadian, white, suburban identity: 'Hippie-type people were even more misogynistic than politicals, which is saying quite a bit ... The more people got into that kind of lifestyle the more they tried to copy what they saw as either American, or black: Hip culture ... [It's about] women being denigrated to prove that you're a hip male.'[85] This cultural model – a set of possible activities and aesthetics which included (but were not limited to) long hair, beards, drug use, free love, psychedelic rock music – was repeatedly underlined as male-centric. Men were the *active* drug users, the *active* rock'n'rollers; women were merely *there*, present, passive recipients of a hip male rebellion.[86] Just as the terms 'youth,' 'tough,' 'rowdy,' and 'beatnik' were code for teenage *boy* in the first half of the decade, to have been a hippie, a greaser, or a biker by 1966 and beyond was to be male – a hip female was merely dubbed a 'girl,' and she was usually perceived to be in some genuine danger, sexual or otherwise. Even the term 'youth' was male first, female second – in all reportage from the period, we read of 'youths' and 'girls,' 'hippies' and 'girl hippies,' 'weekenders' and 'teenyboppers.'

Throughout the 1960s, when it came to sexuality, the Village scene moved between the poles of liberation and exploitation.[87] From 1964 to 1966, as the ethic of freer sexuality became more acceptable, more pervasive in the scene, the shifting between those two poles became ever more erratic. Paradoxical expressions of a hip sexual ethic were not uncommon; in fact, as Beth Bailey has shown through her study of U.S.-based underground papers and 'comix,' the complicated expression of female sexuality (exacerbated by the persistent idea that males were the prime movers in the scene) came both from without and within the hip movement. Bailey argues that, much as they did with drugs and rock'n'roll music, 'members of America's counterculture used sex to create a countercultural identity.'[88]

And yet the uses of sex to this end were often undeniably exploitative, even as they were couched in the rhetoric of liberation. Moreover, as straight and establishment people became aware that sexuality was an aspect of the countercultural arsenal, it (like drugs and rock'n'roll) became part of the attractive (and repellent) hippie trip. Yorkville, after 1964, grew into a kind of tourist activity for many Torontonians, now often dubbed 'weekenders,' a place to come and witness the hip youth culture. But it also, remarkably, became the place to flirt with hip behaviour and identity for the uninitiated, the bemused, or even the diametrically opposed. Yorkville's developing status as a hip playground, and as a centre for Toronto's drug, rock'n'roll, and pick-up scenes, would attract many curious people, young and old, straight and bendy, from all over Toronto and, eventually, beyond.

For suburban youth, Yorkville was beginning to be known as a place to go on a Friday or Saturday evening to meet other like-minded kids and maybe make a romantic connection. One Villager, said to have 'sought identity sexually,' 'became compulsive in constant homosexual relationships' until 'unsatisfied with this he became immersed in another search through heterosexual relationships and a kind of "free love."' His search for sexual identity culminated in his taking up residence in the Village scene by 1966 – the Village offered him a space to seek authenticity both sexual and spiritual.[89] But Village activist Clayton Ruby cautions against equating this with the development of a free-love ethic, as such. 'No, these were teenagers, they had hormones, they wanted to have sex, and they were more open about expressing that than people in the suburbs. That's the principal difference.'[90] This openness was read by these weekend tourists to the Village as an invitation to partake. And, certainly, many found their first big-city partner in one of Yorkville's clubs or coffee houses. Bob Segarini (of the West Coast band the Wackers) offers this little visual: 'I ended up in Yorkville at a place called the Penny Farthing. This is what I remember: I paid a dollar for a bowl of chili and a girl took me downstairs and blew me. The buck paid for the chili.'[91]

Former biker 'Wild Bill' maintains a dark view of the hip sexual performance, and especially in the way it played out among weekenders. 'Some of the hippie guys who were wannabes, they'd get a sixteen- or seventeen-year-old bimbo lubed up and have fun, because she wouldn't say no. It was rape. The point of the drugs then was: it was a policy for raping. For date rape. Which wasn't the way you wanted it.'[92] In early 1967 the San Francisco Diggers (an anarchist collective bent on providing community services and aid to the Haight-Ashbury scene) published a deeply cynical account of the kinds of exploitation lurking in their version of the hip ghetto. Sadly, this famous missive harmonizes with the sentiments of 'Wild Bill' about the Village sex scene, replete with its implicit assumption that upon entering the Village scene the 'chick' lost all agency: 'Pretty little 16-year-old middle-class chick comes to the Haight to see what it's all about & gets picked up by a 17-year-old street dealer who spends all day shooting her full of speed again & again, then feed her 3000 mikes and raffles off her temporarily unemployed body for the biggest gang bang since the night before last.'[93] This persistent trope, then, of the wide-eyed young woman who comes to the Village only to be turned into a drug-addled victim of hip sexual exploitation coloured not just the dire pronouncements of the municipal authorities or the conservative media. Hip sources themselves recognized (or were at least concerned by) the possibility of sexual danger in their Village. And, while there was a tentative assumption that 'true' Villagers could be trusted, it seemed that the expanding ranks of weekenders could not.

Clayton Ruby agrees with the view of 'Wild Bill' that 'wannabe hippies,' or weekenders, were seen as pretenders to this liberated sexual ethic, even as abusers of its unspoken codes. He is very clear that, although the weekenders often came to Yorkville looking to get laid, 'if they got lucky they'd meet other weekenders who felt the same way! For the people who lived in Yorkville it was a status down to pick up a weekender.'[94] Reinforcing the clear delineation – clear, at least to some – that there was an authentic performance of 'Villager' to which only a very few had access, Ruby reminds us that status, hierarchy, and standing were at stake in Villagers' constructions of their own identity. And, since most 'authentic' Villagers tended to be men – my evidence has rarely turned up any women who held power positions or elevated status among their peers – what we are talking about is power. (Male) Villagers knew that they were wanted by (female) weekenders, and that power relationship was maintained through the pairing of true versus false Village identity.

Ralph Sat in the Car and Prayed: A Christian Mission to Yorkville

The post-war period complicated the sense of Canada as a robustly

Christian country.[95] Canada's weekly (Christian) church-going attendance at war's end was around 60 per cent, an impressive figure. But, by the mid-1970s, following a laundry list of upheavals and a series of dramatic culture wars, that percentage had dropped by half, to just over 30 per cent.[96] And yet interest in religion (or, more correctly, *spirituality*) was one of the key characteristics of the counterculture, both inside and outside Yorkville, the Haight, Greenwich Village, and beyond. While criticized by some observers as vapid flirtations with Eastern mysticism, and often dismissed as mere window dressing, spiritualism did help shape hip ideology and discourse in the Yorkville scene throughout the 1960s.[97] As much a subversive activity as going barefoot or taking LSD, hip flirtation with non-Christian religious practices and beliefs helped to distinguish the Village as inscrutable, alien, and separate from the wider cityscape. Adding to the moral panic that accompanied tales of drug orgies, indigence, and random violence, the distinct possibility that Yorkville was breeding a godless youth movement fuelled a certain Christian outrage.

The Yorkville scene (in reflection of wider trends in North American youth culture in these years) had an ambiguous, even paradoxical, relationship with God. Hip visions of the Almighty, whether glimpsed through the immaculate windowpane of an acid trip, elucidated through the searching jams of a psychedelic band, or stolen from the eyes of a lover in a moment of ecstatic communion, did not typically come to their recipients while they knelt between church pews. Instead of being present in the words of the Bible, the infinite was said to be found in the undiscovered country of hedonism, of psilocybin-fuelled vision quests, of stoned group sex, of pseudo-Hindu meditation, and of generalized, unfocused mysticism. And Jesus, although much admired as a revolutionary, as a pacifist and non-conformist par excellence, was still more closely associated with the stuffy air of Sunday morning services than with his splendidly counter-hegemonic activities and teachings. Timothy Leary's much-vaunted ethic of 'dropping out,' which drove many middle-class young people to attempt rejections of the materialism, capitalism, and sobriety of their parents, also implied a rejection of the Judeo-Christian tradition and moral frameworks into which they had been initiated.

And so experimental and unconventional spirituality was central to the identities performed by Village youth. Indeed, Gopala Alampur would note in 1967–8 that the 'search for God' constituted 'an important aspect of the life of each hippie' in the Village. In Alampur's perceptive view, a Villager 'will tend to borrow the theologies while rejecting dogmas, the enforced rituals, the established churches' of all religions, including Christianity, since all 'have something to offer to the hippie as all contain some aspect of an infinite God concept.'[98] Rejection of the blind faith, the unquestioned dogmatism demanded by their parents' churches, fit in with the more general refusals of expected systems of belief. Just as interest in socialism, left-liberalism, and communism began to characterize hip politics, the allure of shifting one's religious association from tired old Protestantism to exotic Buddhism proved irresistible to many. Ultimately, scores of Villagers likely chose none and all points of view simultaneously. As Tom Robbins put it in his countercultural masterpiece *Even Cowgirls Get the Blues*, the trick was to adopt paradox as the centre of all faith: 'I believe in nothing, everything is sacred. I believe in everything, nothing is sacred.'[99] The frustrating tendency of hip youth to adopt religious positions without delving into them beyond superficialities led the Reverend James Smith to despair that 'it seemed like the Hippy's desire was to be an honourary [sic] member of every religion except Christianity.'[100]

Generally, this experimentation extended no further than flirtation with Eastern religions (especially Hinduism and Buddhism), but in some cases Villagers were drawn to more formal expressions of religious non-conformity. 'Among hippies,' reported Alampur, 'knowledge of philosophy, religion and psychology carry prestige.' 'They are particularly attracted to Oriental and Indian religions as well as to mysticism and spiritualism ... Yet, their knowledge of these subjects is superficial. Religious and philosophic terms are used more to make a good impression than to communicate substantial meaning. As might be expected, there is little attempt to struggle with or study these philosophic issues. Philosophical books are carried but infrequently read; religions such as Zen Buddhism are often talked of but rarely understood.'[101] Such bastardized versions of established dogma reflect the individualistic and rebellious spirit of the period. However, not everyone in the scene was so inclined. The advent of so-called Jesus Freaks (the hip forerunners of the mainstream born-again movements of the late 1970s and early 1980s[102]), the Hare Krishna movement, and religio-anarchic communes in and outside Toronto by the early 1970s all reflect the continued relationship between counterculture, community, experimentation, and spirituality throughout the period.[103]

The most significant factor in all of this experimentation after the act of refusal and rebellion – the centrepiece that animated all such countercultural activity – was sacramental drug use.[104] As historian Timothy Miller has demonstrated, 'in such religious esteem was dope held that many ... contended that it should be used ritually.'[105] Of course, newly discovered psychedelic drugs such as LSD were famously capable of exposing the mind to highly transcendental vision and experience.[106] When Aldous Huxley, author and early proponent of the religious qualities of an LSD experience, published his book on the subject, he made an explicit connection between reality, perception, and God.[107] Agreeing with William Blake's lovely suggestion that 'if the doors of perception were cleansed / everything would appear to man as it is, infinite,' Huxley explained that the effect of LSD was precisely such a cleansing.[108] Through LSD, it was said, the infinite God was revealed, not just as some bearded abstraction in the sky, but in the heaven-in-a-wildflower sense that transcendentalists had been dreaming of for hundreds of years.[109]

To be high on acid, to achieve the 'peak' of one's trip into pseudo-schizophrenic weirdness, was to realize a moment of spiritual transcendence – to be suddenly and profoundly able to commune with the infinite, the eternal, the holy. One of the three 'goals' of an acid trip, Harvard-psychologist-cum-psychedelic-pioneer Timothy Leary famously remarked, is 'to discover and make love with God.'[110] Although there were many who refused such a view of psychedelics – musician Paul Krassner quipped that acid simply showed him 'a different God that I didn't believe in' – few could deny the widespread assumption that God was more likely to be found on an acid trip than at the bottom of a bottle.[111]

One former Villager described his first LSD experience in just such spiritual terms:

> It placed me in the universe in a profoundly meaningful way. It relieved me of all of that nonsense, the way we compare ourselves, put ourselves down, pick ourselves up. It just put me in the *continuum*. Actually, I have gone on from this experience to a deeper interest in Eastern philosophy, and in particular Buddhism and Zen Buddhism. I feel that that psychedelic whop to my head at that time really cracked – what I think the Buddha was really talking about – the illusion of ego, and the illusion of separateness. The perennial problem for human beings is the way we objectify the world – consequently, from that process, we are constantly the subject relative to an objective world. That's the dualistic conundrum that bedevils us. It probably does any sentient being. It would have to. But

LSD really penetrated all of that! I had a direct and immediate experience
of myself as an expression of the universe.[112]

For this man, the experience was so intense as to light a fire of obligation
in him. After experiencing the profundity of the LSD trip, this Villager
(he has chosen to remain anonymous) was convinced that his experience needed to be shared: 'Really, I agreed with Aldous Huxley. He had
said that acid should not be generally spread around, because it will be
abused ... But, unfortunately, because of the prohibition, because of the
repression, because of the hysteria, a lot of us came to the conclusion
that there really wasn't an alternative. It was either going to be killed
completely, or it had to be distributed. So I got into the distribution
of acid. I don't know how else to say it, but I really thought it was a
duty.'[113] But, while for this Villager the LSD experience was akin to an
ecstatic vision of deeply religious clarity, for so many others it was (just
as was their lip-service attention to Eastern religions) part of the performance. Another way to make the scene.

In response to these gathering trends, some religious outfits came to
believe that Yorkville was in need of deliverance from such profana-
tion. Launched by the Reverend Kenn Opperman of the Christian Missionary Alliance (CMA) in late January 1966, the Fish Net provided a
new kind of service for Yorkville youth. Set up as a 'free' coffee shop on
Yorkville Ave, the Fish Net operated as an otherwise innocuous establishment, a place to sit and sip on warm drinks, ride out a high, meet
some other local folks. But, as one of the few spots in the Village where
one could find a bit of respite from the move-along prodding of the
proliferating beat cops, its popularity among Villagers grew unabated.
By mid-summer, it was observed that 'the place gets so crowded that
often the door must be locked to keep more from coming in and so kids
sit patiently on the steps and wait their turn.'[114]

Providing free coffee and biscuits, the Fish Net tended to attract
young people without the resources to sit elsewhere – most coffee
houses would force people to move along if they failed to purchase
something once an hour. However, the average Villager likely knew
what would happen if she decided to take the CMA up on their offer
of free coffee and shelter from the storm: eventually, inescapably, one
of the adult staff would sidle up and inexorably steer the conversation
toward Jesus.[115] 'Our primary purpose,' explained Deane Downey, the
twenty-six-year-old University of Toronto student who helped run the
Fish Net during the summer of 1966, 'is to provide a place where we

as Christians can present our beliefs concerning Christ.'[116] Essentially an evangelical operation, the Fish Net went about its mission in a soft-sell, casual manner, using the coffee-shop venue as a kind of front for its chief function.[117] Phyllis McIntyre, who ran the Fish Net six nights a week from 8:30 p.m. to midnight, explained her role as she understood it: 'We never forced religion on any of them ... we tell them we haven't come here to give them religion, but to try to help them sort out their problems.'[118]

Despite its overt associations with evangelicalism, the Fish Net would become a popular spot for Villagers before it was shut down by its landlord later that year. On any given evening, 'scores of them' could be found congregating there and lining up out front for a chance to come in and hang around.[119] However, its success at disseminating Christian ideology was rather less apparent than its success at giving away a great deal of food. According to Frank Longstaff, 'the Church claims to have people at each of its tables leading religious discussions, but instead, most of the workers' time is occupied serving coffee and cookies.'[120] It seems clear that the majority of young people who frequented the Fish Net in the first half of 1966 took the religious discussions in stride, humouring their hosts while taking advantage of the free warmth, victuals, and much-loved caffeine.[121] As Longstaff observed:

> The Fish Net is important mainly as a gathering place for Villagers – a place where they can sit and talk. It is also a contact point for new people coming into Yorkville from out of town, and in the Fish Net, newcomers can quickly make friends and find a pace to stay. Here Villagers plan their entertainment for the night, set up parties for after the Fish Net closes at 11:30 or midnight. All of this kind of action is unplanned and informal, and in fact the Church workers have nothing to do with it ... Their proselytizing attempts are listened to politely by the Villagers, almost like commercials in a television show – and they seem to have about the same impact.[122]

But the counter-mission for the Fish Net was to familiarize its volunteers (primarily adults from nearby congregations and grad students from the University of Toronto theology and divinity schools) with the Yorkville youth scene.[123] Deane Downey referred to this as a 'secondary consideration' in Yorkville, acknowledging the importance of exposing staff to the realities of the world outside the church proper.

The 'ideas and concepts of the Yorkville hippies' were taken to be worthy of study, at least significant enough to merit the attention of the CMA's staff.[124]

The Fish Net experiment proved to be short-lived: by September, Yorkville's only free coffee house had been given orders to vacate the premises. The owner of the building had become fed up with the frustrations that went along with throngs of young people congregating on her site. Moreover, her other tenants had begun to pressure her to do something about the detrimental effect the hippies were having on their business: 'When you have to wade through 20 people on the top step outside your front door, and others on the way down and under the awning on the boulevard, it's too much,' explained Myrl Saunders, proprietor of the high-fashion boutique that sat on the ground floor, above the subterranean Fish Net.[125]

Like many Yorkville buildings in 1966, the one that housed the Fish Net was owned by local landlord Anna Marie Heit.[126] However, unlike most other coffee houses in the district, the Fish Net did not operate under the protection of a signed lease. Rather, according to Heit, 'it was an agreement. It was a signed agreement, but it was conditional.'[127] Heit explained that she was forced to dissolve the agreement after she had seen 'two people move out of the building and a third one threat[en] to move out if they [the Fish Net] didn't move.' This third party, presumably the first-floor tenants Myrl-Andrew (the fashion boutique operated by Myrl Saunders), had complained that customers were afraid of having to step past the crowds of Villagers in order to come up the front steps. And yet the Fish Net never opened its doors prior to 8:30 p.m.; it would seem that Heit and Saunders's argument was a bit forced.

The *Toronto Daily Star* article that announced the closing of the Fish Net was uncritical of Heit and Saunders. However, intrepid *Star* columnist Ron Haggart took it upon himself the following day to attack the closing of the Fish Net as a misguided assault on a truly positive aspect of the scene. Somewhat unsubtly entitled 'How to Throw Kids Back to the Streets,' Haggart's piece aimed to establish the Fish Net as part of the 'other Yorkville, the Yorkville you never hear about.' His tack in presenting the Fish Net as a safe, necessary space for Villagers was none-too-subtle either: drawing a parallel between the riotous events of the previous spring and yet another relatively placid evening in the smoky basement that was the Fish Net, Haggart attempted to demonstrate a kind of oasis of religious tranquillity and sophistication amid the discordance of a derelict youth culture. It was a vision of civility amid the wilderness.

'On the night of the riot in late May,' he began, 'not all the kids in Yorkville were throwing bottles at the cops. Some were praying.'[128] Not only were they praying, but some were busy *actively converting* a former non-believer (referred to as Dave) into a Christian. Interspersed with violent snapshots from the 'riot' was a tale of one man's discovery of light during Yorkville's darkest hour as if it were a lesson from the pulpit; Haggart's conceit, that Dave's conversion happened at precisely the same time as the other Villagers were brawling with Metro's finest, provides for a fuzzy kind of agitprop. We are presented with not so much a vision of the Fish Net on a typical evening as a *version* of the Fish Net in an unlikely context, on a particularly momentous (and somewhat anomalous) night: 'A young man named Dean [Downey (sic)] ... came out of the Fish Net and said to his friend Ralph: "Dave has decided to accept Jesus Christ as his personal Saviour." Deeply touched, Ralph went across the street to join his friends in the car. While a block away the kids threw bottles and popcorn bags at the cops, Ralph and his friends sat in the car and prayed.'[129] Haggart goes on to admit that 'Dave's conversion was unusual' and that 'only three or four people [have] accepted Christ during the eight months the Fish Net has ministered to the kids in Yorkville.' He also concedes that 'they didn't open the Fish Net for that purpose.' However, it is hard to escape the framing device of conversion, even as he later tries to steer us away from it.

The thrust of the article is towards an understanding of the Fish Net as a solitary beacon of middle-class values, morality, and education – the conversion of Dave and those few others to Christianity is allegorical, illustrative of the construction of Yorkville as a contested, fractious, misguided space. Historically, religions (especially Christianity) have converted so-called heathens in what are perceived to be troubled, uncivilized, apparently 'godless' lands over which they aspired to take control. And, as many post-colonial historians have pointed out, this process of *conversion* (again, usually to Christianity, at least in the North American context) was as much about a consolidation of colonial power as it was about a desire on the part of the Christians to fulfil any religious or moral obligations.[130] In striking ways, Haggart draws uneasy parallels between the traditional narrative of the conversion of natives by Christian missionaries and the conversion of the Villagers by modern-day missionaries. He emphasizes the fractious aspects of

Yorkville through recurring mention of the 'riots'; he establishes the beneficence of the Fish Net staff (they freely gave up their jobs to come volunteer here, they didn't *force* religion onto their 'customers'); and he makes a clear delineation between the praying, Christian youth and the violent, Other youth.

Haggart's point, even if I appear to be stretching it, was still, at the root, this: Yorkville appeared to be a foreign land. The Village was like a forbidding jungle, home to an unfathomable, precarious population harbouring backward ideals; in order to save them, missionaries must venture inside, armed with their faith in the righteousness of their beliefs. And the Villagers, likened to natives in need of conversion, of salvation, of deliverance from the evils attendant on their refusal of normative behaviour, appeared to Haggart (and to a growing number of observers) as representing a mounting cultural crisis.

4

Are You Here to Watch Me Perform?

Places are chosen to be gazed upon because there is anticipation, especially through daydreaming and fantasy, of intense pleasures, either on a different scale or involving different senses from those customarily encountered. Such anticipation is constructed and sustained through a variety of non-tourist practices, such as film, TV, literature, magazines, records and videos, which construct and reinforce that gaze.

– John Urry[1]

In the spring of 1964, the *Globe and Mail* reported on a beard-growing contest which, while emphasizing the spectacle of hairy young men, was designed as a bit of levity, not an overt criticism of bohemia.[2] But the *Globe* was deliberate about locating this contest in Yorkville, as though it would have made no sense elsewhere. The hip aesthetic, variously re-defined throughout the period as fashion developed and mutated, was most often represented prior to the advent of long hair by a man's beard. In this, as with most things hip in the 1960s, the masculine performance was repeatedly taken for the expression of the whole.

In general, however, Yorkville's hip aesthetics were lagging behind the curve of most stylish urban centres in Europe and North America. Michael Valpy recalls that 'there was no uniform, no hippie uniform in the early years. That wasn't till much later.'[3] Judy Pocock, who took an overseas job as a babysitter one summer, puts this point into stark relief. 'In 1964,' she explains, 'I went to Europe.' 'And I remember going and hitting Amsterdam and seeing the boys with bellbottom jeans (which I thought were amazing, you know, this contradiction jeans/cowboys, bellbottoms/sailors), and *long hair*. And just, you're thinking:

Wow. I was twenty, or nineteen. You know? This was amazing. And that was *not* Toronto at that point. And I lived on Hazelton, at the corner of Yorkville and Hazelton, and I was still blown away.'[4] While it would not be long before hair and fashion trends crossed the Atlantic (the rushing tide of Beatlemania saw to that by year's end), it is worth noting that Yorkville's bohemian aesthetic was well behind the times during the summer in which it was first widely noted by municipal authorities, the press, and young people alike.[5]

Fashion constitutes perhaps the most significant external expression of identity in the liberal-capitalist context. Pulled on two sides by the decidedly different impulses of conformity and individualism, of normality and originality, fashion offers the means to present oneself most effectively as a member of one, the other, or both camps. The fashions that characterized the Yorkville youth scene, and the hip archetypes that performed them, were thus both mutable *and* consistent. As Joel Lobenthal has suggested (echoing arguments made by Judith Butler, among other identity theorists), in contrast to the more staid fashions of the 1950s, in the 1960s 'the individual remade himself daily, trying out new stances of dress and behavior, internalizing some, [while] keeping others at arm's length as theatrical alter egos.'[6]

The appreciation of this theatrical aspect of hip fashion, and the attendant belief that one's external expression of self could be radically shifted on a day-to-day basis, was central to the mid-1960s youth aesthetic. If fashion in the 1950s was about the apparent contrast between good kids (sweater sets, slacks, crisp shirts, and even neckties for such mundane activities as school) and bad kids (leather jackets, jeans, boots, undershirts), the fashions that reigned in the ensuing years aimed to subvert such class-based normativity. Of course, the 'bad boy' fashion lingered, constituting the basic look for the bikers and the toughs in the Village throughout the period. For other Villagers, as one observer concluded, 'there is no uniform, but there *is* a costume.'[7]

Bearded men constituted the first wave of this fashion rebellion in the Yorkville scene. Months after the Beatles first stormed North America with their mop-top hairstyles, adolescent boys were still trying to grow out their crew cuts. But their older brothers, at least some of them, could grow their beards out much more quickly than the hair on their heads. Beards became a kind of hip argot in Yorkville and on the University of Toronto campus; as an identifying marker, a badge of inclusion, the beard denoted its wearer as a committed member of an alternative world. By mid-summer, 1964, Yorkville's hip archetype was developed around the hirsute male.[8] Following a protracted period in which (in North America) beards were uncommonly worn by men, this sudden re-emergence of the fashion constituted such a novelty that it was counted among the various tourist attractions offered by the Village. In late 1964 the *Toronto Daily Star* ran a piece describing Yorkville as a travel destination, establishing its distinction as a *different* place, even another *planet*, 'a world of little shops selling Finnish rugs, gold bathtub faucets, hand-dipped candles, nutmeg-flavored coffee and bearded guitar players.'[9]

Apart from the charming (but probably inadvertent) suggestion that Yorkville was selling bearded guitar players alongside the candles and rugs, this is a sketch of the popular conception of the Village by late 1964. It was a scene defined by the quaint items on sale in its shops, a scene as near yet as far away from mid-town Toronto as could be, and comprised of a population whose appearances and performances smacked of disparity, eccentricity, and even outright foreignness. In a striking case in point, members of a local Yorkville rock band even changed their names around this time to achieve a more English lilt; it is said that Toronto-born singer Dave Marden (who was now going by Jack London) went so far with this performance as to affect an accent and tell people he hailed from Liverpool.[10] Judy Pocock recalls first seeing this band just after she had returned from a spell in Europe and being impressed by their British pretensions. 'I remember looking out my window, and there was a band practising at the Avenue Rd Club,' she recollects. 'They had long hair! And they were the only long-haired guys in the neighbourhood. And they were Jack London and the Sparrows, which [would eventually become] Steppenwolf! I used to sit in my bedroom window and watch them practice. Wow. And, I thought, *I like* these guys.'[11] Soon enough, this eccentric appearance was taken more and more as the definitive feature of the scene by local media; in early 1966 the *Toronto Daily Star* quipped that there was no point in adding 'Village of Yorkville' to the street signs in the district. 'With all that long hair and all those beards, who needs 'em?'[12]

One notes that this overt male fashion is the only performance mentioned, as though women couldn't make the cut, had no real purchase over this aspect of the scene. In what will be a persistent trope, Yorkville youth are here defined through their non-conformist (long) hair styles, through their propensity for beards and unkempt locks, both specifically male expressions. Aside from a few daring individuals whose *short* haircuts mimicked the French *nouvelle vague* styles of actress Jean

Seberg and, later, British model Twiggy, long hair on women was the anticipated aesthetic in both dominant and alternative cultural expression in the 1960s. Hair, a defining issue, and certainly a politicized facet of youth culture in the 1960s, was yet another category of hipness to which maleness exercised its ownership.[13] A typically long-haired woman's choice of an atypically long-haired man as a sexual partner was as close as she could get to collaboration in *this* particular hip pursuit; yet again, her performance of hipness could be defined through association rather than subjectivity.[14]

Masculinity, fashion, and hairstyles were intertwined in the Cold War years in complex ways. As Leerom Medovoi has pointed out, the advent of suburbia, the rise of the conformist 'Organization Man' ethic, and the repetition of the theme of male domestication in media, film, literature, and television in the 1950s are often misread by historians as constituting a 'new normative model of American manhood.' Rather, he stresses, 'what they in fact connoted was at best a distressed form of masculinity, and at worst a degenerate one.'[15] Medovoi argues persuasively that the development of the trope of the male rebel, the obsession with juvenile delinquency (also typically male), and the sudden vogue of the beatnik individualist (always male) are each indicative of the persistent need for archetypal characters who offer resistance to the male domesticity model.[16] Into the 1960s, the tangled relationship between the rebellious male and the conformist man became further convoluted by the shifting aesthetics of hip. The development of the bearded and long-haired hip archetype played against the hyper-masculinized rebel of the 1950s.[17]

By early 1965, archetypal Villagers sported long hair (over the ears, the eyebrows, touching the collar) and a beard (where hormonally possible), and were ever more taken to wearing such decidedly feminized accoutrements as beads, flowers, and homemade jewellery. For many of my interview subjects, hair and beards were regarded as simple ways to express difference: 'It was a rigid society,' explains Judy Perly. 'Everybody had the same haircut in the early Sixties, you know what I mean? *Everybody*. It was a big scandal when the Beatles had hair to *here*! A big scandal!' She recalls that, since both beards and long hair were inaccessible expressions for women, the thing was clothing. 'Look, when I went to school you had to sit with your hands folded ... I had to wear a skirt all the way through school, and I didn't go to a private school. The year after I left the girls went on strike so that they could wear jeans to school.'[18] But the expression of hip through wearing trousers wasn't long-lived. By 1966, the skirt had returned as the primary expression of hip (hyper-) femininity. Perly was shocked by my suggestion that hip women had fewer means of demonstrating their hipness through fashion than men: 'There were a *lot* of hip women [in Yorkville]. Men had the long hair, the beards and stuff. But women had the long dresses.'[19] Especially with this relational framing, it seems difficult to see the 'long dresses' (often, tellingly, referred to as 'peasant skirts') as emphasizing the kind of progressive rebelliousness that was expressed by long hair and unruly beards. Didn't their parents wear skirts and dresses too? It seems that an aesthetic inequality is an element of a more general inequality within hip expression in the 1965–8 period.

As Joan Didion would emphasize in her steely-eyed account of Haight-Ashbury in 1967, gender relations in the wider hip scene were not necessarily progressive. Rather, one of the more perverse elements of the 'hippie trip' (and an element that was just as apparent in Toronto as in San Francisco) was its adoption of a male-centred social system, a system that seemed to Didion no different from the very feminine mystique from which women were supposed to have been recently delivered. Though she did tend to rely on some already tired clichés regarding women in the scene – the victim, the stoner, the sex toy[20] – for Didion, what this represented was evidence that, no matter how they tried, people were 'the unconscious instruments of values they would strenuously reject on a conscious level.'[21] Bound as they were to the social process, a process that makes the rejection of common sense tremendously difficult, hip youth were, however reluctantly, tied to certain ideological touchstones they found it hard to refuse. Throughout these years, this current runs sharp, icily, and fast.

Hi, Mr and Mrs Tourist: Sightseeing and the Hip Performance

Culture, as Raymond Williams reminds us, is 'one of the two or three most complicated words in the English language.'[22] But if, as Stephen Yarbrough has argued, 'cultures exist by virtue of their being believed to exist,' then identification and performance are their two most significant components.[23] If someone identifies herself as part of a *culture* – that is, she identifies herself through what she and others believe to be the behaviours, appearances, and beliefs of a particular group – she must be in some way conscious of the performative reality of that culture. Although no individual is enslaved to a pre-determined identity which s/he cannot avoid, we must remember that each individual is raised up in (and will begin to identify themselves through, or against) their immediate culture. But this culture is a learned, not an essential, condition, and is thus prone to competing performances, celebrations, and refusals.[24]

Such fundamental signifiers of culture as gender, race, and class are all, at the root, performatively constituted. In making this claim, I am following gender theorist Judith Butler and in particular her assertion that 'identity is performatively constituted by the very "expressions" that are said to be its results.'[25] In her view, gender is not a stable, foundational feature of a subject's identity, but rather the expected manner in which a subject might act. In this supposition, gender (like other apparently immutable aspects of identity) is understood to be a role that one plays, and not an essential feature of one's being.[26] In recent decades, many historians and theorists of race and class identity have come to see both of *these* categories as mutable, as prone to competing discourses, and ultimately as performative categories themselves.[27] In this wider formulation, the common-sense performances of gender, race, and class are shown to correspond to hegemonic beliefs which suggest (or, in some cases, decree) the manner in which to act within the boundaries of normality in a particular culture.[28] Although neither culture nor identity is essential – both are learned and performed by individuals – all cultural and identity performances are dialogically developed through a process of social construction.[29]

Cultures are shaped by the common behaviours (performances) of their adherents, and so a certain collective identity develops around them. These collective identities do not determine how everyone will behave their individual identities; instead, they offer guidelines for 'normal' performances.[30] Under conditions such as these, it becomes difficult to recognize the individual within the group. Once we associate an individual with a particular culture (he is a 'gay man,' for example) we slip him into the melting pot, surrounding his individuality with what we believe to comprise the basic characteristics of his culture. Identity theorists have been wrestling with these primary issues for some decades now, circling around the complex relationship between authenticity, performance, and recognition.

Cultural theorist Kwame Anthony Appiah has referred to 'the Bohemian ideal' of authenticity in his effort to examine 'the politics of recognition.' This ideal – this 'notion of authenticity' – is, he asserts, off beam because 'it has built into it a series of errors of philosophical anthropology ... The rhetoric of authenticity proposes not only that I have a way of being that is all my own,' he claims, 'but that in developing it I must fight against the family, organized religion, society, the school, the state – all the forces of convention.' However, since Appiah sees identity to be constituted through dialogue with 'other people's understandings of who I am,' and also, because it is precisely those 'forces of convention' against which I am in revolt (which presumes that they are already in some ways a part of my cultural understanding), authenticity is not realistically graspable.[31] The beatniks, hippies, politicos, greasers, bikers, tourists – indeed, all those who have variously been invited under the umbrella of counterculture (or whom I am slipping under the umbrella of Villager) – were caught up in competing versions of a politics of authenticity which, by its very nature, was bedevilled by an untenable idealism.[32] Perhaps this is what Marshall McLuhan was pointing to when he famously remarked (in what was seen as a final denunciation of the hippie movement: 'From Tokyo to Paris to Colombia, youth mindlessly acts out its identity quest in the theatre of the streets, searching not for goals but for roles, striving for an identity that eludes them.'[33]

Oversimplifying the complexities of a variety of youth cultures which were by no means unified in their responses, their ideological positioning, or their identity performances (to name but a few points of comparison), many commentators have used the incoherent term 'counterculture' to refer to a vast array of events, behaviours, and identities as though they were simply the *No* to the establishment's *Yes*. And, while Yorkville might be examined through such a lens – reducing the conflicts in and over the Village to an ideological war of position between a young, hip bloc and an old, stodgy monolith – this reconstruction would bury much of the colourful complexity of the historical moment. As we have seen in the preceding chapters, the Village scene did not constitute a unified whole. Neither did the establishment, the municipal authorities, parents, the police, nor any of those comprising the system that many Villagers claimed to reject.

The Interim Research Project on Unreached Youth, part of a wider study on alienation headed by John A. Byles, stumbled into such murky waters when it sent a field worker into Yorkville in 1966 as an observer. On the suggestion of lawyer and social worker Jim Felstiner, the group hired a sociology master's student named Frank Longstaff to undertake the study.[34] The idea was that Longstaff, a young man who might move surreptitiously in the scene, would live in the Village for the better part of three months and collect his findings in an 'Observational Report.'

Since it was well understood that an effective *performance* was key in order to achieve any kind of status or respect in the Village, Longstaff was told to go into the field undercover, so to speak. And so, throughout the summer of 1966, the twenty-two-year-old student tried to pass himself off as a Villager, asking veiled questions, hanging around, taking clandestine notes. Somewhat predictably, his report concluded that, although he had indeed *observed* a lot, in the final analysis he hadn't truly cracked the Village nut. 'The covert approach was something of an obstacle,' he admitted. 'Because I didn't exactly fit in, there was some suspicion as to what I was doing there. Villagers knew there were undercover police in the area, and I'm sure that some suspected that I was one of these. As a result, my acceptance was limited; as someone told me later, I "wasn't completely bought."'[35]

At the end of 1965, Michael Valpy – among the first to highlight the performative dimensions of Village identity – concluded that Yorkville had become a place where 'teen-agers stand about to see and be seen.'[36] In an interview with Dr Robert James, president of the VYA, he revealed that 'we have considered Yorkville a national attraction for the last two years or more.' His belief that 'Torontonians [were] starting to pick Yorkville as the first place to show out-of-town guests' perhaps explains the accelerating influx of tourists to the district over the preceding summer. Indeed, Valpy reported that, throughout 1965, 'the number of non-Ontario license plates in the nightly bumper-to-bumper parade along Yorkville Avenue's two short blocks [grew] steadily larger.'[37]

The phenomenon of gridlock on the two short parallel streets is both crucial and difficult to comprehend. 'And then you got the cars,' recalled Judy Pocock, 'and, I mean, *that* was the weird thing. Because you had chock-a-block from Bay [Street] to Avenue Road. It would be *cars*! And it would take people, what, two hours, three *hours*, to drive that far? But that was their night out. They would sit in their cars and they'd watch people.'[38] 'We sit around and watch the tourists go by in their cars, gawking at us and pointing at us,' complained a 'bearded, chubby-faced 19-year-old' to Valpy. When asked why people went to Yorkville, former Villager Jeanine Hollingshead reckoned: 'for music, and to look at the people. It was the place to be.'[39] But many Villagers were feeling uncomfortable about this new form of tourism; one young man told Valpy that he had taken to antagonizing such voyeurs. 'Hi, Mr and Mrs Tourist,' he would begin. 'I'm a beatnik. Are you here to watch me perform?'[40]

Pocock agrees with the suggestion that performance was at the root of the Yorkville hip scene. 'God, you know, they were *watching* you.' The crowds were so thick that 'I would … basically have to *fight* my way home, and you might run into somebody, and you might talk to somebody, and there's all these people coming to watch … *us*. It's a very strange dynamic. There was all kinds of back and forth performativity, I'm sure. The people in the cars are performing for the people outside the cars, who are performing for the people inside the cars, who are also boys looking for girls, girls looking for boys, people looking for dope, whatever.'[41] Performing, of course, can be fun. And, for the adventurous, the curious, and the simply *bored*, going to Yorkville to perform their version of hipness was an attractive activity. It mustn't go unmarked that both Pocock's and Valpy's recollections of the Village in this period are peppered with words relating to performance, acting, and spectacle. 'I mean it was just *wall-to-wall* kids from Avenue Rd over to Bay,' Valpy explains. 'It was just a constant parade; you walked down one side, turned around, then walked down the other. It was then just … come and be seen, and see others. It was just a great sort of urban parade area.'[42] Presaging his recollection, Ron Thody (writing in the spring of '67) referred to 'the changing Village scene' as 'the Yorkville hip parade,' at once making the connection between Yorkville and performativity while also suggesting a link between the Village and pop music (or commercialized entertainment).[43]

Theorists of 'visual culture(s)' emphasize the primacy of 'seeing' in the modern era. Arguing that the project of modernity has in fact been predicated upon (or at least has been so successful *because of*) a privileging of sight, such scholarship suggests that 'the modern world is very much a "seen" phenomenon.'[44] To be sure, Yorkville operated for many as a visual experience – a spectacle that scores of people crossed the city (the province, even the country) just to witness (or, in the language of visuality, just to gaze upon). The phenomenon of tourism in the Village scene, especially in the years after 1964, exaggerated the spectacular quality of Yorkville both among its resident habitués and among its steady streams of weekend visitors. John Urry, in a seminal study, explained that 'what makes a particular tourist gaze depends upon what it is contrasted with; what the forms of non-tourist experience happen to be.'[45] So much being made of the apparent foreignness of the Village, and of the expected 'forms' of non-tourist (Villager) experience therein, Yorkville became the subject of an intensive, persistent tourist gaze based upon a shared assumption of Yorkville's hip authenticity. And yet much of what people were witnessing in Yorkville was a self-conscious imitation of the idea of Village authenticity. As Jeanine Holl-ingshead recalls, 'for the few hundred of us ['real' Villagers], there were thousands of others, and we used to call them "weekend hippies," you know? They were kids that lived at home with their families and they had short hair cuts and they'd put on long hair wigs to come down to Yorkville. To *look* cool.' Former Village drug dealer Eric Deveaux con-curs: 'The weekenders ... were pretending to be like the others, the real ones. They'd even buy overalls and dye them, or put all this bleach ... on them ... and show up down there and look like the hippies.'[46]

But, as Urry has emphasized, the tourist gaze 'is constructed through signs, and tourism is the collection of signs. When tourists see two peo-ple kissing in Paris what they capture in the gaze is "timeless romantic Paris." When a small village in England is seen, what they gaze upon is the "real olde England."'[47] In other words, tourists tend to see what they expect to see – 'we're not here to capture an image, we're here to maintain one,' in novelist Don DeLillo's memorable words – and their interpretation of this spectacle relies on the information they have brought to it.[48] A recent study by some of the leaders in this field, persua-sively entitled *Performing Tourist Places*, speaks to precisely this notion. 'Tourism,' goes the authors' argument, 'is a way of being in the world, encountering, looking at it, and making sense. It incorporates mindsets and performances that transform places of the humdrum and ordinary into the apparently spectacular and exotic.'[49] In Yorkville, tourists came to see Toronto's Haight-Ashbury, Canada's 'hippie ghetto' – the district becoming famous as a 'foreign country.'[50] And although the signs they were looking for – drug use, free love, outlandish clothing, bohemian artistry, heavy bikers, long-haired boys, and barefooted girls – were often being performed by people who were themselves tourists in the scene, come to the Village on their days off school to dress up as Villag-ers and play the part, it didn't matter.

But it wasn't just suburban Torontonians making their way to this ongoing happening – young people from around the country were appearing, seemingly with each successive Greyhound that rattled into town. Attracted to the Village from every corner of Canada (and beyond), they came in droves, some with more success than others.[51] As former Villager (and Ontario premier) David Peterson recalled, there was an 'unbelievable infusion of humanity from all over Canada. The [Village] had little coffee shops and a cultural scene, but that wasn't what really dominated. It was sort of a Mecca for dispossessed kids.'[52] Judge Jim Felstiner recalls presiding over a constant flow of young people brought up on Yorkville-related vagrancy charges. One story in particular stands out in his mind: 'Two kids from Winnipeg or Regina decided that they were going to go to Yorkville,' he began.

> And they hitchhiked all across the country to get here ... They were thirteen or fourteen, and had gotten all the way from, let's say Saskatoon! And they got it wrong, or their driver got it wrong, and he let them off at *Yorkdale* which was a brand new shopping plaza. OK? And they got arrested there for being vagrants, so they ended up with me ... The Children's Aid Society, since these were children needing protection, the CAS in each province flew the kids back. I remember calling some 'higher up' in the police department and saying: 'Look. Would you do me a favour, and these kids a favour? Pick them up two hours early and take them to Yorkville so that when they get home they can say that they've seen it?'[53]

Young people looking for a piece of the action, for drugs, sex, perhaps even some of that political conflict that was so much the order of the day in the era of student activism and sit-ins – they all came. And, while they may not have moved to the Village proper (according to most reports, the ever-increasing rent kept many prospective Villagers from living exactly *in* the district), it didn't stop them from spending much of their waking lives there. Mike Waage, himself a young émigré from Greenwich Village, has explained that 'it seemed a much more casual and relaxed kind of place, superficially anyway ... A bunch of people from all over the city were there. [But] not as residents – [they were] *hanging out*.'[54] 'Wild Bill' tries to quantify the phenomenon of the weekender invasion: 'The true number of hippies? I would say that at no time there were more than 150 or 200 of them. But every weekend there was crowds of people. That street was *packed* from one end to another with wannabe weekend hippies.'[55] Of course, it wasn't just hippies who moved freely from role to role. In a key scene in Donald Shebib's 1965 short film on the Satan's Choice motorcycle club, one biker gets razzed by his mates for having 'a double standard. Like, at night he likes to become a dirty motorcycle bandit. But when he's working, he's just one of the rest of the professionals!' His response: 'I live in two worlds!'[56]

As Waage recalls, living expenses, rooming issues, and such were generally remedied by doubling, tripling, and even quadrupling up in squalid garrets with single beds. 'People lived wherever they could afford. A lot of the time people weren't really renting, they were just staying with other people. Or they were renting with a whole bunch of other people. I come from a street-kid demographic. The university crowd, or something like that, might have done things a little differently. Although I expect they were all rooming together as well.'[57] Longstaff reported that 'often five or six may sleep on the floor of a room designed for two. At other times the halls of a rooming house may provide nighttime shelter for Villagers without a definite place to stay, or, as is more often the case, week-enders who choose not to return home for the night.'[58] One former Villager agrees that such arrangements made sense among her friends because they were unable to cope with high rents. 'Communal living was a big deal. They all started adopting the style of communal eating. They started sharing food, so they were always concerned about living as cheaply as possible. Probably because they were spending so much money on drugs!'[59]

There was a great deal of mobility among young, usually college-aged North Americans by 1966. And so, with this movement came a certain mutability of the meaning of community, even as Yorkville maintained a kind of hierarchical identity structure. Hip youth could arrive in Toronto beginning in about 1966 and be assured of contacts, a place to crash, and, most likely, food, drugs, and sex. 'There was a real infrastructure in those days,' explains Judy Pocock. 'You could arrive in town, and say to someone, *Hey, where can I crash?* And people would help you. You knew somebody who knew somebody who knew somebody. And so there were *always* places to crash. There were tons of places where people could stay. If you're young and if you're not straight, I mean, you know. There was the straight world, and it was sort of the enemy. And you had the sense of being part of a group ... there was the straight world, and us. There was very much this feeling. You kind of felt a responsibility to people.'[60] Judy Perly agrees that responsibility and community were the glue that held the transient community together after about 1966. 'You also had a lot of hitchhiking that was going on. People would hitch across the *country* to go to Yorkville. I even did some hitchhiking. And there was this thing of, you could just go to someone's house and who cared? Sleep on the floor, whatever. It was all woven with the drugs, you know: drop in, get stoned, get laid. It was [often] this total sexual, physical thing. No responsibility.'[61]

Yorkville's summer of 1966 was defined by crashers, parties, psychedelic music and dope, and a fluid, irrepressible turnover of people, faces, ideas. Trying to find something of permanence amid all of this mutable energy was like staring into a waterfall.

War Resisters in the Village Scene

Mike Waage was of draftable age in 1965, as the U.S. military was busy with the vast expansion of its role in a civil war in Vietnam that it had helped to foster in the first place. While a slight stream of draft resisters (including some outright deserters) had come to Toronto in the few years before the Gulf of Tonkin incident (August 1964), the current gathered strength following the advent of open warfare between the United States and Vietnam.[62] To many, the escalation from mere 'advisers' to the South Vietnamese Army to full-on grenade-and-M60-wielding commando units was deeply distressing. By 31 December 1964, some 23,000 U.S. troops were stationed in the faraway nation; 365 days later, that number had swelled to 184,300. New Left groups across the United States and Canada took up the cause with gusto, primed by their respective work on civil rights campaigns and in university politics. For many U.S. teens who were appalled, disgusted, or simply terrified by the illegal war, the writing was on the wall: north to Canada and safety. In Canada, the New Left umbrella group Student Union for Peace Action began to offer a variety of services to these reluctant immigrants, including housing, legal advice, and even employment. By 1966, SUPA was offering counselling and developing safe spaces for resisters to hang out, get information, and make contacts.[63]

David Churchill's academic study of resisters demonstrates, among other things, that 'as young Americans came to Toronto,' and especially in the first few weeks prior to establishing any foothold in the city, 'they gravitated toward the city's counter-cultural venues, quickly becoming another ambient detail in the expanding youth scene.'[64] By the spring of 1966, a new identity performance was developing in the Village as American draft resisters, along with their wives, girlfriends, and, in some cases, boyfriends, began to make the scene in greater numbers.

'A popular pastime in Toronto is visiting Yorkville Village to spot the beatniks, oddballs and bohemians,' began a 1966 CBC television report, 'but now the name of the game is to spot the American draft dodgers.' Standing in front of the Penny Farthing coffee house, reporter Larry Bondy openly propagated gossip and conjecture in his opening statements: 'Some rumours say there are ninety draft dodgers here, others say there's a whole battalion. Well a day-long search by this reporter has uncovered just one.' But this failure to find 'draft dodgers' wasn't ascribed to the dubious practice of believing in the veracity of rumours; rather, Bondy insinuates that it was simply that Yorkville provided too dense a jungle from which to 'flush them out.'[65]

According to two recent studies of Toronto's draft resisters, Yorkville was indeed a site for entertainment and recreation, but it was never a primary site for expatriate American community building.[66] That's not to say that Yorkville didn't amuse a variety of U.S. resisters in the 1960s (along with their partners, the oft-forgotten parts of this whole). Rather, both studies emphasize that Toronto's growing ex-pat community was centred, for the most part, on Baldwin St, about a kilometre southwest of Yorkville, and that the Village was a much less significant star in their constellation.[67]

Importantly, this piece of journalism, like so many other reports on the Village explored in this book, uses a discourse of foreignness to locate, discuss, and bound Yorkville. In his search for 'draft dodgers,' Bondy has transgressed the boundaries of the Village, entered its confused and confusing community, a community that operates on rumour and speculation. His report is fraught with an underlying frustration (or is it fascination?) with the elusiveness of his subject and, by extension, of the Village community in general. They are inscrutable; in this case, *literally* foreign. In a final fit of poetic reportage, Bondy summarizes all of these themes in one neat pair of phrases: 'Well, there may be two or three recently-arrived American draft dodgers here in the Village, but if they're here, they're hard to find. As for that Battalion, well we looked in garrets, communal pads, discotheques, and even a pizzeria. If they're here, they're as difficult to flush as those Viet Cong in the Mekong Delta.'[68]

The inanity of Bondy's attempt to find draft resisters (whose legal situation was precarious at best in these early years of the war) willing to appear on camera, to admit their status before LBJ and everybody, is fairly obvious. A letter from an anonymous nineteen-year-old 'draft-dodger (so-called)' to the underground Village newspaper *Satyrday* from later that year demonstrates the weakness in Bondy's plan: 'I regret that I can't join in on the action [in Yorkville],' he complains, 'since I appear to be an ordinary tourist because I have a job here and I must conform to a certain degree.'[69]

Besides, it seems that Bondy was asking only the wrong people. For, if he had asked anyone in the know, he would surely have been directed to John and Nancy Pocock's house at 12 Hazelton Ave (just perpendicular to Yorkville Ave). Ever since the early days of the war, the Pococks,

who were Quakers (and so practising pacifists), had been operating an
informal asylum for resisters at their house. David DePoe bristles at the
suggestion that Yorkville wasn't much of a home to draft resisters, and
recalls the significance of the Pocock family to this end: 'Where [the
Pococks] lived was a hub, a Mecca for all these war resisters who came
into town. They housed them. So that was right in Yorkville, *happening.*'[70] 'Otis' Richmond, one of Canada's most important black power
activists and advocates, fled his native United States as a resister and
was directed to the Pocock house by local activists. 'When I came to
Toronto in '67, I landed in Yorkville and I was assisted by hippies,' he
recalls. 'For the first couple of weeks I was assisted by the hippies, and
the Quakers.'[71]

Judy Pocock – who lived with her parents on Hazelton Ave until 1968
– remembers her house as a kind of refugee's haven. Her parents, left-
leaning and highly active in the Ban the Bomb movement of the 1950s
and 1960s, became well known for their devotion to pacifism and their
unfailing resolve to provide for U.S. war resisters of all kinds.[72] 'They
were Quakers. They were both real activists in the anti-war movement,
and the anti-draft movement. And, my Mum, who just passed away,
was a refugee activist [at the time of her death]. That really had started
in [the 1960s] because we had a lot of draft dodgers living in the house,
especially after I left home. And Vietnamese. We had a number of about
fifteen who had deserted the South Vietnamese army, ended up in the
States, and then heard of my parents and came up.'[73] The Pocock house
remained at the centre of the resister movement throughout the 1960s,
but as the community of transplanted Americans expanded alongside
the increased demand for new recruits into the disastrous war, Yorkville
lost ground as a resister scene. The establishment of an American ex-pat
community on Baldwin St and the promise of open rooms at Rochdale
College (after 1968) both pulled people away from the Pococks and
Yorkville.[74]

The Expanding Role of Drugs

Historian Doug Owram reports that 'as late as 1963 the Annual
Report of the RCMP was confident that there was no real drug problem in Canada. The new Narcotic Act of 1960, the excellent work of
the police, and severe court sentences had, the report concluded, actually reduced the low level of drug usage in the country. As for cannabis, a grand total of *fifteen ounces* were [sic] seized during the year.'[75] In

fact, 1963 saw a mere 394 drugs charges laid in all of Canada – when we compare this to 1970, which saw that number increase to 8,596, we see that something has clearly changed over these seven years.[76] Following the Graeber bust in 1961, drug use in Toronto was becoming more visible for a number of reasons, not the least significant of which was the advent of tighter police controls on marijuana sales and consumption.[77] Whereas by mid-July of 1964 Metro Toronto Police had nabbed a mere five people on marijuana offences, they had charged about twenty by the same time a year later. And marijuana had clearly overtaken all other narcotics as the most popular street drug – by mid-1965, charges for marijuana possession had swollen to outnumber all other drugs arrests in Toronto.[78]

Prior to the sustained media spotlight, the Yorkville drug culture was a markedly different animal from the one that would become infamous in the late 1960s. It is, of course, difficult to characterize the Yorkville scene in any of its incarnations, but it can be said with some authority that, prior to 1965, illicit drug use in the Village was fairly quietly confined to marijuana, amphetamine pills, and (*much* less commonly) LSD.[79] Even alcohol was not much of an issue in the Village, considering the paucity of liquor licences in the area. British transplant Martin Barber dryly recalls that 'it was a lot easier to get a joint back then than it was to get a drink. In Toronto, you couldn't even find a place *worth* drinking in!'[80] His friend Miguel Maropakis concurs: 'On Saturday night,' he reminds us, 'you couldn't get a drink after 11:30!'[81]

In 1965 Yorkville drug use, heretofore an allegation, perhaps at best an assumption, suddenly became a full-blown reality. As reflected in an alarmist front-page article in the *Toronto Daily Star* – in which drugs (namely, pot and LSD) were still treated as a largely unknown proposition – there was growing anxiety that Villagers were degenerating into a ghettoized culture of addicts and criminals.[82] But anxiety was not the only thing that the article suggested was growing in Toronto: the ostensible point of the report concerned the allegation that Villagers were harvesting marijuana themselves in 'Yorkville patches.' Although immediately dismissed as unlikely by police officers in the ensuing article, this baseless contention figured into the prominent front-page headline anyway. And so here was one more reason to see Yorkville as different, strange, foreign: not only was it a place where people took drugs, but it was a place where they grew pot unchecked! (Of course, this notion is laughable, if only for the simple reason that, if one were to grow marijuana in Toronto in 1965, one would likely not be stupid enough to grow it precisely in the location where people were expecting to find it.)

Indeed, by the mid-1960s, marijuana was Exhibit A in the state's case against the hip youth culture.[83] The shift from mere conjecture to the plain expectation of marijuana possession among Villagers occurred swiftly in these years, and can be traced through the gathering surge of media reportage on drug use in the district. The notion that Yorkville was overcome with a new kind of hip activity, and one that was inextricably tied to a subversive criminality creeping among the shadows in alleys off the main conduits, pushed a shift in the treatment of the sophisticated versus bohemian (or its corollary, beatnik versus tough) framework. No longer was the divide merely drawn along the lines of activity, expression, and age: now the cleavage separating Yorkville's sophisticates from the hip youth kicking down its sidewalks could be established along legal lines. Drug users were increasingly understood to be hip youth; hip youth tended to congregate in the Village; ipso facto, Yorkville must be drug centre *numero uno* in Toronto.

Put simply, it was now becoming apparent that, if Yorkville was a stage, its most authentic performance was drug use. As Frank Longstaff discovered, Villager 'status' was earned through 'turning on.' Through doing drugs, he concluded, 'they establish themselves in the Villager subculture, for it sets them aside from outsiders, from "squares who don't know where it's at."'[84] But the perils of working towards this status were well understood: since mid-1965, drug busts and arrests for simple possession in cases related to the Village had soared over the numbers from previous years.

In a powerful example of the accelerating normalization of the drug-scene-as-Yorkville framework, Michael Valpy reported in the late summer of 1965 that marijuana supplies had dried up in the Village, promoting a palpable uneasiness among its 'entrenched beatnik habitués.' 'Finding Marijuana Tougher for Yorkville Pot-Lovers,' his headline declared, simultaneously relating his pseudo-human-interest story while underlining the natural association between marijuana availability and the viability of the Yorkville scene. His main character, a 'chunky, net-stockinged redhead' (whom we'll have to assume was female), was actively surveying the Stork Club (an all-night café on Avenue Rd) for a line on pot. It was two in the morning, a pre-dawn Thursday in September. 'The restaurant … was crowded and smoky. Customers – young, long-haired, raggedly dressed – stared solemnly into their coffee cups … They listened to the redhead's whispered question and shrugged.' Two major drug busts, both of suppliers from New York who had been feeding the Yorkville market, had ebbed the flow. '"They had good stuff, too!" said a 19-year-old bearded beatnik. "It was cured with tincture of opium and really turned me on."'[85]

Of course, resourceful Villagers could always find their ways around such supply shortages. LSD was available, as was a variety of other pharmaceuticals offering a wide range of psychotropic, depressant, or uplifting effects. In the case of LSD, or psilocybin mushroom pills (both of which were becoming available to Villagers following a surge in their popularity in the hip communities of the United States), this entire range of effects was offered in one small capsule. As one LSD user described his experience, the drug offered a means of total re-evaluation, and reappreciation, of the immediate environment. 'I remember sitting with my buddy … on the stoop out in front of this house,' he began. 'We were totally mind-blown, both of us. It was towards morning, and they were collecting garbage. And the mounds of garbage were *exquisite*. The aromas were just *pungent*, and so interesting. Seeing the garbage truck make its way, and those tender human beings moving through this environment, it was just … *phew*. It was super duper acid.'[86] The magnetic effect of such tales of radical drug experiences was inviting many curious hipsters to partake in so-called mind-expansion drugs – and the Village was the centre of the Canadian psychedelic universe.

'These kids will try anything,' lamented a police inspector, pointing to a fundamental paradox of prohibition. Although all that the vast majority of Villagers wanted to do was to smoke marijuana, and occasionally to take trips on LSD or psilocybin, continued shortages in supply and fear of prosecution led them to engage with a range of other, often highly destructive, pharmaceuticals in their stead. Cough syrups, amphetamines (usually in the form of 'diet pills'), and muscle relaxants were all legal, inexpensive alternatives for the more benign marijuana that they were being denied. Still, the resourceful Villager who wasn't willing simply to 'try anything' was prepared for the inevitable shortages of marijuana which go along with black-market realities. 'We of the elite,' one claimed, 'always keep a spare ounce of pot around in the event of shortages.'[87]

The previous year, Yorkville had likely been among the safest and best spots in urban North America to be a regular marijuana user. Prices were the lowest in the country (no more than $40 per ounce), and virtually no one got into any trouble with the law over their indulgence – less than one person per month was brought up on charges for marijuana possession over the course of the year.[88] However, 1965 was a much more difficult year for pot smokers in the city, and as criminal charges mounted, so did the politicization of the act of taking drugs. As American historian David Farber has argued, since 'society had declared that everyone who dropped acid was a criminal' and since countercultural identity seemed ever more predicated on drug use in general, what was soon to be named 'the counterculture' took on a distinctly criminalized aspect. To enter into the Village scene was to engage with the illegal; to be a Villager meant taking drugs that made you high, but also a criminal. This process, perhaps more than any other, helped to radicalize youth in the Yorkville scene to the idea that they constituted an embattled minority within the wider community, and were prone to unfair, violent coercion from what was vaguely formulated as the 'establishment.'

Still, something of that former obliviousness had ingrained itself in the minds and habits of Villagers: even as drug busts continued to increase in frequency, many visitors to the district from other hip centres would remark on the continued offhand nature of drug use in Yorkville. 'They're so really uncool in Yorkville,' explained a recently arrived beatnik to Valpy in 1965. 'They take no precautions at all.' Valpy's description continues: 'He and other users talked of pushers peddling their wares through the Yorkville Avenue throngs, of young Beatniks holding noisy street conferences on their flowering marijuana plants, of pushers openly handing the narcotics out to the customers of restaurants.'[89] This openness, while shocking to some hip travellers from cities with more vigorous drug squads, was likely even more shocking to the morality unit which had been assigned to Yorkville. 'You could walk into at least half a dozen of the coffee houses and be offered the drug!' commented an exasperated RCMP officer.[90] The reality was that, even though they had been more than a little successful at ferreting out some of the key players in the drug-trafficking networks actively supporting the Yorkville scene, somehow the marijuana culture was still spreading.

By the end of the summer of 1965, it was disclosed that 'every person arrested on a marijuana charge this year was either picked up in Yorkville or was known to frequent the district.'[91] By the end of the year, police had charged more than seven times as many people for pot possession than they had in the previous year, and were loudly proclaiming that all of them were connected to Yorkville. In Yorkville, drug use and Village status were increasingly tangled up in the local common sense. In these years, for example, Solveigh Schattman and Jutta Maue, two German au pairs, had become local celebrities, renowned for their profuse consumption. Giving up on their au pair responsibilities, the two women made their way through the scene, working at a variety of hotspots including the 71 Club, the Half Beat, the Riverboat, and the Penny Farthing. Before long, they were 'the most popular waitresses in the Village,' famously 'using their tips to buy everything from amyl nitrates to acid and heroin.'[92] Such a quick entry into full-blown drug consumption was still rare, but the numbers of Villagers willing to experiment were growing. Then again, so was the police presence.

'Yorkville [Is] Breeding Crime' read one headline late in the year. This 'new breed of criminal,' the middle-class beatnik youth (the average age of those arrested was estimated at twenty), was 'of above-average education and intelligence,' and most had no prior criminal records.[93] This issue of middle-class drug consumption was so galvanizing among members of the criminal justice system that efforts were stepped up to rid the district of this scourge. But at least one lawyer, concerned that the sentences were too harsh, expressed his uneasiness over the blindness of all of this justice: it seemed that 'the court had warned sharply that such conduct could not be tolerated from young persons, *whether they are students or riffraff.'*[94]

For this was the real issue. While the fact that drug use was becoming a dominant feature of a Toronto district was hardly comforting, the prospect that the Village was populated by a new breed of criminal comprised of alienated middle-class Torontonians was plainly unacceptable. The old assumption was that it was mainly working-class, immigrant-reared youth who would be attracted to criminal activities (or, even, that they were simply prone to such activities). To have middle-class youth engage with the underworld was the world turned upside down – would Toronto need to set up Settlement Houses for suburbanites too? Of course, the middle-class youth were being drawn into criminal circles for different reasons (and under vastly different pressures) than were their working-class counterparts; while working-class Villagers came into their identity performances through a certain celebration of their class identities, middle-class hip youth came into their identities through the *performance* of authentic criminality. As drug use became a primary marker for middle-class Village identity, excess and capriciousness haunted the scene. One detective attempted to outline the situation: 'Young persons – particularly those who have had many of the luxuries of life – are being attracted to it by the Beatnik philosophy ... : if you haven't tried everything, you haven't lived.'[95]

Arrests and lengthy jail terms loomed as sagging branches over the Village. In late February 1965, one young man was sent up for six months after pot was found in his apartment;[96] in mid-August, marijuana charges were laid against a sixteen-year-old Villager, the youngest person ever charged with such a crime in Toronto;[97] in mid-autumn, two 'under-18s' were arrested trying to fence stolen morphine ampoules to an undercover police officer – both received twelve-month sentences;[98] months later, a young man was hit with two years less a day for an eight-ounce bag of pot;[99] in July 1966 a pregnant sixteen-year-old who had been in the Village for 150 days pled guilty to pot charges and was sent home to Stoney Creek, Ontario;[100] later that month, police found a loaded gun along with a half-pound of marijuana in a twenty-three-year-old's apartment;[101] by late September, a bust of seven major dealers in the district resulted in one woman being sentenced to three years in the penitentiary for possession of heroin;[102] by the end of the year, there could be little doubt: Yorkville was a criminal territory.

The rise in charges and convictions relating to marijuana and other drugs in Metro Toronto was indeed staggering. While there were a mere seven drug-related offences in 1964, there were sixty-eight such convictions in 1965. But, really, that was nothing: in the first ten months of 1966, 130 people were arrested on narcotics charges. Before Judge Harry Weisberg delivered sentences to ten young, mostly middle-class men and women who had (all but one) been arrested in the Yorkville area, Department of Justice prosecutor Arthur Whealy took the opportunity to blame Yorkville's 'subculture' for promoting an environment in which 'drug offences are tied to a way of life.' Citing this litany of drugs arrests and convictions (so often of middle-class suburbanites), he declared that 'Yorkville can no longer be called an artistic community,' since it 'has become a hangout for bums and hoodlums.'[103]

The Process of Co-Existence:
The Changing Face of the Drop-In Centre

Faced with a dwindling interest in the church Drop-In Centre and well aware of the maturing scene around the corner, the Reverend James Smith turned his attention to what he understood to be his new mission. However, selling the Drop-In Centre to these Villagers proved more difficult than it had been with the greasers years before; although he tried 'every gimmick' he could think of, Villagers weren't interested in hanging around at his church. 'Then we remembered that alienated kids relate to natural leaders,' Smith recalled, and when 'we sought out the natural leaders [we] ran into Mike Waage.' As vague as this explanation might seem, the story of the Villagers and the Drop-In Centre is, at least in Smith's version of events, all tied up with Mike Waage's incarnation of the hippie archetype.

The seventeen-year-old son of a New York subway conductor, Mike Waage had arrived in Yorkville in the summer of 1965 to find that 'there was no intellectual rat race like there was in New York ... [Yorkville] was pretty easy going, pretty casual, and I made hundreds of friends. They were warm, sincere, and much more beautiful people.'[104] Articulate and charismatic, Waage fit the profile of a 'natural leader' sought out by Smith, and by mid-fall he was recruited to help bring Yorkville to the centre. 'I was sitting in Webster's restaurant perhaps in September or October 65, and Rev. Smith started bantering with me ... And he had a program for gang kids from the immediate neighbourhood, that area above Davenport or whatever it was, and I think he wanted to reach out to the Yorkville kids too, but this didn't necessarily go over too well with the people he was already servicing. In fact it *didn't*. So he engaged me to start a little Art Group there [at the centre]. Not that I was necessarily qualified in any formal sense, but he thought it was a good idea. And our relationship started with that.'[105]

As Waage suggests, getting the working-class youth to give up what had for years been their hangout wasn't going to be easy. Smith knew that he needed Waage not only because he was a leader, but also because he was tough. Given the media-driven sense that a climate of potential violence surrounded the Village, Smith was hardly being over-cautious in his preparations for a kind of turf war between two rival factions over the use of the Drop-In Centre. Still, he courted the clash, believing it to be a battle worth waging. In short, it seems apparent that Smith saw the Villagers as the preferable choice to fill his basement. According to his version of the key showdown:

> One night by prearrangement, Mike [Waage] led 100 Hippies to the youth centre. Knowing that the few Greasers would present problems, he came prepared. With a fag hanging from his lower lip he told a Greaser who was mouthing off at him, 'Look friend, Smitty says we're welcome here and we're going to stay.' Then he explained in his own enigmatic way,

'We're peace-loving co-existors [sic] we don't want trouble.' Then putting two fists together he twisted them as if to wring a neck and explained, 'If we have to, we can take you man.' ... So began the long process of co-existence. The next morning we found the boulevard strewn with fence pickets, rubber hose lengths and other grievous crabtree cudgels that were never used.[106]

This macho performance, replete with clichés of casual cool (cigarette-hanging-from-bottom-lip, kind-words-big-stick attitude), may be no more than a fanciful recollection, but it leaves little doubt as to which side was favoured by Smith and the Community Services Organization. The hippies, led by this young, charismatic New Yorker 'with a command of English worthy of a professor,' are clearly elevated in this construction of the events, even though it was they who threatened the greasers with violence in order to usurp their turf.

In the context of an understanding of the greasers and the hippies as two distinct and even antithetical youth cultures (a position clearly held by Smith, who always capitalizes the terms), such an argument over territory is demonstrative of the privilege of one class and culture over another. The violence was never (fully) borne out, but, as Smith makes clear, it was not because the kindness of the hippies prevailed over the bellicose sensibilities of the greasers; rather, it was through the overt threat of force (backed up by some one hundred followers, all apparently armed) that the hippies were able to appropriate the greaser space as their own. What Smith refers to as a 'process of co-existence' sounds more like a street-kid version of *might makes right*.

Bill Clement recalls this showdown as a demonstration of, if nothing else, the depth of Smith's betrayal of the working-class youth who for years had built a sense of community in that basement. In his inimitable style, Clement recounted in an interview a defining moment for him on the way towards this realization:

It used to be a working-class kids' Drop-In Centre. So one of the long-haired-drug-crazed youth is talking to one of the kids from the Drop-In Centre. The long-haired-drug-crazed youths are in the process of forcing the locals out. The greasers. The long-haired-drug-crazed youth says to his newfound friend who he [wants] to encourage to get the fuck out cause we're taking over this Drop-In Centre, he says: *my Mum and Dad told me I could take 18 months off to find myself*. And the greaser kid says: *Oh, shit! If I dropped out of school, my old man would kick my ass all over the*

floor and tell me I'd better find a fucking job before I came home in the afternoon.
I mean, *that* kind of social conflict! Basically, the middle-class kids just
moved the greaser kids right out of the operation.[107]

Out of the operation, and back onto the street.

Is it surprising then, given the rejection many of these young people
must have felt, that there remained a considerable animosity between
the two groups right up to the end of the Yorkville hip scene? The greasers, whose numbers expanded far more dramatically over the next few
years than did those of the hippies (at least according to one anthropolo-
gist who studied the Village), would always be regarded by authorities
and observers as second-rate Villagers, even when they came to constitute the thrust of the Village population. For, while identity performance was the name of the game in the Yorkville scene, working-class
youth always had fewer options than did their middle-class counterparts. As Clement's story demonstrates, the disjuncture between wilful
poverty and actual *need* was inescapably real.

Nevertheless, Smith's gambit paid off in the sense that it infused the
centre with new life, new faces, and a fresh new character. The basement, neglected for much of the summer of 1965, boomed into a primary meeting space for Villagers by late fall. Offering showers, food, and
shelter from the rain or the cops, and operating at least on one level as
a hip pick-up bar, the church caught on with the teens who were flock-
ing to Yorkville in ever greater numbers. According to Smith's (likely
exaggerated) estimates, 'attendance at the centre rose steadily from 150
to 300 and even went up to 600 or 700 per night in 1965 and 1966.'[108]
Waage's estimates are not too far afield from those of his former boss;
he recalled that, by early 1967, the church hosted 'maybe hundreds,
some nights.'[109] The church basement underwent a dramatic renovation
in order to accommodate the much larger groups of young people that
now used the centre. 'Well, it was already established,' explains Waage.
'[The centre] just went through considerable alterations, conceptually.
The size of the space over the years increased considerably ... Certainly
[as a result of] the number of people that Yorkville brought into it. But
in a small way it was already fully functional, it just got bigger and
bigger.'[110]

By late 1966, the significance of the church as a necessary and potentially useful project for the protection of otherwise alienated Villagers had begun to trump allegations of impropriety therein. 'Grants
began to come in from the Corporation of Metropolitan Toronto and

the Addiction Research Foundation. United and Anglican Headquarters both became supporters. The Kiwanis of the Kingsway contributed many items such as a pool table and a stereo.'[111] At its height, the budget for the church's Drop-In Centre reached $50,000. On top of this, some Villagers, recognizing their responsibility to the maintenance of the church, had begun a campaign in 1965 to levy ten cents as an entrance fee. Rather impressively, by the end of 1967, they had raised $4,000. Over the following summer, 'a work-camp for kids saw 40 loads of clay removed from under the church and soon the whole area was cemented and partitioned. The $4000 was spent in wages, food and material.'[112]

For some, Smith's bourgeois values and the uncomfortable association between the United Church and the middle-class establishment was a problem. '[Smith] maintains certain traditional, middle-class concepts,' observed Frank Longstaff, 'which make some of the kids think he is a sell-out. For instance, he encourages all kids to work, at least on a part-time basis to make enough money in an accepted manner to keep themselves going in Yorkville. If this necessitates a haircut, then Smith says they should see a barber.'[113] His status as mediator between the Village and middle-class society was, to Longstaff, central to both the successes and the failures of his Drop-In Centre. 'Part of the problem is that neither he nor the kids can ever forget that they are in a church, and someone else's church at that. This seems to place something of a damper on the spontaneity hoped for.'[114]

Famously branded as a 'dope dealer's post' by Chief of Police James Mackey, and derided in a well-publicized sermon in front of a neighbouring congregation as 'the church that sold dope,' the Drop-In Centre and the Reverend James Smith were soon under fire for what was seen as a tacit encouragement of a Village drug-and-sex culture.[115] The *Toronto Daily Star*'s David Allen, for example, argued that, along with nearby Webster's restaurant, the church was 'drawing the drug and flesh peddlers' to the district.[116] One anonymous LSD dealer recalls finding his clients in precisely this area: 'In those early days when I had first turned on ... I started out dealing, really, on the streets ... I can recall doing my deals around the Church, around the Mont Blanc, the Matador, the Upper Crust ... [Smitty] wasn't allowing anything, but he also wasn't strip-searching everyone coming and going, so ...'[117] Raising enough money to keep the Drop-In Centre alive in the face of such denigrating media and municipal (not to mention irate parental) scrutiny was a constant struggle. In the early 1960s, while it was still a hangout for working-class youth, a number of Toronto's more wealthy churches

had come together to help support the centre. Now, amid wide speculation that the church was simply a front for criminal activities (activities
that were being, de facto, sponsored by the centre), it had become ever
more difficult to secure financial backing for the project. To make matters worse, the church was in the position of being the primary meeting
place for an ever-widening swath of middle-class weekenders whom
many believed should not be coddled.[118] When *Telegram* writer Aubrey
Wice dubbed the centre the 'Lone Oasis for Troubled Kids,' Smith joked
that it had become 'the drop-out's Granite Club,' a reference to the toney country club in North Toronto frequented by many of the parents of
his current flock.[119]

Local musicians, poets, acidheads, politicos, and teenyboppers alike
turned to the church from time to time as a hangout, an escape, or for
the free meals that local activists began to distribute there in 1967. The
one guy everyone could count on being there was David Clayton-
Thomas, the irrepressible rock'n'roller who made Yorkville his home
while pursuing that big break which would eventually see him front
the 1970s powerhouse band Blood, Sweat and Tears. After he was
released from prison in the mid-1960s (Clayton-Thomas had a legen-
darily short fuse, and a real love of the fisticuffs, something that set him
apart from many of his contemporaries in the music scene), the front
steps of the church became his haunt, and his impromptu stage. Since
he was famously tough to approach, people generally left him alone to
play away. David DePoe recalls of his old friend: 'He wasn't really a
very nice person when he first got out of jail, you know? He was pretty
fucked up. But he was trying to sort of find his better side, y'know?'
Night after night, Clayton-Thomas would park himself on the church
steps and hone his craft, playing away for anyone who'd listen. DePoe,
then driving a cab to make ends meet, used to work till the wee hours,
often until 4 a.m., and would still be able to find Clayton-Thomas at
his usual spot when he got off work. 'I used to park my cab on Avenue
Road in front of the church and take my guitar out of the trunk and
we'd sit and jam,' recalls DePoe.[120]

Meanwhile, inside, a typical Saturday night. The record player blast-
ing the new Stones record. Teens dancing, meeting, grooving, stunning
and high. Long-haired Villagers leaning intensely over chess or cards,
guitar cases by their sides. Long gray doobies in the backlot. Blotters
on the tongue, waiting for the rush. *Paint It, Black* and *Tomorrow Never
Knows* and *Brainwashed*. Teenaged boys and girls clutched in nervous
and bold embrace. It was a scene, a happening. The centre had lost its
original mission, to be sure. But, in the process, it had gained a new,

significant status within the ever-growing Village scene, and with it, a new mission altogether. For the next three years, the church would be known to many as a central site for Village activity. It became, in one Villager's recollection, 'like our community centre.'[121]

The Martyring of Hans Wetzel: Ron Haggart, *Satyrday*, and the *Yawn*

Following the winter of 1964–5, Yorkville fell under the media microscope in earnest, as articles and reports on the goings-on, the highs, lows, trials, and tribulations of the district piled up, week after week, even day after day, in local and national newspapers. Throughout the year, the energy spent on reporting even the most insignificant arrest or disturbance was striking. But most remarkable of all, considering the rosy way this period (and this year in particular) is remembered by many observers of post-1967 Yorkville, was the uninterrupted emphasis on the dangerous, subversive, and violent aspects of the district's youth scene. For this is when the supposed 'real' or 'true' hippies were afoot in Yorkville. However, it is also the period in which Villagers were fighting over things as insignificant as wearing sunglasses at night.[122] Perhaps as a symptom of the ousting of working-class youth from the church, animosity bubbled over from time to time, never failing to make its way into reportage over the conflicts afoot in the Village.

The underground newspapers *Yorkville Yawn* and *Satyrday* (the one became the other in late 1966) were born out of what was decided was a gap between the reality of Village life and the stuff being printed in the mainstream press. Editors Andrew Mikolasch and Ron Thody (a.k.a. 'the Thud')[123] emphasized underground bands, printed locally produced artwork and poetry, and featured often furious attacks on what was invariably decried as the police state of Toronto and its insistence on destroying the Village scene. Like any local newspaper, the *Yawn* and *Satyrday* aimed to provide a neighbourhood view of local personages, events, and ideologies.[124] The editions were roughly twenty-five pages long, and were published somewhat unpredictably, with lapses lasting as long as a few months.[125] Their mandate, summarized in a late 1966 editorial, was to 'knock and satirize the Establishment, attempt to promote new Canadian sounds and culture on all levels and carry on the fight for personal freedoms.' This emphasis on libertarian politics was, perhaps, their most coherent theme – in general, their concern for the sanctity of individual rights and freedoms lies at the fore of their view of the political relevance of the Village scene. 'We seek to unfetter

the individual from all restrictions imposed on him and his freedom,'
as they put it, 'whether by government, police, or corporation. However, we draw the line at the point where personal liberty would create
harm or injustice to a fellow human being.' Their argument, written
here in an overture to the non-Village population – '[this issue] is not
necessarily aimed at Yorkville villagers and tourists. It's aimed at everyone' – tends to take for granted that the Village represents precisely
such an unfettered politics of individual liberation.[126]

'They were good,' recalls DePoe, 'because they got the news out, you
know? And from people who weren't the big media. You know, the big
papers always got *everything* wrong.'[127] But were they read? Michael
Valpy, who, admittedly, was of the other camp as a writer at the *Globe
and Mail*, disagrees with DePoe's assessment. 'I don't recall them as
being significant,' he told me. 'I don't recall anyone talking about them
or thinking about them as significant. They were very small-scale operations. They were an attempt to tell the other side, and things like that.
But my recollection is that nobody paid too much attention to them.'[128]
At least some people were reading them – most issues included a 'Letters' page, which promoted a dialogic relationship with the papers'
audience.[129] (Indeed, *Satyrday* claimed to constitute a 'forum for hip
people.'[130]) A sampling of such letters (the selection process behind
which got printed and which got discarded is unknown) demonstrates
a sense of community shared both among readers and with the editorial staff. Some letters offered encouragement ('keep firing the spark of
rebellion,' wrote Trevor Goodger-Hill, an aspiring poet), some offered
personal views of the Village ('I can't see a comparison between yours
and ours in N.Y. [but] I still dig it,' wrote a '19-year old New Jersey
draft dodger [so called]'),[131] and some reported terrible stories of run-
ins with police, judges, and Village phoneys ('the true villain is the
establishment,' summarized 'Anonymous,' 'infringing on the personal
freedoms of each of us').[132]

Valpy reminds us that, although there were conservatives and reac-
tionaries at all of the media outlets, including at the *Globe and Mail*,
there were also young sympathetic reporters like him.

> I was covering it, reporting on it, until I got banned for awhile by the
> *Globe*. It didn't last long. They felt that I was, I guess with some justifi-
> cation, getting too close to what was going on there. There were huge
> debates that went on nightly within the *Globe*'s newsroom as to what our
> coverage was like, and how [the *Globe*] was inclined to be beating these

kids up, and denigrating them, really treating them as a classic Other. And it just *enraged* me. There was one particular news editor: he was the senior guy on the newsroom floor, and it was he who banned me from going to Yorkville. He just loathed the hippie kids, and he, you know, felt that the cops should clean them out. He sort of rejoiced whenever there were arrests. It was just so irrational.[133]

This may have seemed irrational behaviour to Valpy, and perhaps to some of his cohorts, but the reality of the period was that the divisive-ness of Yorkville made for a certain absurdity; at the very least, there was a sustained incapacity of the one to comprehend the other, on both sides.

Martin Barber, staff writer at the *Toronto Telegram* after 1967, recalls that the story of Yorkville, as it was presented to the public by the mass media, tended towards sensationalism. Emphasizing the most spec-tacular aspects, media framed the Village as a drug-infested youth centre and tended to refuse any more complicated assessments of the scene.

We had three pages in *Time* magazine – that was the Canadian edition, three pages stuck inside *Time*. So I remember writing this long flowing piece – because I got paid by the page – about things that were going on [in Yorkville]. Not one line of which survived the edit. When the piece came out … it said: 'Hippie Revolution' and 'Drugs in Park'! It empha-sized all of the things that I had given a paragraph or two to, but missed out on all the music, on what I called the new entrepreneurs, the business people who understood youth. The people who were making stuff for your pad, lava lamps, and all those things … But all this stuff, all kinds of things, was cut out! Basically, they were saying Yorkville was copying Haight Ashbury; that it was Haight Ashbury north.[134]

DePoe's exaggerated opinion that 'the big papers always got *everything* wrong' harmonizes with some, but not all, of the evidence. As we shall see below, the mainstream press, at least some facets of it, was coming around on the Yorkville issue. At the very least, the mainstream-under-ground divide was a lot more complicated and nuanced than many people recall.

Typically, Villagers (often referred to as *Yorkvillians* for some reason) were presumed by the *Yawn* and *Satyrday* to be male, and their activi-ties were easily reduced to 'balling.' But such an underlining of male sexual conquest as the primary hip occupation (alongside getting high) was ubiquitous throughout the North American alternative press in the 1960s. Historian Beth Bailey notes that, in such publications, sex, and the female body in particular, was routinely conflated with freedom and with the revolutionary potential of radical youth. Even a casual reading of the *Yorkville Yawn* or *Satyrday* establishes female nudity, especially breasts, as a dominant aesthetic theme. Breasts are objects of fascination – symbols, perhaps, of freedom and liberation, but objects nonetheless. The Villager (as presented by these papers) is male, into dope, and looking to get laid. A one-liner from late 1966 finds Ron Thody boasting that the kinds of 'adult problems' Villagers face from day to day are 'how to ball the chick in the next pad or where to get the next turn-on.'[135] There are Villagers, you see, and there are chicks.

But this was knowingly disingenuous. For, if *Satyrday* and the *Yawn* were concerned with anything, it was the very 'adult problem' of escalating police presence in the Village. In one illustrative example, the case of a local nineteen-year-old hippie named (Gunter) Hans Wetzel was turned by the Village papers into a cause célèbre, a signpost and warning to any who might fail to appreciate just how totally the legal deck was stacked against them. Stemming from the final realization of a fracas between greasers and hippies that spilled over into a fully borne insurgence in the streets, Wetzel's arrest on dubious charges turned him into both the scapegoat for the mess and a martyr for the hip cause.

At the height of the anxiety surrounding greaser/hippie confrontations in Yorkville in 1966, a group of twenty-five working-class boys from east Toronto armed with scissors roamed around the Village one Saturday night, aiming to cut off the hair of their chosen enemies.[136] A disturbance ensued, as around six hundred greasers and hippies faced off on Avenue Rd, shouting obscenities at one another and marking their turf. Meanwhile, up the street, Hans Wetzel and two friends were being denied service at the Mont Blanc café (presumably for their long hair and shabby appearance). On their way out the door, they bumped into two men (about whom little is known apart from that their skin was black) and a fight ensued.[137] Wetzel ran to get help and, according to the police, randomly attacked one of the officers who was trying to break up the ongoing street battle.

In the wee hours of Sunday morning, 29 May, the corner of Avenue Rd and Yorkville became a mob scene, as some two thousand young people engaged in a full-blown riot, replete with bottle throwing,

sporadic brawls, and chants of 'kill the cops' directed at the two officers who were first on the scene. As the officers stood on parked cars
trying to restore order, one of them trying to restrain his seventeen-
year-old prisoner, Allan Eggleton, the other trying to restrain the
unfortunate Wetzel, the crowd surged and began to tear at the two
cops' uniforms, even making off with a billy club and one of their
hats. Soon enough, a further twenty policemen arrived and the clean-
up began in earnest.

Eggleton, Wetzel, and two other hippies were the only people arrested. In at least one account of the ruckus, this was explained as a result
of the class character of the two groups in the face-off. 'The Greasers,
who have had long experience with [police], ran and were lost in the
crowd,' mused Frank Longstaff, while 'the Villagers, with their middle-
class backgrounds, did not know enough to get away quickly.'[138] (Note
that Longstaff refuses to allow greasers under the umbrella of Villager,
plainly assuming that they do not belong.) Wetzel, it was reported (by
the *Toronto Daily Star*, which carried this story on the front page), was
charged both with assaulting one of the police officers and with a count
of obstruction; he was being held without bail. By noon the following
day, Wetzel's supporters had begun to congregate outside the College
St police station (about 1.5 kilometres south of Yorkville) where he was
incarcerated. Protesting unfair, trumped-up charges, they chanted and
marched in his defence. By Sunday evening, police had begun to arrest
the protestors for 'causing a disturbance,' among the vaguest and most
effective of the weapons in their arsenal.[139]

As Alderman Helen Johnson called for a curfew for Yorkville youth
which would effectively shut down the scene at midnight, Villagers
in general began to rally around their martyred comrade. 'Alderman
Helen Johnson,' complained *Satyrday*, 'is still ranting stupidities that
would never make the public prints, were it not for the publicity prone-
ness of the Yorkville Village itself. Any ridiculous thing she says about
the Village makes the papers.'[140] Wetzel, it was said, was being blamed
for the whole fiasco and had become a whipping boy for a frustrated
police force, sick of dealing with Yorkville politics. But those politics
would come back to bite them. The day following Wetzel's conviction on
all counts, but before he was sentenced to four months in prison, thousands of protesters gathered around Nathan Phillips Square carrying
yellow placards decrying 'Police Brutality' in Yorkville and announc-
ing that 'Christ Had Long Hair Too!' Warned that if they set foot in the
square they'd be arrested, protestors milled on the sidewalks. 'Isn't the

square public property?' a mainstream reporter asked Ron 'Crowbait' Masters, a staffer at *Satyrday* and one of the leaders of the event. 'Not if you have long hair,' was his spiked reply.[141]

Satyrday and the *Yawn* recognized the symbolic significance of the case and began their coverage from the perspective that Wetzel was simply an innocent man fallen victim to the repressive and corrupt police, who seemed unwilling to protect the Villagers from interlopers who were shaking up Yorkville. For his part, Ron Haggart of the *Toronto Daily Star*, the greatest defender of Yorkville in the mainstream press apart from Valpy, argued very nearly as strenuously – as did the underground papers – that Wetzel was a victim of circumstance. Calling him a 'brilliant boy' with a 'near-genius IQ,' Haggart presented Wetzel's case to Torontonians as sympathetically as could be. As Wetzel went on trial that July and then on to appeal in the fall, both *Satyrday* and Haggart were reporting that everyone from Justice Walter Shroeder (of the Ontario Supreme Court) down were destroying Wetzel out of collective spite for the Village. '[Shroeder's] condescension came when he bowed to an Establishment ruled society which frowns down it's [sic] long, collective, frustrated nose at the long-hair and new ideas of youthful Villagers,' *Satyrday* (somewhat awkwardly) proclaimed.[142] In the *Star*, Haggart reminded his readers that 'the Magistrate believed Wetzel was guilty of a senseless assault on a harried policeman,' underlining both the implausibility of Wetzel's decision to randomly assault a cop and that officer's own inexperience and anxiety, and he reported that, after his conviction, Wetzel 'was led downstairs to the cells, where he cried.'[143] In an issue from early 1967, a *Satyrday* editorial referred to Haggart as 'the *Toronto Daily Star*'s formidable truth-seeker.'[144]

In all, five defence witnesses told the court that Wetzel and two friends had been attacked by two black men outside the Mont Blanc coffee house on Avenue Rd. One crown witness testified that Wetzel had yelled 'I'm going for the cops' as the fight erupted. Wetzel had run up the street to find some help, only to emerge into the riot at Avenue Rd and Yorkville.[145] Foolishly, he rushed up to one of the two police officers and grabbed him on the arm from behind to alert him to the situation at the Mont Blanc. 'They [the five defence witnesses] then testified that the officer, without any warning, whirled around and belted Wetzel and then arrested the youth for assault.'[146] During testimony, the same officer admitted to being new to the Yorkville beat, and that at the time of the alleged assault he had been extremely nervous: 'To tell you the truth,' he had testified, 'I expected it [an attack] at any minute.'[147]

Although the obstruction charge was thrown out, Wetzel was given one month in prison for assaulting a police officer. Haggart's response was truly impressive in its scope: he published a new editorial on the young man every day for nearly a week, each one more complimentary than the last, each one designed to demonstrate Wetzel's strength of character, obsession with honesty, overall excellence at school, and probable innocence. 'He was advised to get his hair cut,' Haggart explained, 'but he didn't because he felt that would be a dishonest representation. In other words, to cut his hair for his trial would be, to Wetzel, the same thing as a lie.'[148] *Satyrday*, reeling from the injustice of the decision, concluded that anarchy was the only plausible response to the magistrate's decision. 'In effect he is telling the public – particularly the Yorkvillians – not to seek the aid of police when trouble brews. If you do, baby, you'll only get thrown in the pokey.' Just as Yorkville was entering its most crowded, most closely watched, and most diverse period, the Village newspaper finally capitulated. 'So,' it sighed, 'let the riots begin.'[149]

PART THREE

Under Yorkville's Spell, 1967

5

Village Politics and the Summer of Love

The Diggers became the face of it. They were the people who gave it form and structure. I mean, there was nobody else. Everybody else was ... they were backdrop in a way. What would you call them? They were the cast of thousands. They were the scene.

– Michael Valpy, 2006[1].

By mid-summer 1967, Yorkville was a tumultuous, contradictory, and exciting place. Spared no respite from the glare of media, authorities, and young people alike, Yorkville was decidedly a spot worth discussing, exploring, decrying. All of the practices, activities, and behaviours that were said to have characterized the youth scene in the first half of the 1960s (namely, sex, drugs, and rock'n'roll, not to mention violence) now seemed to proliferate with every passing day. By year's end, a humanitarian crisis was in the works, exacerbated by widespread amphetamine use and perpetuated by the continued (if inadvertent) glamorization of the district by media and municipal authorities through repetition of the mantra that Yorkville and what it represented was a foreign, contaminated, destructive element in modern society. To young people who tended to empathize with the Village and its attendant critique of authority, such a mantra was nothing short of a brilliant advertising campaign.

Throughout 1967, Villagers got younger, their hair grew wilder, and their outfits became ever more peculiar. By summer's end, one might have little noticed a barefoot, shirtless dude with curls falling past his chin, a bandana holding it roughly in place, wearing outsized pants first hemmed circa 1955, picked up for pennies at the local Sally Ann.

He could have been seventeen, twenty-two, or twelve. But, most important, he was no longer probably a Torontonian. The social make-up of the Village was changing, complicated by fresh numbers of fed-up farm boys and girls, eastern and western Canadian small-towners in search of big city excitement, draft resistors, and, most significantly, otherwise homeless and needy youth looking for community and escape. It was in this latter cohort of Villagers – a group boasting of little money, few social connections, and often scant urban experience or sophistication – that many saw the beginnings of a crisis. What was just as bad, in the eyes of many, was that ever since the Hans Wetzel fracas of the previous year, police presence in the Village had expanded in kind, increasing the likelihood of getting arrested, charged, and sentenced for drug use.[2]

By the time the first autumn rains began to cool the September air, there was almost nothing in place to protect Villagers from their illusions. Yorkville had no shelters, and just a very few safety nets, usually provided by the Diggers (a new Village-based humanitarian group based on their forebears in the Haight) and other responsive members of the community. The dream that had set so many of these newer Villagers hitchhiking to the 'Big Smoke' (the promise of a perpetual block party, replete with whenever-orgasms and jubilant, giggling highs) faded swiftly in the rearview mirror after a few nights in the slammer for vagrancy, a couple weeks of those persistent hunger pains, or the realization of an unshakable burning sensation down below.

The truth was that, while drugs were plentiful, sex abundant, and rock'n'roll ubiquitous, security, health, and comfort were as elusive as a midday shadow. The city authorities had become so frustrated with the Village that they were now weirdly blind to the harshest realities of the very district they decried. As, one by one, their predictions came true (of widespread indigence, disease, violence, rape, and drug addiction), they stood back, perhaps unsure of how to respond. Or was it that they were unwilling to respond? By the end of 1967, Yorkville was entering a darker period characterized by a distinct lack of support for its indigent Villagers and the disintegration of what had been a seedbed for radical lifestyle experimentation, for the great pursuit of living otherwise.

The year 1967 marks a turning point in the role of media coverage of Yorkville, and of North American youth movements more generally. As Alice Echols, Todd Gitlin, and Thomas Frank have each explored in landmark studies, spurred by exaggerated and often hysterical media coverage of the counterculture, the relationship between youth and big business reached new degrees of complexity in the months surrounding (and following) 1967's so-called Summer of Love.[3] As with the case of Rent-a-Beatnik schemes in the late 1950s, media often played complicated roles in the production and propagation of hip codes. Part advertiser, part emissary, part detached observer, part vicious critic, and part giddy optimist, Toronto's major newspapers each looked into the Yorkville scene at least once a week in 1967, and nearly every day during the summer, offering a perpetual reconstruction of a scene which was hurtling towards critical mass, its seams bursting under the unrelenting pressure of a daily influx of ever more searching youth from across the country and beyond.

This chapter considers the tangled politics of hip identity in 1967, emphasizing Villagers' various attempts to foment local political responses in the face of an ever-spreading set of challenges. As myriad new problems surfaced in the Village – some of which were fed by media and corporate reification of hippie identities during the famous Summer of Love – many people from within the community worked to reimagine Yorkville as something other than an empty spectacle, a magnetic, but too often unfriendly, place. Through it all, questions of authenticity, purpose, and identity coloured the debates.

Hippie Wonderland or Festering Sore?

As others have rightly pointed out, the standard binary opposition of counter versus straight culture in the 1960s made a very smooth transition into a product of media and corporate framing reinforced by consumption and identification.[4] The commodification of hip, an enterprise that had legs long before it marched into the 1960s, hit new levels of sophistication and success during this decade of a thousand slogans.[5] Advertisers, famously exposed as the 'hidden persuaders' in Vance Packard's 1957 bestseller, expanded their chances for success in the 1960s through the revolutionary innovation of market segmentation.[6] To take a famous example, the 'Pepsi Generation' campaign (1961–6) saw the mass of consumers as divisible into fractions and components, each comprising its own market segment, each apparently demanding its own particular brand of advertising. But the illusion of segmentation was the very genius behind the campaign's success – advertising hip to the hip and youth to the young worked best when both 'hip' and 'youth' were themselves demarcated and controllable categories. What was the real coup, however, was the development of a means of advertising hip to the decidedly unhip, and youth to the ripened.[7]

By appropriating hipness (a move that was consolidated through-out the 1960s) and taking up a position behind its wheel, steering it around the corners, advertisers (and, by extension, the corporations they worked for) helped both to entrench the binary understanding of hip versus square and to demolish the sense of authenticity that many of the first waves of Villagers had cherished about their community. As this trend towards commodification advanced with abandon during 1967, its parallel (and no doubt the advertisers' greatest ally) was the stepping up of anti-hip proselytizing from hopelessly (and proudly) un-cool conservatives across North America. Yorkville and Haight-Ashbury, by then the two most significant centres in Canada and the United States, respectively, were not just the implied subjects of scores of advertising campaigns (Pepsi, Columbia Records, Volkswagen, etc.), but they were also subjected to near-daily publicized attacks from an ever more vitriolic political establishment. The rub, the paradox: both the exploitative advertising campaigns and the vociferous conserva-tives fed the counterculture even as they dismantled it.

Yorkville's political enemies made up in bombast what they lacked in subtlety. Led by Allan Lamport, the anti-Yorkville politicians were also rarely out of the media spotlight in 1967, as each took up a parallel posi-tion on the front line. Unlike their predecessors in this pursuit, whose main concerns tended towards making Yorkville safe for commerce, they went so far as to suggest that the Village be emptied of its deni-zens. Emphasizing the unkempt aesthetic and lackadaisical work ethic displayed by many happily impoverished Villagers, these politicians generally shared in a new figurative notion that Yorkville constituted a sickness, a kind of moral and social vortex which could no longer be condoned.

And, since Toronto's psychedelic drug culture had metastasized in Yorkville (getting stoned had by now emerged as a defining activity for Villagers), they had piles of evidence to back their position. In mid-March, provincial cabinet minister George Ben lifted public discourse over Yorkville to the rare air when he formally called for the legislature to 'break up' the Village, citing sexual and mental (not to mention mor-al) degeneration.[8] Basing his comments on a personal 'investigation' of the district, Ben emphasized the seamiest aspects of the scene, and unmistakably failed to note anything positive. Furthermore, in case his account appeared too one-sided to be representative, he offered up as evidence a harrowing recording he had made of a seventeen-year-old girl who told him she had just come down from her fortieth (!) acid trip.

'A little bit of Europe' at Das Uppenbrau Café.

The Dirty Shames, a venerable Village jug band, onstage at the Riverboat.

The city fathers tour Yorkville.

Making the scene by day.

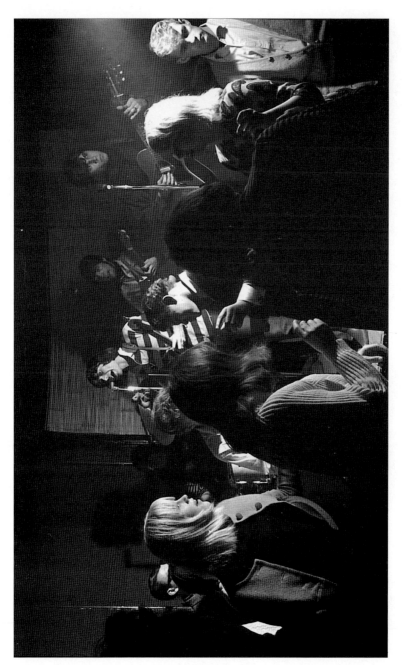

The Sparrows at Chez Monique.

Critical mass at the traffic protest.

'The Crawl.'

The generation gap personified? DePoe and Lamport at the 'Talk-In.'

Satyrday endorses Trudeau (sort of).

PUBLISHEDITORIAL

Satyrday

Box 12. 340 Bathurst st.
Toronto 2B Ont.
Canada

Publisher
ANDREW
MIKOLASCH

Editor
GERALD
MELLING

Business
Laima Matule

Advertising
Alison Hewer

THE FUTILITY OF DROPPING - OUT

Here it is. Come and get it. Futility is now available as an instant dose of existential suffering reality.

Take my mythical hippie friend, for example. He'll be walking barefoot again as soon as weather permits.

Oh......! The luxuries of modern Christhood send holy flashes of euphoric slobbery up my chagrined spine!

Yes, the coarse cement and warm asphalt feel good against the tender soles of dirty feet. You may join him by simply removing your shoes. Like a good hippie, he'll resent you with love.

How dare you intrude upon this original concept of selfless suffering, you dirty little plastic teenybopper you?

But don't worry about it, man. Like, sooner than it takes to count measureless time (yeah, baby it will creep up on you) you'll find yourself by the glaring headlights of good times passing. Honk honk...Eeeeck.....! You look funny there, old man, standing on the corner holding your lonely cock in your hand. But you're undernourished and can't even masturbate anymore.

This may sound like I'm bitching and blowing my cool about the influx of 'drop-outs' to the shady grottos of downtown pads (in the Megapolis of Toronto, Yorkville in downtown) but I was born here.....
....in the sense that I grew up on the street corners and Yorkville is just another corner of my life. Here I found love, companionship, and ways to make a living. And now you come here on a luxuriously adventurous middle class choice.

Some of us never had a choice. Some of us are forced to live by our wits, and play the game of urban survival. And you think it's fun. You think you can make a philosophy and a way of life out of it, from intellectually rationalised choice. So you want to remove your shoes, sit on the ground and chant Hare Krishna, groove on the Universe and let the Diggers feed you. That's cool with me. I hope you are as sincere as you think you are in whatever lack of purpose you possess in your non-motivation.

It is good for a man to go off into the jungle of whorehouse emotions and drug induced schizophrenia. Madness can be fun as long as it is our choice to go mad. Some of us like to escape into madness. Others, with no choice, would like to escape from it.

A permanent freakout is a loss of choice. When you reach this stage, man, you've got it mad.....
....you're beautiful!

Be like Jesus and dig suffering. Bullshit. The so-called suffering we impose upon ourselves these days is nothing but middle class luxury of a freakish nature. Jesus has been sold out by the hippies, and at a pretty cheap price at that. No, baby, the spirit of enlightenment cannot be bought for a dime.

Being unshod is fine as long as there are no poisonous snakes and insects to attack your bare feet. Walking around in bizzare rags of affected poverty is groovy as long as it blows the spectator's mind. It's too easy to play Jesus or Buddah the Holy Beggar on the fringe of an affluent society. The holy dropouts live off the society they drop out of. In its great affluence, society can afford a few clowns on its fringe for amusement and diversion. But beware, boys and girls! Any time now another type of clown may come into vogue.

So much for the exterior. How about the inner self? States of mind at different levels. Where the thing is at. Dope. Yeah.

So we smoke. Maybe drink, too. We indulge in every possible way to find pleasure. All this is not a search for answers to mystical problems. We should not make ourselves saints for taking dope.

Perhaps it is our Puritan Victorian heritage that causes so many 'heads' to have all those self-righteous excuses and pseudo-religious reasons for turning on. They can't admit they like to have a good time of sinful pleasure.

This has made some of us sick enough to quit all three-letter drugs, and to smoke on rare occasions simply for old times sake. We've never been busted mainly because we don't seek the status of martyrdom by going to jail.

So let us not be the heroes of our own fantasies (real or drug induced) it would be just another of the many futilities of our fucked-up generation. Making a way of life out of dope shouldn't be anybody's cup of tea.

For all the years I've been in the thick of where things are happening, I still can't help giving those professional dropouts a quizzical look (mixed with side-glances of contempt and sick pity) it's not that I'm jealous of the teenyboppers taking over, or anything like that. why drop out? I happen to be a 'pushed-out' person who cannot understand why any fool wants to drop out when he has a chance to stay in. To me and many other guys with the same socio-economical background, such a person is a brick.

But the sidewalk is public property and the street is open to any misguided fool who is stupid enough not to appreciate his nose.

If he wants a taste of what the simplicity of the 'La Vie Boheme' has been perverted into, by all means let him have it.

Brothers and sisters, I bid you welcome. And in your futilities, I wish you happy suffering.

BABY, ITS SPRING!

IF THAT DOESN'T TURN YOU ON

SATYRDAY WILL!

SUBSCRIBE
$2 ~ 1YEAR ~ 8 ISSUES
SEND CASH ~ CHEQUE ~ M.O.
BOX 12 ~ 340 BATHURST ST

'The Futility of Dropping Out,' *Satyrday.*

June Callwood with friends at Digger House.

A trio of bikers make their allegiances known.

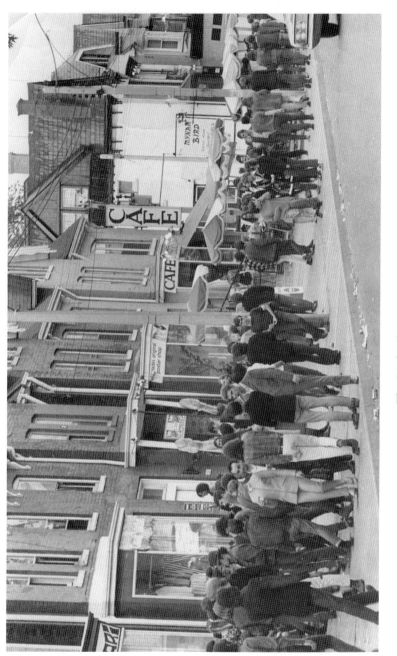

The 'Yorkville Hip Parade.'

Summer 1968

The Penny Farthing Coffee House

Soup du jour .35 — We don't have soup on hot days, our replacements are really groovy. cantalope, strawbrys, melon, etc.

Baguette Sandwich [french stick, buttered, ham, salami, cheese and lettuce] .85

WE ALSO HAVE GREAT ROAST BEEF SANDWICHES ON FRENCH STICK 1.05 OR CORNED BEEF ON RYE BREAD .65

WHEN LADY BOSS FEELS CONSTRUCTIVE

Salad Plate 1.25

Chili con Carne [with french stick] .75

THE FAME OF THIS GOURMETS DELIGHT HAS SPREAD NEAR + FAR [SCARBORO' DON MILLS IS FAR?]

French Pastries .35 — Very good, nice Hungarian man makes them.

Ice Cream .35 — Coffee or strawberry. Nice ice.

CALLED VIENESE WITH WHIPPED CREAM .55

COFFEES

Espresso small .35 — VERY BLACK VERY STRONG
        Double .45

THE ORIGINAL FROFFEE COFFEE

Capuccino .40 — trés milky

Cafe au lait .40

Cafe au rum .65 — No. you won't get stoned, madam!

Hot Mocca .65 — hot chocolate, espresso & whipped cream in a glass hummy good!

Milk & a dash .50 — wot they drink in Blighty mate
    COLD DRINKS

Iced Tea .40 — REFRESHING

BLACK OR WHITE WITH A RUDDY GREAT DOLLOP OF REAL WHIPPED CREAM

Iced Espresso .65 — BLOODY COLD!

Fresh Lemonade .50

Pespi Calo .40 — POLISH COKE

AARRR JUST LOIK THEY ARV IN ZUMERZET!

Cider .50
    PENNY FARTHING SPECIALS — THE VERY BEST IN TORONTO!

Hot Chocolate .50

English Breakfast Tea .40 — A REAL CUPPA ROSY LEE, MATE!

Café Penny Farthing [coffee, ice cream + whipped cream in a glass.] .75 — First famous at the half beat coffee house eight years ago - wonderful.

AFTER 7 PM ALL DRINKS UNDER .50 + GO UP TO FIFTY CENTS.

Penny Farthing Coffee House menu.

105 avenue road

925—7794

day & night

The Trailer's calling card – day and night.

'Hippie Hepatitis' mocked by the Grab Bag's Reuben Bernatt. Nancy Dymond, pictured here selling *Satyrday*, was the daughter of the Ontario health minister at the time, Matthew Dymond.

According to Ben, the young woman was a former prostitute and the victim of violence of the ugliest sort, her arm bearing the name of the 'Detroit pimp' who had carved her up for failing to hustle enough business. And, as a coup de grâce, Ben reminded his (likely) stunned audience – stories of this nature were quite unknown to the provincial legislature – just exactly where these young people were coming from, who they were underneath their insane performances, what lay beneath their hip masks. 'Places like these foster drug addiction and crime … [yet] many of the youngsters come from good families up north – ·from [wealthy Toronto suburbs] Forest Hill and Leaside. They're just children coming down for kicks.'[9] The gauntlet was thus thrown: your *middle-class* sons and (especially) daughters are being lost to Yorkville – what will you do to save *your* children? In a valiant effort to obscure the forest with some trees, Ben's argument (and the case taken up by those who would follow his lead) appears to victimize *everybody*, relying on the assumption that what happens to young people in Yorkville isn't their fault but is rather the fault of degenerated *Yorkville* itself. The solution: empty Yorkville and save Canada's middle-class children from their ruination.

No piece of news reporting amplified Ben's argument as successfully as David Allen's prominent multi-instalment exposé, which ran throughout April in the *Toronto Daily Star*. Foregrounding sexual degeneration, but sure to establish Yorkville as home to all manner of temptation and moral chaos, Allen's first piece heralded spring in 'The Acre of Action Where the Teenyboppers Are Prostitutes.' 'It's *the place* which attracts teenagers by the thousands,' declared Allen. Yorkville 'hooks them, and won't let them go.'[10] 'Yorkville today is the place where: the prostitutes are teenyboppers; a 15-year-old can buy and sell marijuana in a church basement; you can live in an all-night restaurant for days on end; a 16-year-old lost her virginity to a man she'd known only a few hours; the same girl – she's almost 17 – tonight will sell her favors for $20; fifteen-year-olds boast about how much marijuana and LSD they've taken.'[11] Allen's litany of sin, while rather obviously comprised of only two or (at most) three personal narratives – the fifteen-year-old who sells drugs at the church is likely also the one who boasts about how much dope he takes; if it was the same 'girl' who lost her virginity and then became a 'teenybopper prostitute,' this would satisfy the rest of his examples – had the intended effect.

As Allen, Ben, and others stepped up their invective, Villagers found their sense of community solidifying, deepening. Feeling embattled and misunderstood, and in need of a medium through which to respond to all of this criticism and allegation, many turned to the one figure in the scene whom local media had already singled out as a hip representative. Charged with defending Yorkville against its mounting army of detractors, this Village emissary would become, overnight, a sensation, the face of the summer of 1967, and, for better or for worse, the de facto leader of the Village scene.

Politicos and the Emergence of a Hippie Archetype

David DePoe materialized on the cultural radar very early in 1967, appearing in profile articles in the major newspapers to discuss his expected role in the Yorkville community. A fieldworker with the publicly funded youth initiative the Company of Young Canadians (CYC), he had been dispatched to help develop humanitarian efforts in the Village.[12] Overnight, DePoe, a well-known Villager, became the kind of media darling that Yorkville had been missing: a face, swagger, and voice for the scene. His middleman status further enhanced his credibility – for this wasn't just a Villager, but also the estranged son of one of Canada's top journalists (Norman DePoe), a paid worker for a government organization, and by all accounts a clever leader.[13] With both local media and the city looking for someone in particular on whom to focus their attention, to put a face on the scene, DePoe seemed a perfect fit: a well-spoken, aesthetically appropriate, and seemingly media-hungry young man, whose ability to attract controversy was apparent from the start.

With his first act as CYC representative in the Village, DePoe had managed to attract the disapproving glare of no less an authority figure than the former prime minister, John Diefenbaker.[14] On the second day of the new year, DePoe had taken part in a demonstration at the U.S. Consulate in protest against the still-escalating American war in Vietnam. By all accounts, it was an uneventful manifestation – no beaten heads, no property damage. But, because of allegations that a young man who was on the government payroll may have been the director of the protest, a new story emerged. A political uproar ensued, culminating in Prime Minister Lester Pearson's call for an investigation into the still-adolescent CYC and its practices. Meanwhile, DePoe struggled to put out the fire by clarifying that neither he nor Lynn Curtis, the other CYC volunteer at the demonstration, had intended to take charge. 'I had better explain that I didn't lead the damn thing,' he wrote to fellow

CYC-er Bill Poole. 'I fell into a leadership role simply because I had my guitar with me.'[15]

But DePoe clearly relished this media and political attention. In his words: 'I used the media consciously. I grew up in a house with a media person. My father, you know, was a print, radio and TV journalist. And so I knew people at the news desk at the CBC. I could phone up and say, "There's something happening up here." I'd phone the guy at the *Toronto Telegram* ... I mean, I could phone these people and go, "There's something interesting going on, you should send someone down to cover it."'[16] By the spring of 1967, DePoe had a significant ally in the *Globe and Mail*'s Michael Valpy (himself involved with the CYC for a time in these years), along with additional contacts (including his old roommate Bill Cameron at the *Star*) and acquaintances at the other major outlets. The stage was set for the emergence of a celebrity.

Having recently defected from the Student Union for Peace Action to the fairer fields of the CYC – a move that did little to endear him to the tumultuous New Left scene on the University of Toronto campus[17] – DePoe was familiar with the vicissitudes of youth politics and the role of Yorkville in the politicization of hip identity. His belief was that Yorkville represented a kind of unconscious political bloc, a sleeping giant that needed to be awoken to its power, strength, and political influence. 'Because I was media savvy, and because my name was a recognizable name, I would very consciously use [the CYC] to promote the cause and values of the counterculture, of Yorkville, of the youth, the generation thing that we were trying to get across, to the media and the public. I saw myself as a conduit to get that out there.'[18] He, like all CYC volunteers, had been given explicit directives not to become a *boss*, but rather to remain a facilitator, an enabler of positive change.[19] Young volunteers like him were sent out across Canada under similar orders, but few were sent to such a well-publicized neighbourhood.[20]

DePoe's greatest contribution to the scene was his development (with a small group of other Villagers) of the Diggers.[21] An anarchist humanitarian collective, loosely based upon groups with the same name in San Francisco and New York but not officially affiliated with either, the Diggers took to ministering to the needs of Yorkville's hip youth.[22] 'In the fall of '66,' DePoe explains, 'I moved onto Hazleton Avenue and I was starting to just lay the groundwork for community organization. And the Diggers was the first thing that kind of happened, as a way of organizing the community into something.'[23] The core group of Diggers was comprised of DePoe, fellow CYCers Don Riggan and Brian

'Blues' Chapman, and, to a lesser extent, former martyr Hans Wetzel and law students Clayton Ruby and Paul Copeland.[24] (DePoe, clearly uncomfortable with his legacy as Yorkville's emissary, stresses: 'I was probably important. But you see, it wasn't just *me*.'[25]) Their popularity among Villagers (for all had been on the scene, as it were, for months and years), combined with their consistent drive to keep Yorkville healthy, safe, and progressive, put them in ideal stead to promote the cause. In fact, even their critics conceded of the Diggers that 'the lives they saved could probably [alone] justify the cost of CYC.'[26] But, while the CYC was still footing the bill for their controversial endeavours, it was through their greatest ally, champion, and fund-raiser that they would achieve the level of recognition and support they needed to keep afloat.

June Callwood had caught on to their humanitarian concerns from the get-go. 'When I really got my nose rubbed in it,' Callwood has recounted, 'was when our nineteen-year-old son (who was doing a bit of drugs) clashed with me and moved out and found a room over the Grab Bag. Through him I met Blues Chapman, Don Riggan, and David DePoe. Clay Ruby, who was then a law student, was interested in [their group]. All these were the kind of people I understood.'[27] Unlike most parents of her generation, Yorkville began to make sense to her, even to become *attractive*. '[About] our son's rebellion,' she admits, 'vicariously I was *thrilled*!' Thrilled, that is, until something fundamental seemed to change. 'He [her son] began bringing home kids who didn't fit. You couldn't talk Nietzsche with them, they had almost no education. They had teeth rotted from neglect. They were strung out – I'd never seen kids like that. They weren't like kids of the Depression when I was a teenager who were kind of *whole* kids. These were *broken* kids.'[28] Callwood, hearing that the Diggers were setting out to help this growing number of transient, unhappy youth who had come to latch onto the Village as a refuge, approached them with an offer of support.

'To us this was good,' explains DePoe. 'This middle-class woman who came in and cared for these kids and decided that *yes*, homeless kids need a place to sleep, and food, and so on.'[29] The Diggers worked with Callwood to get word out that the scene was growing at too feverish a pace, and that shelters, food, and health counselling were badly needed. By early 1967, they had secured a base of operations (next door to the Grab Bag convenience shop on Yorkville Ave), were working towards the inception of a youth shelter called Digger House, and were busy developing a variety of local initiatives in preparation for what was expected to be the biggest summer yet in the Village. 'We were all very close friends,' recalls Ruby, 'and [we] worked together on every project, along with June Callwood.'[30] Together, they rapidly became the public face of the Yorkville scene. With DePoe as their principal, the Diggers assumed the mantle of Village leaders; as Ruby puts it, quite simply, 'David, Blues, and Don were the head of the [Village] hierarchy.'[31]

But some Villagers prefer not to look at it in those terms. 'We were consciously trying to set aside notions of status,' explained one man, who has chosen to remain anonymous. 'These were the contact people. Remember that what was going on was an attempt at *overthrowing* the notion of hierarchy, so, really ... most of us were dismissive of all of that. Obviously they were sort of contact people with the press, so we valued that. They were capable spokesmen and they said things that were in line with our own attitudes. We valued that, and appreciated that. But we didn't really look *up* to any of them.'[32]

Certainly many Villagers concurred with this sentiment in the period. For its part, *Satyrday* had laid the groundwork for hip resentment of the CYC's attempts to 'send the cream of Canada's youthful do-gooders ... into the deepest jungles of Toronto's Yorkville Village.' Under an irreverent sketch by Ron Thody – of Peggy Morton, a prominent left feminist activist and recent convert to the CYC, being boiled in a cauldron by a gaggle of Villagers – the editors complained that the CYC was treating Yorkville the way missionaries treat heathens. It seems that their ire had been raised when Morton had referred to Yorkville as unhealthy and suggested that it was in need of help. 'Cool it Peggy,' began *Satyrday*'s pointed response. 'Yorkvillians are not disturbed children. They are adults, disturbed or not. If you treat them as lost, unhappy waifs, you've had it.'[33] However, the case remains that the Diggers, by positioning themselves as the contact people, did indeed foster the impression (however self-constructed) that they represented and spoke for a majority of their fellows.

Thing was, the CYC never achieved much credibility in the activist scene – it began and ended as an *always already* co-opted initiative.[34] A government-run youth organization with aspirations of becoming a Canadian version of the Peace Corps? How could any self-respecting politico with counter-hegemonic objectives sign on to a government program predicated on the old liberal shibboleths of social responsibility and material guilt?[35] In her memoir-cum-history of the Canadian 1960s, Myrna Kostash summarizes that many 'SUPA activists ... repu-

diated CYC, saying that a government agency could not make the revolution.'[36] But, Kostash suggests, some were tempted by the promise of
funding. '[The] CYC had money,' she explained, 'it offered salaried jobs
and consultants' fees and all the accoutrements of a real office, and it
had lots of publicity.'[37] Myrna Wood, Peggy Morton, and many other
decidedly dedicated left activists took up the CYC's offer of subsidies
for their work, even though they were aware of the probable consequences. There was always the hope, as Art Pape put it, that through the
CYC the activists might 'use the system against itself' – and with money scarce, especially for social activists who had been trying to operate
apart from 'establishment' humanitarian organizations, the CYC's offer
of much-needed cash was hard to resist. Myrna Wood recalls this situation as 'one of the real contradictions of the era':

> The CYC bought off the leadership [of SUPA] ... A number of people like
> Peggy [Morton] and I were put on the payroll, and most of us were very
> suspicious about the whole thing, and said this whole idea of the CYC is
> contradictory to our aims, but I guess we thought we could use it for a few
> months. And for most of us, that's what happened ... Then, after a year
> and a half had gone by, we found out retrospectively that our leaders had
> been paid huge amounts, huge compared to us, and that they had socked
> [the cash] away in their bank accounts before going to law school, or what-
> ever. So, while [Peggy and I] were writing that paper,[38] part of that time we
> were working in that office.[39]

For his part, David DePoe agrees; the money made a lot of people excited that they could now find the funding they needed to effect real positive change: 'A bunch of us in SUPA decided that we were going to go
into the CYC and use their money in order to do our stuff, you know,
what we wanted to do. There was this big debate about "you're gonna
be a sell-out 'cause you're taking government money." And we said:
"Whatever! It's free money and we can use it to do what WE want."
You know? In other words: organize poor people, organize native people, organize youth, organize people to get what they deserve in the
broadest sense. Power to the people.'[40] Perhaps the most arresting thing
about this construction is the casual comparison drawn between Village youth and native people, as though the oppression and class/racial
identity issues were analogous. Yorkville was, in this formulation, a site
rife not just with needy youth but with youth who might be organized
into a political bloc defined around their minoritized subjectivity.

Such connections were often made in the late 1960s, as the category 'youth' came to be viewed through a Third-World prism. Yorkville, for DePoe, seems to have represented a worthy site of oppression, and its Villagers a people in need of liberation, rights, and representation: 'In other words, young people should have a voice that's respected, native people need to be organized and respected ... And we strongly believed that we could create a more democratic society by going out and organizing how people power people. I, having been in Yorkville, decided that these young people ... we could do some organizing so they could have a voice. They could, in all their diversity and difference, they could be listened to.'[41] Many of the politicos in SUPA (and some of the CYC volunteers) looked to such attempts to connect Village identity with minority prejudice and social violence as (at best) misguided. Myrna Wood explained the general reaction she (and many of her peers) had upon seeing Villagers' attempts to politicize a carefree lifestyle:

There were hippies who clearly believed that their lifestyle could change society. I don't know how they ever got that impression. They were ignoring reality. They were also, I would have said, innocent and naive, ignorant children of fairly well-off middle-class society. To have been around, as they were, in those years when the most horrendous things were going on, to black people, to poor people of all kinds ... I mean, in the midst of all that, to think that by, I don't know, by *singing* and just maintaining the attitude that everything is just going to be peaceful, man, and we're just going to chill out, and be peaceful, and there is harmony, and there's no room for this disharmony in our lives, and ... well, *excuse me*! I mean, that was racist, if nothing else. There's no other way I can explain it. This kind of escapism defined the hippies.[42]

This view (echoed by other former Villagers) appears to demonstrate a straightforward adversarial relationship between class- and youth-based politics in the period. For Wood, Yorkville was a non-issue, an insignificant battleground in a wider war in which the stakes were so very much higher.

Historian Van Gosse argues that although 'the counterculture was never synonymous with the broader New Left ... there were clearly links between them.'[43] Part of the reason for this separation between these two groups, he notes, is grounded in the reality that many who self-identified as part of the activist New Left looked at the hippie phenomenon with disdain. In Wood's recollection, political youth regarded the Yorkville scene with a mixture of frustration and disparagement: '[We thought them to be] selfish little bastards, many of them, in fact. What I would have said, and I think what most of my political friends would have said was: *those people are just wasting their time*. If we don't change society, then there will be no freedom for those people, or for anyone else. Still true today. So it was kind of useless.'[44] While Wood surely speaks for many of her contemporaries from the political movements, her vitriol obscures the degree to which her New Left contemporaries interacted with these same 'selfish little bastards.'

Judy Pocock, who was both an activist and a Villager, complicates this either/or dichotomy separating Villagers from politicos but cautions us against blowing it up. 'The whole Yorkville thing was *connected*; it was much more of an *environment* than a political movement,' she explains, with characteristic incisiveness. 'And within that environment there were many, many different types. And there were a lot of politics, and there were a lot of people who saw themselves as political. And some people were sympathetic with politics. And you know there was also a very anti-political strain within that: you know, *do your own thing, don't bother me I won't bother you*, you know, *be cool*. So, I would say it was more of a culture rather than a movement. I think that's valid.'[45] But DePoe happily distances himself and the majority of Villagers from the wider activist movement. '[Villagers] just looked at them [politicos] like: *Ahh, you guys have your own agenda. You people are like ideologues, and we're against all that*. Oh yeah. We were against ideologues and ideology and we just wanted to be who we were, that kind of thing. They came with their little speeches, and we would just say: *Go away*.'[46]

For her part, Judy Perly sets up her view of the disjuncture between Villagers and the New Left in much the same way: 'My brother went on to become an ultra lefty, a Maoist. Canadian Liberation Movement. So at the same time as the hippie culture, you have a lot of very left wing politics going on in Toronto. The intelligentsia was into the left wing politics [while] the less intelligent were into arts. Like me. *I* was into the light shows.'[47] Though she is joking, Perly's assertion is perceptive. In her experience, the intelligentsia (as she calls them) represented a real antithesis to the Yorkville scene. Their politics were stultifying and enervating while she and her friends just wanted to be free, have fun. 'It definitely was like that,' she explains.

There were different layers going on. There was art, there was music, there

was politics. Which group were you going to join? Political people were
... *horrible*. They were going to change the world, and be very authoritarian about doing it. My brother was one of the leaders of the new left, and
he was NOT a hippie. He didn't smoke dope, didn't get into folk music,
whatever. He never *went* to Yorkville ... Yorkville was mostly really busy
on the weekends, with suburban kids trying to change the world by smoking dope and doing artistic things. Having different kinds of relationships.
But the political ones were trying to change the world in a different way.[48]

The Village, then, even in this most politically charged of years in
Yorkville's 1960s, was not generally regarded as a site of political organization, ideology, or activism. The intervention of the CYC was meant
in some way to remedy this, to marry the political leanings of the New
Left to the hip hedonism of the Villagers. But whatever credit the CYC
might have accumulated through its early endeavours was squandered
when, in the waning days of August, DePoe and the Diggers chose to
focus Yorkville's mighty voice, population, and media presence on the
astoundingly unnecessary issue of traffic jams.

Feminism, Pregnancy, and the Limitations of 'Free Love'

Alice Echols has argued that 'for women, the so-called sexual revolution was a mixed blessing. Women were having more sex (and with less
guilt), but they were also more sexually vulnerable. Instead of undoing
the deeply rooted sexual double standard, free love only masked it in
countercultural pieties.'[49] Indeed, while providing a context in which
people were freer to have sex with more partners and with fewer repercussions than ever before, the famous 'free love' ethic also reinforced
an atmosphere which equated female sexual freedom with male sexual
gratification.[50] Or, in the pithy phrasing of a foundational Canadian
position paper on women's liberation: 'We are allowed sexual freedom
but are still faced with a loss of respect on the part of many males if we
take advantage of that freedom.'[51] Besides, this much-ballyhooed ethic
was ill-defined at best; how free was too free? Unlike their bohemian
forebears in the Greenwich Village scene of the 1910s, some of whom
were known to keep their doors open during sex so as to protest the
bourgeois convention of 'privacy,' Villagers (like most of their contemporaries elsewhere) tended towards a far more casual approach.[52]

After a few years of frustrations, doubletalk, and contradictions,
many women turned away from the free love espoused by their con-

temporaries, disappointed to have found that this freedom referred to *male* sexuality, while women were cast as shiny satellites orbiting around their sun.[53] In her widely read kiss-off to both the male left and the hip scene more generally, radical U.S. feminist Robin Morgan very deliberately equated hipness with misogyny. 'Goodbye to Hip Culture and the so-called Sexual Revolution,' she pointedly declared, 'which has functioned toward women's freedom as did the Reconstruction toward former slaves – reinstituted oppression by another name.'[54] Denise Kouri, a Canadian feminist, is no more sanguine in her description of male responses to feminist arguments: 'Men would actually say things like, "You're ugly and just need a good fucking."'[55] While many feminists have written about their disillusionment over the failures of their male contemporaries in the New Left to recognize female oppression, there is a dearth of discussion of the parallel blind spot for women's rights at work among other youth movements in the era.[56] Among the few assessments at our disposal of the relationship between Villagers and Toronto feminists is the one offered by Myrna Wood: 'We certainly took to the idea of free love, in our meaning of that phrase, but, at the same time, you know, we couldn't help but be conscious of how males used it. And so, if there was one dominant theme of consciousness-raising [sessions], it was that! How to deal with the constant arrogance of male attitudes and ideas [about sex]. And that was just more so among the counterculture, the hippies. I mean, it was bad enough amongst the politicals, but it was worse among the hippies.'[57] Whether or not it was worse among the hippies, free love did operate in Yorkville in predictable ways. It tended to be tied to an identity performance, yet another badge associated with hipness and anti-establishmentarian authenticity.[58]

Today, it is not uncommon for men to publicly recognize their inability (or failure) in the 1960s to appreciate the depth of their own chauvinism. David DePoe offered this anecdote by way of explanation of the emergence of feminism in the Village: 'I had a very personal experience with this. This woman that I slept with, she wasn't very happy because it was a real quickie and she said: "You didn't treat me with any respect!" Right? And: "You son of a bitch you just used me for yourself!" The personal is political! … They said: "Guys, you bunch of sexist pigs, wake up!" Male chauvinist pigs – that was what we were.' Such language mirrored developments in the wider activist communities around this time. Both in June 1966, and again in the autumn of 1967, the Toronto Women's Liberation Work Group (a University of

Toronto student group) had presented papers to SUPA outlining theory and proposals for positive change within the organization.[59] In both cases the male-dominated SUPA responded dismissively.[60] The plight of women was simply invisible to many SUPA activists, whose eyes had been trained on noticing the inequality issues attached to people of colour, people of limited resources, or (to put it more generally) those to whom they felt that the labels of Third World or Colonized People would most clearly fit.[61] As it was with the American Students for a Democratic Society, the bell was tolling for SUPA by late 1967, yet the leadership failed to appreciate the root cause.[62] Feminism – specifically the emerging radical feminist movement – would play a vanguard role in pulling both organizations apart.[63]

In response to this maddening stonewalling, women from within the New Left began to organize consciousness-raising (CR) sessions around Toronto, meetings geared towards empowerment and educating women about the destructive influence of male chauvinism.[64] Open to any woman who was interested, and often advertised in the Village, such groups 'were usually made up of eight to ten women who met regularly over a period of time. They operated without a leader, and discussion could include ... personal relationships with men, sex and sexuality, body image, or friendships and attraction between women.'[65] The fruits of such grass-roots organizing became apparent right away as the alternative ideologies generated through these informal 'teach-ins' were disseminated through the city, suggesting alternatives for women who felt constrained by gender expectations.[66] As activist Nancy Adamson notes, 'more formal political meetings were essential to organize those women who had been reached, but it was the CR group that got so many out to those meetings in the first place.'[67]

As CR sessions helped to reveal, many of the problems facing women in Yorkville were no different from those facing women elsewhere. Repercussions (most notably pregnancy) for women in this era of limited sexual education were often severe. While oral contraception was available to many women (usually through a certain subterfuge or nod-and-a-wink relationship with a sympathetic doctor since it was still legally restricted to married women), it was by no means universally taken; nor was it 100 per cent effective.[68] Pregnancy was rarely understood by Villagers to be a mutual responsibility – it was the woman's fault she got pregnant, and anyway, how could she prove who the father had been? As a result, more often than not, a surprise pregnancy meant the end of one's Yorkville experience. It seems that performing

Village identity with a protruding belly was unsustainable. According to one observer, 'a few have left because of unhappy love affairs and a very few to get married to villagers and settle down in a conventional way. A number have also returned home because of pregnancy. There is no opportunity for an unwed pregnant girl to find security in Yorkville. Her baby is believed to be her responsibility and the fathers usually do not help in any way.'[69] A poem (entitled 'a poem') printed in an early 1967 issue of *Satyrday* supports this construction, painting pregnancy as a female responsibility, something she must face on her own:

> It's all quite complicated,
> Double-talk at its best.
> But you'd better go through it all, my dear
> (Please get a pregnancy test).[70]

A young man explained that, in the view of many Villagers, 'when a girl gets pregnant, she gets motherly and she wants a home and family and to be respectable.' This 'motherliness' is what calls them home, to their parents. Regrettably, he admitted, if they do not (or cannot) go home, 'many girls in the village give up their babies to the Children's Aid Society when the guys take off.'[71]

Colleen Riley, who moved to the Village in 1967 with her six-year-old son, came for the work, the scene, and the music – but was never under any illusions that she, as a single mother, would be one among many. 'Even my son hailed me as a pioneer woman in those days,' she recalls with considerable pride.[72] But what was it like to raise a child in that environment? By way of response, she offers this instructive story, emphasizing the contrasts that characterized the scene: 'There was a little milk store across the street. And my son would go to get a quart of milk or something, and have to walk by the seniors, you know, at Mt Sinai, the [nursing home] on Yorkville, and the hippies would be sitting up against the fence, while in the background there would be the ladies in their wheelchairs out enjoying the sunshine. And as [my son] walked by they'd say: "Hey kid, want some drugs?" and he'd say: "No thanks."' To Riley, such a scenario is illustrative of two simultaneous realities of Village life in the 1960s: on the one hand, here was the danger represented by drug culture and hippie irresponsibility, while on the other, here was all of this potential danger taking place under the watchful eye of the seniors at the old folks' home. Riley reminds us that, from 1967 until she moved away in 1971, the Village always felt safe to her and her son. Even as young people in the scene got deeper into the needle drugs, and as the general impression was that Yorkville was descending into disrepair, 'the [Rosedale] ladies would come with their poodles! They'd walk their poodles up and down [Cumberland]!'[73] This is the continuing counterpoint to the narratives of sex, drugs, and rock'n'roll – Rosedale ladies, wheelchair-bound seniors, and errand-running six-year-olds, right there amid the Villagers and their vice-ridden scene.

The flipside of Riley's view: Marilyn Brooks, Riley's counterpart in the Cumberland fashion world, declares that 'I was happy I was on Cumberland, and that I wasn't on Yorkville, because it was too much, like a sort of cesspool of desire.'[74] Desire for escape, and for a chance to perform a new version of the self; for many young women and men, weekenders arriving in the scene looking to perform at hipness, to try drugs and sex, and generally to explore this scene, a typical series of experiences may have run something like this:

> It's hard to describe the scene. But you'd go into those houses: people would be passed out, you'd have art always on the wall, tie dye was big, incense burning, stuff from India, Afghanistan. There would always be strangers dropping in, backpacking, what not ... It wasn't like it is today where it's like a social thing, you smoke a joint, *blah blah blah*. In those days, you'd go to parties to get stoned. People were not smoking at home particularly; they'd go to these parties. But people wouldn't know how much to smoke, you'd go to these parties and we'd smoke so much dope that in an hour everyone would be on the floor! But it was all the incense, and the hookahs, and then you're on the floor. You didn't even know who you were next to, and in a half an hour you were making out with somebody you didn't even know who they were.[75]

While group sex, nude parties, and other such daring manifestations of sexual adventurism were few and far between, the media made sure to report on any that caught their attention, suggesting to those not in the know that such activities were nightly affairs along Yorkville Ave.

In one shiny instance, the *Toronto Daily Star* alerted readers in late May to the break-up of a Village three-way by police, ostensibly on the grounds of combating 'drunkenness.' The three people directly involved, two male and one female, had been found naked, drunk, and sprawled out when police officers burst in on them (the precipitating reason for the bust is unclear). The girl, a thirteen-year-old runaway

from Winnipeg, was said to have been so drunk she was nearly unconscious. A sixteen-year-old girl who lived in the apartment, but who had
not been present for the police action, took the stand in defence of the
two boys, aged nineteen and twenty. Described by the *Star* as 'wearing
a short, short skirt under a short plastic coat,' the young woman testified that, although she did indeed live there, she did not know who
paid the rent. The magistrate, as he handed out sentences, explained:
'Anyone involved in any way in the debauchery of young ladies should
be sent to jail.' To this statement, and to what was no doubt the pro-
foundest displeasure of the judge, the nineteen-year-old defendant
insolently returned: 'The *what*? De-*bitch*-ary?' The two young men were
given thirty-five- and ten-day prison sentences, respectively.[76]

For his part, 'Wild Bill' relates stories of the sexual availability of
weekender and runaway young women that very much suggest a free
and liberated sexual landscape: 'It was easy [to pick up girls]. Because
three-quarters of the weekenders were down here for that. Girls would
stay at my apartment every weekend. They'd come in by GO train, or
VIA [sic]. They'd come into town, see me, and say: *Can I come up to your
place?* I'd say: *Sure, I'll be home at 8:00.*' These young women, having
come to Yorkville for a weekend of illicit fun from suburban Toronto,
often had no pre-arranged places to stay, so such arrangements were
worked out casually and with no-strings attached. There to take drugs
('what usually happened was that they would come in on Friday afternoon and take blotter acid') and to try out some of the free love that
they had heard about, Villagers like 'Wild Bill' had no trouble accepting
their offers. Nevertheless, the dark side of such casual sexual dealings
emerges early and often in his recounting of his adventures with inex-
perienced young women: 'One night I said to a girl, *I got one question.
Everyone calls you a virgin, are you a virgin?* She says *Yeah, but I don't
wanna be.* So I said, *Well, why don't you and me go into the bedroom?* So we
went in there, and I knocked her up. She told me she was on the pill,
but she wasn't. [Meanwhile], her girlfriend, same thing! She went home
knocked up that weekend too. But neither of them were on acid. When
they were stoned I would never do a thing. They were straight sober
that weekend.'

Some former Villagers describe this type of story as phoney, sensa-
tionalized. 'I think the girls felt quite free to say no, and they said no
lots,' stresses Clayton Ruby. 'There wasn't that much of *that* really; it
was more like a buzz in the press. People were freer and were experimenting more, and so on, but lots of people were in stable relationships

and so on.'[77] But freedom and experimentation in an era rocked by shifting sexual and gender politics were noisy propositions, especially when performed in such a spectacular space as Yorkville.

The Siege of Yorkville Revisited

On the night of 22 August, a throng of some four hundred Villagers staged a silent march out of the district that had come to be their weekend address, down Bay St and into the heart of downtown Toronto. Led by a visiting American activist named Mary Kerson, the protesters marched in a snaking file of twos south to city hall and, after being asked to move along by the police, back north to Queen's Park where they staged a sit-in until just after midnight.[78] This demonstration, among the largest to emerge from the Yorkville scene, did not simply express the flawed but oft-repeated argument that Villagers were basically peaceful and harmless. The real effect here was to illustrate to all observers (followers and detractors alike) that, without them, the 'Village of Yorkville' would *cease to exist*. Their *absence* from the Village, not their hushed, peaceful excursion into the greater Toronto cityscape, was what characterized the exercise.

Following years of build-up, mounting coverage in the press, and viral word-of-mouth, Yorkville was now unquestionably synonymous with hippies. As such, their absence from the district on that August night was deeply conspicuous. For the first time in months, traffic flowed freely along skinny one-way Yorkville and Cumberland. The couple dozen coffee houses sat empty, undercover police were unable to make any significant drugs arrests, and, as the *Toronto Daily Star* pithily noted, pedestrians were allowed to move 'unhampered on the sidewalks.'[79] But, at the same time, the neighbourhood seemed vacant, staid, colourless. The 'Hippies,' read a headline the following morning, had 'Show[n] It's Not Yorkville without Them.'[80] Their identities had become so intertwined in the popular imagination, so fused following years of sustained media exposure of the Village and its denizens, that the counterculture had redefined the expected map of meaning represented by Yorkville. The little neighbourhood was no longer simply *associated with* countercultural activity – it *was itself* a countercultural activity.

In a sense, Yorkville had come to represent the Canadian counterculture at large – for both the silent demonstrators and the municipal authorities who would have had the Village rid of these milling young people, this erroneous assumption had become accepted, endorsed, even (as in this case) celebrated. As synecdoche for the youth movement, Yorkville was powerful and dominant; by the end of the summer of 1967, the fate of the hippies (and whatever they had come to represent) was seen through the prism of the Village. And so the perceived failure of the Villagers to wrest ultimate control from the municipal authorities, a failure that is understood to have culminated in their eventual wholesale removal from the district by the early 1970s, was born of this commitment to the equation of Yorkville and countercultural activity.

No one appeared to represent this activity more clearly than David DePoe. As the son of a famous CBC broadcaster, controversial CYC-er, and peace activist, this bearded, guitar-playing, LSD-taking sex symbol provided a comprehensible pin around whom to revolve the Village scene. In nearly every way, DePoe represented the archetypal Villager. And it didn't hurt that DePoe's archetypal adversary was himself a caricature of Mr Jonesism. Allan Lamport, the blustery and unswervingly old school mayor-of-Toronto-cum-city-controller, had quite comfortably settled into his role as defender of all things conservative by early 1967. Recognizing a base of traditionalist voters who were anxious over the bunch of raucous young people that had been getting louder every year, Lamport singled out Yorkville as *his* issue. And, as a result of his persistent attacks on the district throughout 1967, Lamport emerged in media frames as the establishment's answer to the question posed by DePoe.

'He selected himself [to be a leader] as well,' maintains DePoe. 'He was outspoken and colourful ... so he set himself up as the opponent.'[81] By throwing his hat into the ring, and taking up the role as spokesman for a traditional Toronto, Lamport indeed finagled himself into a position from which his 'colourful' attacks on the Village could be given their widest possible audience. His self-styled role as arch-nemesis to DePoe and his band of Diggers was eaten up by media sources only too pleased to be offered such a deliciously reductionist frame for their coverage of the Village. Throughout 1967, Lamport (often dubbed Lampy in the press) matched DePoe's every move with yet another stunningly angry denunciation of Village youth. In mid-June, for example, Lamport called for police action to 'disperse Yorkville's beatnik-type' teenagers, claiming that he was prepared to 'go to the limit' to rid the city of this 'sore' now that Yorkville had become a 'generator of delinquency.'[82] A week later he was calling for federal assistance in the fight to erase this 'blot on the city,' since hippies seemed to be coming 'from all over.'[83] By early August, he was calling for the institution of identity cards for Yorkville youth. In DePoe's incendiary words, what Lamport was really casting about for was the 'final solution' to Toronto's hippie problem.[84]

As both an active hippie resident and a self-styled community organizer, DePoe was a bridge between political activism and hip Yorkville. His efforts to facilitate communication between what he saw as clashing generations and ideologies were inevitably shaped by his unambiguous association with the scene, his past work with SUPA, and his current capacity as CYC volunteer. But his media-friendly performances of 'Villager,' and his proselytizing on the virtues of the anti-conformist ethic, served to place him in the position of group leader rather than mediator in the cultural conflict. Eventually, his was the only voice that garnered any sustained attention – his friends and colleagues in the Digger outfit were routinely referred to as *other hippies* while he was quoted at length, described in detail, and referred to as *Mr* DePoe.

As the summer built towards an inevitable showdown between the two sides, the Diggers planned and executed a series of protests designed to promote their cause (in this case, their call to turn Yorkville into a pedestrian mall). The Diggers, having attracted considerable attention through their various initiatives (they had opened a storefront 'Free Shop,' they were negotiating with the city to create a shelter for hip street youth, and Digger lawyers Clayton Ruby and Paul Goodman had recently started the Village Bar, a legal-aid service), now had the ears of the community, and of observers of the scene. People seemed prepared to pay attention to their calls for change, to their ideas, and to their peculiar but meaningful criticisms of the status quo.

On 17 August, the Diggers were invited to a 'talk-in' at city hall. 'I took it upon myself,' explained Lamport just prior to the meeting, 'to talk to these people called hippies. Now, they're not all bad, not all kids are bad. But sometimes you get a cancer area ... and we're trying to ferret that out.' In a few sharp sentences, he cut right to the core of his vision of Yorkville as a sucking void, a 'cancer' that pulls otherwise good kids off of their productive path: 'If we stop some of this – and this meeting today will do it, I'm sure – we'll get these fellas back on the right track, and try to help them out.' For Lamport, the right track was, above all else, occupation, industriousness, and embrace of a work ethic that to him was lost in the haze of Yorkville's coffee bars.

The Diggers arrived at the 'talk-in' in a flamboyant manner.[85] Flanked by various film crews and a couple dozen Villagers, they filled the room with their noise, their disdain for hierarchy, and what can only be called their aggressive naivety. While Allan Lamport tried to find some kind of middle ground between his side and the brazen throng before him, DePoe sat largely silent, apparently deferential, even aloof. The Villagers in the audience joked, cajoled, and proclaimed their irreverence as Lamport outlined his vision for the outright commercialization of Yorkville.[86] 'Why do you wish not to work?' he demanded. 'Do you want more recreation? Something to give you aims and objectives?'[87] Exasperated (although forcing a studied, patronizing calm), Lamport allowed 'Blues' Chapman to respond. Well spoken, and decidedly placid, the striking young man began by explaining that work, as he saw it, offered little to those who viewed any job as drudgery. Voicing the hip pursuit for a more authentic way of being, he explained that he and his contemporaries shouldn't be tied to the kind of 'personal pride and dignity people have, and their ability to be happy, or satisfied, with a job.' Lamport leapt after this: 'But you refer to the word *dignity*. Now that's a very good word.' Pointing to the Villagers, he exclaimed: 'A number of them there haven't been washed for weeks. Now, they aren't seeking dignity, are they?'[88] When one young man (off camera) yelped: 'Practice leaving us alone!' Lamport snapped: 'Unfortunately society doesn't work that way, just exactly the way *you* like it.' In a decisive moment, the young man fired back with a retort that the 1960s had taught him, and that had become a kind of mantra for the disaffected, the bored, the curious, the fed up: 'Well, that's why we dropped out.'[89]

The shambling 'talk-in' marked the beginning of a week of protest – a few nights later, the Diggers gathered together hundreds of Villagers and inspired them to sit down on Yorkville Ave in protest. Close the street to cars, return the street to the pedestrians, and respect Yorkville as a youth centre – the Villagers had found their political issue, and, organized by the media-savvy Diggers, they were prepared to make their voices heard. The sit-in, which lasted for a few hours as a simple protest, suddenly turned violent when, inexplicably, the police broke ranks and began beating, dragging, and brutalizing the Villagers, throwing them into the backs of paddy wagons. DePoe was among those arrested for his part in the protest, and spent a night in the Don Jail, along with June Callwood. The *Toronto Daily Star*'s front-page headline the following day proclaimed: '"Jail-In" for 46 after Yorkville's "Worst" Brawl.'[90]

After having watched for years as televised U.S. civil rights protests ended in bloodshed, bottle tossing, and arson, Torontonians were genuinely frightened by what seemed to have been a real political confrontation in Yorkville.[91] But what was worse was the realization that Toronto's police force may have responded with unjustifiable violence. Well-publicized allegations of police brutality hit the city like a firestorm by the end of the week. The Canadian Civil Liberties Association called for a royal commission into charges of brutality in Yorkville, noting that, for some time, police had been 'pressing their authority [in Yorkville], particularly in regard to the movement of pedestrian traffic, well beyond legal limits.'[92] Its concerns over the pervasiveness of injuries to the protesters, of 'broken bones' and other evidence of maltreatment, were listed in front-page articles in the *Star*, the *Telegram*, and the *Globe*, and as top stories on the television news reports.[93] In the end, Toronto's police force would have a great deal to answer for, not the least of which being the fact that the phone call to the fire department during the protest – a false-alarm call that brought fire trucks to an impassible Yorkville Ave and that precipitated the ensuing beat-down – had originated in the police phone system.[94]

City hall's Nathan Phillips Square became the site of ongoing protest, as hundreds of Villagers and sympathizers made the scene. Some held a 'starve-in,' essentially a hunger strike designed to protest the traffic issue, but they were foiled when police busted twelve of them for trespassing.[95] Hundreds of others, however, managed to avoid arrest as they joined in chants, sing-songs (*Frère Jacques* and *Alouette* were among the tunes heard by a *Globe and Mail* reporter, for some reason), and recitations of the 23rd Psalm.[96] Most significantly, this week of protests demonstrated a virtually united Yorkville: not only were there hippies carrying placards and chanting, but here were activists and radicals standing in solidarity, here were greasers and toughs come to show support. 'When we did our thing down at city hall,' underlines DePoe, 'the Vagabonds Motorcycle Club came down and protected us. They sat down with us, all night, in their black leather jackets, and made a ring around this bunch of hippies to protect us. They were like our bodyguards.'[97] Still, for many Villagers, all this noise simply wasn't worth getting involved with. Bruce Cockburn, a Village-based musician, speaks for many when he confesses that 'I remember hearing about the sit-in, but I really wasn't involved in things like that then.'[98] By no means were all Villagers geared towards politics and protest, even at this most fraught political moment.

Now a political hot potato, these protests had garnered serious national attention. Some Villagers, however, felt they still hadn't been given enough opportunities to air their grievances at city hall. And, riding a surging tide of energy, antipathy, and the sense that perhaps this time they were undoubtedly in the right, they acted out a little street theatre for their city fathers. Some thirty Villagers, led by a U.S. army deserter known as Smokey, streamed into a chamber at city hall that was being set up for an impending Board of Control meeting, took over the room, and (outrage of all outrages) sat in the members' chairs. Ostensibly a protest over the council's refusal to hear DePoe earlier in the day, the so-called 'chair-in' was pretty innocuous, but highly disruptive.[99]

The chairs were given up after about forty-five minutes, when the floor was ceded to DePoe. Listing demands and presenting arguments over the closing of Yorkville to traffic, he spoke for an incredible three hours – routinely interrupted by board members and Villagers alike, the latter cheering and shouting from the seats in the back – and terminated only after other citizens who had been waiting in line for their own chance to speak on municipal matters grabbed the microphone and complained.[100] The major papers very happily covered this wild scene – it made for dynamite copy. Here was the brawny, shaven-headed Smokey (described by DePoe as 'like security for us; a tough, *tough* guy') leading a group of long-hairs into the Board of Control, sitting in the mayor's chair, and literally usurping the stage.[101] Infuriated, Lamport did exactly what everyone was expecting, and angrily denounced the event, grumbling about 'anarchy.' In response, the protesters booed him resoundingly.

The following day, Smokey and several associates were arrested at an early morning raid on their Hazelton Ave house. Busted for a variety of offences including drugs, trespassing, and possession of a 'spring knife' were twelve men and two women, including at least two protesters from the previous afternoon. Smokey was in fact the very protester who had occupied Mayor Dennison's chair; few Villagers believed this to be coincidental. Nor was it deemed an accident that another draft resistor, a twenty-year-old named Frank Michalski, was picked up by immigration authorities in Webster's hamburger joint (a twenty-four-hour Yorkville mainstay) that same day and threatened with deportation.[102]

The public response to all of this is tricky to gauge, but a variety of opinions is apparent from the letters-to-the-editor sections of the Toronto papers which, for a time, were wholly given over to debate over Yorkville.[103] From a minister at the Bayview Church of Christ ('Where would Canada be if the United Empire Loyalists merely grew long hair and beards to protest the Revolution of 1776?') to a former resident of the Village ('The trouble started when adolescent suburbanites and unemployed out-of-towners swarmed in'), a diversity of views of the hip scene crowded the pages. 'If the theory of dialectical development is correct,' wrote one hopeful Hegelian commentator, 'then the meeting of the "lost" youth of Yorkville and the city fathers in the Metro Chambers recently was history in action.'[104] Even as some Torontonians wrote in to the papers in support of the initiative to close Yorkville to traffic – 'I feel that the city fathers are confusing hippies with good planning' – there was scant support for Villagers' behaviour or perspectives.[105] Commonly, the sense was that, throughout the melee, the hippies had shown that they were 'empty-headed'; they were living in a 'rat-den village'; they were 'low-grade simians.'[106]

On 23 September, the *Toronto Daily Star*'s weekly insert magazine *Star Weekly* ran a cover story on DePoe, famously dubbing him the 'Super Hippie' and cementing his status as a national celebrity.[107] The article, written by DePoe's old university friend Bill Cameron, glamorized DePoe as had little else before, offering colour photographs (one of which pictured a shirtless DePoe for some reason) and a full-scale interview. 'Oh man,' recalls DePoe, 'I was so embarrassed by that!'[108] 'It was like I was Paul McCartney! Oh my god, it was scary. I mean, I couldn't believe it the first time I went to a high school ... and I walked down the hallway and all these girls started to scream! And they all had my picture from *Star Weekly*. In their *lockers*. Oh my God, you know? It was certainly an ego trip, but at the same time it was scary. Like, I'm sort of thinking inside: "This is just me – I do what I do, trying to be honest and true to my values. I'm not a friggin' *rock star*!"'[109] Rock star or not, DePoe had solidified his place in the firmament. Though he is adamant to this day that he was too often singled out, that it was never only him behind these famous events, the case remains that he was consistently presented by the media and at the Board of Control as the man at the helm.

If it 'wasn't just *me*,' as Depoe maintains, then who *was* it? Who were these people, and what were they trying to accomplish on those days in late August 1967, in front of the cameras and the reporters and the police and the cheerleaders? 'We thought of ourselves as a *community* who wanted to welcome people in,' DePoe concludes. 'The motivation for that [protest] was we wanted them to close the street and get out and walk so they could meet us like human beings. I mean, we really truly believed that, right? And we rejected the values of the mainstream society – we wanted it to be an alternative way of living and so on. A counterculture, if you want to call it that. We were against the mainstream culture. Fair enough, but, we believed in peace and love and understanding, essentially.'[110]

Set against the monolithic authority of the mainstream culture, the Diggers' carnivalesque protest-debacle could claim no measurable victory. While some sympathy was generated for the Villagers after images of their heads getting busted were broadcast, Yorkville Avenue was not closed to traffic nor were Villagers rendered any less incomprehensible to the average Canadian. Throughout the remainder of the year, and into the following three summer seasons in the Village, this 'Siege of Yorkville' loomed as a moment of excited futility, an example of the insubstantiality, even the arrogance, of Village politics. One Villager took out a page in *Satyrday* on the one-year anniversary of the protest to announce his disdain for the constructed significance of the event. 'Why,' he demanded, 'was sitting down in mid-street to stop traffic indicative of anything at all?'[111] In the mid-1980s, Jeanine Hollingshead looked back to this famous moment with some sheepishness: 'I mean, what were we protesting? The right to be able to sit in the middle of the road? ... It seems to me that it was pretty shallow ... we were just a bunch of people, we didn't have any real cause.'[112]

This whole affair was immortalized in two documentaries prepared that summer by the National Film Board of Canada (NFB). In anticipation of the impending showdown between the Village and the city, the NFB had sent a film crew to Yorkville led by a young filmmaker named Mort Ransen. The plan was simple: explore the curious forms of social rebellion taking place in midtown Toronto. However, while Ransen's crew was at work (filming what would become *Christopher's Movie Matinee* [1968]), it became clear to everyone that more was at stake here than just a collection of peculiar young people vying for an enclave of freedom – as political tensions began to rise leading up to the protests of late August, another film crew was sent in (under the direction of Robin Spry) to chronicle the deepening conflict.[113]

But, somehow, the filmmakers managed to inculcate the sense that they had incited the whole affair. Recalled to Ottawa on 24 August amid allegations that they had tried to orchestrate a Queen's Park protest, had paid their interviewees, and had encouraged their subjects to act up in front of their cameras, directors Ransen and Spry had no choice but to comply. However, within two days they were reinstated by the NFB, under the condition that upon returning to Toronto they would stay away from Yorkville. Accusations that they had paid their subjects were dropped after a review of the film crews' respective 'kitties.'[114] Ultimately, the incident did little more than make for a great scene in Ransen's *Christopher's Movie Matinee*, in which the young Villagers read about the NFB's ejection in the newspapers. One of them smiles and says: 'I didn't even know I *was* a hippie!'[115]

6

Authenticity among the *Fleurs du Mal*

Toronto's Yorkville district was blamed yesterday for the downfall of Herbert Beed-
ell, 21, who was jailed one year for trafficking in narcotics here [St Catharines,
Ontario] ... Troubles began for Beedell, a musician, when he went to Yorkville and
'came under the spell of the hippies,' his lawyer, Frank Keenan, said.
                                        – Toronto Daily Star, 19 March 1967

My son's beautiful and I'm terrified! What's going to become of him?
                                        – Toronto Daily Star, 31 March 1967

In early September 1967, the popular CBC program *Newsmagazine* sent
host Knowlton Nash into Yorkville to make a fifteen-minute documentary on the Village. The result, a captivating glimpse into the district as
framed by the nation's public broadcaster, featured a lengthy conversation with a young man named Bill, a soft-spoken, aspiring writer. He
was, according to Nash's narration, 'a *real* hippie.'

This notion of the 'real hippie,' or the 'true Villager,' had begun to
matter a great deal. While down in San Francisco the Diggers were
preparing to hold a funeral for their co-opted community following
the hypefest that was the Summer of Love, Villagers were also struggling to draw lines around authentic Village identity. Nash's attempts
to define Villagers were coloured by such confusion. 'The real hippie
drop-outs,' he offered, 'who probably number only a few hundred,
have left society to contemplate their individual souls, usually with the
help of mind-expanding drugs like cannabis (that's marijuana), or LSD.'
But, to complicate matters, Nash then included a brief interview with a
young woman who declared that she didn't know what a hippie even

was. She then relented, drawing distinctions between 'real hippies' (of whom she figured there were only four in Yorkville) and what she called 'summer help.' Nash then returned to Bill, his central character, a supposed representative of these 'real hippies.' 'If enough people drop out of the society, it'll be altered,' Bill proclaimed, in his sleepy manner. 'It may eventually be the creation of a subculture. A large enough sub-culture could modify the existing culture.'[1] But Bill, though articulate and informative, was not being at all ingenuous with the CBC reporter. Nor was he even any kind of authentic hippie, at least in his own esti-mation. Rather, he was a paid volunteer, an expressive kid trapped in Yorkville by a lack of funds. Yet another one of Yorkville's soon-to-be famous artists, musicians, and authors, the star of Nash's documentary was none other than a young William Gibson.[2]

Years later, Gibson, by then an internationally renowned author of speculative fiction, was asked about his appearance in the CBC docu-mentary. 'Yep, that is indeed me,' was Gibson's reply, 'though nothing I'm saying there, at such painful length, is even remotely genuine. They were offering $500 for someone to monologue about the summer of lurve [sic]; And I was (1) somewhat articulate, and (2) wanted desper-ately to get my ass out of Yorkville.' He continued:

> In a universe where a furnished bedsit [sic] on Isabella Street (comfortably far from the site of this taping) rented for $25 per week, $500 was serious money. That isn't my girlfriend, by the way, but another media-opportun-ist, someone who smelled CBC money and welded her unshowered hip to mine as soon as she saw the cameras. They paid her, too, though not as much, as she didn't have a speaking part. So there are multiple layers of irony, in this ancient footage. I'm not, in spite of what they say, from Vancouver; I'm from Virginia and rightly anxious not to be recognized as such. I'm thoroughly fed up with the particular Children's Crusade being examined here, and want nothing more than a ticket out of it. My love-beaded sweetheart is someone I only know well enough to cordially dis-like.[3]

As the Village entered its fractious, desultory late period, distinctions between true or authentic Villagers and 'plastic hippies' or weekend-ers highlighted many discussions and appeared in most reporting. This authenticity – loosely defined, impossible to quantify – seems at the very least tied to commitment.[4] Dropping out of school, moving out of one's parents' house, taking acid and other mind drugs, accepting, supporting, or at least admiring radical politics, and generally distancing oneself from the establishment (whatever one takes *that* to mean) all combine in the ideal archetype of the true Villager. While William Gibson's little subterfuge was a means to an end (and in retrospect makes Knowlton Nash and his team look the fool), it also demonstrates the subjectivity of the authenticity gauge. Performance was everything – Gibson knew it, and he played the part on command when the offer looked good. As we survey Villagers' complaints over an influx of poseurs, weekenders, and plastic hippies, we would do well to bear in mind Gibson's performance, and what it tells us about the muddiness of the distinction between true and inauthentic performances of hip.

This chapter looks at key Village pastimes (namely, sex, drugs, and rock'n'roll) as they tangled with the dichotomous relationship between authenticity and imitation. With Village performances gaining ever more widespread exposure, 'Yorkville' events started to take place outside the confines of the district, offering new public sites for Village performances. As hundreds of curious newcomers flooded the scene, their degrees of commitment debated and decried by those who had come before, stark class divisions came to solidify categories of identity among Villagers, leading many to believe that, finally, hippies (who were always treated as the real Villagers by observers) were comprised of middle-class youth and defined against the working-class Others in their midst. Meanwhile, as sensational Village performances associated with LSD and other drugs, free love, biker coercion, and sexual violence were becoming widely acknowledged, many observers amped up the rhetoric around the idea that Yorkville represented a creeping menace.

Perception '67 and the Case against LSD

While marijuana had been a somewhat familiar proposition for Torontonians in the years prior to the mid-1960s, LSD was still undiscovered country by the end of 1966. A veritable artifact of the 1960s, and intrinsically linked to the character and verve of its youth culture, LSD promised a virtually authentic, total, and indelible experience. If the defining attributes of the 1960s youth movements were existentialism and the search for authenticity in pre-fab North America, LSD claimed to offer immediate gratification on both counts.[5] Here was a quick fix for your false consciousness, your angst, repression, and alienation: eight hours in Owsley's wobbly kitchen.[6]

Inexorable as love or madness, an LSD trip could last anywhere from six to ten hours, and might offer up myriad visions, perceptions, sensations, revelations – all apparently genuine while being, at least empirically, unreal. And so LSD offered an easy-access authentic experience, tailored to one's own psyche, immutable and iridescent and highly personal. If the existential quest is the unending pursuit of an authentic state of being beyond the *mauvaise foi* through which one has been conditioned, LSD's promise of near-total escape from social constructs and structures of normality established it as the existential drug par excellence. But its 'total experience,' for years thought by researchers and psychiatrists to be a chemically induced schizophrenia, did indeed mimic the effects of a psychotic break in its users. At its root an LSD trip has always been about wilful madness.[7]

One former Villager put the significance of LSD in bold relief:

> What happened to me was, after smoking a bit of pot, and really being quite embraced by the community as it existed, it just enlivened my imagination, broadened my scope. In short order I lost my virginity which was an enormous relief. And, as well, I took an acid trip. I'll never forget it: it was in one of those big old houses, I think it was on Bernard Avenue … It transformed life, it transformed the world, it broke down my sense of isolation, and all the constructs of the ego, you know, that we (not to get too philosophical or spacey on the whole thing), but we define ourselves through these internal constructs that we make our way through the world with. And it just swept all of that away.[8]

But for conservatives – for *most people*, regardless of politics or station – LSD's cosmic draw was simply impossible to comprehend. Here was a drug that was said to promote synesthesia (the profoundly disorienting perception-jumbling of, for example, hearing colours and seeing sounds), and people *wanted* to take it! This was deliberate insanity, a kind of self-induced psychosis – what did it mean that the children of the baby boom were trying to escape reality with such sincerity? But, since it was still legal in Canada to take LSD (it was illegal to sell it, but possession and consumption of the drug was allowed, if proscribed by virtually everyone), its place in the narcotic constellation was unclear at best.[9] Unclear, that is, until the right disaster turned LSD from a weird, provocative proposition into a malevolent, hulking killer.

On 16 March 1967 a twenty-year-old student at the Royal Conservatory of Music plunged to his death from the Bloor St viaduct, becoming Toronto's first LSD casualty.[10] John Stern, an aspiring musician, son of an upper-middle-class family from the Toronto borough of York, took the drug for the first time in his life at around 5 o'clock in the afternoon and was dead before midnight. With this tragedy coming less than a month after the much-vaunted Perception '67 festival at the University of Toronto – a three-day event designed around the idea of mind-expansion and psychedelic experience – Stern's apparently drug-directed suicide led many to speculate whether too much support was being afforded the chemical brew. It didn't help that Stern's father, grief-fuelled and biting, put the blame squarely on the shoulders of 'pseudo-experts' who glamorized the drug by suggesting that it might 'expand the horizons' of creative people. 'They murdered my boy – there's no doubt about that,' he declared.[11]

Initially designed around the artistic conceit of re-creating the psychedelic experience through sensory and aesthetic experimentation and stimulation, the centrepiece at Perception '67 was a kind of *faux* fun house replete with eerie sounds, disorienting visuals, and other unidentifiable sensations. The brainchild of twenty-four-year-old visual artist Michael Hayden, the Hayden Environment (also known as 'The Mind Excursion') was designed to imitate the psychedelic experience without drugs.[12] Employing a combination of film, slides, sound bites, lights, prepared textiles and other materials, and blaring music, it would attempt to offer disorientation, discomfort, and a vertiginous psychic experience to people presumably fearful of actually doing drugs.[13] This watered-down version of the LSD experience was, it seems, well publicized as part of an attempt to de-emphasize the centrality of drug use to the theme of the festival; it would allow non-drug-users to feel involved, to feel somehow connected to the goings-on, but ultimately offer nothing of the profundity of an actual eight-hour LSD experience.[14]

This is likely apparent even to the uninitiated, but taking a 'trip' through a fun house, which might last anywhere from ten to twenty minutes, during which one is surely at all times aware that the exit is right around the next corner, can hardly be compared to (for example) the often terrifying time loss that can accompany an LSD experience, an overpoweringly claustrophobic bewilderment that makes seconds drip by like minutes.[15] Still, according to journalist Robert Fulford (who was the first subject to explore the installation), this baffling ten-room LSD 'environment' comprised of 'horrible screams in the darkness ... eerie pulsing music ... creepy-crawly black plastic walls ... blinding lights and deafening sounds ... floors that don't feel like floors at all ... [and]

gigantic staring faces' was, as far as he could imagine, 'a remarkable success.'[16]

Perception '67 participant Judy Perly remembers the environment as less an attempt to re-create the LSD experience than just another in a series of sensory art exhibits popular at the time. 'They had these *environments*. University of Toronto had one. You would go in and feel like you were in a womb, very touchy-feely. What had happened was that smoking marijuana was getting people more into their bodies, more focused that way.' But these types of 'environments' were somehow understood to be diminished experiences. What was more popular, says Perly, was the developing art of light shows: 'You have to remember the Sixties were very visual. People were doing all kinds of stuff that was interesting. They had these light shows where they would paint discs with oil – it was all to do with drugs, to tell you the truth. So the whole idea was that you would smoke marijuana, or a lot of people were dropping acid and then they would go to these light shows.'[17] Perception '67, then, was part of a developing artistic movement towards invoking the sensory disarmament that accompanies psychedelic experience, but it was also part of a new paradigm in artistry devoted to creating art that was best experienced while under the influence of psychedelics.

Most of the installations and venues at Perception '67 were designed around a specifically drug-induced version of 'mind expansion.' Such notable (American) figures as Allen Ginsberg, Richard Alpert, Paul Krassner, Ralph Metzner, and a pre-recorded Timothy Leary all made the trip to Toronto to attend what would be a weekend-long celebration of the 'there' out there. (Dubbed a 'prohibited person,' Timothy Leary, who had been recently convicted on a drug-smuggling charge, was denied entry to Canada by Minister of Immigration Jean Marchand.[18]) Speeches, jam sessions, teach-ins, and Happenings comprised the two-day line-up, tickets for which sold out in a mere four hours to inquiring Torontonians eager to catch a glimpse of such psychedelic luminaries.

The brief festival, which culminated in a performance by New York-based rockers the Fugs at Convocation Hall, ultimately did little to foster new appreciations of LSD and the psychedelic pursuit. Rather, the festival seems to have been about preaching to the converted, about proselytizing on the richness and brilliance of LSD experience to a group of the 'Experienced.' Media coverage remained generally aloof, detached, and mildly amused by the sheer weirdness of the whole event. After they had registered such offhand praise as 'Groovy!' (Paul

Krassner), 'A Blast!' (Alpert), and 'Fantastic!' (Ginsberg), the *Star*'s Gary Dunford concluded that approval had been bestowed, at least by the super-famous-psychedelic-American community.[19]

But their praise for LSD was much less direct, and a good deal more complicated. Perhaps the most straightforward speaker was Leary associate and former Harvard professor Richard Alpert (who would be reborn as Ram Dass while studying in India later that year). Alpert took the provocative position that his use of LSD was a means to 'break the *status quo* and get to a meaningful future,' even if it meant '10 years of living like a psychotic.' But Paul Krassner, hip journalist extraordinaire, was more blasé about the role of LSD in his life. '[LSD has] about as much effect as an ice cream soda – I refuse to look upon it as a panacea,' he proclaimed, with trademark cynicism. What's more, he cautioned, 'there are far too many idiots taking LSD trying to avoid seeing their own idiocy.'[20]

Perhaps the most exciting session of the weekend was the head-to-head between writer-in-residence Earle Birney and *ur*-hippie Allen Ginsberg, an occasionally fascinating discussion of the role of the transcendent in the artistic process. 'There are times when art, or lovemaking or solitude or mountain-climbing or any human experience produces the same experience as LSD,' proclaimed the great bearded Beat poet, more than a little disingenuously. 'All the pill does is inhibit conditioned responses,' he concluded, instructing his audience that, while LSD can be transcendent and influential, so could Shakespeare or personal creativity itself. In a final bluff, Ginsberg underlined his hollow assertion that an acid trip and a *really good read* comprised basically the same event: 'Poetry,' he reasoned, 'offers a psychedelic experience.'[21]

But it wasn't poetry that inspired twenty-year-old John Stern to leap to his death off the Bloor St viaduct a few weeks hence. At least, that was the conclusion reached by his father, by MPP George Ben, and by a variety of influential Torontonians who worked to put LSD on the agenda in a much less celebratory way than did the organizers of Perception '67. Stern's death was front-page news, as was the fact that the young musician had attended a number of sessions at Perception '67.[22] Apparently Stern and a friend (identified only as Les) had been planning to take LSD 'for some time,' before they (somewhat inexplicably) went out to a hotel near the Toronto Airport (outside Toronto proper) to take their trip. Believing that 'if he tried LSD it would give him greater creative power,' Stern had read up on as much acid lore as he could find. He even tried to prepare his body for the maximum LSD effects by starving himself all day long, and dissolving the drug in hot water. At the last minute, Les got cold feet, and Stern took the drug on his own. After some initial euphoria, he began to fall into a 'deep depression,' and, while the two friends shared a cab back to mid-town Toronto, Stern became 'panic-stricken.' At this point, tragically, Les left his terrified friend and went his own way home. Some two hours later, Stern dove to his death, four miles from his parents' home in the borough of York, with a handwritten note in his pocket reading: 'The most important thing is to love God.'[23]

As the investigation into Stern's death picked up steam, fuelled by public concern and the kind of persistent media reportage usually afforded perfect cases in point such as this, information came to light which began to lay in some weight behind the claim that this death could be blamed on the recklessness of LSD's proponents. It turned out that not only had Stern attended Perception '67 with his friends, but he had also been present at a house party on Avenue Rd at which Richard Alpert himself had held court, preaching to his young flock on the value of the psychedelic experience. Sidney Katz, staff writer for the *Toronto Daily Star* and frequent commentator on the Toronto youth scene, concluded that 'much of the criticism directed at the US psychologists [Alpert, Timothy Leary, and Ralph Metzner] is justified,' citing what he called their 'irresponsible enthusiasm.'[24]

But, while it may have been Alpert's encouragement that had inspired the young man to take LSD for the first time, it turns out that what Stern ingested can only be described as a rather heroic dose of pure, 'clean' acid. The long-awaited shipment of uncut LSD had arrived from Chicago only a few days prior to Stern's death on 16 March, too soon for word to get around warning of its astonishing strength. Rather than being packaged in 200–300 microgram capsules (a standard 'dose'), these pills were each packed with about 500 micrograms of the mind-bending chemical.

If the only on-record account of dropping this particular batch of the drug is any indication, even the experienced were powerless to retain any form of control while riding that much pure acid: 'I took [two capsules for] what I thought to be a healthy dose – 400 micrograms. Judging by what happened, it must have been 1000 micrograms. I was so frightened I sat on the floor with my legs crossed, in the same spot, for five hours. I flipped out completely. I went through a complete mental and physical death. I was disoriented. I achieved a state of non-being. I wanted to go even further and get out of my body [and] one way of doing that is to destroy your body.'[25] So many trippers were finding the LSD experience too intense that psychedelic dealers began to realize that demand for their product might start to suffer. One former Village LSD dealer explained the situation: 'So what happened was that as people started having bad trips – and of course the press was relentlessly negative on the whole thing, throughout North America – I think the dealers cut the doses way down ... In fact I *know* it. The classic dose was about 250 micrograms – that's 250 millions of a gram. It was cut down from that to about 40 mics. Which will give you a buzz, but nothing like before. Later on, when I was intending to take a trip, and when I knew what the source was, I would often take six doses, which would move it up to the classic dose.'[26]

But *was* John Stern the victim of the hype surrounding LSD? Not according to *Satyrday*, which ran a scathing article condemning the 'sensation-hungry' press for propagating a fabricated story making out Stern 'to appear untarnished' in his personal life. 'What the fearless press did not report was that those who knew Stern in Yorkville say that he had at least 20 to 30 previous "trips" on LSD, and was obviously no stranger to its effects.' 'He was known by many as "Stern the Burn," a reference to his connection with the dope business in Yorkville ... Our informant and others said Stern kept his stash at his parents' home ... Did [his father] know, for example, that his son was pushing hashish and marijuana in Yorkville? His father charged that Yorkville was a bad influence on his son. Perhaps it was the other way around.' With this, one of the clearest examples of disagreement between *Satyrday* and the mainstream papers, we are left wondering: How did the mainstream papers miss this information? Or why would it have been suppressed? *Satyrday* offers its own interpretation: referring to Stern's death as 'the event our Establishment has been waiting for,' *Satyrday* suggests that whitewashing Stern's character might have been deliberate, a ruse to stir up anxiety over a new danger to middle-class youth.[27]

Oddly, while Yorkville found itself again at the centre of a drug hysteria (this time over LSD and suicide), some hip youth were turning away from the district while on their acid trips. 'Certainly for the first few trips,' explained an anonymous Villager, 'until you get your feet under you (so to speak) in that new world, it would be unwise to go into Yorkville.'[28] LSD-high Villagers were said to avoid the scene because folks were known to play 'mind games' on them, especially if it was clear that they were tripping. In one young man's description, such mind games could prove terribly frightening, even damaging to someone in such an altered mental state. (Of course, one man's 'terribly frightening' is another man's 'total experience' – the unpredictability of LSD was part of its allure.[29]) According to one unidentified Villager, some of the things these unfriendly people did (such as 'putting your face close to his and staring into his eyes, explaining that you can see directly into his brain') could make the defenceless tripper come unglued. The same young man (who, for these reasons, avoided Yorkville while tripping) was decisive about the potential damage such 'games' could cause. 'To the person under LSD,' he warned, 'the effects can be demolishing.'[30]

A demolishing experience on LSD was known in the Village as a bummer, or a 'bad trip.' One of the most pressing concerns for young people experimenting with the volatile and unpredictable drug was that, in general, Toronto hospitals and clinics hadn't the faintest idea of how to treat bum LSD cases. That is, until a newly minted, deeply non-conformist doctor came along. Having just completed in-depth research into the potent tranquillizer Valium, Dr Bill Clement was perfectly suited to the unpredictable field of Village medical treatment. Unlike most other doctors in the city at that time, Clement looked at LSD trips scientifically. While other doctors would simply strap stoned kids to a bed in the psych ward, zonk them on anti-psychotics, and watch them have a horrible time, Clement refused to avoid the issue so neatly. And so, at his clinic at Queen Street Mental Health, 'I developed a treatment procedure for bad trips.'

> Bad trips are, actually, acute anxiety-inducing synesthesia. Bear in mind that when we see somebody, when we saw somebody at Queen St, they walked in off the street usually accompanied by four or five of their friends who tried to talk them down. We had a limited staff, and limited resources. *No* resources. So, I came up with the brilliant idea: Valium is a neat little drug ... And here we had these kids coming in with acute anxiety. Why not give them, since the usual dose for Valium is ten mg, why not give him *fifty* mg? Because the drug results [for Valium] were incredibly safe.[31]

Clement's gambit worked. In fact, it worked so well that, before long, Villagers knew that if their trip went south, he was the man to see.[32]

Clement's deep knowledge of Valium also protected Villagers from the most common treatment at hospitals at the time, the anti-psychotic Thorazine.[33] 'No! Bummer! Some brilliant soul, a truly creative young man, discovered that if you added Ajax cleanser to your LSD you would get increased visual effects. And I mean, who doesn't want *that?* [*laughs*] I mean, you're getting the picture of the environment I found myself working in! So when you put the Ajax cleanser into the LSD for big visual effects, if you give the person Thorazine their blood pressure goes way up, and they die.'[34] The work Clement and his staff were doing at Queen Street didn't go unnoticed, especially in the LSD panic that engulfed the city after 1966.

Having been informed that a Toronto pharmacologist had developed a treatment strategy for LSD, the Poison Control Branch of the federal Department of Health came to Clement, asking for guidance. 'They say: will you write poison control cards for us? [I said] OK, give him fifty mg of Valium, put him to bed, and tell him to fuck off. In the morning he'll wake up and say: Oh boy, what a night. You'll say: how'ya feeling? He'll say: alright. Fine: you're discharged, fuck off. There are no after effects, no nothing. The only reason you keep them in the hospital [overnight] is that you've given them an overdose of Valium.'[35] (It is not impossible that Clement's recollection of this conversation is somewhat more colourful than the actual discussion. Still, the point remains the same.[36]) While the media and city hall fanned flames of fear with their repeated reports painting LSD as a leap off the precipice, Villagers (and, increasingly, young people all over the city) knew that if things got too weird, if their reaction was too intense, or if their friend seemed to have broken free of her moorings, there was a doctor a few blocks away who, perhaps uniquely in North America, had a method of treating their case that was both safe and effective.

Village Excursions: A Love-In, Wasaga Beach, and the O'Keefe Centre

As the Village approached critical mass, its population so swollen with the young, the curious, the lost, the enlightened, and the deeply stoned, it also spread beyond the confines of the Village proper. There simply wasn't enough room in Yorkville, which was crowded to the point of discomfort. Most Villagers didn't, *couldn't* live in the Village – even if they did spend many of their waking hours there. Still, it was the undisputed site for congregation, for community, for connection. And, in the absence of any other recognizable sites for the expression of Village identity, young people looking to partake in the counterculture simply headed for the one place they knew they could find it and play along.

Until the advent of large-scale rock concerts and festivals – which came into their own following San Francisco's successful Monterey Pop Festival in the late spring of 1967 – 'Yorkville' tended to take place in Yorkville. But now that the Village was becoming too hard to hold, too full to be contained, external sites for the expression of Village identity suddenly made more sense. Such expressions of Village community and youthful rebellion *outside* their expected and defined territory posed a confounding question for those who were busy railing against the horrors of *Yorkville*. The question was epistemological: How to understand a phenomenon, a youth identity, a 'foreign territory' that seemed ever more able to bleed through the figurative confines of its terrain? If this youth culture isn't Yorkville, what is it?

One way to approach the issue, and which managed to maintain both the heuristics of foreignness *and* geographic specificity, was to treat events at which significant numbers of Village youth congregated at sites *outside* their expected area as aberrations. Yorkville was a place, but it was also an attitude, a belief, a look, and a culture – and it did not belong outside its confines. When it appeared to be trying to spread to new areas, as it was seen (and feared) to be doing throughout 1967, authorities and residents collectively responded with distress and panic. Such events provided instances when what had come to be known as 'Yorkville' was most overtly exposed as a performance – it was a character that could be carried from place to place, all the while remaining tied to its apparent meaning: 'hippie.' The words now interchangeable in both the press and in the public imagination, Yorkville and hippie denoted place and identity as if they were the same things – as one study of the district concluded, 'the most important thing that we found out about the Yorkville image was that *Yorkville is hippies.*'[37] Consequently, countercultural congregations were, throughout 1967, treated as Yorkville field trips, populated by 'Yorkville types' and, in one memorable case, even decried as colonization schemes.

Toronto's first 'Love-In' was held on Victoria Day (a holiday Monday in late May) at Queen's Park, about a half-kilometre south of Yorkville. The (almost) impromptu and unstructured gathering attracted thousands of people from across Toronto and beyond, eager to participate in the unstructured celebration. An earlier attempt at developing a Love-In-type event, an Easter parade organized by Don Riggan and 'Blues' Chapman, had been a stale affair, marred by cold weather and a lackadaisical turnout. Ron Thody, writing in *Satyrday*, complained that 'it was hardly successful.' But, he quickly added, 'who's to put it down? At least the small, Yorkville hippy parade was a beginning and, as spring explodes in Toronto, bigger parades and a projected Human Be-In ... are being discussed.'[38] The main thing, explained Thody, was that the parade, replete with a theatrical crucifixion of a Village habitué named Spider, 'proved that Yorkvillians are doing more than sitting in loud cafés and dim coffeehouses and decrying the state of the world in relation to their own existence and that of straight society's. In other words, they are learning that it's great to dig the idea of love and brotherhood.'[39] Riggan and Chapman were equally inspired by the parade, even though it was somewhat less exciting than they had hoped. Collaborating with DePoe, they planned another, much larger event to be held in late spring, when the weather was more amenable. And so the Victoria Day Love-In was born.[40]

The Love-In was a variation on a theme established on 14 January in San Francisco at the famous 'Human Be-In' at which tens of thousands of young people had gathered to celebrate themselves and their community. This highly successful and symbolic event was soon repeated at another hugely attended Be-In on Easter Sunday in New York City.[41] By all accounts, Toronto's Love-In was equally successful – there were no arrests, no drug 'freakouts,' and none of the milling teens were nabbed for causing 'disturbances.' Rather, there was the spectacle of a concentrated phalanx of Villagers (and more than a few 'non-Yorkville' observers) whose colourful, jubilant performance of hip was on display outside the confines of Yorkville for the first time. For many observers of the scene, it was as if Yorkville itself had moved a block south – media sources used the words *hippie* and *Yorkville* interchangeably in their reports. And, just as Yorkville was known to be a favourite tourist destination for Torontonians looking to escape the reality of the rest of the city, the Queen's Park Love-In attracted so many 'sight-seers' that, according to the *Toronto Daily Star*, they outnumbered even the four or five thousand hippies.[42]

Bryan Palmer, Myrna Kostash, Doug Owram, and Pierre Berton have each emphasized this Love-In in their capsule histories of the Yorkville scene. For all, it represented a romantic, Dionysian moment, a happy calm before the inevitable storms of controversy that would overtake Yorkville later in the summer. To Kostash, writing roughly ten years after the event, the Love-In was characterized by 'languorous crowds meeting under the sweet greenness of the newly leaved trees, in long skirts and hand-painted rubber boots, carrying enormous paper flowers and kaleidoscopes, there to play music for each other and join in large dancing circles around the flute players, to admire young men with earrings and a rose behind the ear.'[43] Young Villagers approached passersby, offering them flowers and their love. Police, unsure of what their role should be, spent their time pulling long-haired teenagers down from trees. Leonard Cohen (with flowers behind his ear) and Buffy Sainte-Marie, by now established international stars, famously made the scene, playing a few songs. To Pierre Berton, the crowd was 'peaceful, naïve and winning.'[44]

Hans Wetzel, having recently formed a short-lived organization called the Yorkville Cultural Activities Committee with his fellow Diggers, had applied to the city for the necessary permits for the gathering. Although some bureaucracy snuck into the process, the city did issue the permits, leaving little in the way of legal obstacles for the throng at the jamboree. The police couldn't issue citations, not unless something unreasonable happened. Apparently, the only real offence reported all day was that a half-bed of yellow flowers had been picked by revellers looking for horticultural ornaments; still, the *Toronto Daily Star* managed to slip this minor infraction into its lead paragraph, for good measure.[45]

One month after the Love-In, as the oppressive heat of a Toronto summer descended, clinging as it does to the walls of high-rises, like a stifling bedspread no one can lift, a fair number of Villagers got the itch. Just north of Toronto, about an eighty-minute drive up the recently-completed Highway 400, lay escape: the long stretch of Georgian Bay beachfront known as Wasaga. Yorkville, of course, didn't really move en masse to Wasaga – the summer months saw the Village fill to overflowing with young people, pouring in from around the country – but a significant number of 'Yorkville types' *did*, at least for a time. Predictably, just like their counterparts back in Toronto, locals (especially merchants and residents) were none too pleased by the sudden arrival of long-haired youngsters. By 11 July, Wasaga Beach councillors were formally requesting more police to aid them in their drive to eliminate the 'long-haired bearded vagrants who sleep on garbage cans' from their vacation community. Citing shoplifting, all-night parties, and 'lovemaking,' Wasagans in the packed council meeting complained bitterly that the seven-mile stretch of beach was being overrun by 'hippies from Yorkville.'[46]

This conception of 'hippies from Yorkville' scattering through other areas was potent. Only a few months earlier, MPP George Ben had referred to Villagers as 'a cancer that is spreading through Metro' – now here they were colonizing a sleepy vacation town! Again, Yorkville was being treated as an identity all its own. In this case, Yorkville had spilled out of its expected locus, carrying the Villagers to Wasaga. However, this time their presence wouldn't stick. Armed with reinforcements from the Toronto police force, the Wasaga authorities managed to round up most of the offensive 'Yorkville types' and have them sent back either to the Village or, if they were young enough, into the arms of their parents.[47]

Reports of shoplifting and noise were the violations that precipitated this crackdown – and while the latter charge was likely pertinent and wide-ranging, one hesitates to believe that *all* of the young people beaching it in Wasaga were up to no good or (even less likely) stealing from shops. This crime simply wasn't reported in Yorkville; why should it be different in Wasaga? Reports of poverty, dirtiness, and hunger were more likely accurate (and they harmonize with most reportage on Yorkville in the era); but, still, none of these is a criminal offence. How could the Wasagans justify their round-up of hippies and 'drifters'? It seems that, having heard about what had become of Yorkville, the village council in Wasaga Beach was prepared to do whatever it took to rout a comparable takeover of its little town. And, for what it is worth, it worked: this would be no Yorkville North.

Meanwhile, by the end of July, Toronto had found a place on the map of North American youth scenes. This fact was not lost on San Francisco impresario and concert promoter extraordinaire Bill Graham, who could sniff out a market at fifty paces. In the Haight, his efforts at turning derelict buildings into premier concert venues had hugely influenced the development of the psychedelic rock'n'roll scene. With so many guaranteed stages to play, copious free publicity, and stoned, focused, dedicated audiences, bands had a degree of freedom in the Haight that they simply didn't have in most other scenes in 1967 (or, perhaps, ever since). It is no accident that some of the most exciting American groups of the psychedelic period happened to surface out of Graham's stable of local artists. The Grateful Dead, Jefferson Airplane, Quicksilver Messenger Service, and Big Brother and the Holding Company all honed their crafts on stages in rickety old buildings like the Fillmore and Winterland, two of Graham's best-known hotspots. But the Haight couldn't hold them for long – after the massive success of the Monterey Pop Festival in late spring, a veritable coming-out party for the San Francisco sound (as this new music was being called), Graham took his most popular bands on the road. 'That's when the fun began,' recalls Grateful Dead bassist Phil Lesh.[48]

On 23 July, around 20,000 turned out to see the Jefferson Airplane play a free show at Nathan Phillips Square, in front of Toronto's new, space age city hall. Perhaps the finest and certainly the most popular psychedelic band of the moment, the Jefferson Airplane's mix of blues, rock, folk, and even classical styles (the inexorable march of their acid-washed missive 'White Rabbit' is clearly based on Ravel's *Bolero*) defined the psychedelic sound. Boasting three vocalists, duelling guitars, and daring, un-encoded drug references in their surreal lyrics, they offered a new vision of the commercially successful rock'n'roll band. Loose, jarring, frequently sublime (but just as frequently inharmonious), the Airplane set a standard for scores of psychedelic rockers to follow.

Bill Graham's gambit – throw a free concert and then reap the financial windfall as kids clamour for more at a series of five subsequent paying gigs – demanded that the Airplane nail this first, teaser performance. Realizing what their promoter had gotten them into, the stress level in the band reached a peak in the days leading up to the show. 'If we are bad in Toronto, if we blow it,' moaned an apprehensive Spenser Dryden, drummer for the band, 'then nobody, but nobody is ever going to come and see us again.'[49] But he needn't have worried; Toronto was ripe for a *scene*, and a scene is what the Airplane would bring. As July slipped by, anticipation was peaking in the Village. Here was the authentic 'hippie trip,' the real deal, and it was coming to Toronto! Light show artist Joshua White sums up the exaggerated enthusiasm shared among many Villagers: 'For us this show *was* the San Francisco scene – the good vibes, the love – coming to Toronto.'[50]

For most of the psychedelic neophytes experimenting with the form in the Village, the city hall show was the first opportunity to see their forebears live. Peter Goddard, then a young rock journalist, was decidedly keyed up by what he witnessed on the makeshift stage. It was a happening, he was quick to recognize, that seemed to unite 'hippy havens from the Haight-Ashbury district of San Francisco to Greenwich Village to Yorkville' in praise of the 'one avant-garde God' that is rock'n'roll music.[51] The communion between artists and audience members was central to this presentation – the stage appeared somehow superfluous, everywhere at once, as the band and the audience united in a shared performance of psychedelic identity. The unity was remarkable: Jorma Kaukonen, crack guitarist for the Airplane, told Goddard, 'I've never seen such a crowd! Usually they come too [sic] look and sometimes to touch. But this group seemed to be getting into the swing of things.'[52] The audience splashed in the fountains, danced and spun in effortless circles, sharing the apples and candy tossed out to them by the band. 'Flowers, pagan amulets, tiny bells on girls' ankles, a general assortment of baubles, bangles and beards were in abundance, as were bare feet,' observed Goddard. For the thousands of Villagers, here was the opportunity to perform their Yorkville scene alongside some of their Haight-Ashbury contemporaries. But this was only the beginning: next stop was the decidedly high-brow O'Keefe Centre for a week-long engagement.

'*This* is the O'Keefe?' demanded the front page of the *Toronto Daily Star* on 1 August. Underneath an oversized photo of two gyrating Villagers, the *Star* marked the arrival of the 'San Francisco Scene' (as the tour named itself) with a mixture of shock and excitement. The Grateful Dead, the Jefferson Airplane, Yorkville band Luke and the Apostles, and hundreds of Villagers had taken over the venerable building, reports agreed, verily refiguring it with their incongruous presence.[53] But, while the audience helped to inspire the bands to perform (and vice versa), a series of stumbles threatened to overshadow the celebration.

Plagued by sound problems – 'the sound system had a buzzsaw noise in it,' according to Phil Lesh – the O'Keefe concerts led to mounting frustrations among band members. Exhausted from their hectic schedules, too many drugs, and the pressure of what they felt was an all-important show, the Grateful Dead came close to cataclysm: 'For the first time, Jerry [Garcia] and I started grumbling to each other about the music,' recalls Lesh. 'With too many shows and not enough rehearsal, the music wasn't moving forward to our satisfaction; [guitarist and vocalist] Bobby [Weir], being years younger and a bit spaced, became our target. We confronted him after the show about working harder to keep up.'[54] Long-time Dead fans may not realize just how close their favourite band came to breaking up after that first muddy performance at the O'Keefe. It probably didn't help that they were savaged the next day in a famous review in the *Globe and Mail*, panned in terms so vicious that Lesh recalls it as the worst appraisal he has ever read of their work: 'The review of our first night still cracks me up: "five simian men, presumably reeking with San Francisco authenticity … not volume, but noise … a jet taking off in your inner ear, while the mad doctor is perversely scraping your nerves to shreds." Wow, we got his attention, huh? At least we now know what we are – we're *Musimians*!'[55] Importantly, it is 'San Francisco authenticity' that the reviewer, Urjo Kareda, emphasizes, subtly including in his review of the Dead a denunciation of the whole scene that they were ostensibly there to represent.

The Dead may have played badly on that first night, but so did Yorkville mainstay Luke and the Apostles. The band, among the biggest draws on the Village scene, was ruthlessly denounced by a clearly exasperated Kareda. 'Amid their self-conscious, pretentious and stupefyingly awful performance, there was not a shred of talent,' he wrote.[56] Kareda's hostility was, again, not simply aimed at the music – he pointed fingers at the *scene* as well, attacking it for its flimsiness, for what he believed to be its insubstantiality.[57] Although preposterously harsh, his assessment reminds us just how central all of this performing was to the Village community, especially when it was occurring here, on a field trip (as it were) to the O'Keefe Centre. 'It was a pity,' he wrote, 'that the audience response which the group [Jefferson Airplane, which he actually enjoyed] inspired was frequently so superficial.' 'One revolting sub-teen stood onstage trying out a variety of Judy Garland gestures with no greater interest than having himself photographed. There were many like him; an objectionable distraction for those who had come to listen, and not to indulge in ludicrous self-exposure.'[58] Of course, not everyone was there to 'indulge' in such theatrics. For many, this first chance to experience a full-on San Francisco-style acid party carried great significance. For Villager Judy Pocock, it was a threshold moment. 'I do remember the first time I smoked marijuana,' she confided, 'and it was David DePoe that gave it to me! And that was the summer of 1967. We had come down from [a summer camp] to go and see the Jefferson Airplane and the Grateful Dead.'[59]

Heralded as a 'cultural revolution' in the *Toronto Telegram*, the O'Keefe shows are widely remembered by Villagers as a high point in their Yorkville experience, even though the concerts took place some two kilometres south of the district.[60] Getting high, hearing the blissful insanity that was the San Francisco sound, Villagers (and especially the musicians among them) found in that week-long engagement room to spread their wings, to explore, and to exaggerate their performances of Village identity. Dancing in the aisles, even on the *stage*, throwing flowers at the musicians, stoning themselves on acid, pot, and pills, the audience made the scene. The shows (which improved dramatically with each successive performance, leading up to a spectacular finale as all three bands jammed together onstage for an hour on the final night) have been collectively called the moment 'the old Toronto Sound died,' as, in the churning wake of that O'Keefe run, dozens of psychedelic bands were formed.[61] And, for Luke and the Apostles, it marked the end – they disbanded in triumph after that last epic jam session, as leader Luke Gibson (perhaps influenced by what he witnessed that week) found himself drawn to more psychedelic material than his blues-based Apostles could handle. Within a couple of weeks, he'd be asked to join the newly formed Kensington Market, a band that found itself almost immediately at the forefront of the Yorkville psychedelic sound.[62]

Bikers, Villagers, and Outlaw Chic

The First Annual National Convention of the Satan's Choice motorcycle club was held over a weekend in late September, in a farmhouse in Markham Township, just northeast of Toronto. Designed to 'promote good will and sociability within the club,' the two-day meeting of the notorious organization was also built around the inclusion of erstwhile rivals the Vagabonds into the fold. Some three hundred members of the Ontario-based Satan's Choice, representing eleven chapters including Oshawa, Kitchener, Windsor, Montreal, Peterborough, Guelph, St Catharines, and Kingston, were united for a weekend of partying, planning, and discussion. On Saturday, an all-night bender was held in the farmhouse, to which the Vagabonds were invited, and a football game between the Toronto chapters of the Choice and the Vags was on the books for the next afternoon.

Around midnight, some twenty-three policemen tried to break up the party but were beaten back under a shower of beer bottles, rocks, and drunken threats. They did, however, manage to come away with a case of beer and the cashbox from behind the makeshift bar inside, proof that the party was breaking more than noise regulations. According to the *Toronto Daily Star*, the officers were 'jostled, punched, kicked and spat on before they piled back into their cars and made what one officer said was "a tactical withdrawal."'[63] Within ninety minutes, scores of police officers were assembling, planning a raid to knock out the two clubs in one fell swoop, now that they could be charged with both liquor violations and assaulting police officers.

Back at the party, it seems that little was done to prepare for the raid, even though they must have known it was coming. Sure enough, at 4:00 a.m. on Sunday, the party came to a decisive halt as some thirty police cruisers, manned by eighty-four officers representing nine municipalities, descended on the farmhouse in what was one of the biggest raids ever conducted in Canada. Sixty-four bikers (including nine women whose allegiances are unclear) were hauled off to jail, including Bernie Joseph Guindon, the Choice's national president (and 'supreme commander'). Among the items seized were weapons (ranging from sawed-off shotguns and revolvers to axe handles and bike chains) and a giant stash of liquor. Some marijuana was also found, although it was specifically attributed to two of the men, while all sixty-four were charged with possession of dangerous weapons and being 'found-ins' under the Liquor Control Act. When the smoke cleared, those arrested faced a total of 131 charges. (The football game was cancelled.)

Since the riot of May 1966, the Vagabonds had been expanding their presence in the Village and, by the summer of 1967, were an integral part of the Yorkville landscape.[64] At first, their presence was considered by many Villagers to have been benign, even beneficial – in Frank Long-staff's account of the summer of 1966, the Vagabonds were described as the performers of 'an important service' in the Village. 'Not only do they keep other troublesome elements out, but in squabbles between different elements of Villagers they are often called in as arbitrators and policemen.'[65] Some of the Vagabonds also sold drugs, which many Villagers believed was a necessary service. But, as their interest in the district increased, so did reports of the more untenable performances associated with the exaggerated masculinity of biker culture – especially intimidation, violence, and sexual assault. The Vagabonds, having taken over a house in the Annex 'which serves as their headquarters and a place to take their girls for parties,' began to colonize other local spots, seeking to expand their area of influence. Over the summer of 1966, for example, they tried (unsuccessfully) to oust the university students from the Place Pigalle (or the Pig) and turn it into their own haunt. Eventually, they gave up and subsequently set up shop in the El Matador. While one observer could optimistically claim that, by September, 1966, 'they [Vagabonds and other Villagers] live in a state of peaceful co-existence with co-operation but few friendships crossing the group lines,' there is no doubt from his report that the main reason they were tolerated was that their presence in the Village helped to demarcate the space as a Vagabond area – a trick that tended to keep out *other* biker clubs such as the fearsome Satan's Choice or Para-Dice Riders. For many, the Vagabonds constituted the lesser of some fairly serious evils.[66] 'For them, of course, it was all about predation, basically,' explains a former Village dealer. 'They were there to exploit a market, you know, muscle their way around. It was a kind of, you were kind of dealing with the devil in a sense. But at the same time, we were trying to get this [LSD] experience to people. So you found yourself agonizing about it a bit.'[67]

The relations between bikers (hardly the poster boys for peace, love, and good vibrations) and other Villagers were thus often strained. Running as they did along class lines, these identity categories appeared incompatible on a pretty fundamental level. And, in many cases, it was the question of aggression and violence that kept bikers and other Villagers apart. 'I mean, we didn't have much to talk about,' goes one recollection. 'You just don't share the values. But, of course, they engineered the *importations*; I mean, they brought in great whacks of pot, so there'd be *that* interaction.'[68] However, in their parallel attempts to articulate a performative distance from mainstream society, the two groups could often sound rather similar. 'I don't care what society thinks,' explained John 'Tiny' Taylor, president of the East Toronto chapter of the Satan's Choice in 1965. 'But, they're nothing anyway. They're no better than me. Out there you just have to fit into a pattern that somebody's already laid out for you. Life we live, you have to set your own patterns, your own ideals. You have to handle the whole job yourself.' As it was for other Villagers, this reverence for authentic individualism was undergirded by a central refusal of acquisitive material culture. 'To them, life is getting a college education and making ten or fifteen thousand dollars a year and being able to keep up with the Joneses, being able to make enough money to spoil their kids rotten. Money, to them, is life. But it's not. It's not.'[69] Coming together on such issues, many hippies and bikers alike were willing to look past the chasm that separated them (ideologically, materially, philosophically) after word had come down from the Haight that their counterparts there were working, living, and partying together. As Murray McLauchlan recalls, beginning at or around the same time, 'people in the Village attached a certain kind of glamour to bikers in those days.'[70]

At a month-long party in California, Ken Kesey and the Merry Pranksters had thrown one of their famous Acid Tests at which they dosed the Hell's Angels (the most fearsome bikers in California, if not the whole of the United States at the time) in an effort to convince them that their anti-establishmentarian pursuits were not mutually exclusive. 'We're in the same business,' the psychedelic prophet famously told the Angels. 'You break people's bones, I break people's heads.'[71] Even their language was shared: the Pranksters had borrowed (and disseminated) the Angels' term for a lousy ride (a bummer) to describe a bad trip on

LSD.[72] For the Angels, the motorcycle represented freedom, authenticity, community; for the Pranksters and a growing mass of 'heads,' it was acid.

To the shock and dismay of many observers, the Angels seemed willing to try this supposed wonder drug; but some of their fears were assuaged when, at least at first, tripping seemed to make the Angels peaceful.[73] Allen Ginsberg notoriously called them 'angelic barbarians,' as excited as was Kesey by what was thought to be the bikers' primitive authenticity and utter disregard for order and convention.[74] According to Charles Perry's history of the Haight, the shock of witnessing the scene at Kesey's ranch during that period of first contact between the Pranksters and those 'angelic barbarians' was nothing short of paralysing: 'You'd come over the footbridge to Kesey's wooded retreat, get your LSD-dosed pill, watch the Angels gang-bang some willing girl, chip in for spaghetti, [or maybe] wander around the woods among the sculptures and unexpected microphones.'[75]

In the Village, this merging of worlds took place at a slower rate, and minus the crucible of Kesey's LSD-themed yard. However, it was happening through 1966 and into 1967, as a group of Vagabonds took up residence and began to hang out at the El Matador. Their leader, Edjo, was a familiar sight, cruising his big red convertible up and down the streets, looking for someone to cop his dope or a few girls who might be interested in trying out their free love on him.[76] 'The Matador was the bikers' coffee house and clubhouse,' explains 'Wild Bill.' 'Anytime you'd walk in there you'd see three-quarters of the guys in there were bikers.' But that other 25 per cent were those who, taking a page out of Kesey's book, felt unthreatened by the outlaw culture of the bikers.[77]

In the context of a *Bonnie and Clyde*-infused hip scene – the angrily anti-establishment film's mid-August Montreal première met thunderous support from young audiences – violence, especially political violence, was harvesting consent, respect, and even a certain existential appeal.[78] As the gorgeous, youthful, and vivacious criminals blazed across the screen late that summer, a braless Faye Dunaway sporting an equally historically inaccurate beret, Warren Beatty embarrassing the authorities with a winning smile and a gun, the idea of violence seemed that much more viable, that much more *fashionable*, to the gathering youth movements. As Pauline Kael argued in an extraordinary review of the film, the significance of *Bonnie and Clyde* lay in the way it invited its audience to identify with its frustrated, disaffected, bored, murderous, and yet somehow *glamorous* anti-heroes. 'By making us care about the robber lovers,' she concluded, '[*Bonnie and Clyde*] has put the sting back into death.'[79] *Their* death, that is – the sting was never felt so keenly as in the movie's final moments, as horrific hales of tommy-gunfire riddled the eponymous couple. Somehow, the good guys killing the bad guys here seemed disgusting, oppressive, ferocious in its excessive, uncompromising violence. Bonnie and Clyde were killers, sure, but they were also beautiful, young, sexy, unfettered, and free – until the establishment, cowardly hiding in the underbrush, tore those perfect bodies to shreds in a chorus of a thousand bullets.

If an existential search for authenticity animated the hip appreciation of identity, then revolutionary violence, if understood as an authentic expression of radical selfhood, may be considered distasteful but can never be denied.[80] The late 1960s saw the glamorization of violence (especially when directed against the establishment, however loosely defined) take hold of a variety of youth social movements, many of which had previously been focused upon the pursuit of peace through non-violent means. Into this context, hip respect for (and pursuit of) the bikers fits somewhat more easily.[81] Although recognized as dangerous, the bikers represented the radical refusal of normality that many Villagers professed to respect above all things. (As one rider with Satan's Choice put it: 'I just like to spit in society's face because I'm doing what *I* want, and they're doing what everybody *else* wants. That's the whole thing.'[82]) Theirs was an apparently authentic performance – of working-class angst, perhaps; of primitive masculinity, id-fulfilment, anti-establishmentarian self-interest, radical carpe diem. A young biker woman – one of the precious few whose voice I have uncovered – told a filmmaker in 1965 that the reason she rode with Satan's Choice was primarily 'the thrill. The feeling you get … it's like all your words are gone. That's what I always feel.' But she added that she was drawn to the biker scene for its authentic lifestyle. 'I like the people. They're genuine people. They're not phony at all. A front is put on, but it's not a real front. It's just their way of life.'[83] Frightening, mysterious, and darkly attractive, bikers were thus mythologized as fellow travellers in the great pursuit of living otherwise.

By no means were all Villagers over the moon about the presence of bikers in their scene. Ambivalent Villagers often avoided them but knew that to be tight with these hulking dudes was to have achieved a certain status in the community. DePoe, Riggan, and Chapman, for example, all hung around with bikers and made a point of trying to include them in Village politics. Indeed, some very colourful charac-

ters became known to the Villagers after the Vagabonds began to inte-
grate into the scene. As DePoe recounts: 'Murray McLauchlan lived
on Hazleton with this guy called Moses, a member of the Vagabonds,
who was sort of a philosopher type. He was a deep thinker, y'know?
He read, which was unusual for a biker. Every winter he would take
his Harley apart in the front room of the house and fix it all up and
then put it back together. He had this mighty Wurlitzer in his kitchen
with the most amazing collection of 45s on the planet. Blues, y'know,
just an amazing collection: early rock'n'roll and R&B, and all kinds of
stuff. And he just played whatever he wanted in his kitchen.'[84] And yet
these lively characters were also part of a gang structure which was
well known to practise terrible violence.[85] McLauchlan was under no
illusions about what his roommate was involved in: 'They knew there
was money to be made in Yorkville, with a healthy market in grass and
speed ... Make no mistake about it, your average motorcycle gang *is* a
criminal organization.'[86]

Gang splashes (as gang rapes were known to Villagers at the time)
cannot be divorced from other biker involvement in the Yorkville scene.
The offhand definition of the practice offered by 'Wild Bill' suggests
just how routine such violent exploitation of Village women may have
been for some bikers: 'The splash thing ... they would literally, four
or five guys were sharing a place, and one of the guys would pick up
a girl. Well, if you're gonna bring her back over to the house, we're
gonna all have fun with her. Get her stoned, and splash her.'[87] The
Diggers' and other male Villagers' wilful ignorance of this side of the
biker scene remains confounding today. DePoe, for example, doesn't
pretend that rape and sexual exploitation wasn't going on between the
bikers and other Villagers, but he never suggests that much was done
to stop it from happening. 'The Vagabonds. I mean, they did things
that we didn't like. Like gang rape. You know? They would call girls
a *splasher*. And they'd take her to their clubhouse and they'd, ten guys
would, y'know, basically fuck her, and that's what they did. Right? So
I mean *that* stuff we didn't like.'[88] Interestingly, DePoe's fellow Digger
Clayton Ruby doesn't recall bikers as being of much importance in the
scene. 'I think they wanted to exploit the women,' he recalled, but he
remembered there being 'no [sexual violence] that I would see.' However, his reasoning as to why the bikers likely didn't have to resort to
rape seems problematic: 'There was lots of sex everywhere. So the need
for sexual violence, people would scratch their heads and say: "Why,
what's the point? Go meet somebody down the block, somebody that's

interested."'[89] The reality was that, over the following years, rape, gang splashes, and a variety of other degrading and outrageous acts of violence against women were indeed a part of the Village scene, as they would be in other hip centres around North America.

Bikers, often as part of initiation and hazing rituals, would use women from the Village as entertainment, preying on their youth, relative innocence, and what they hoped was a naive toeing of the free-love line.[90] If the biker philosophy was 'booze, fuck and ride,' as one Vagabond member put it in late 1967, all were expressions of identity and status – how much could you drink, ride, fuck?[91] 'With sex, with girls, I'll admit there were certain things done,' discloses 'Wild Bill.' 'The girls would, literally, if you had a place to crash, would put out. Now, you can have a girl come and stay in your apartment, two girls, three girls, their friends, they'll come to your apartment thinking that by three of them coming to one guy's apartment they're protected. That they'd protect each other. It don't work that way. Because [once] I walked girls home, three or four girls together, from the Village scene and ended up screwing all three of them.'[92] Safety from sexual violence, then, wasn't found in numbers. And its pervasiveness is apparent in all of the material at our disposal when studying the post-1966 Village scene.

In one of the few extant contemporaneous interviews with a Village biker, violence and sex were indeed foregrounded, even conflated. The interview subject, described as a working-class, eastern European immigrant, explained that biker violence, including sexual violence, was always about status. 'The girls we picked up were horrible,' he began. '[But] it was a desperation type of thing. You have to participate in sex to keep up. Toughness was important – being able to show scars, carry around knives and beat up guys. When you have a car, you drive around and you pick up some sluts – basically they were sluts ... And you have a little party, not much of a party, just where you can get drunk so you don't see how ugly the broad is. The broad is also drunk and she doesn't know what is happening to her either.'[93] With everyone overdrinking to insulate themselves from their mutual disgust, this was sex for the sake of sex, violence for violence's sake, more about peer pressure than satisfaction. At least in this formulation, the women were objects used to promote male power within the organization; the purpose of sex was to impress, to justify a guy's presence in the biker club. Certainly the epithet 'slut' – used here to in some way blame the young woman for what was done to her – seems misplaced when one learns that this apparently sexually promiscuous woman still has to be obliterated on booze before she will submit to their advances.

Even the *Voice of the Annex*, a community newspaper prepared by and for the residential neighbourhood immediately west of Yorkville, openly reported the presence of biker gang-rape apartments on their blocks, whose residents were 'using strong-arm methods to extort money and girls from Yorkville Hippies.'[94] This commodification of women, and the open expectation that trade in money and women could be somehow equated, colours numerous such reports from the period. Women within the biker fold were often treated as property and were subject to severe repercussions if they ever tried to escape their man. Gopala Alampur, observer of the scene in 1967–8, outlined the kinds of horrors perpetrated upon one woman who tried to leave the Vagabonds: 'The motorcycle girls are vulnerable if they are abandoned by their "old man" because they face the alternative of cutting their association with the gang or possibly being gang splashed. There is kudos [sic] associated with unusual sexual practices such as oral-genital stimulation and intercourse in groups of three to fifteen people. One girl was forcibly taken by 12 motorcycle gang members to Windsor where she was gang splashed three times in 36 hours. The resulting extensive vaginal hemorrhaging over several weeks may have caused permanent damage.'[95]According to June Callwood, such an outrage was 'common' but only very rarely reported to police, parents, hospitals, anyone. 'You get raped by a million people,' she explained, 'and the last thing you want is that anyone knows. It's your shame that it happened. Well, that culture prevailed at the time. You got gang-raped and you didn't tell anybody.'[96] Such a culture of silence was exacerbated by the apparent alliance between Villagers and bikers. How does the 'do your own thing' philosophy fit into a context in which my 'thing' is gang-raping women? This debate was just as significant in other hip centres around North America: recall Tom Wolfe's famous depiction of the gang rape of a semi-coherent woman by a throng of Californian Hell's Angels 'until she had been fenestrated in various places at least fifty times.'[97] And this in the context of an alliance of sorts between the Angels and the local hippies?

Among the revelations following the raid on the Markham biker convention in September 1967 was that the Satan's Choice had been conscripting Villagers to come up to the party to be assaulted. Shortly before the raid on the farmhouse, an eighteen-year-old woman was discovered lying naked, semi-conscious and in serious condition, in a ditch near the party. Rescued by a passing motorist, she was rushed to Scarborough General Hospital where she was found to have severe internal injuries, the result of a brutal gang rape. All she was able to tell police was that she remembered nothing after leaving Yorkville to go to the party. Her boyfriend had reported her missing just around the time that she was found. Terrifyingly, one of the bikers interviewed by the press explained that the reason only around eighty-five club members were present at the farmhouse at the time of the second raid was that everyone else had gone down to Yorkville to 'pick up something to eat and pick up some fresh girls.'[98]

To be sure, rape was not only a biker issue in the Village. For example, the rape of an eighteen-year-old woman in a Prince Arthur St flophouse had recently raised the attention of humanitarians, media, and authorities alike at the time of the biker outrage in Markham. The young woman had been walking along Yorkville Ave looking to meet a girlfriend when she was grabbed by a twenty-two-year-old man and brought back to the nearby house. She was raped in a locked room, upstairs, screaming loudly enough to alert neighbours to the assault. While the dozen or so others living in the house attempted to break down the door to the room, she managed to get free, escaping to the street where she hailed a taxi to bring her south to College St and the police. Everyone in the house, even those who had tried to save her from her attacker, were busted for vagrancy and spent the night in jail.[99]

In the ensuing weeks, attention picked up in the courts and among City Council members to the possibility of widespread sexual violence in the Village. Young women, often arrested on vagrancy charges, were routinely sent home to their parents under the condition that they would never return to Yorkville.[100] In early October, following a Ravi Shankar concert at which some two thousand Villagers revelled in his suddenly hip take on Indian classical music, a thirteen-year-old girl was busted on drug charges, fuelling the debate.[101] By November, the *Globe and Mail* was reporting on what it feared was rampant prostitution in the Village as young women had no other means to make ends meet. As ever more young people seemed to be disappearing into the vortex at Yorkville and Avenue Rd, anxious parents were seen wandering the streets holding photographs of their missing children, frequently shockingly young.[102] Taking advantage of the apparently lucrative situation, a Toronto-based private-detective agency began running ads on the CHFI radio station under the slogan: 'Lost your son or daughter in Yorkville? We'll find them for you.'[103]

The Self-Fulfilling Prophecy: Violence and Authentic Village Identity

On the evening of 10 May, a thirty-seven-year-old father of four named William Brigaitis was murdered in front of the Penny Farthing after a brief confrontation. Following a dinner for insurance underwriters at a nearby hotel, Brigaitis and four colleagues had decided to walk through Yorkville, apparently 'to see how the Villagers live.' Along the way, the men got into a fight with a pair of teenage boys – it was never made fully clear as to who started the scrap. At some point during the altercation, one of the teens jumped onto a three-foot brick wall and, from this elevated position, kicked Brigaitis in the head. Reeling from the blow, Brigaitis dropped hard. Too stunned to put his hands out to break his fall, he struck his head against the concrete on his way down, fracturing his skull and causing bleeding in his brain. As the assailant ran off, chased by the victim's friends and some other witnesses, Brigaitis's limp body was carried into the Penny Farthing. He never regained consciousness and was subsequently pronounced dead on arrival at Toronto General Hospital.[104]

The following day, City Council members were offered what stands as the most remarkable suggestion for legislating youth out of Yorkville. Citing Brigaitis's awful fate, Controller Herbert Orliffe concluded that Torontonians (and Canadians in general) needed to go further to take back control of their teenagers and (by implication) their streets. Something had to be done to 'help these undisciplined young people,' he explained. And so, although admitting that this solution might not 'fit in well with our democratic way of life,' he proposed that Toronto 'send these people to work camps.' His plan was simple: if unemployed young people drifted into Yorkville, they would become eligible for a 'draft,' 'just like the U.S. Army does it.' Then they would be sent to camps, where they would be instructed in a 'useful trade' and where they could 'work off their frustrations.'[105]

Although Orliffe's suggestion was generally disregarded as extremist, its significance was not lost on Villagers sensitive to the idea that the Brigaitis murder was being used as an example of Village reality. One Villager (writing under the name Kama Gilboe) suggested in a letter to the editor that Orliffe's remarks were 'asinine' since murder was by no means a commonplace occurrence in the Village.[106] Not only that, but 'the young man who has been jailed is not a "villager" and does not characterize what the Yorkvillians believe in and stand for.'[107] The murderer's performance was all wrong – although the incident did indeed take place in Yorkville, in front of one of its most popular hangouts, and although the battle was between a young man and an older man, Gilboe emphasized that this wasn't to be connected to Village identity. It wasn't, Gilboe stressed, 'true' Village behaviour.

But violence was, for at least some of the young people frequenting the scene, a reality, and a vital identity performance. As one Villager put it, 'I love fighting – I can be mean and I can be good.' For this young man, the basic moral and ethical divide was most starkly proclaimed through the relationship between might and right. 'You can tell by fighting whether you are right or wrong,' he declared. 'If you lose, you are wrong.' Unsurprisingly, perhaps, the young man believed that 'fighting [was] one way for the greaser to establish his identity.'[108] Thus, in the eyes of some Villagers (and a growing number of observers), the line between 'true' Village performances and inauthentic versions of said same ran along the class divide.[109] In one key editorial, Ron Haggart, known as a staunch defender of the Village, condemned outbursts such as Orliffe's while suggesting that the real problem with Yorkville was everyone *but* the peaceable Villagers themselves. Citing the lamentable failure of the Fish Net, the recent refusal of the Diggers' request for a shelter for Village youth, and persistently ignorant editorializing from the *Toronto Telegram*, Haggart concluded that 'Yorkville may eventually become the crime belt and the centre for bums and hoodlums that the magistrates, the politicians, and the crown attorneys thought it was a year ago … But the people to blame will not be the kids of Yorkville, who tried so desperately to make Yorkville their own.' Haggart argued that repeated assertions that Yorkville was rife with violence, vice, and criminality were the reason violence, vice, and criminality were on the rise in the Village. Accepting wholesale the assumption that authentic Village identity was reflected in a middle-class hippie performance, and thus viewing the presence of the working-class toughs as aberrant, Haggart stood by the vision of Yorkville as a hippie space marred by the intrusion of these others. 'If Yorkville now falls apart,' he chided, 'if Yorkville now fails as a centre for peaceful and passive nonconformity, essentially controlled by young people themselves, a great deal of the blame will rest on an arrogant officialdom unable to distinguish in its own middle-aged mind between hippies and hoodlums.'[110]

For the next six months, William Brigaitis's murderer, a seventeen-year-old named Ziggy Nowoszynski, sat in prison, charged with man-slaughter.[111] Although young, at no point was he fashioned into a cause célèbre for Villagers. Instead, he was treated as an outsider. Nowoszynski was a teenager from the Danforth area of Toronto (an immigrant-[especially Greek-] heavy enclave three kilometres east of Yorkville). Judging by his neighbourhood and his non-Anglo name, he fits the umbrella description of greaser and was treated as such. Even though he and his comrade both testified that they were being threatened by Brigaitis and his four friends, and that those men had come to Yorkville specifically to start a fight with Villagers, it seemed that no one believed his testimony. When both of the teenagers testified that Nowoszynski had kicked the man out of fear for his own safety after being cornered by Brigaitis and being called a 'punk,' there was no public outcry, and no Villagers came to his defence. And, when Nowoszynski was finally found guilty by the Supreme Court in mid-October, there were no protests on his behalf, and no editorials decrying his scapegoating.

Given the extraordinary coverage of the Village and all things connected to it, it is surprising that this case received so little press attention. Apart from the initial flurry of interest in the days after the event itself, little was written on it in the major papers until the trial, and then only short, matter-of-fact articles were slipped in towards the back of the editions. While Hans Wetzel had the details of his case (hearsay and otherwise) outlined by champions like Ron Haggart, and had his life story laid out for a wide audience in lengthy articles, Nowoszynski's biography remains a mere sketch. He was seventeen (or was it eighteen? It seems the newspapers were unsure). He was on probation at the time of the altercation with Brigaitis (but for what?). He was from a working-class area. He was named Zigmond (or Zigmonde?) Nowosynski (or Nowoszynski?). The one thing about him that was most loudly proclaimed, that seemed indisputable, was that he didn't *belong* in Yorkville. ('There are two kinds of people who frequent the Village,' wrote Yorkville poet Eric Layman in late-August 1968, 'those who belong there; and those who don't but think they do.'[112]) Ultimately, all that was made public knowledge about this case was that a teenage boy came to the Village, got into a fight, killed a man with one kick, and was completely disowned by the community. As Kama Gilboe had proclaimed, regardless of what he may have thought about himself and his place in the scene, Nowoszynski was inauthentic, an outsider, a pretender to the 'true' Village identity.

Perhaps this is why Nowoszynski, while awaiting sentencing,

removed his reading glasses, broke one of the lenses, and tried to tear open his wrists. A guard, hearing him moaning in pain and fright, found the teenager lying in a pool of blood. Nowoszynski survived the attempt, only to be sentenced two days later for manslaughter. Although it was generally agreed that he hadn't meant to kill Brigaitis, he *had* intended to kick him. During the sentencing it was revealed that the probation officer who had visited Nowoszynski the day before the suicide attempt had warned officials at the time that he had concerns the young man would try to kill himself. Nothing was done to protect him. Instead of pity, a bandaged Nowoszynski was offered censure for his suicide attempt. 'I am giving you the opportunity to learn a trade,' scolded Justice Eric Moorhouse while handing the seventeen-year-old four years in the penitentiary. 'Don't feel sorry for yourself,' he advised.[113]

The tragedy of Ziggy Nowoszynski, who took a life for no good reason and paid with so much of his own, doesn't end in the Kingston Pen. In early October 1972, a few months following his release, he attended a house party on Gloucester St, less than a kilometre south of Yorkville. At the party, Nowoszynski was handed a rifle to admire. The loaded gun went off, killing the twenty-two-year-old.[114]

White Slavery Just North of Bloor: Narratives of Sexual Danger

In the mid-1950s Herbert Marcuse, German émigré and soon-to-be hip philosopher par excellence, prefigured the embattled role that liberated sexuality would play in the coming counter-hegemonic struggle: 'In a repressive order which enforces the equation between normal, socially useful, and good,' he predicted, 'the manifestations of pleasure for its own sake must appear as *fleurs du mal*.'[115] Indeed, the 1960s saw both an increase in youth activities that appeared to be chasing the 'pleasure principle' and a proportional increase in often hysterical reactions from authorities, unable or unwilling to comprehend the refusal of the equation between *socially useful* and *normal*.

Throughout 1967 we have seen various incarnations of this hysteria, this confusion, this sometimes over-the-top rhetoric and condemnation of hip behaviour. But, just as this frenzy maintained distinctions between the degeneration of middle-class youth and the (less-unexpected) corruption of Others, the gendered response to Yorkville was equally uneven. While men, the archetypal Villagers, and certainly the expected embodiment of the category 'authentic hippie,' were castigated for their apparent rejection of work, mainstream fashions, and masculine responsibility, women were repeatedly constructed as victims, powerless to resist the magnetic sway of this archetypal Village man.

Late autumn saw a spate of articles published in all three major newspapers exploring narratives of sexual danger in the Village. In each, the dominant themes were older (male) hippies using drugs to lure young, otherwise uncorrupted girls (read: *virgins*) into their 'pads,' stoning them on pot or LSD, and making them into their sex toys. In each article, the young women are presumed to have little sense, few tools at their disposal, and a marked inability to make decisions for themselves. They stray innocently into Yorkville, drawn by the docile allure of hip authenticity, and they leave (*if* they leave) fallen, corrupted, damaged.[116]

Drugs played a significant role in this construction. The repeated warnings that male Villagers would coax young girls to their apartments with the promise of dope worked on two levels: on the one hand, they stressed the fascination with marijuana and LSD that had become endemic over the past few years, and on the other they played on fears that 'innocent girls' were making decisions while suffering drug-induced incapacitation. Both of these arguments were no doubt fair, inasmuch as many young women were indeed coming to Yorkville, especially after 1965, drawn by the promise of sex and drugs. Many teenager girls were indeed trying pot and sex in Yorkville for the first time, and often with men who were older and more experienced. But the way media framed such activities failed to appreciate that perhaps a great many of these young women *wanted* to get stoned and laid. Because their desires, decisions, and intelligence were assumed to be either wrong, naive, or drug-induced, and because they were imagined to be under the spell of some authentic hippie ideal, such frames stripped Village women of agency. *Satyrday*, perhaps in an attempt at a backhanded feminist argument, responded to such allegations with a shrug: 'The parties that are so concerned with the widespread use of pot and L.S.D. ... blame the cheap movie image of the corner dope pusher for seducing the minds of twelve year old innocents. [But] he is, as far as we're concerned, a friendly neighbourhood figure, or at worst an opportunist.'[117]

Historian Catherine Carstairs's work on the social history of narcotics in Canada prior to 1961 explores the ways in which 'white slavery' narratives were employed in the 1920s to vilify Chinese Canadians. It is remarkable how the race-based anxiety that she describes can be used to illustrate the discourse of hip sexual danger so prevalent throughout 1967 and beyond. 'The "victims" of the "evil Chinese drug traffickers" were always young,' she explains, 'and the narratives of their corruption fed into long-standing fears about the dangers posed by urban environments and unsupervised leisure.' Notions of female vulnerability allowed authors to portray some women as blameless victims of 'drug addiction disease.' Many stories of female drug users were copied directly from 'white slavery' narratives – a young woman was taken in by an older person, drugged, and then forced to earn a living through prostitution.[118]

In a curious update on those old anxieties that used to keep anti-drug activists like Emily Murphy hunched over their typewriters, such frames reinforced the notion that Yorkville's foreignness was inherently wicked. While Murphy, writing in the early 1920s, vilified Chinese Canadian men by propagating the myth that they used opium to turn white women into drug-addled sex slaves, Don DeLaplante of the *Globe and Mail* disparaged hippies in much the same way in late autumn of 1967. 'Older hippies,' he reported in a seminal front-page exposé, 'are preying on the girls as a form of free sex and leading them into prostitution.'[119]

DeLaplante's article is dominated by alarming quotations from police officers, each one reinforcing the claim that young girls (helpless, pathetic, and immature) were bound to suffer sexual exploitation in the Village. Deputy Chief Bernard Simmonds, for example, offered an uncomplicated vision of the degenerative powers of the district: 'The real evil of Yorkville is what is happening to these young girls. They come to the Village as good kids, mixed up perhaps, many from fine homes, and these beatniks grab them and within two days they are ruined.' For his part, the sergeant in charge of Yorkville's plainclothes unit was dramatic and pointed in his explanation: 'The course a girl runs in Yorkville is very short.'[120]

The word 'ruined' here is, we can assume, code for what happens when women lose their virginity.[121] The lingering obsession with protecting virginal women from the crude advances of men may seem antiquated today, but it was still a potent rallying cry in late 1967. DeLaplante's article was but one of a series of reports on the sexual danger young women faced from the inherent evil of Village depravity. The persistent depiction of Yorkville men as rapists – or, at the very least, sexual opportunists – seems predicated on a notion of female vulnerability and inherent physical weakness. In most reports from police officers, for example, the young woman over whom all of this concern is being lavished is reduced to a nameless, powerless, sex object. A *Toronto Daily Star* article from early November reads as a bleak post-mortem assessment of the scene. 'The once colourful Village,' it explained, 'is now a place where girls are sold for prices ranging from a few cents to $15 by boyfriends who no longer want to sleep with them or who need the money for something more important.'[122]

Accelerating such fears were the climbing numbers of runaway teen-agers across Canada and the assumption that a great many of them had slipped into the Village vortex.[123] By early November, Toronto police were searching the Village for some 123 girls under the age of sixteen, and another seventy-three young women between the ages of sixteen and twenty, all of whose parents or wards had reported them missing and heading for Yorkville.[124] What would they find when they arrived there? One police officer emphasized the iniquity inherent in the Vil-lage, tarring its female residents with a wide brush: in Yorkville, sex is 'a communal affair. The girls are fed a little marijuana and in a few days they are passed around to everybody.'[125] By August 1968, *Satyrday* ran an article exposing the problem of the exploitation of runaways, admonishing those 'exploiters' for their negative presence in the Vil-lage: 'To entice a young, uninformed, un-self-sufficient [sic] person into using methedrine, being a prostitute or even worse, the exploiter relies on his victim's ignorance and inexperience,' admonished Eric Layman. Having established the aggressor/victim frame, Layman then divid-ed the victims into two categories: 'Those enticing young people into crimes like petty thievery, etc., can already be punished for contributing to juvenile delinquency; but turning a young girl into a prostitute or a speed freak is something far worse.'[126] In Layman's analysis, echoing to some extent the line favoured by both media and municipal authorities, the danger of Village exploitation was gendered. Boys might end up in prison, having been pulled into 'petty' criminal activities; but for girls, 'something far worse' lay in wait.[127]

It seems clear that much of the concern over the 'ruination' of young women was tied to a wider disgust over the casual sexuality practised in Yorkville. The *Globe and Mail*, in an attempt to offer these largely silenced women a chance to defend themselves and their decisions, printed brief vignettes on five Villagers. After a lead paragraph explain-ing the stakes involved here (some 196 runaway girls in Yorkville, 50 active carriers of venereal disease, marijuana charges, vagrancy charges, etc.), the floor was given to the young women. The first, a sixteen-year-old from Oakville (a Toronto suburb) named Beth, explained that 'I just like to ball, and I don't care what anybody thinks. I'm never insulted when a Villager asks me. I like to give ... Everybody balls here. It's quite a common thing. I mean, sex is enjoyable, so why not do it? At least we're honest about it.' Linda, also sixteen, offered a different perspective, claiming that she had yet to sleep with anyone in the Village, even after having been there for six months: 'The boys will leave you alone, if that's what you want. Even if you crash where they're staying. A lot of them respect you for it.' Karen, a seventeen-year-old from Sault Ste-Marie (some eight hundred kilometres from Toronto) complained that she was broke, hungry, and sick. 'I haven't had a meal in two days,' she admitted. But she explained that 'I don't intend to go sleeping around and there are a lot of girls who feel as I do.' Susan, also seventeen, had crossed the country from Vancouver to make the Yorkville scene. She claimed not to be worried about venereal disease, even though she was sexually free. 'It happens. That's the chance you take with free love ... Pregnancy? Now that's a problem ... When you're pregnant, the people here won't have anything to do with you. But, they'll welcome you back after it's over. Sure, the girls come back – and do it again.' Finally, Rita, whose age was not provided, was not a Villager per se. Rather, she was from Forest Hill (a wealthy nearby neighbourhood). She liked to sneak away to Yorkville to find what she felt wasn't available at home. She agreed with Linda that in Yorkville one didn't have to sleep with anyone if one didn't want to. 'I don't do anything if I don't like the guy,' she maintained.[128]

This glimpse into the scene suggests, right there on the page below the headline 'Wasn't Molested, but She Came Close,' that the supposed universality of female sexual exploitation, prostitution at the hands of villainous hippies, and drug-fuelled mindlessness was more a product of panic than truth. If anything, this collection of voices stands to reaffirm the centrality of sex as a Village activity, and one in which both men and women could share, if not equally, then clearly with some degree of power exercised on both sides. Of the five young women, none suggested that she had been the victim of Yorkville's sexual-exploitation machine – rather, all conveyed the relative *safety* of the scene and the freedom that they felt therein to 'ball,' or not to ball, and to choose their partners deliberately. If the *Globe and Mail* was looking for evidence to support the rising anxiety over sexual danger in the Village, it was unsuccessful.

Still, city hall was on the alert, and, in reaction to what they had read in the *Globe and Mail* on 2 November, a few distressed council members loudly proclaimed their renewed intentions to rid Yorkville of its hippies. One controller, Margaret Campbell, expressed her exasperation at the thought of such activity among these children: Yorkville, she declared, represents 'something sick in our society.' The question of whether to raise the juvenile age of consent from sixteen to eighteen years of age was tabled, as was the notion of instituting a 'Yorkville curfew' of 6 p.m. for anyone under the age of twenty-one. 'We should be getting rid of this element,' raged Allan Lamport, 'not making a haven for them.'[129]

PART FOUR
Hold It, It's Gone, 1968–70

7

Social Missions in the Teenage Jungle

Probably, there are no more than 300 hippies involved, together with about a thousand greasers and about two hundred motorcyclists. Perhaps the hippie population is the most strikingly small; it is smaller than skid-row, the drug addict, and delinquent populations of Toronto. But the amount of interest in Yorkville expressed by the news media and people in general is very great.
                                    – Smart and Jackson, 'The Yorkville Subculture'[1]

In the late summer of 1968, *Canadian Welfare* magazine published the substance of June Callwood's recent speech to the Women's Canadian Club. Discouraged in tone, Callwood's speech unleashed upon her audience of upper-middle-class, largely white, and Christian women a hail of horrific and damning revelations. Opening with a reminder that she had spent the past months playing landlady to Digger House, a shelter designed to house the kind of young people who 'disgust' her audience, Callwood criticized the erroneous belief – which she evidently thought her audience held – that troubled Villagers were responsible for their lot. Not so, explained Callwood: these 'children' were 'society-damaged.' The fault for their predicament was, according to her assessment, anyone's but their own. 'Let me tell you who they are,' Callwood offered.

> They are the loneliest, most frightened people in this land. They are the children of the poor who are made wretched by living at the lowest level of subsistence we can manage without the embarrassment of having them die of starvation. They are the children of alcoholics and prostitutes and child-beaters; they are the children no one wanted in the first place; they

are the children who went to eleven schools and lived in 14 foster homes and can call any woman mother; they are the children of middle-class parents whose own despair and ambition and anxiety occupied all their attention, with nothing left over for a child; and of the parents who truly thought that love is something that can be given in the form of toys and television sets.[2]

Furthermore, this 'damaged' swath of Canadian youth, comprised of unfortunates from all social classes, all walks of life, was 'the visible mark of our disgrace [as Canadians].'

Callwood's pronouncements, vividly realized and rhetorically insistent, were based on a belief that 'the original hippie movement' (which she brazenly romanticized) had come and gone, leaving behind a 'new wave of badly mangled and desolate kids who now form the core of the movement.' Her argument was that the 'original hippies' had been concerned with 'trying to find room somewhere on this crowded earth and practice simple generosity, from the heart and to strangers [sic],' while these new Villagers were merely troubled pretenders to that fine pursuit. 'They have the aspiration to be beautiful, loving people,' she explained, 'but their mental and emotional faculties are almost destroyed. They could imitate, but they could never understand' those 'original hippies' and their lofty goals. In other words, the 'authentic hippies' were all but gone – only their imitators remained.[3] Within a year, Callwood's impressions of the scene would darken even further. 'The regulars now' she wrote in late 1969, 'are those too tired to move. Plugged into drugs that are killing them slowly, they languish. They came to find love, but it's gone, and what can you do? As they decay, the police pick them over; so do the dealers who cut the product with poisons and the thugs who take the girls and sell them.'[4]

This was not simply an outsider's view – Callwood was echoing the opinions and concerns of many Villagers by mid-1968 about the advent of new performances of Village identity. In a detailed examination of the scene, entitled 'Positive and Negative,' Village poet Eric Layman reported in late August 1968 that, 'despite the changes in Yorkville in the past few years, it has not yet lost all the people who, in the final analysis, are the ones who hold it together and give it the positive aspect of its identity.' Still, he cautioned, there were far too many new people in Yorkville 'whose conduct threatens to turn the Village into a combination of Orphans' Home, Den of Vice, Refugee Camp, and 12th Century Insane Asylum.' 'If things continue as they are developing now,' he concluded, 'the Village might soon end up being nothing at all.'[5] For its part, a new underground newspaper named *Harbinger* reported on 'The End of Hippies' in mid-summer, 1968.[6]

A variety of media sources toured Yorkville as autumn descended on the scene following the protests of 1967, and tended to agree that Villagers were becoming restless, dissatisfied with the current situation. Michael Valpy remains convinced that Yorkville's fall can be traced to 1968: 'You have to understand that only very early was this sort of a middle-class rebellion phenomenon. It increasingly, and quickly, became a phenomenon of kids who were *wounded* in a lot of ways. There were a lot of psychological problems, kids who had been abused in many ways at home. They were running to Yorkville as an alternative to a life that they couldn't cope with ... My memory is that by '68 it had definitely changed. It was more of these [wounded] kids.'[7] The contemporary media reports and on-the-street interview respondents tended to agree. 'Today, it's a small stretch of jungle all but deserted by real hippies,' concluded the *Star* in early November 1967.[8] Who was left behind? Some journalists found this impossible to answer. They had come to find hippies – an apparently stable, visible, and coherent community, and the expected exemplars of Village identity – but instead had found something else. 'Its new inhabitants are runaway girls, small-time hoodlums who sell marijuana, motorcycle gangs, young men dodging the military draft in the United States, and the lost.'[9] Writing in the popular women's magazine *Chatelaine*, Catherine Breslin referred to the Village as a 'teen-age jungle' before facetiously claiming that since real live hippies were so hard to find, 'in ten years of tackling tough magazine subjects, from Montreal underworlds to a bare-footed royal wedding in Luangprobang [sic], I have never tackled a tougher assignment.'[10]

By mid-summer, 1969, the conservative daily the *Toronto Telegram* even went so far as to declare that *all* of Yorkville's 'hippies are gone.' The article, entitled 'Yorkville Re-visited,' took a retrospective view of a bygone era, an era that was said to have reached its zenith in August 1967, that two-week period characterized by sit-ins, confrontation, and police overzealousness. But this zenith had come into focus only with a little perspective: 'Looking back now from the distance of two years, the famous hippie sit-down in the middle of Yorkville Ave takes on another coloration. It seems, if anything at all, rather quaint.'[11] Written on the occasion of the culmination of the last of the criminal trials of participants in the protest – David DePoe had been recently acquitted of two counts of causing a disturbance – the article reads like a dark eulogy. Casually reducing the phenomenon of Yorkville youth culture to a quadrumvirate of conflated shorthand, the article relates, but certainly does not lament, that since 'David DePoe is gone, the hippies are gone, the Yorkville of 1967 is over, [and] the trials have ended,' Yorkville can now move on.[12]

The assumption that there was some kind of 'original hippie' whose sudden absence from Village life amounted to the spiritual death of the hip experiment informs most sympathetic reportage and studies of the Village in this period. The memory of a first wave of hip youth that was replaced by a disastrous second cohort is widespread and commonly used to define the late Yorkville era as shady, fetid, and dangerous. Between Rochdale College, which opened its doors in September 1968 to hundreds (eventually thousands) of college-aged youth right on the edge of the Village, and the already budding hip community on Queen St West (a diffuse area four kilometres to the south and west of Yorkville), it was increasingly apparent that 'hippie' didn't need to be performed in the city centre – it could be performed anywhere, everywhere.

And so the perceived necessity for Yorkville to remain a demarcated space for hip congregation, the core belief that Yorkville somehow *belonged* to the young people who flocked there most evenings, became increasingly redundant as the mainstreaming of the counterculture accelerated throughout the city, the country, the Western world. If, in 1966, one could be said to perform 'Yorkville' in suburban Toronto by dressing the part and smoking dope, by 1969 to do so would simply be to perform 'hippie.' The idea of a specific hip space was losing relevance as such hip spaces became decentralized, more democratic, less constrained. Performances of 'hippie,' from outlandish clothing to psychedelic music, from the spread of dope through public schools and universities to the liberalization of sexual relations among young people, were no longer specifically tied to Yorkville in the Toronto imagination. Indeed, 'hippie' went mainstream so quickly in the 1960s that such superficial rebellion seemed merely a cliché by the end of the decade.[13]

Thus, the notion of 'Yorkville youth' took on new connotations in the late 1960s as people like Callwood emphasized the essential differences between these new Villagers and the so-called original wave that had colonized the Village. No longer was 'Villager' mere shorthand for hippie. By the summer of 1968, it had become synonymous with a certain needy, distressed, and alienated portion of the community: its homeless, its disturbed, its junk-sick, its infected. And the truth is that, from 1968 to 1970, as developers tightened their hold on the district, as police managed to arrest ever more Villagers on dope offences, as disease and drug addiction spread like oil on water over the young people who congregated in Yorkville's all-night restaurants and cafés, the Village scene fell into a complicated, and often bleak, downward spiral into irrelevance.

As Valpy puts it: 'For sure the first period is over-romanticized, and the media played a role in that. But I don't think the latter period is over-dramatized [because] there *was* a scary number of wounded kids [coming to Yorkville].'

> I'm just not certain enough of my sociology here, but we were going through a truly phenomenal period of social change in the 60s, and kids were just falling through the cracks. I mean, you can blame the urban-rural divide, you can blame the prioritization of post-secondary education (what happens to kids who can't make it in?), the pandemic use of drugs, going from OK drugs to the really bad stuff, and kids frying their brains on God knows what chemicals. These very lonely, failed, hurting kids. I don't know how many of them there were [in Yorkville]. Maybe it was over-dramatized, I mean, maybe the numbers weren't all that huge, but they were in pretty bad … a lot of them were in *really* bad shape.

Ultimately, we must consider the late 1960s in the Village as a period of breakdown, of declension. While it certainly was a bright and joyful time for some Villagers – and their experiences mustn't be diminished – for a great many other Villagers this period was defined by pain, addiction, and disillusionment. As Miguel Maropakis bluntly recalls, 'there were [still] a lot of right kids here. From a lot of rich families. And they got totally lost here in the crowd. In the drugs, you know. Junkies. There were a lot of junkies.'[14]

This chapter explores the ways that Villagers struggled to save themselves in the late 1960s from the scourges of hard drugs, the schemes of developers, expanded police activity, and a growing popular view that their very identities were becoming *passé*, irrelevant, even pathetic. At the same time, this chapter considers the paradoxical reality that the Diggers', Callwood's, and other humanitarians' efforts to attract attention to alienated Villagers served to flesh out the impression that Yorkville was more or less a disaster area, an impression that played no small role in its final dissolution.

For, if the true or 'original' hippies were gone by 1968, then who *were* these young people, sporting long hair and headbands, smoking dope and dropping LSD, playing at 'free love,' hanging around Gandalf's head shop, wearing beads and baubles, cowboy hats and patchwork skirts? If the hippies were gone, who was filling the Cumberland St rock'n'roll clubs, or the Yorkville coffee houses? Some exciting music was still there to be heard – Yorkville's folk musicians were as exceptional as ever, with the likes of Murray McLauchlan, Bruce Cockburn, David Wiffen, and Eric Andersen all fighting for a chance to play the Riverboat in those years. And a new wave of bands like Mashmakan, Kensington Market, Mainline, and Mandala all rocked the scene in the late 1960s. Who were the hundreds in the audience at the Rockpile, the newly opened concert venue at the corner of Davenport and Yonge that was staging performances by international sensations Led Zeppelin, Cream, and the Doors alongside these homegrown heroes? Who was dancing all night long with the body-painted go-go girls at the Mynah Bird? Or checking out the Rockshow of the Yeomen at the Night Owl? The Sunday night jam session at Flick? The Church basement, the Mont Blanc, El Matador, and Webster's burger joint were still popular hangouts, still scenes that got moving every evening as young people piled in, many of them blazing, beautiful, and stoned, just like the old days. But these weren't the old days.

An Ethnography of Village Identity:
Greasers, Hippies, Weekenders, and Bikers

The Addiction Research Foundation (ARF) was by no means the first to consider Yorkville as comprised of distinct, inscrutable cultures. The discourse of foreignness had always served to inculcate the view of Yorkville (and the aspect of white middle-class youth culture that comprised its expected inhabitants) as an aberration. The Village was a space in which something must have gone wrong, where some divisive, transformative element had been introduced. Alternative identity performances (especially as evidenced through increasingly peculiar clothing, affected mannerisms, obscure figures of speech, and even predilections towards certain hyper-modern genres in music and the arts) were of principal interest to observers, but through it all, no apparently alien aspect of the Yorkville scene garnered more attention from media, municipal authorities, and youth culture alike than its appetite for drugs.

On 27 October 1967, under the auspices of the ARF, a twenty-seven-year-old graduate student named Gopala Alampur went to live as a hippie in Yorkville. According to the ARF's famous report of early autumn, 1969, Alampur, recently arrived in Canada from his native India on a student visa, 'grew a beard, wore typical Yorkville clothes and beads, and took part in the life of the "Village" until May 1, 1968.'[15] For a period of six months, the undercover Alampur infiltrated, observed, and interviewed a wide swath of Villagers, amassing a sizeable cache of ethnographic information on the 'cultures' of the community.[16] The ensuing report, prepared by the ARF's Reginald Smart and David Jackson, synthesized Alampur's field notes into a fascinating but gloomy vision of an alien community in crisis, a factionalized, dangerous, and foreign ghetto.[17] But it also did much to define a set of class-, race-, and gender-based divisions within the scene: a simplistic, clear-cut system for decoding and representing Yorkville's diverse and diffusive populations. And, crucially, it never failed to underline the assumption that Yorkville and its denizens constituted a kind of anthropological curiosity – a spectacle of anti-modern difference right in the heart of a modern city.

The ninety-page report began by setting out its theoretical position and framework. 'Yorkville was studied as a viable subculture or set of symbolic and material arrangements made by a society embedded in a larger society,' it explained.[18] Yorkville, then, was conceptualized by the study as a distinct locus for deviant or subcultural activity – the study would not question the veracity of this foundational premise. However, this conceptualization was said to have been the only assumption deliberately carried into the project by its participants, since 'an effort was made to minimize conceptual presuppositions and free the study of any special position.'[19] According to Gopala Alampur, the raison d'être for the project was laid out very succinctly to him and was free from any theoretical scaffolding: 'Jackson and Smart brought me down to figure out who these people were,' he explains today.[20] That 'these people' were unknown to them, that the question *who are they?* was so central, underscores the foreignness associated with the scene. The known versus the unknown – such a dynamic opposition should have made for a straightforward reconnaissance project.[21]

Alampur wasted no time in setting apart four main cultural groups within the context of the Village and (as had Frank Longstaff during the previous summer) establishing them as the dominant categories of identity in Yorkville. 'I like simplifying difficult concepts,' Alampur explains. 'So when I saw these people, there were various types of behaviour.'[22] These categories – 'hippies,' 'bikers,' 'greasers,' and 'weekenders,' terms that were already in use in the Village to describe subgroups – were then carefully filled out in the ensuing pages as Smart and Jackson interpreted and synthesized Alampur's findings. The result is a hugely informative but often bizarre bit of scholarship, complete with a makeshift survey (conducted by looking out of a window over Yorkville Ave at various times during the day and night and counting the people on the street, before dividing them into what were assumed to be their four respective categories), a lexicon of Yorkville terms, and four lengthy character studies designed to personify these four Village identities. Throughout, drug use is the report's leitmotif. Smart and Jackson never stray far from the argument that drug use and hanging around in Yorkville are to be understood as simultaneous occupations – in fact, each of the identity categories is in some real way defined by its degree of predilection for psychotropic substances.

Unlike the typical khaki-shorted ethnographer who moves into a tribal community and, for a time, attempts to live with and become a part of a foreign culture, Alampur donned instead the very garb of his expected subjects in an effort to blend into the Village. With the ARF perhaps unaware of Frank Longstaff's warnings following his botched undercover experience the previous summer, a certain subterfuge was at the core of the enterprise. Importantly, Alampur's choice to get into a beard and beads immediately positioned him inside one of the four distinct identity groups to which his study would adhere: his clothing, and general preoccupation, was based on preconceptions about hippie aesthetics. As such, a further level of suspicion of his questions and observations was likely at work when he approached bikers and greasers (since weekenders, as 'plastic hippies,' might have been more comfortable with his performance). Unsurprisingly, the report admits that 'hippies and weekenders were more readily encountered than greasers or motorcyclists,' although it does not suggest that Alampur's disguise was the root of the issue.[23]

Moreover, Alampur's adoption of the name Krishna (his middle name) worked to associate him with the Hindu religion (which was, in fact, his own). As the interest in and veneration of Eastern mystic and spiritual traditions was passed from the Beats and early Villagers on down to the current scene, this association tended to inspire some Villagers to seek him out for spiritual guidance. 'They thought I was guru,' explains Alampur. 'Some people used to come and see me from all over. Haight Ashbury, Greenwich [Village] … and say "Krishna was the guru." People came to see "Krishna" lots of times.'

> My life became easy mainly because if you asked people in Yorkville, no matter who they were, they'd say: 'I'm an artist,' 'I'm a poet.' Some people think they're Jesus Christ or whatever, you know, which is fine. So they dressed like that, and walked like that, and presented themselves like that. And so they asked me: 'What are you?' They asked me, 'Why are you here?' 'What are you?' I mean, 'narc' was the term used for suspicious characters, foreigners, the new people who came in. Because they were thinking, hey, there're gonna be drug busts! Lots of undercover [police activity]. So my method was … I'd say, 'I'm a writer,' which was fair. And then I used to record all the people's conversations, just like you do.[24]

The report argues that Alampur was able to overcome the suspicions of the Villagers at large for three key reasons. One, he was able to offer his Village apartment (paid for by the ARF) to people as a place to crash, to have a snack, to stay warm, and to use a bathroom; two, he was in the habit of giving away food and clothing, but never money, to Villagers in need, citing a kind of social responsibility based on a hip ethic of anti-materialism and sharing; and three, most significant of all, he had convinced the Villagers that he was an experienced drug user himself. Early upon his arrival, likely by way of introduction, Alampur passed around some Indian cigarettes (the popular brand Charminar) which were widely thought to contain marijuana. They, of course, did not, but people were fooled by their exotic flavour and curious smell. The association between Alampur and this unfamiliar type of pot (people claimed that they experienced a kind of intense euphoria when 'on' the stuff) stuck.[25]

In an environment in which drug use and identity were so closely interrelated in the local common sense, by associating himself with drugs, Gopala Alampur became an active participant in the scene. He even began to collect and give away narcotics that Villagers left in his apartment. 'People gave me [drugs],' he recalled. 'I used to smoke anyway, cigarettes. So all these people come and give me drugs of all kinds. And I used to store them under the air conditioning filter or something. I got a stash, a good spot. And I used to get: "Hey Krishna, lay some stuff on me, man." So I used to give any guy that wants to smoke this or that.'[26] Alampur, then, *did* involve himself as an actor in the very drug scene that he was assigned to study; not only would he tacitly encourage people to use drugs around him, he would supply them with the drugs they were looking for.

'I used to tell them: "Hey, in India, the culture is: we smoke,"' he explained. 'Opium is normal. It's natural. A lot of poor guys do smoke, in the streets. He can go buy a big ball of opium, put it in the hookah then smoke, and sit down, sleep under a tree, and live happily.' This emphasis on the 'natural' served as a major factor in Alampur's identity performance in the Village. He would use his status as Indian (and all of its attendant cultural generalizations) to protect himself from the drugs he was uncomfortable with. 'I did drugs,' he explains, '[but], no, I don't do all of this LSD and, what other stuff was there? Speed. Right? Any chemicals? No. I'd tell them: "Being an Indian I don't believe in any of this chemical stuff." [Only] natural stuff. So that played better. So, only marijuana, hashish, and opium.'[27]

Unbeknownst to his new-found friends/objects of study, Alampur was in no danger of being arrested or prosecuted for his participation in the drug scene. Aware of the potential dangers that faced him upon infiltrating a world in which illegal activities would be taking place around him at every turn, he had voiced his concerns to his employers early on: 'Firstly, I didn't want to take any chances, going there without protection ... Listen, I don't belong in this country. I'm a foreigner ... So somehow I think they got me immunity of some sort. I recall that they paraded me in front of the entire RCMP [sic]. They said: "Hey, you see this guy, leave him alone. Bust him, but then let him out of the back door. Take him for a couple blocks." I felt a little more secure.'[28]

Although Alampur claims he could never keep straight who the narcotics agents were and weren't while living in Yorkville, it seems fair to assume that *they* would have remembered *him*: an Indian undercover ARF field agent nick(code)named *Krishna*.[29]

As a result of this relative safety, this freedom from prosecution, Alampur was able to operate out of his apartment without fear that he would be interrupted by the otherwise commonplace police incursions into private residences. He established his apartment as a kind of free space; he hoped to encourage Villagers to drop in to his rooms at all times of the day or night, and maintained a steady store of supplies which he would use to entice them to stay, to open up, and to tell him their stories.[30] When asked whether he felt accepted by the Yorkville community, whether they bought his line that he was a writer at work on a book, Alampur responded without reservation. 'Absolutely, no doubt about it – *absolutely*. I used to have a place that was *open*. I used

to have a *one-bedroom* apartment or something. It was a studio apartment. It was always open. And I always had bread and peanut butter
sandwiches. And they would come. Sometimes bananas! Sometimes
for people that smoked pot and hash and all this I'd have orange juice
and stuff.'[31]

Although the report claims that Alampur's apartment attracted 'all
types of Villagers, male and female, drug users and criminals, weekenders and hippies, motorcyclists and greasers [who] came to his place
at various times and talked spontaneously,' it is unclear as to how freely
in fact these people talked.[32] Were they truthful? Accurate in their representations? Or were they hiding behind a veil of paranoia and self-
preservation? For, in light of escalating drug busts and increasing street
violence, it was hardly unlikely that this strange new Villager was an
undercover police informant. There was, of course, an imposing spool-
to-spool tape recorder running all the time in his apartment, and the
ever-present microphone in one's face tends to throw even the most
unselfconscious person off his game. Given the already paranoiac climate of a neighbourhood plagued by the spectre of undercover police
work and surveillance, we must presume that, as was the case for Frank
Longstaff the previous year, any information provided to Alampur was
passed through the sticking web of suspicion.

The four identity categories developed and defined through Alampur's report serve as the backbone for all its attempts to rationalize the
activities and ideologies in the Village. As each category serves to place
boundaries around behaviours, and establish difference and commo-
nalities between various types of youth cultures and countercultures,
each category also simultaneously reinvents and propagates the notion
of Yorkville as a factionalized, contested territory. But, crucially, by
dividing the expected denizens of Yorkville into distinct categories
of identity and performance, Alampur (and subsequently Smart and
Jackson) presented the scene (however unconsciously) as a kind of
gangland, split along lines of class, ethnicity, and gender. Obvious from
the fact that Alampur chose (or was given) the disguise of the hippie
(beads, shaggy hair, and beard) is the conclusion that the ARF, like so
many observers, saw this group as archetypal. However, it was later
surprised to find that 'hippies,' by their definition, were outnumbered
by the group it defined as 'greasers' virtually all of the time. Moreover,
the report stressed that, blind to the reality of a diverse Village scene,
the general public (whom it termed the 'straight world') believed that,
in effect, *'Yorkville is hippies.* When everyone questioned gave us their

opinion on the village, they were actually talking about the hippie phenomenon. There was no recognition of the motorcycle gangs or the greasers … In general, Yorkville was seen to be long hair and beads.'[33]

Although critical of the public's oversimplification of the Village scene, the report still offered the bulk of its attention to the hippies. One comes away from the report with a rather more comprehensive vision of the structure and criteria of this category than of any of the other three. At the very same time as the report repudiated the claim that hippies comprised the most significant group in the district, it served to propagate this same notion. To the ARF, as it was for many Canadians by 1968, Villagers and hippies were simply the same thing. And yet the very word 'hippie' was rejected by Villagers as unrepresentative. Indeed, Alampur was forced to acknowledge the awkwardness of the hippie category almost immediately. 'During the interviews for this study,' the report admits, 'no one was willing to say they were a hippie.'[34] Still, Alampur thought he knew what hippies were, and his notes clearly emphasized the hippie as a readily identifiable category of identity and activity. He constructed for this group a somewhat hazy visual description which he then used to identify hippies as he observed the street: 'There is no uniform, but a costume – a style characterized by comfort, freedom, and eccentricity … The costume aspect in the hippie dress is designed to reflect individuality so that hippies may look alike in characteristics such as long hair, dirty clothes and beads, but each is dressed to portray a unity.'[35]

Alampur's 'weekender,' closely connected to the 'hippie,' is otherwise somewhat of a catch-all category.[36] Ostensibly made up of inauthentic performances of all three other categories, the weekender category seems most often to be comprised of pretenders to the hippie mantle. (Weekenders, recall, were referred to as 'plastic hippies' by many Village residents.[37]) Thus, the weekender tends to be described by Alampur in somewhat contradictory terms. While he maintains that weekenders wear costumes designed to 'harmonize with [either] the motorcycle gang, the hippie, or the greaser,' he explains that weekenders in general can be seen wearing 'bell bottom pants, brightly coloured shirts, and psychedelic patterned mini-skirts,' decidedly atypical garb for either greasers or bikers as he sets them out. Nevertheless, he is quick to point out that weekenders are easily distinguished from hippies because they are 'always clean and well groomed' and because they wear 'more expensive and more colourful clothing than the other groups.'[38] Class, then, or at least affluence, is a distinguishing factor here. 'When the weekenders come, they bring money,' explains Alampur – which is to say that one can distinguish a hippie from a weekender by her spending habits. If a person is buying something from the Grab Bag convenience store, for example, odds are she is a weekender; in Alampur's recollection, hippies were unlikely to have much disposable income.[39]

The key to understanding this category is to see it as the transitional stage between a typical young person and a Villager. Alampur saw the weekender as someone who dressed up, came to Yorkville, did drugs, had sex but did not otherwise inhabit the Village – as an aspirant who was both absent from and actively engaged in the meta-culture of Yorkville. But, as weekenders became more enamoured of the scene, as they began to engage more and more freely in the culture, Alampur recognized that they were likely to sever their connections to the outside world (high school, suburban home, university) and move wholesale into the Village. 'People from Toronto who enter the Village as permanent residents generally begin as weekenders,' he explained, 'and will eventually become committed to a Village group.'[40] This process wasn't inevitable, of course: it was also possible that, after a time, 'they will leave [after] having satisfied their curiosity.'[41]

In the most egregious instance of class determinism underwriting the analysis, Alampur's report routinely groups 'bikers' and 'greasers' together, casually conflating them owing to their mostly shared working-class, often immigrant, and non-Anglo backgrounds.[42] Meanwhile, their hippie and weekender contemporaries were assumed to be of middle-class, white, Anglo-Christian backgrounds. The old assumptions about pacifism/violence running along class lines rear their head early and often in the report: bikers were presented as frequent gang rapists and infrequent murderers, while greasers were often speed addicts and thieves and, sometimes, prostitutes (gay and/or straight), whereas hippies and weekenders were well educated, docile, and only infrequently violent or involved in criminal enterprises (beyond drug use).

The one key distinction between bikers and greasers lay in the bikers' emphasis on *community*. Greasers tended towards individualism and maintained few fraternal bonds, concluded Alampur, while bikers constituted a kind of family with firm and easily apparent codes, rules, and hierarchies of power.[43] Greasers were roughly the same age demographic as their hippie counterparts ('between 16 and 25 years of age') but were characterized by a vast majority of males over females

– Alampur judged their ranks to be about 70 per cent young men.[44] However, here the similarities plainly end: while hippie youth tended to receive rather laudatory, if condescending, tributes and descriptions by Alampur, greasers were immediately set up in the report as a violent, unfriendly, opportunistic fraction of aberrant, immigrant youth.[45] 'Greasers are more aggressive and more delinquent than the other groups ... Within the greasers, there are basically two subgroups – the young criminal on his way to becoming a rounder and the drug addict whose habit has caused him to be completely alienated from the straight society.'[46] Significantly, Alampur found that greasers 'resent the hippies as drop-outs and lazy ne'er-do-wells'; as one greaser told him: 'Rich people can afford to be bums. Poor people can't.'[47] However, this class-based resentment is somewhat neglected in the subsequent discussions of the uneasy relationship between the two principal groups. Rather than emphasize the exploitation of hippies by greasers as a gleeful attack on middle-class asceticism by lower-class have-nots – an interpretation that, going on the information presented in the report, is entirely plausible – the report avoids the issue entirely, instead criticizing the greasers for taking advantage of relatively meek hippies. Alampur repeatedly emphasizes the greasers' penchant for violence: 'The value they place on aggression is another characteristic which unites all greasers ... They often carry knives or guns.'[48] This emphasis on greasers as the most immoral constituents in the Village is maintained unabated.[49] Alampur clearly did not come to respect or admire the greaser identity category in his time in the Village. Seeing greasers as working-class youth harbouring aspirations to move up in the world, Alampur noted that as they talk about their criminal activities 'it becomes apparent that they take craftsman-like pride in such activities as stealing or peddling.'[50]

The origins of their nickname is interrogated by the report not as evidence of a dangerous, racialized division between identity categories but rather as an instance of *inadequate* racialization: 'The term "greaser" is used because "They put grease on their hair and grease in their food," to use the words of one Villager. This statement implies that many have come from eastern and southwestern European backgrounds. [However,] Greasers also have large representation [sic] of people from countries, such as the United States and the West Indies, although there are many Canadian-borns among them.'[51] In other words, the report seems to conclude that the racialized assumption that all greasers are swarthy eastern and southern European immigrants is actually an *insufficient* racialization. This is as if to say that, while some are those *naturally* greasy types, not *all* of them are naturally greasy. In the one case study that appears near the end of the report, there appears a telling reiteration of this accent on the natural predisposition to dirtiness shown by eastern Europeans: '[Jay's father] made sure he was wearing a clean shirt, often having to change it three times a day ([this is] typical behaviour of a "greaser").'[52]

In general, all four groups were characterized in the report as being primarily male, even though women were clearly as important (in both their numbers and the significance of their performances) as men. Throughout, the expected occupants of each category are *always* male – women are, however improbably, left to perform supporting, insignificant roles. Alampur observed that 'women are property and are afraid to be unfaithful' in the greaser scene. His report demonstrates that there were many more men than women who fit the greaser mould, but that those women who did tended to be in some real danger, sexually, physically, or emotionally. 'Many of these girls are lesbians who work with a male greaser as a prostitute,' he observed, even though they 'have no sexual interest in men.' Elsewhere, he claimed: 'In the greaser group both male and female turn to homosexuality and prostitution in large numbers.'[53] For their part, 'the male greasers are very interested in "hustling broads" from the hippie and weekender groups ... To the male greaser who is not a junkie, sex is more important than drugs.'[54] Ultimately, the picture we receive of these gender relations is sketchy and unstable.

In short, greasers are undoubtedly painted as the least admirable Village category: they are variously described as 'feared and despised,' 'less intelligent than hippies and weekenders,' and 'grandiose and loud.' It is difficult not to sense some perverse pleasure, however unconscious, in the offhand remark that 'motorcycle gangs enjoy an opportunity to beat them [greasers] up because other Villagers condone this activity as justified.' Such blatant disrespect for this, the most populous category in the Yorkville scene in the winter of 1967–8 (according to the ARF's own survey), further inculcates the view that the expected Yorkville inhabitants were suffering at the hands of outsiders, an uninvited force. 'Usually the greaser lives outside the Village, at home, with relatives, or in an apartment,' reads the report, subtly reminding us both that they don't belong in the Village and that they don't have *parents*, per se, but rather the much vaguer 'relatives.' 'They come to Yorkville for the same reasons the motorcycle gangs do – "To get some action." They find victims and customers among the weekenders and hippies.'[55] 'Victims and customers': hippies and weekenders are reduced to the objects of greaser oppression.[56]

Finally, bikers receive a somewhat more sophisticated rap in the report, but there is very little sense that Alampur was able to infiltrate their world, or to gain their confidence. What results is a distant, hearsay-influenced overview of the category. For example, while the report is clear that most motorcycle-club members came from working-class families, and that, generally, 'their early experiences include violent or delinquent behaviour on the part of their parents,' it provides no evidence to support either position.[57] Such generalizations, pervasive and fundamental to the report in the main, seem even more central to the depiction of biker identity in Yorkville. For example, when faced with a gap in information about how bikers must support themselves financially, the report opts to speculate rather than to admit insufficient research: 'One can only suspect that they get money from their families, or other gang members, or from illegal activities.' Finally, the only interview with any biker offered by the report comes from a *former* biker, who has 'sold his bike and left the gang to go back to school.'[58]

Judged to be between eighteen and twenty-eight years old, bikers were, on average, the oldest Villagers. Described as 'generally bigger and more strongly built than the other inhabitants of Yorkville,' '[bikers] wear leather jackets or levis [sic] jackets with the sleeves cut out, with jeans and cowboy boots ... Many wear long hair and beards.' This aesthetic is gendered masculine because all 'official motorcyclists are males' although there were women who were acknowledged to be 'associated with them in roles carrying lesser status.' The report describes the interior of a Vagabond clubhouse (located 'across town') – though it doesn't explain how this information was gleaned – and testifies that the club has about fifty members, with 40 per cent of these men being married.[59]

The case study of 'Jay – a Motorcycle Gang Member' that appears towards the end of the report seems to be the primary source for much of the information on offer about bikers in Yorkville. Jay, the American-born working-class son of a delinquent father and battered mother, had quit school after grade 9. He fell in and out of associations with biker clubs for a period of time until, after quitting his odd jobs and getting serious about starting a motorcycle-repair shop, he became a full-time active member of a club that frequented the scene. Alampur's respect for Jay is apparent – he refers to him as 'obviously intelligent.'[60] However, he seems to have been unable to elicit much information from him regarding anything but drinking and sex.

These descriptions of biker culture conflate the various activities of the five or more clubs into one, monolithic Motorcycle Gang – a representation that, it seems, is based upon the case study of this one (former) Vagabond. In a lengthy passage outlining the procedure for joining a club, the report relates what appears to be Jay's own specific experience as if it were the regular biker practice. 'To join,' Alampur explains, 'a member must sponsor [the guy] and the club would accept him as a "striker." The probationary period for a striker can last from two to eight weeks … When a member acts "smart" during striking the club may make him suck a female's genitals before the assembled members.'[61] Alampur explains that 'there is a good deal of talk in the club room about perverted sexual acts carried out by various members. "Eating a girl out" (male sucks the female's genitals) is not uncommon.'[62] That the performance of cunnilingus in front of the gang might be an embarrassing punishment for the man is implied; that the act might be humiliating for the woman is jarringly absent.

The report concluded that bikers were less likely to use drugs (apart from marijuana) than the other groups, but stressed their obsession with alcohol. It was put to Alampur by a biker that 'booze, broads and bikes' were all that he cared for.[63] Nevertheless, biker ties to the underground crime world often put them in the position of messengers for the drug trade. Greasers, it was explained, also abused alcohol, but tended towards amphetamines, glue sniffing, and even heroin, eschewing the psychedelic drugs. Hippies and weekenders were understood to be preternaturally obsessed with being high on psychedelic drugs such as LSD and marijuana, but were also said to be interested in trying any and every drug they could get hands on. Typically, they smoked marijuana and hash on a daily basis, and did LSD at least once a month. In general, the report concluded, they largely refused alcohol as a 'down trip,' preferring the kind of high they got out of pot and hallucinogens.

Ultimately, what is most arresting about the ARF study is the utter banality of these conclusions. Such trite and expected generalizations betray the complex relationships between the Village and its inhabitants, visitors, and observers. And yet this report, issued in 1969, came to be accepted as the standard study of the Village, its inhabitants, and its expected meaning as a countercultural centre.[64] Although there were blotches of inconclusive results and incompatible accounts splattered throughout the report, the authors were so intent on relying on the four distinct categories of identity and performance that they seem to have been unable to engage with inconsistency. The 'hippie,' for example, who explains in an interview that he had been a heroin-addicted gay prostitute before arriving in the Village, would seem to contradict their treatment of the 'hippies' as a promiscuously heterosexual, strictly soft-drug-using category. But there is no interrogation of this evident discrepancy.[65] Moreover, the simple fact that women are virtually silent throughout the report suggests the utter neglect of a central population in the Village.

But, for all of its faults, the report still stands as the most detailed first-hand account of the scene in that winter, 1967–8, as the Village was entering its final phase. If nothing else (besides being a fascinating document), Alampur's observations and conclusions, inconsistent though some may have been, establish the multifarious, contradictory, and downright complex identity pool at work in the Village after the enveloping hype of 1967.[66] The report was unambiguous in its conclusion that bikers, greasers, and weekenders had come to outnumber the hippies significantly; hard drugs were rampant, sexual violence was a serious concern, and poverty and alienation were on the rise. Were the identity categories too distinct? Certainly. But these circumscribed groupings *were* relevant, at least in the general sense, to the Villagers who surrounded Alampur that winter, and in the years before. As we have seen in previous chapters, the Village community *was* comprised of various competing and overlapping identities, and the quest for authentic Village performances animated them all. The problem with Alampur's formulation wasn't that he employed these four faulty categories, but that he hewed so closely to them in his search for meaning that he failed to appreciate just how intertwined they were both in the real sense and in the public imagination. For his part, when asked how he felt about the rigidity of the four categories outlined in the report, Mike Waage's response was both apposite and fittingly contrary: 'I'd say there was a diverse variety of people [in Yorkville]. And some may have gone through *all* of those categories, some might not have gone through *any* of them. You know?'[67]

The Trailer and Innovative Social Welfare, 1968–70

On 27 May 1968 the Jewish Family and Child Services of Metro Toronto established what it called a 'Mobile Counselling Unit' right in the heart of Yorkville. The 'Trailer,' as it was named (for it was, indeed, a forty-foot mobile home), sat at 70 Avenue Rd and was initially introduced to the Village as part of a three-month study designed to test new initiatives to help troubled youth. The poetry of using an actual trailer (a vehicle, capable of quickly re-establishing itself wherever the action was) was not lost on the post-1967 Yorkville scene. Over the next two years, the Trailer would go through a series of permutations, each one mirroring and mimicking shifting realities among its young constituents. Naturally, it also spoke to the realization, however unspoken, that Yorkville was no permanent hip enclave – if the events of 1967 had taught Villagers anything, it was that the Village could move, but only if it stuck together. The Trailer, a mobile centre, reflected the gathering mutability of the Village scene.

'We have no interest in trying to channel the Village kids back to straight society,' explained twenty-one-year-old volunteer Greg King in 1968. 'Unless, of course, that's what they really want.'[68] This position, yet another solidification of the boundaries between the 'straight' world and Yorkville, also demonstrates the peculiar and highly effective position taken up by the Trailer for the two years of its existence. Responding rather than ministering, listening and helping rather than teaching and enforcing, the Trailer was built on the idea of Yorkville as a self-contained community, altogether separate from the rest of Toronto, with its own particular problems requiring its own particular set of solutions. From late May 1968 to mid-July 1970, the Trailer would move with the Yorkville scene, an integrated and expected facet of the performance of Yorkville; from the Village to Rochdale to rock festivals at Mosport Park and the Canadian National Exhibition, the Trailer was relied upon as a local, friendly, and necessary Yorkville charity.

As Eric Layman explained in his lengthy discourse on the problems besetting the Village scene: 'Acid and speed freaks, panhandlers, and others … will listen more seriously to their better oriented friends – if to anyone at all – than to a policeman, social worker, or any other authority symbol.'[69] In recognition of this reality, the principles, or 'working concepts,' underlying the Trailer project included 'youth's right to self-determination,' servicing youth 'on their own ground,' a 'youth serving youth policy,' and a restructuring of services to the 'pace and rhythm of youth's needs.' The plan was uncomplicated: provide a space in the midst of the Village in which medical and legal issues (many of which were otherwise dismissed and/or avoided by Villagers because of the ties of hospitals and aid agencies to the establishment) could be freely and safely discussed. Like the Fish Net and the Church Drop-In Centre, the Trailer quickly became treated as another hangout in the Yorkville landscape. As Trailer staffer John Kileeg explained after that first summer, 'Villagers tended to think of the Trailer as a Haven, meeting place, or general "gab" spot. They casually came into all parts of the trailer and settled as one of the group. The trailer staff accepted this and freely promoted a fairly relaxed, casual atmosphere which appeared to encourage some of the Villagers.'[70] But it is worth mentioning that, unlike the more explicitly religious Fish Net and, to a limited extent, the Church Drop-In Centre, the Trailer was merely Jewish by association. Neither was the Trailer preaching from any moralistic dais, nor was it even obvious that it carried an association with a Jewish organization. The Trailer was, instead, a secular experiment, funded by a Jewish charitable group but run by young people from within the community itself – and, it is clear, this was the reason for its high degree of success at persuading people of its good intentions and remaining an effective mission within the Yorkville scene.

The real centre of the operation was a middle-aged former army doctor named Anne Keyl. Loved by many, feared by all, Keyl showed a professional dedication to the enterprise that was as extensive as it was anomalous. Michael Valpy's recollections of the scene are limned by a variety of fond memories of the 'tough old bird': 'She was an expert in Venereal Disease, and she had acquired that expertise at Camp Borden during the war! She ran a VD Clinic at Women's College where, most of the time, she was treating prostitutes. I think either Chapman or DePoe made contact with her because the hospitals were turning away a lot of kids. I mean, Toronto General wouldn't treat *any* of them unless it was truly an emergency. If they were dirty, and the hair was long, and the rest of it … So my recollection is that she used her own money to fund a clinic, and that became the medical arm of Trailer.'[71] Famously militant and organized, Keyl was the antithesis of her laid-back customers and patients: 'Anne Keyl just intrigued me. I still have this image in my mind of her organizing her interns and residents sort of two by two to march from Women's College Hospital up around Queen's Park circle carrying tables and medical paraphernalia, everybody in their white coats! It was done at night, in this little parade up Avenue Rd to Yorkville.'[72] But she was thorough and professional and may well have saved a lot of young lives during her tenure with Women's College and the Trailer.

Kileeg's report to the Social Planning Council of Metro Toronto, written in September 1968 (at the culmination of the initial three-month

Trailer 'experiment'), detailed his observations and criticisms of the endeavour. Alongside these more significant assessments, Kileeg illuminated the daily routines of the average Trailer volunteer, and in so doing established the types of services provided by this innovative enterprise:

> My daily program included the following: The transportation of Villagers who were medical emergencies to the hospital. The transportation of Villagers to regular medical clinics at Women's College Hospital every Tuesday evening, and to VD clinics at Toronto Western and Women's College Hospitals every Tuesday, Wednesday and Thursday evenings ... Referral of a) Village clients to the Good Shepherd Refuge, Salvation Army hostels, Fred Victor Mission, Seaton House and the Digger House; b) applicants to emergence welfare; c) emergency legal problems to legal aid or to the volunteer legal back-up person; d) under-age youth to the police Youth Bureau; e) various clients to appropriate psychological or psychiatric services.[73]

The Trailer was indeed involved in a wide variety of initiatives: consider the multiplicity of issues the Trailer claimed to be prepared to remedy in its advertising leaflets. These flyers, ubiquitous on Yorkville Ave throughout 1968 and 1969, invariably listed a diversity of common Village problems, brightly described in local language: 'Just got into town? Got no bread? Got busted? Kicked out of your room? Pregnant? Need Welfare? Freaking? Need legal advice? On a bummer? Hassled by the man? Need a job? Got a dose? Trailer 70 Yorkville.'[74] Clearly, the Trailer was a multifaceted operation, aiming to meet a wide assortment of needs.

As the *Globe and Mail* reported, underlining the language of religious conversion, 'everybody at Trailer stresses that they are not there to save but only to help the young Villagers.'[75] Rather than working from without, ministering to the flock from the morally elevated position of pastor or missionary, the Trailer operated from within – while the Church Drop-In Centre or the Fish Net could be transformed into community spaces, could become incorporated into the landscape of Yorkville a few nights a week, the Trailer was immediately an integrated facet of the Yorkville performance. And one cannot discount the fact that the Trailer offered a safe environment for otherwise embarrassing, socially awkward, or otherwise potentially shameful circumstances and symptoms. Anne Keyl was tough, but she was a professional – her patients would not be turned away nor would they be insulted or made to feel like failures. In a scene in which venereal disease was as common as nicotine fingers, this was undoubtedly a good thing. 'Funny story,' recalled Michael Valpy: [*Name Redacted*] was very good looking. Very attractive to girls. And, of course, he was constantly getting gonorrhea. There's this funny story of Anne down on her knees treating him, and looking up and saying: [*Name Redacted*], we've got to stop meeting like this!'[76] Dispensing with ethics lessons couched in religious rhetoric, and sidestepping the deleterious association between the church and the middle-class ideology that was avoided like Black Death in the Village, the Trailer was taken up by Villagers in the summer of 1968 as a locally sanctioned alternative.

Kileeg's 1968 report highlights this line above all others. 'The Villagers suspect anyone from the establishment,' he began, '[such as] social workers, church workers, Youth Bureau, etc. Several workers moving into Yorkville have met passive resistance which has approached hostility.' The Trailer avoided this pratfall – even though it was funded and overseen by the Jewish Family and Child Services, hardly an anti-establishment outfit – by allowing its on-site operations, and the majority of its counselling, to be performed by Yorkville youth volunteers sympathetic to the beliefs, aesthetics, and age of their constituents. Because the volunteers 'dressed like their clients and talked their language' – in other words because they performed 'Yorkville' themselves – other Villagers found them approachable and disregarded the association between the Trailer and the establishment.[77]

In Kileeg's estimation, '[The Trailer] demonstrated the value of using "in" people to make the initial approach to alienated youth when back up services were available … it was recognized and accepted where other attempts have failed.'[78] However, the staff was so young (ages ranged from eighteen to twenty-three that summer) that Kileeg, in the same breath as expounding on the success of employing youth volunteers to treat Villagers, blamed the overcrowding, clutter, and disorganization of the Trailer on their inexperience. The trick was simple, if awkwardly performed: there was an obvious need, in Kileeg's view, for 'continuous "behind the scenes" overall control and supervision' of the site. And yet this need was overshadowed by the reality of the situation: the very success of the Trailer at insinuating itself into the Yorkville scene was reliant upon its being peopled by (apparently unadulterated) local youth. As Kileeg warned, 'further supervision and planning may have the effect of disturbing the relaxed setting of the trailer and may tend to repel the Villagers.'[79]

Trailer legal volunteers, such as Clayton Ruby, Paul Copeland, and John King (all law students at the University of Toronto), made it very clear to the press what their intentions were with regard to their clients' practices. 'We're not here to drag people in and tell them not to take dope; we're not here to moralize or reform,' King told the *Toronto Daily Star* in June 1968, mere days after the Trailer's inception. Ruby and Copeland had begun to conceptualize the Village Bar Association in late 1967, a legal-aid project based in Yorkville which would eventually become a key facet of the Trailer's operation. As Ruby recalls:

> The thing that I did was set up a street legal project. Nowadays you grow up in a universe in which there [are] all kinds of free legal services available in community centres or whatever, called clinics now. We had the first clinic in North America – the first legal clinic. For a while we were actually on the street. So we set up a little table, a school table, and I'd organize law students and lawyers to man that table for a certain number of hours of the night, in the early evening. And we'd sit there and give legal advice to people who were being hassled by landlords, or hassled by cops, or stores that wouldn't let them in, stuff like that. We'd intercede, we'd threaten law suits, we'd put up bail sometimes.[80]

The kinds of cases taken up by these young lawyers and law students tended to revolve around the key issues of drugs, vagrancy, and the ubiquitous 'causing a disturbance' charge: 'My first case,' Ruby recounts, 'was done with Ian Waddell [today an NDP politician in British Columbia]. He and I did our first case together as law students. We defended twenty-odd hippies, including the "world's oldest hippie," a guy who was about eighty-two, or seventy-two, for trespassing. They were living in a house that was abandoned. They broke into this abandoned house, and that's where they were all living. There was about twenty-odd of them, from about sixteen up. And they were all acquitted. This was the Village Bar.'[81] In short, explains Ruby today, the majority of the cases were really about civil rights for Villagers. He and Copeland even set to work penning what would become an extremely successful pocketbook guide to civil rights for Villagers who might find themselves entangled with the Canadian justice system.[82] Whimsically titled *law law law*, and eventually published by the nascent House of Anansi Press (run by a collective of youthful Toronto writers), the guide would go on to become among the biggest sellers in the country.[83] However, not everyone was pleased with the idea. Police officers stood to lose ground if their constituents were able to represent themselves as victims of bullying and prejudice. Moreover, the Law Society wasn't about to let these young upstarts sully the name of their institution. 'One day Paul Copeland and I, he was a first-year lawyer, we got a summons from the treasurer of the Law Society [of Upper Canada],' recalls Ruby.

> And the summons was, 'come to the Law Society, we've had some complaints.' So we show up at the treasurer's office and the secretary Kenneth Jarvis is there, with Arthur Martin who was then treasurer (and later a Court of Appeal judge): a stern, older man. And he demanded that we change our name because it was misleading [... and he said]: 'We want you off the street! It's not becoming for a lawyer to be on the street giving legal advice.' Of course, we were on the street because that's where the kids were! They didn't want to go to a lawyer's office, or *any* office. They were on the streets, you've got to go to where they were. Seemed perfectly sensible to us, but we were forbidden from doing that, so we stopped, and we rented a storefront at that point, a basement storefront, on Yorkville Ave.[84]

The Trailer's balancing act on the straight razor of this apparent cultural divide was fraught with difficulties, beyond the clutter and disorganization of Village youth. Other established and well-funded aid agencies in Toronto, whose help the Trailer (with its tiny, under-trained staff) could surely have used, tended to mistrust the operation. It was too Village-oriented, too haphazard in its procedures to be considered an ally. On the other hand, the young Trailer staff had little time for these established agencies, predictably regarding them as too clinical, too formal, and too rigid in their procedures. As a result, very few aid agencies (such as the Children's Aid Society [CAS] and the Canadian Mental Health Association [CMHA]) were able to sustain any serious dialogue with Trailer staff. Both the CAS and the CMHA found that their only response against the charge that they were too set in their ways, that they were too much of the establishment, was to send their own youth representatives in as advisers.

The Trailer would shut its doors in mid-July 1970, with then-director Judy Johnson citing a general belief among its staff that it had become 'an irrelevant institution. Trailer helped kids for a long time,' she explained, 'but in many ways we became an institution ourselves, and institutions are what many kids are fighting against.'[85]

Toronto's Hippie Matron: June Callwood and Digger House

'Our family joke,' smiled June Callwood in an interview not long before she died, 'is that our kid got out of Yorkville and I didn't.'[86] She explained that her commitment to the Village was born out of her frustration over the misconceptions and false assumptions propagated by media reports about the supposedly middle-class character of the scene. 'I knew first-hand that these were *not* the middle-class kids that were being portrayed. Everybody thought they were still the middle-class kids.'[87] This misapprehension seemed to her the root of the problem of Yorkville. The impression of the scene as being comprised of 'drop outs' from middle-class homes in suburban Toronto, a hippie scene that was bullied and cajoled by outsiders like the greasers and the bikers, was not at all representative. The Villagers she observed simply weren't like her son Barney and his friends 'Blues' Chapman and Clay Ruby in 1965–6. They were younger, and far less prepared (emotionally, physically, intellectually) for the Yorkville that received them. What frustrated her most was that, even after years of intensifying migration to the district, there was still very little support for them, no social institutions, no shelters. And, because Torontonians had false impressions about just who Villagers were, no one appeared to be concerned about the escalating problems in the scene: 'What had happened was that the middle-class kids [had only been] *imitating* poverty: they were wearing shabby clothes and torn jeans, and letting their hair grow. [But] right across the country the message went out to all the kids who'd been in thirty foster homes that there was a place where they would blend in, [where there'd be] lots of drugs, lots of sex, and [where] everything was going to be great. But there was nothing here to welcome them, nothing at all.'[88] Since Callwood didn't see much residual evidence of the positive side of the scene that she remembered from the mid-1960s, she found herself taking up a lonely occupation. As a respected middle-class journalist working among hard-drug-taking, socially ambivalent, under-educated, homeless youth, and openly enamoured of the central refusals that had once underwritten the scene to which these young people had hoped to become a part, Callwood was castigated on both sides as a member of the opposition. Was she a hip apologist or yet another establishment figure trying to undermine the Village scene?

Perhaps because she was of the media herself, Callwood was quick to recognize the complicated way that reportage on Yorkville (whether slanted anti or pro countercultural activities) tended to act as 'a super-lative aid to recruitment.'[89] Michael Valpy agrees with Callwood's assessment but puts the media obsession with Yorkville into some per-spective: '[Yorkville] was now attracting not just kids who were sane and upwardly mobile and all the rest. As a result of the media cover-age, it attracted this *new* population. So I guess in that sense the media was responsible in some way. But it had all the elements of a major media story: it had political conflict, police versus citizen conflict. It had images (real or not) of sex, of drugs, of deviant behaviours. I mean, it was stuff the media would just love. And they did. And then, because of the coverage, it began attracting this whole different population. That's when it tanked.'[90] The proliferation of magazine articles, news-paper updates, television specials, and National Film Board-sponsored studies offered contradictory assessments and treatments of the scene: the Village is powerful, beautiful, ideologically sound, and necessary; the Village is disastrous, violent, unsafe, and wretched; the Village is illusory, *passé*, a home for poseurs and wannabes; the Village is vibrant, exciting, sexy, fun, and cool. Such a complex brew of contradictory val-ue assessments was part of the allure of the scene; very often, the nexus of bohemianism develops at the site of ambiguity.

Indeed, bohemianism usually coheres around an admiration for pov-erty, for the authentic life of the desperate. The search for an authentic experience in a commodified world often translates into a fascination with, even a *pursuit* of, danger, even death. No less an authority than Terry Southern, author of the gleefully filthy novel *Candy* and eventual co-author of the screenplay for the film *Easy Rider*, defined 'hip' as a dance between death and junked-up bliss: hip, he wrote to Paul Krass-ner, implies 'a certain *death* of something near the center ... About the hippest anyone has gotten so far, I suppose, is to be permanently on the nod.'[91] Poetically, there can be no more authentic experience than the fatal moment: the *like a dog!* instant, the final existential crash. This is the needle push, the *petit mort* of the orgasm, the gathering storm of the acid rush. This is the ashes-in-your-mouth hunger of junk-starved street life. (This is also, of course, hardly a new idea. As long ago as the seven-teenth century, John Donne was exploring the connection between 'the nod' and death. 'And poppy or charms can make us sleep as well / And better than thy stroke' ran his mocking rebuke of death's dominion.[92]) Because so often the respect, the hushed-toned reverence, is saved for those who can touch the void and return unscathed – changed, per-haps, but *alive*. At the root, the hip performance has always been about surviving death until you don't. Indeed, the hip pantheon is an assembly of corpses, a slow motion montage of young people who chased, and finally caught, oblivion.

June Callwood believed that she was watching as her son's new friends realized a black taste for death. For their part, the newly formed Diggers came together around the same apprehension. But how to curb this enthusiasm for horror, for the knife-edge thrill of peril? The immediate response was the obvious one: shelters, community building, welfare programs, and counselling, little of which had ever been tried in the Village. Coming together, Callwood and the Diggers agreed that money was the key. She went first to see if Toronto's welfare system was inadequately processing cases from the Yorkville district, because Villagers seemed to be unable to receive benefits: 'I went to the city to see if there'd be a faster way to get them welfare. Well, there wasn't – "No address? Well then, you have to get an address."'[93] Next, Callwood turned to the hospitals, especially the emergency rooms, and discovered their unspoken policy of refusing to treat Villagers: 'One [kid] that I knew very well, she stayed with us over the weekend many times, she was suffering from hunger. Very emaciated. And she went to one of the hospital emergency [rooms] and was turned away ... It was appalling. The rejection in hospital emergency wards – it was *shocking*. I mean, you're supposed to take care of people, not make moral judgments!'[94] What was needed, above all else, was a shelter at which counselling, safety, and understanding were available to these young people.

Establishing such a shelter, it was agreed, would solve a number of the problems the Diggers were facing in their attempts to provide aid to needy Villagers. In the absence of any central shelter, young, broke, and homeless runaways were holing up in crash pads, flop houses, and such, often hiding there for days on end from the realities of their illnesses, their addictions, their fears. Such overcrowded places tended to be unhealthy environments, full of the junk-sick and often the deranged. Spread throughout the university housing areas around Yorkville, crash pads were the new Village community housing, a sign of the rising rents and general disrepair of the Village itself. 'Crash Pads were proliferating, and these kids were hidden,' explains Michael Valpy. 'One of the problems DePoe and Chapman and [Bill] Clement had was in actually *knowing* where they were so they could get help to them.'[95]

If the hospitals weren't prepared to provide these services, and if homeless shelters were inaccessible to most young Villagers, what was needed was a shelter run *by* Villagers *for* Villagers. And so Digger House was born. 'The city was buying properties along Spadina for the Spadina Expressway,' recalled Callwood. Since the Spadina Expressway plan (a wildly unpopular initiative that would have seen a freeway carve through western downtown Toronto) was beginning to falter under pressure from protesters and homeowners, Toronto was suddenly stuck with a whack of houses it had been busily buying up. 'So [the city] would rent it to me, a house that had about eight bedrooms, for about $600 a month. So I put down $600. Now, I was not going to be able to do that for very long. It was a lot of money. We had four kids [my husband and I] were still contributing money to!'[96] Municipal money was scarce. Ministering to the masses of hippies and greasers was hardly a priority for a City Council that preferred to see them die out, rather than be coddled back to health. Undaunted, Callwood turned to prominent Toronto churches and synagogues to remind them of what she believed were their social responsibilities: 'I thought: This is Biblical! You're supposed to give shelter to the helpless. So I went to the churches and two synagogues, with varied results. Nothing from the Catholics. Nothing from the Presbyterians. $200 from Beth Tzedec [a large conservative synagogue]. $200 from the Anglicans. $5,000 from the United Church. And not only $2,000 from Holy Blossom Temple (a large reform synagogue), but also the help of their Social Action Committee, which at that time the leaders were Howard Perlmutter and Fred Zemans. They became active in trying to help.'[97] With money in hand, young allies among the incipient Digger crew, and a renewed outrage fuelled by her discoveries of such clear municipal failures to respond to the escalating social crisis she envisioned, Callwood and her volunteers began to focus their energies on their Spadina Rd haven for Villagers, about one kilometre west of Yorkville.[98]

The house was, by all accounts, a dump – at least at first. Before long, Digger volunteers and the first rounds of residents had transformed the place into a somewhat less squalid version of itself, boasting that 'every room has been painted, the wood varnished, there are even rugs on the floor. The front of the house received a wild Chinese red coat of paint. In their bedrooms, each wall, in fact each panel of a door is usually a different colour.' (One wonders what the neighbours thought of the aesthetic incongruity of a 'wild' red house full of Villagers having suddenly appeared on their otherwise red-brick and plain block.) 'Drop down to the house and look. It *was* a dump. It is now a beautiful, old, distinguished looking house,' entreated one volunteer in a request for funding from the city. 'It looks great!' she enthused.[99] Meanwhile, Callwood continued a relentless campaign of letter writing and speech-making, rallying support (money and food) from all over the city.[100] This aesthetic transformation of Digger House was cast as a kind of group-therapy exercise by Sheila Pennington, an early volunteer. 'As the house begins to shine, so do its occupants. Care and respect are contagious. These youngsters are beginning to care for themselves ... their hair is clean, they bathe regularly. For the first time they are beginning to think and care about who they are as individuals.'[101]

For a year or so, the money held out, if only barely. The story of Digger House (typically referred to as 'Hippie Haven' by police and media) was driven by this constant shortage of funds, and a parallel paucity of support from the city. And yet, by early 1968, it had become an integral and utterly vital service for the Village-based street youth in need of support, shelter, and guidance. As Callwood was quick to point out in her frequent requests to the city for funding and supplies, there was nowhere near enough in the way of support options in place for these young people: 'In Yorkville there is only the magnificent and gallant Community Services Organization of St-Paul's-Avenue RD United Church (which on weekends these summer months closes its doors on the maximum it dares to contain, some *six hundred*). It is a drop-in center which cannot provide overnight shelter, but does distribute free food: about 100 meals a day. [There is also the Trailer.] And then there is the Digger House, with 20 beds.'[102] In its first incarnation, the Board of Directors for Digger House understood the shelter as 'a half-way house between running away and returning to society.'[103] Comprised of a lawyer, a psychiatrist, a professor from York University, a house-wife, and Callwood, the board was decidedly middle class and well connected. However, its first round of applications for financial support went unheeded; apart from a successful application to Ottawa for an income-tax exemption, nothing in the way of institutional or governmental assistance was received for the first year.

The first live-in house administrator, a social worker named Vance Davis, was well liked by his colleagues and directors for his 'maturity' and 'ultimate faith in the potential of these youngsters'; however, his presence, both as an on-site counsellor and as a responsible adult, surely rankled many of his wary charges.[104] Besides Davis, two other live-in staff (one male and one female) helped to maintain order, safety, and cleanliness in the crowded, snug environment, often helping with the cooking (when there was any fresh food to cook) and the enforcement of rules such as curfew and (relative) quiet. Indeed, fresh food was a persistent issue at Digger House. While the occasional casserole or lot of baked goods was donated by benevolent souls, in general the Digger House pantry was bare, and its residents often went rather hungry. As a rule, whatever money they managed to acquire was to be directed to the communal food fund, but drugs, so central to the identity structure of many of the residents, frequently won out in the battle between empty stomach and empty head. In an effort to promote self-sufficiency, some practical Diggers planted a vegetable garden in the backyard of the house, but the few carrots, heads of lettuce, beans, and tomato plants it produced were but small pebbles thrown into the grand canyon of rumbling teenage bellies.

The typical letter to the Metropolitan Welfare and Housing Committee from Digger House stressed the certainty of social disaster if its mission to house and shelter young people went unsupported. The young people were invariably presented as 'desperate,' while their complete and unambivalent distrust, even hatred, for adults was emphasized at every turn. 'These youngsters,' explained one such letter, 'starved both physically and emotionally, view adults as hostile, rejecting, suspicious, and authoritarian.'[105] It seems that, in requests for funding, the association between working-class youth, broken homes, and alienation is counterpoised against a vision of the middle class as successful and emotionally secure.[106] The general refusal of complexity here, the deliberate presentation of these needy young people as uniformly mentally deranged, disturbed, even hopeless, is sensationalist in every way, and not a little disingenuous. In their efforts to secure the view of these young people as unquestionably in need of municipal financial support, such letters often strayed into the territory of excess, even absurdity. One request, from a female volunteer assistant at Digger House, went so far as to characterize the facility as the 'Humane Society' for youth: 'Instead of preventing abuse and misuse of animals, it protects teenagers.'[107]

The residents of Digger House were, of course, a mixed bag of young people, mutable and therefore all but impossible to characterize in any meaningful way. Since it would have been patently absurd to approach the city for funding for a shelter designed to house productive and happy if slightly alienated young people, the emphasis was instead placed upon the extreme cases of truly disturbed, unwell young people who were washed on their shores. 'These were young people the hippies had never imagined,' Callwood wrote in 1969. 'The broken-hearted and nearly destroyed victims of multiple foster homes, parents who were drunks, or insane, or hotly hostile, homes that were bleak and dangerous because of bitter, angry poverty.'[108] The 'real hippies,' as Callwood and others seemed to agree, 'had health to squander.'[109] Since they had come from the middle class – 'because no source but affluence and liberalism could have produced them' – 'their childhood legacy of warm beds, orange juice, pediatricians, regular dental checkups, and summers at the lake' paradoxically steeled them for the 'reckless adventure' of poverty and privation.[110] In one of the more astute observations of the hip refusals of affluence and authority, Callwood recognized that 'few can live for extended periods in a state of risk without having safety in their bones'; in her view, despair needn't creep under the skin if one always feels the enveloping blanket of security.[111] Caught up in the hip death chase, there is a yawning, fundamental gap between the vanishing sense of confidence one feels when alone on the darkened street with no money and no options, and the exhilarating sense of adventure the same situation might inspire in a suburban teen with his parents' phone number in his pocket.

8

Toronto's Hippie Disease

In theory, any visitor to Yorkville who ate in a café, bought any object or contacted any person, may have been exposed to the disease, a liver infection which can eventually lead to death.

– *Toronto Daily Star*, 7 August 1968[1]

THE NEW ANTI-SEMITISM ... DESTROY THE HIPPIES.

– *Satyrday*, August 1968

As the Church Drop-In Centre began to wind down (both as a result of mounting criticism and of the belief that it was no longer serving a positive purpose in the scene), the Reverend James Smith began to withdraw, his role filled by a Catholic layman named John Reid. Described by Smith as someone who 'wrestled with the deep despair of man' and who understood 'the depths of [Villagers'] agony,' Reid had a tough time with what he saw in these young people, what he learned from them, and what he saw in their future.[2] Wrestling with the daily turmoil, the persistent crises, and the mounting cases of overdose and violence that characterized his scene – by the end of 1967, the staff spent 'much of its time policing the crowds,' taking 'ODs out of the centre on stretchers nightly while others "talked down" their friends on acid' – Reid (already once published as a novelist) turned to his writing to help him come to terms with what he was witnessing.[3] By 1969, a new book was coming together, envisioned as an 'historical novel' set in the present, which would provide a detailed, harrowing, and bloody narrative of Yorkville's rise and fall. The result, an epic, vertiginous ramble through philosophical posturing, mysticism, moralism, and debauchery, was the fascinatingly overwrought *The Faithless Mirror*. The novel (which was also, according to reviewer Herbert Rosengarten, the longest work of fiction published to that date in Canada) amounts to a vast denunciation of the Village of the late 1960s and a stirring endorsement of the view of Yorkville as a once beautiful, now desperate community.[4] While Reid's novel begins in a bright, hopeful place, it ends in apocalyptic, gothic horror – his characters mired in an intractable hell, bloody, coarse, and sinister, as the godless and recklessly individualistic Yorkville scene implodes on itself.[5]

Reid's vision of Yorkville as an antediluvian disaster area was not just confined to his novel. By late 1969, he was making public pronouncements on the recent history of the Village and on the grievous state of its current incarnation. Positioning himself alongside June Callwood as another middle-class person with knowledge of the scene, Reid penned a desperate, damning missive for the liberal *Canadian Welfare* magazine which was reprinted in the *Globe and Mail* in early October.[6] Using a young woman named 'Lynda' as a stand-in (something he would do to great effect in *The Faithless Mirror* with the synechdocal character Steyl), Reid offered a capsule history of the Village, of its slip from the precipice of idealism into the inferno of aimlessness.[7] 'The first Yorkville died,' he explained, 'about September 1966; it was composed of a hard core of older and more serious hippies, of above average intelligence, dedicated to a way of life inherited from the beatniks of a decade earlier.' These 'serious hippies,' and their Yorkville, didn't die any natural death; rather, they were killed by rampant 'publicity,' which brought in tourists, and by the subsequent inauthenticity of their Village performance. 'By the summer of 1966,' Reid complained, 'many of the tourists were teenagers, made up to resemble each other, and mistaking other groups like themselves, in beads, bell-bottom trousers and long hair, for the authentic phenomenon.' Immediately, drug use swelled, as did the spectre of sexual violence. 'They came looking for girls,' he says (reminding us that *they* were assumed to be men) and, as if by some cause-effect response, 'girls became available.'

After 1967, Reid reckoned, 'most came, now, from broken homes; they brought their emotional problems to Yorkville, where, in contact with others like themselves, the problems augmented.' But it was 1968 that marked the beginning of the third period, the fall of Yorkville, according to Reid's article. 'Something had released upon us a mob, many of them under age, from all over Canada ... they were young innocents who corrupt faster.' Caught up in this cohort was Lynda, his charge and demonstration subject. A rape victim, speed freak, and suicide survivor (all before the age of seventeen), Lynda had come to the Village because it was the 'in' place, and her life was destroyed. But now, following a devastating string of highs and lows while cranking speed and heroin, Lynda, desperate to get clean, has come to Reid for help. The scene is appalling, paralysing. Reid is holding her down in bed as she shakes through her withdrawal, delirious and agonized. 'At 4 a.m. she went slack. Then she began talking; she saw herself and Yorkville in a sterile light of utter contempt.' She slipped back under, writhing in his arms, until suddenly, in a moment of clarity in the eye of her storm, Lynda knew her attacker, knew where to point her finger. 'And with a low despairing howl [she] filled the dark room with: "God – damn – the *Star Weekly*."'

A certain portion of the post-1967 Village scene was indeed burdened with fear, confusion, and danger. Following a hepatitis scare in August 1968, Yorkville was widely regarded by editorialists and other observers, by many Torontonians, and by many of its own, as having run its course. This hepatitis 'epidemic,' so voraciously consumed by press and public alike, both ready to pounce on any tale of danger and depravity connected to the Village, seemed definitive proof that the Village community had finally hit bottom, was at last being punished for its sins. As Reid's story suggests, the end days for the Village played out for some as a journey through flames. But we must bear in mind that it was not all doom and gloom from the tomb – for every Lynda there was another young person whose experience of the Village in the late 1960s was carefree. It is just that that version of the scene no longer mattered to anyone very much. Instead, the idea of Yorkville as a sick community dominated discourse and press reportage. This chapter considers the months and years following the hepatitis 'epidemic,' years when Yorkville was increasingly known to be a hazardous space, a repository of failure, years when it had few remaining defenders, and even fewer optimistic representatives. The attenuation of local hangouts and rock'n'roll clubs, a disastrous rise in amphetamine abuse, and the advent of Rochdale College a few blocks away, with its irresistible invitation to erstwhile Villagers to come and partake in a new, dynamic, and virtually irrepressible hip scene, left the Village without much in the way of draw. The scene remade, this was the end.

A Day in the Life: Performing Yorkville, Performing Dope

In early 1968 Gopala Alampur asked a variety of his interview subjects to describe a typical day in the Village. Acutely aware of the lack of 'regular schedule' in the lives of these young people, Alampur was curious to know how Villagers understood and articulated their own aimlessness and indigence. His first respondent, whom he dubbed a 'weekender,' provided his version of a typical day in the life.

> About noon there are signs of motion, yawns. Everybody sleeps in. They walk around, sit around, go down to Queen's Park. They are usually just sitting around. They talk about drugs and sex … Around 5–6 p.m. the drug thing starts. 'Where am I going to get my next joint so I can do up tonight?' is the question in everyone's mind. By nightfall everybody is out and they all get together and talk about where the next joint is going to come from and then they go to the Church. People gather together in groups. Hippies go from one group to another. They know everybody. It is like a community. The general attitude is that nobody seems to care about anything. Later on the clubs start opening up and cars start driving through. It is like a Zoo. At night the village is *the* night spot. After midnight the tourists have gone and the hippies wander around until 2 a.m. Then they go to a restaurant.

Alampur concurred with his interviewee's remark on the lack of sleep indulged in by many Villagers. Because the typical scene during the day was rather uneventful, Villagers 'go to sleep whenever they are tired,' just as they 'eat whenever they can get food.' 'When they visit their friends,' he found, 'people take the opportunity to sleep on chairs, on the floors, or wherever they can find space.' And, since all-night parties were common occurrences, 'often one encounters people who haven't slept for over 24 hours and when they do get to bed, they are totally lost and do not know when they will awake.'[8]

For those who did wake up and face the daylight, Alampur agreed with this interviewee that 'most of the Villagers spend their day around the Village looking for drugs on which they can get "high." Their main concern is drugs; how they can procure drugs, to whom they can sell them, or where they can find a place to take them.' Another interview subject provided a much more drug-focused description of a Village day in the life: 'When you wake up you go to restaurants in the Village, go to the Church to meet different people, talk about various people that have been high the night before; and try to find a place to crash. Most of your time is spent talking to your friends. You talk about how and with what you have been "high," how many trips each one had, and several other things. I am usually awake all night talking. Whenever me and my friends are stoned, we sit around and "blow our minds."' Indeed, according to most reports, visiting friends and a general wandering about was tempered by persistent discussions about pot, about the joy of doing up, and about the general plan for getting stoned that night. Perhaps curiously for a community comprised of hormonal teenagers and twenty-somethings, 'drugs and talk about drugs form the main sort of recreation in Yorkville, with sex a poor second.'[9]

By Alampur's estimates, Yorkville was indeed, by early 1968, utterly overrun by substance abuse. 'The variety of drugs used freely in Yorkville,' he claimed, 'can only be astounding to the outsider. It is almost impossible to inventory them, as reportedly new drugs or new mixtures are introduced each week. The substances in regular use for kicks or mood changes include, marijuana, hashish, LSD, amphetamines (speed), frost, cough syrups, asthma preparations, codeine pills, morning glory seeds, STP, airplane glue, nose drops, strammonium [sic], opium, DMT, nail polish remover, cigarettes, depressants of all sorts and, of course, alcohol.' But it wasn't just the range of drugs that impressed Alampur; it was the commonplace, casual use of drugs (*any* drugs) by people with no sense that this activity was dangerous. 'There is virtually no consensus that drugs in general are harmful enough to discourage use.' In fact, apart from heroin (which he claimed only greasers would dare to try), the general rule with regard to drugs was: give it a try. 'I don't like to criticize any drug,' a hippie told Alampur, 'until I have tried it at least once. I would like to try everything once and find out the best and stick to it.'[10]

In that quest for the 'best' drug, many Villagers put themselves through some fairly ghastly experiences. Some, for example, experimented with shooting 'ordinary sugar into their system' and even water directly into their veins, both of which would produce results more painful than euphoric. Since sugar is used to cut heroin (and other injectables), and water is necessary to mix and cook the stuff prior to shooting it, Villagers may have (quite wishfully) been hoping that some of the mix would still bring them some of the way. Another example that fascinated Alampur was the sudden flare-up of interest in nitrous oxide (which users referred to as 'frost'). 'Some of the Villagers fill a balloon with it and then inhale it. The first reaction is almost a sort of choking sensation. As soon as the user recovers from this he begins to speak with a queer bass voice. During the frost ritual, people laugh at one another, giggle, scream and hold their heads, probably to feel if their heads have frozen. The frost reaction lasts only a few minutes.' One greaser told him that 'he could go on 100 trips with a two-dollar frost can.' 'When you close your eyes,' he told Alampur, 'it is beautiful.' Captivated, Alampur witnessed a 'session' (indeed, he may have even held it at his apartment) and recorded various people's comments while under the influence of the stuff.

> Groovy stuff, baby, putting me right out of my mind, wow! wow! wow! I don't understand this at all. God, am I stoned ... Never gotten stoned like this. Really weird. Best stuff ... Little green lights running down your head. Your veins are green. Holy God, does it ever screw up your mind ... Do you understand what I am saying? I don't know what I am saying. Does my voice sound like I think it's sounding? It's blowing my mind. Holy God, does it ever fuck you up ... You can feel it on your teeth. Cold mouth. Feels like going real fast, then slowing down. Is it harmful? This won't kill you ... I can't even feel it now. He's gone. I think it's kind of dangerous. It kills one thousand brain cells. It's like a pick in the crowd. You'll freeze your fuckin' fingers. That will fuck him this time. Am I all fucked up. Baby you know what I like. I am so stoned, what's happened, I have gone way out. I don't believe my fuckin' eyes. All gone. Can't be all gone. Hold it, it's gone.[11]

This bizarre scene, and others like it, led Alampur to the unhappy conclusion that, on a day-to-day basis, many Villagers were deliberately putting themselves in harm's way, chasing down the death trip. Paradoxically, he concluded, 'many Villagers are very worried about the physical and psychological effects of various drugs, but they continue to use them.' Indeed, Alampur puzzled at the fact that, although 'many Villagers believe that their drug use has done them irreparable harm,' this knowledge did not inspire them to give up the practice. Even though 'in numerous conversations they say that "their minds are fucked up" ... few seem to stop using drugs for that reason.'[12]

But, as we have seen, throughout the 1960s Yorkville and drug use had been regularly conflated in the popular press, in municipal reports, and within the Village. Given all of this build-up, how else could these young people perform Yorkville if not through using drugs? By mid-1968 (in what was surely part-goof, part-public service announcement), the underground Toronto paper *Harbinger* was publishing a 'Yorkville Stock Exchange' which detailed the going prices for various drugs, while simultaneously performing a critique of the economy of narcotics in the scene and positioning Yorkville as the centre of the drug trade.[13] As Alampur himself had discovered, 'one could not maintain status as a Villager without frequently using drugs.' Although 'crucial to the definition of a Yorkville hippie is that he uses drugs,' it was now also crucial to the definition of the Villager at large.[14]

Hepatitis Attacks!: Yorkville, the Hippie Quarantine

In mid-summer, 1968, Yorkville became the very 'festering sore' that Syl Apps and other conservative city councillors had claimed it to be.[15] Throughout July, Dr Anne Keyl (through her role as medical supervisor of the Trailer) had admitted an 'unusual number' of patients suffering from hepatitis and had been forced to concede that 'most of these individuals, both in-patient and out-patient, were associated with the Yorkville district.'[16] June Callwood explained Keyl's role in the fostering of an epidemic: 'Dr Anne Keyl ... she was sympathetic ... And she wanted to know what was going on in Yorkville. She was worried about their health and [for me, it was:] finally, here was the establishment starting to worry about them. She was in her fifties, a short stout woman, plain spoken. And when I told her about the conditions, the health condition of these kids, she was appalled. Then somebody came in [and was] diagnosed with Hep B. And she took off on it, huge. Everybody had to get immunized.'[17] She (and her staff) met with the medical officer of health for the City of Toronto and the provincial epidemiologist on 30 July, and then again on 2 August, when it was concluded that, although 'the number of cases of infectious hepatitis reported in Toronto in July 1968 ... was still less than half the number reported in July 1966,' the right move would be to undertake a survey to try to determine the extent of hepatitis in Yorkville.[18]

According to the final report of the hastily assembled Hepatitis Coordinating Committee which was published the following September, 1969: 'Subsequently, two unforeseen events took place, either of which would have been sufficient to transform the "quiet" survey into a front page news story.'[19] 'On the afternoon of the first survey clinic (August 2), at least two newspapers received telephone messages advising that the clinic would begin work that day and suggesting that this would be a good opportunity for a news story. The second incident was the wide distribution in Yorkville, on August 5, of a typewritten single-sheet flier headed, "Danger! Danger! Danger! Hepatitis." The source is unidentified but the news media were in possession of copies in time for the daily papers of August 6.'[20]

The well-timed invitation to the survey clinic as well as the leaflet were actually the brainchild of Dr Bill Clement, chief pharmacologist at Queen Street Mental Health Centre. Following a particularly unproductive meeting with local health officials, the indomitable Clement took matters into his own hands. 'I recall being in a meeting [regarding Yorkville and hepatitis] with the people from Toronto General and Women's College Hospital ... The nice ladies from Women's College Hospital were asking the Province to put up the money for needles to score the blood. The Province doesn't want to pay for it. This goes on for half an hour – they're arguing about the fucking spikes!'[21] Clement, infuriated by this apparent lack of interest in helping the Villagers – Toronto's hospitals were notorious for a paucity of concern for Villagers – was also dumbfounded that the province wouldn't pay for the needles necessary to measure the spread of the illness.[22] 'We're talking about maybe $1,000,' he explained. 'We were also talking about an epidemic that we were trying to nip in the bud. That's the whole purpose – we're going to nip this fucking thing in the bud!'[23] In the end, Women's College Hospital found the money to buy the needles, but not before Clement, enraged by the apathy he had witnessed in the meeting, had alerted the local press to the situation.[24]

The Trailer played a central role in the humanitarian effort to contain the hepatitis outbreak, being (with the Grab Bag) among the first sites in the district to offer free testing for the disease. The incendiary leaflet, it must be assumed, was designed to coax certain otherwise indolent Villagers into action on this potentially devastating issue. Yet, in constructing the possibility of a hepatitis epidemic as a kind of foregone conclusion, the flyer acted as an extraordinarily effective *anti*-advertisement for the district. Compounding this, when Clement alerted the media both to the flyer and to the hepatitis testing stations, he helped to re-establish boundaries around Yorkville and to reinforce the perception that it was a sick community. Yorkville was no longer figuratively ill, it was now quite literally *infected*.[25]

Almost immediately following the initial newspaper articles of 3 August, Villagers started to evacuate. Although the first report in the *Toronto Daily Star* made it plain that the suspected cause of the outbreak was needle sharing, it also explicitly claimed (incorrectly) that intravenous drug use was typical Village behaviour: 'Ten doctors from two Toronto hospitals spent last night in Yorkville looking for cases of a form of hepatitis *often found among hippies*. The disease is believed to be transmitted by hippies using contaminated hypodermic needles.'[26] The Globe and Mail went a step further, referring to an apparent epidemic of 'a little known variety [of the disease] that has come to be known as *hippie hepatitis*.'[27]

Meanwhile, police officers, hugely overrepresented in Yorkville in their efforts to curb the drug trade, vandalism, and underage vagrancy, became concerned that their beat was hazardous to their health. Perhaps as a result of hearing that Women's College Hospital had set up a clinic in anticipation of an epidemic among Yorkville youth, many cops from the Yorkville beat refused to get their prophylaxes anywhere but there. 'There was a cop ward at Toronto General,' explains Bill Clement, but 'the cops refused to go to the cop ward to get shots. The cops were terrified! They insisted on going to Women's College because they didn't trust anyone else.'[28] The following morning, photographs of a swarm of uniformed police, all lined up to get inoculated, appeared in local papers.[29] 'Some asshole ... seems to have phoned all the newspapers,' Clement winks. 'I was shocked and appalled – I open the paper, what a lovely picture!'[30] As the Trailer and the Grab Bag established their testing stations, reporters and observers from various media took up their vantage points in the Village.[31] And, because frenzied reports of a probable epidemic were floated by doctors and the police even before the results of blood testing came back, reporters were left with an easy front-page headline for the following Tuesday morning: 'Hepatitis among Villagers Now an Epidemic, Doctors Fear.'[32]

Toronto was about to get a crash course in epidemiology. A combination of serum hepatitis (now known as Hepatitis B) and the more communicable infectious hepatitis (Hepatitis A) was apparently found in up to twenty Villagers on that first weekend.[33] While the serum form of the liver disease had been expected (since it was well known to be communicated through needle sharing and sexual contact), the second form was not. The evident presence of infectious hepatitis, which could be spread through contaminated food, water, human contact, and a variety of other media, threatened to move the epidemic beyond the boundaries of the Village.[34] But A.R.J. Boyd, the city's medical officer of health, was quick to make it clear in press statements that infectious hepatitis had yet to be conclusively found in Yorkville, and he emphasized that, until it was found, the word *epidemic* was being misused. He cautioned: 'The word epidemic is *itself* sometimes misleading. All the word means is that a great many more cases of a certain disease are showing up than is usual. So far, that is not the case with hepatitis. After all, there have been some years we've had 500 reported cases of the disease.'[35]

Rather than heeding his words, reportage of the apparent epidemic continued unabated and Dr Boyd, along with those city councillors who took up his line, was castigated for dragging his feet.[36] Even on 8 August, when Boyd was forced to admit that two cases of infectious hepatitis had been conclusively found among the stricken Villagers, he still refused to bend to pressure from the press (and, increasingly, the community at large) and to dub the situation an epidemic. He also attempted to clarify the muddied results of the initial rounds of testing in Yorkville which variously reported up to five hundred possible cases of the disease. '[These] blood tests are inconclusive,' he stressed. 'The same test could be positive if someone were beaten up and badly bruised. It just shows tissue damage. I want more than that. The picture is still not at all clear.'[37]

Suzanne DePoe, David's younger sister, had a unique perspective on the hepatitis epidemic. As one of a very few full-time volunteers at the Trailer, DePoe was alerted to the prospect of a hepatitis predicament very early on. 'So that was my next job,' she recalls, 'pinching sick kids off the street and getting them into the clinic for blood tests.'[38] But her proximity to the disease – she had, for months prior to August 1968, been working with the sick and addicted Villagers who came to the Trailer seeking help and advice – proved to be a problem when, very early on in the development of the 'epidemic,' she was felled by the disease. 'And then *I* got hepatitis. I got taken out just as it got big. You see, I was getting a blood test once a week because I was dealing with them [sick Villagers]. And the minute my liver function went off the tiniest bit they whacked me into isolation in Women's College [Hospital]. And there was a picture of me in the *Globe and Mail* in bed in the hospital.'[39] And so the young woman became a cause célèbre for both media and a public who were, by now, very familiar with the name DePoe and its close association with the scene.[40] Meanwhile, the nefarious tourist activity that was Yorkville was being explicitly reconstructed in media reportage, and likely in the minds of many frightened Torontonians, as potentially lethal. Just *going* to Yorkville could kill you. The *Toronto Daily Star*, on 7 August, underlined this characterization with a dire front-page pronouncement: 'In theory, any visitor to Yorkville who ate in a café, bought any object or contacted *any person*, may have been exposed to the disease, a liver infection which can eventually lead to death.'[41]

Newspaper reports in the following days painted a grim portrait of a community in peril. As the apparent numbers of victims escalated – almost 150 people, including as many as six policemen, were reportedly infected by 9 August – editorials appeared which were critical of the city for its slow response to such an obvious catastrophe.[42] Before the end of the week, the province had taken over the investigation 'because people in Yorkville may have spread the disease outside the city of Toronto.'[43] While Dr Boyd attempted to calm a frightened public by blaming the press for overzealous and inflammatory reportage,[44] downtown hospitals were overrun by spooked Villagers 'desperate' for a test.[45] Panic, knowing no boundaries, was in no way confined to Toronto: it was reported that, three days after the initial accounts of the Yorkville outbreak, a public swimming pool in London, Ontario (some two hundred kilometres away), was being drained as a 'precautionary measure.'[46]

The following Monday, the provincial government formally asked the public to 'stay out of Yorkville,' appealing to them to 'satisfy their curiosity at a later date.'[47] Businesses began to suffer. Coffee houses and rock'n'roll clubs sat empty. There were reports that, even in 90° heat, cars passing through Yorkville were rolling up their windows.[48] One Villager, who provided the pseudonym Luke the Drifter, explained to the *Star* that people like him were being treated as pariahs, more than ever before, on the streets surrounding the Yorkville district. 'All sorts of guys are swearing at you if you come near them. They all think you're going to give them hepatitis. One lady screamed at me, "Don't breathe near me, you —!"'[49] Even local celebrities found themselves subject to a new kind of prejudice. Three members of the psychedelic rock band Kensington Market, among the biggest local draws on the Toronto scene, were asked to leave a coffee shop on Bloor St (at Lothian Mews, just adjacent to Yorkville) because they looked like Villagers. 'I don't care too much about who we serve,' explained Stephen Kefkoto, manager of the Coffee Mill. 'But, you know – the hepatitis scare. They were obviously Village residents. Usually they don't come in here.'[50] For most Village businesses, though, it was not as much a question of turning people away as it was of *attracting* them. On the first Friday after the outbreak was reported, it was estimated that the crowds on Yorkville Ave were but a tenth of their usual size. Coffee houses and other hangouts were sparsely populated, and dining spots were reporting a dip (by up to 80 per cent) in reservations. As Marilyn McHugh (of the Penny Farthing coffee house) put it: 'The whole street is down.'[51] Many wondered openly if the Village would ever recover. On 12 August, York Council voted five to four to ask the province to close off Yorkville to the general public – establishing a makeshift quarantine – and to order all of the restaurants and coffee houses in the district to close down.[52]

Fears of diseased Villagers spreading their infection throughout Toronto, along with an apparent desire to keep such youth activity in one place, culminated in the scuppering of a project to build a badly needed youth shelter at the corner of Queen and Bathurst streets, about four kilometres southwest of Yorkville. Originally *for* the project, if only grudgingly and apprehensively, the Queen-Bathurst Merchant Association now turned vehement in its attempts to quash the venture. Armed with the profoundly effective (apparent) evidence that Villagers carried a lethal disease, the group petitioned Mayor Dennison and Controller Margaret Campbell to shut down the plan. 'We said we would go along with the shelter,' explained George Starr, president of the Merchant Association, 'but that was before the sickness.'[53]

By 15 August, blame for the outbreak was ascribed to a culture of permissiveness that had allowed Yorkville to become a hotbed for infection. As a result, city controllers concluded that 'stronger laws [were] needed to put down hippies.' Now afforded the opportunity that many on the Board of Control had been looking for – a viable reason (and workable mandate) to rid Yorkville of its indigent young people – the move to 'clean up' the district was under way. 'As strange as it may seem,' speculated Controller Fred Beavis, 'this [hepatitis outbreak] may have done a lot of good for Yorkville.'[54] In a sense, Beavis's assumption was correct: Yorkville was beginning its long goodbye, fading into the twilight of the late 1960s. The hepatitis 'epidemic' was another signpost along the way, but it was the one that clearly marked the beginning of the end; following almost a month of constant media and municipal announcements that it was the epicentre of an incurable infection, the Village scene would never recover.

And yet the truth is that the famous Yorkville hepatitis epidemic never really took place. When, more than a year later, the report by the Co-ordinating Committee for the Ontario Department of Health was published, it admitted that the vast majority of the (very few) cases of the illness were easily traced back to the unsanitary practices of intravenous drug users, never more than a small minority in the Yorkville scene, the basic point that Dr Boyd was making all along. In fact, the report concluded that, of the total of thirty-two patients hospitalized for probable hepatitis during the outbreak, 'the 27 who were classified as *probable* [serum] hepatitis and the three as *possible* hepatitis used drugs intravenously. The remaining two, who did not use drugs intravenously, [were] classified as probable infectious hepatitis.'[55] According to one clinical account which was included in the report, only twenty-five patients with a diagnosis of hepatitis were admitted to Women's College Hospital during the period from 3 July to 30 September – a period three times the length of the epidemic episode. Of these twenty-five patients, twenty were male, and the age range spanned sixteen to twenty-seven, with a mean age of nineteen. Only one of these patients did not use any drugs, but the remaining twenty-four *all* used drugs (amphetamines) intravenously.[56] In effect, what the report demonstrated was that all of the turmoil and confusion had been massively exaggerated.[57] This was no epidemic – rather, it was, as Dr Boyd had maintained throughout the panic, a minor outbreak which was virtually confined to intravenous drug users and had nothing to do with the water, food, or sanitary practices of the vast majority of Villagers.[58]

Violence, Junkies, and Crime: The Press and the Village, 1968–70

David DePoe's last word on the scene came in early July 1969, following his final victory in court over charges stemming from the sit-ins of August 1967. His appeals successful, DePoe, now twenty-five, was interviewed by the *Toronto Daily Star*. In what must have been a striking revelation to some of his former followers, fans, and friends, DePoe took the opportunity to condemn the Village in its current incarnation. 'The whole dropout thing in the sense of kids coming to Yorkville is over,' he explained. 'Hippies aren't going to make a revolution.' Two years on, the events of the summer of 1967 seemed irrelevant to a more jaded, more deeply radicalized DePoe. Within a year, as a final refusal of the viability of a hippie revolutionary movement, he would join the Communist Party of Canada.[59]

A study of newspaper coverage of Yorkville in 1969 and 1970, the final two years of the Village scene, and the beginning of the serious push towards redevelopment, yields predictable results. With the waning of the expectation that 'true' Villagers were comprised of middle-class hippies, and as ever more troubled youth descended upon the Village in search of community, comfort, drugs, sex, and escape, the press turned paternalistic, condescending, and dismissive. Yorkville was *over*; what remained was refuse and castaways, the busted detritus after a fearsome storm. Although some former residents dispute, one might say *rail against*, the reports of street violence and danger in late 1960s Yorkville, at the time they continued to pile up, effectively dominating coverage of the scene.[60]

As Callwood decried Yorkville's inability to take care of its own, as DePoe finally removed himself from the Village stage with a stunning refusal of the scene, and as bikers and greasers seemed to have effectively taken over the drug trade, the press simply gave up on the Village. The years 1969 and 1970 saw continuing coverage of Yorkville in the *Globe and Mail* and the *Toronto Daily Star*, but few articles gave more than a halting appreciation of the current version of the scene. With the press having turned up their collective nose at what they now continually framed as a violent, speed-addled Yorkville, this late period in the Village is when one finds the complaints of an anti-Yorkville bias in the media to be most accurate. Indeed, there is very little light here. But, given the mounting evidence of illness, addiction, mental disease, violence, and criminal activity in the Village, coupled with the growing resentment of the scene expressed by many of its former champions (all of whom had moved on), what was left to report?[61]

Anyway, the stories coming out of the scene were sensational and unavoidable by 1969. In late May an undercover police officer named Jack Campbell was approached in the Village and 'asked if he wanted a woman for $5.' He bit, and followed the apparent pimp to a room over an Avenue Rd restaurant where he met another man. From there, Campbell was led by the two men across Avenue Rd and onto Bedford Ave. There, he was jumped by the two men he was with, along with two others who had appeared behind them. He identified himself as a cop, even while he was being kicked and punched by the four men, but he wasn't left alone until he managed to pull his revolver and fire a shot into the ground.[62] Another policeman, an undercover RCMP officer, after spending six months in and around the Village, reported that he was 'convinced these people do not contribute to the dignity of man and do try to destroy all they can through slothfulness, indolence and eventually violence through the use of drugs.'[63]

Even more chillingly, guns, rarely heard of in the Village prior to these years, began to haunt the scene. In late June, two police officers found a .32 calibre automatic pistol in a crash pad on nearby Howland Ave, after they were led there by a suspicious character they found hanging around in front of a 'Yorkville restaurant.' It belonged to the

man's twenty-year-old girlfriend.[64] Less than a month later, Gordon
Clark, a nineteen-year-old Villager living on Huron St, was killed by a
shotgun blast to the face by his flipped-out friend, insane in the throes
of a methedrine overdose. Flying high and full of the horror of what
he'd just seen – and done – John Bouweraerts ran to the Trailer for help,
telling them his friend had accidentally shot himself. In the courts, the
whole awful story came out. It *had* been an accident: a stoned, edgy mis-
fire while Bouweraerts was showing Clark how to load the gun.[65] On
top of this, in August and September, at least two stabbings occurred
in Yorkville and its environs, both involving Villagers. In one case, a
nineteen-year-old was stabbed in the back in Yorkville by another teenager.[66] In mid-September, an American ex-pat was slashed in the face
by three youths in an apparent anti-American attack.[67] One young man,
arrested for packing an offensive weapon, explained to police that he
always carried his hunting knife when he went to Yorkville out of fear
for his life.[68]

As more violence, more hard drugs, and more disturbed youth
flowed through the scene, the police presence was expanded in kind.
The courts saw a veritable parade of Villagers throughout 1969, most
on drug charges. Some examples: in early March 1969, a twenty-year-
old woman was handed a four-year sentence for heroin trafficking in
the Village;[69] a series of coordinated busts in late August nabbed nine
Villagers on a variety of drug charges;[70] in September, a would-be
speed dealer was busted while trying to sell fake pills to the police;[71] in
November, a Villager known as 'Judas' got three years for dealing;[72] in
mid-December, a Villager was handed a three-and-a-half-year sentence
for his trafficking in LSD.[73] In response to such frustrations, Village
police officers began to fear that they were being targeted by brazen
criminals. In mid-August, for example, one officer was jumped by a
gang of Villagers and kicked in the throat, damaging his voice box.[74]
The sheen was off: the Village was now undeniably a land changed.
One LSD dealer told the *Toronto Daily Star* that autumn that he no longer dealt his chemical in the Village, but only partly because of the police
presence. 'It's dangerous,' explained David Lewis Stein in a special
report, 'and anyway he doesn't dig the Village people anymore.'[75] The
young man now sold his drugs in the wealthy, old Toronto enclave of
Rosedale. It was safer.

Perhaps feeling emboldened by such revelations, a series of developers – who had been quietly buying up properties throughout
the Village since 1966 – announced plans to build high-rises, hotels,

and parking garages in the spring of 1969.[76] When Toronto planning chief Dennis Barker 'warned' the Planning Board that building
high-rises in Yorkville would spoil the character of the Village, three
members replied that such projects were needed in order to 'clean up
Yorkville.'[77] By mid-March, Barker had softened his position, and the
high-rise construction went ahead amid a trickle of letters to the editor complaining of prejudice towards hippies and a lack of respect for
the character of the Village. This time, the fight was brief, and the victory decisive. By 1970, noise, debris, and dust dominated the Avenue
Rd portions of Cumberland and Yorkville, effectively keeping people
(read: Villagers) from congregating in those areas. In May 1969 New
York Congressman Adam Clayton Powell (who was famously dealing with the deepening crisis in the South Bronx) toured Yorkville and
made a dramatic, and influential, statement. 'Where I come from,' he
told the *Globe and Mail*, 'they call it nigger renewal ... I guess they call
this hippie renewal.'[78]

The Health of Yorkville, 1968–70

One of the most significant findings that came out of both Alampur's
report and the hepatitis panic was that a Villager was unlikely to seek
out medical assistance, even in the face of demonstrable proof that
his or her condition demanded attention. This phenomenon, clearly
endemic among the embattled, much maligned Yorkville scene, was
also reflected in San Francisco's Haight-Ashbury, which had begun to
suffer from the pernicious effects of needle drugs and mental illness
at roughly the same time as its northern cousin. However, as with all
examples in the Yorkville/Haight comparison, the American epicentre
for countercultural identity performance experienced the crisis more
vividly, and on a much grander scale.

By 1968, the Haight was entering into its own period of decline,
largely precipitated by a municipal failure (whether deliberate or not)
to respond to the arrival of impoverished and often disturbed youth
in the months and years after January 1967. In 1970 three health-care
workers familiar with the district wrote a report detailing 'The Health
of Haight-Ashbury.' Their prognosis was dire, to say the least. Building
on the premise (astute and eminently applicable to the Yorkville scene)
that 'people who do not measure up to middle-class standards pose
a problem for organized medicine,' their summary of the collapse of
the district relied on the persistence of the problem of *avoidance*.[79] They

concluded that people in the Haight were avoiding medical attention, even when they clearly needed it, out of a combination of fear and mistrust of authority and establishment symbols of any kind, along with an epidemic of disdainful and unhelpful physicians who discouraged hip youth from coming to see them.

Although violence, chronic diseases, malnutrition, viral infections, and drug-exacerbated psychosis had become ever more rampant in the Haight in the years following the Summer of Love, the report complained that 'physicians appear unwilling to attempt to solve the local health problems. Like many policemen, the public health representatives seem to look on young drug abusers as subhuman.'[80] This, coupled with the legitimate fear on the part of such young people of being handed over to the law if they reported their drug practices to a 'straight' physician, had forced many in the Haight to avoid medical attention entirely.

And so, as the Haight-Ashbury Free Medical Clinic, the first privately operated facility in the United States to cater to adolescents in such conditions, struggled to provide aid to a population too large, too diverse, and too needy to be adequately served by such a small, under-funded, and experimental operation, some of its physicians set out to determine the cause of the crisis of avoidance. Their response, both prescient and hugely perceptive (and, again, in some ways reflective of the Yorkville scene), was to argue that the San Francisco Public Health Department, rather than responding positively to its role as host city to an expanding hip counterculture, 'attempted [instead] to isolate and thereby destroy their community.'[81] By allowing the 'hippie ghetto' (which, by virtue of its proximity to the low-rent Fillmore district, was much less geographically valuable to middle-class San Franciscans than was Yorkville to affluent Toronto) to slip into a state of disrepair, with the dramatic fall in property values that this produced, and by exposing its residents to the scourge of hard-drug use and burgeoning epidemics of poverty, illness, and homelessness, the Public Health Department – if not gladly then at least unsympathetically – had facilitated the sudden crisis in the district. As veterans of the Haight scene moved away in droves in the months and years following the media frenzy of 1967, the arrival of alienated, disaffected, troubled youth looking for a little of what the newspapers and their parents had warned them against only increased. And with them, inevitable as a hangover, followed the death knell for the once vital district.

Up north, it was instead a government-funded commission that took up the study of 'The Health of Yorkville' in October 1968.[82] The response of Ontario's Department of Health following the unsettling revelation of hepatitis was to initiate a massive, full-scale study of the drug and sexual practices of the district, centring on the 'sociological aspects of health problems prevalent among this segment of the population.'[83] The emphasis of the study was to be placed not only on determining the degree of and types of illnesses active in the scene but also on coming to a conclusion about why Yorkville youth chose to avoid medical help. What was it about this disease of the spirit which had deranged Yorkville youth to the point that they had become so utterly self-destructive? What was the linkage between Village ideology and behaviour, drug use, and the Toronto medical services?

From the opening statement of the nearly two-hundred-page unpublished report, 'hippies' is the name given to the 'study population' at issue, though this term is never properly defined. While the report claims to outline the 'hippie subculture' of Yorkville, and to explain the various reasons why this subculture has tended to avoid seeking out medical assistance for its ills, in reality what it is about is the small, but by no means insignificant, portion of the Village scene that used needle drugs. Again, the category 'hippie' was being used to connote 'Yorkville'; and, again, 'Yorkville' was being used to connote 'drugs'; finally, again, all three terms were being used in their monolithic, one-dimensional senses: 'the people,' 'the place,' and 'the activity' were synonymous, as though each was all and all was each. Although the study's methodological approach aims towards a coherent understanding of the place of the Yorkville scene within larger processes both inside and outside Toronto, it remains married to a vision of Yorkville as a hippie zone in which speed has become the drug of choice, further complicating, confusing, even obscuring the history and development of the district.[84]

The study opens with a lengthy examination of ten hours in the life of a particular subject (known only as John) as he attempts to secure medical treatment for his apparent drug addiction and attendant liver problems. 'John is a sixteen year old speed freak' is our introduction to his plight, his identity. He is described in terms that suggest his falling into Alampur's hippie category ('long, abandoned-looking hair,' 'does not try to control events around him, but rather lets things happen to him,' 'comes from a well-to-do middle-class family,' 'adopting the "spokesman of peace" role with anyone who can stand it'). However, his amphetamine use frustrates Alampur's view that only greas-

ers indulged in needle drugs, suggesting either a new development in
the Yorkville drug scene – Alampur's report was completed some four
months prior to the start of fieldwork towards the Health of Yorkville
study – or, more likely, the over-simplification inherent in Alampur's
categorization of behaviour.

Either way, John is presented as a boy who, although 'not representative of all the young people we shall be describing,' is confronted with problems defined as 'typical in their complexity and
diffuseness.'[85] These problems – drug addiction, symptoms of pressing
medical issues, and a general apathy towards seeking out medical care
– are presented in the form of a 'diary' by a 'detached youth worker' who tries to help John to secure treatment. The youth worker's
attempts to this end are complicated by a variety of problems, not the
least of which is a Toronto General Hospital (TGH) Emergency Room
which is openly hostile to treating any drug-addicted Villager. John,
with the aid of his mediator, argues with various doctors and nurses at the TGH, but does not receive any actual treatment, for six and
a half hours. Eventually, John is shipped to the Queen Street Mental
Health Centre after it is suggested that there might be 'an underlying
schizophrenia' at work.[86]

Such antipathy towards Villagers and their problems promoted a
dangerous trend in Toronto's emergency rooms.[87] Villagers, struggling
with the various stigmas associated with the scene, faced an uphill
battle once they made the decision to try to escape their drug addiction, social alienation, mental illnesses, or physical discomforts. Villagers hardened by months of street life, addicts aching for a hit, and/
or paranoid teens scared that the cops (or worse, their *parents*) will be
informed that they have been taking injectable amphetamines were
treated by various Toronto hospitals as hopeless cases, as being somehow not worth the time and attention of physicians. When it came to
understanding the reluctance of medical professionals to deal with
the Village health issues head-on, the study found that 'the majority
of doctors and nurses in the two major downtown hospitals surveyed
would like to see the treatment of drug-related cases *removed* from the
hospital setting, and place high priority on the provision of alternative
facilities outside the hospital.'[88] The main concerns expressed by the
doctors and nurses in the study orbited around the frustration they
felt towards treating drug addicts with band-aid solutions rather than
offering them long-term, effective cures. This response was dismissed
by the study as an excuse to continue to offer truncated care: 'If the

attitudes expressed by medical personnel in our survey can be regarded as expressing medical and nursing opinion in general, there is a poor prognosis for improving the quality of care available to young people ... in our study.'[89]

This was, according to the study, a terrifying prospect. All of its findings pointed to a growing epidemic of mental illness, drug addiction, and physical deterioration at work among Toronto (especially Yorkville) youth. There was unsettling, alarming evidence that nearly 77 per cent of the study population in the report was unhealthy – and that fully one-third of this unhealthy fraction was decidedly ill. The study based this gloomy conclusion on the findings of a survey which asked if Villagers had experienced any of a list of thirty-six signs and symptoms in the past two weeks. These responses had been organized into categories ('healthy,' 'low symptoms,' and 'high symptoms') based upon the number of times respondents had ticked the various boxes beside the list. The symptoms reported, ranging from the somewhat innocuous ('Loss of Appetite,' 'Loss of Weight,' 'Headache,' 'Sweating,' 'Easily Startled') to the severe ('Urethral Discharge,' 'Blood in Stool,' 'Excessive Vaginal Bleeding,' 'Lump in Abdomen'), paint an ugly picture of the types of infirmities endured by many of these Villagers. Such symptoms, indicative of anything from malnutrition, dehydration, and/or sleep deprivation to hepatitis, venereal disease, and/or cancer, were found to literally plague the respondents to the survey. Ultimately, 22 per cent of the sample was deemed 'healthy' (i.e., they failed to check any boxes) while 53 per cent were 'low symptom' subjects and 24 per cent were 'high symptom' subjects.[90]

Unsurprisingly for a group of people prone to drug use and fear of police persecution/prosecution, and whose perceived identity (as hippie, Villager, greaser, whatever) remained a source of scorn and derision for many fractions of society, the two most commonly reported symptoms were 'Restlessness and Agitation' and 'Nervousness and Tension.' 'Loss of Weight,' a common side effect of even simple drug use, poverty, and an unsettled lifestyle, figured prominently as well, appearing in over 75 per cent of the cases in the 'high symptom' category. According to the study, 'a similar picture [was] presented by the following symptoms: Excessive Fatigue, Pain in the Chest, Loss of Appetite, Nausea, Pounding Heart, Shortness of Breath'; again, such symptoms could easily be explained as related to excessive, but generally benign, use of marijuana, tobacco, alcohol, even caffeine.[91] However, they could also be indicative of more severe, chronic illnesses. Because these respondents were so unlikely to have any of these symptoms checked out by a physician, we are left with a high percentage of youth who, judging by their check marks on a questionnaire, could be suffering from anything from thyroid cancer to a particularly vicious hangover.

More than any other element, it was speed that transformed the character of the Village in the late 1960s.[92] As younger, more disaffected, more troubled youth continued to frequent the Yorkville district in these years – rearranging the social structures that, although always in flux, had been fairly well established prior to the advent of harder drugs – the disintegration of so-called 'true hippie' ideologies occurred rapidly and irrepressibly. Psychedelic drugs such as LSD continued to be used, but the emphasis on this particular substance as the dominant 'hard' drug in the district was fast disappearing as speed, and other needle drugs, became the predominant issue among observers of the scene. One LSD dealer in the late 1960s complained that, as a result of the lumping of LSD with other, less beneficial drugs such as speed and heroin, not only was LSD seen by many young people as an escapist drug, a *party* drug, but it was also being dealt by increasingly dangerous criminal elements. 'It is not in *any* sense a party drug!' he stresses. 'And people take it in combination with other things! You know, they'd drink a bunch of beer and do a few lines and this and that, and then drop some acid, and then they'd wonder why the acid didn't do for them what they had heard it would.' As a dealer, and as a Villager who saw the LSD experience as a sacrament that needed to be shared, he found himself torn between his belief that Villagers had an obligation to keep LSD available, and the necessity of dealing with dark criminal elements in order to do so. 'As I got into the dealing scene,' he laments, 'there were a lot of unholy alliances. You wanted to get your stuff distributed, but, unfortunately, because of the way the law was fucked up the way it was, you were forced to deal with criminal networks.'[93] But criminals, preying on the ever more destitute and transient population, made less money on LSD than on addictive drugs like speed. While LSD may have been illegal, and therefore at least somewhat lucrative (especially in a concentrated community of acidheads such as the Village), no non-addictive drug could ever compete with amphetamines for return customers.[94] Young people, happy or unhappy, indigent or affluent, were all vulnerable to the addictive, unstable, and suddenly highly available chemicals as they drifted through the collective consciousness of the Village.

The Health of Yorkville study discovered, to its considerable horror, that speed had become a tolerable (if not quite conventional) performance of Village identity. Even worse was the way many Villagers
seemed to be interpreting the symptoms of their various illnesses –
many of which were directly attributable to their drug use – as badges
of honour. The study suggests that, 'although such symptoms [chest
pain, shortness of breath, persistent backaches and headaches] are
sometimes viewed with alarm by the user of drugs, they can also be
seen as "desirable" attributes of risk-taking ... the threat to life involved
in such experiments seems to heighten the user's pleasure.'[95] In the
bewildered common sense of a drug culture that saw itself as inevitably disconnected from the 'straight' world, any such sign of community
interconnectedness was to be celebrated.

Instead of perceiving the symptoms of, say, hepatitis as miserable,
adverse results of their drug use, many amphetamine users reported
to the study that they enjoyed, *even sought out*, such a distinction. In
an interview with an 'ex-speed-freak,' the study's investigators were
informed that, 'if you got hepatitis, it sort of implies that you were shooting with one of the big time somebodies and you got it from them. So
that is what they do – it means that you are a registered speed-freak.'[96]
This use of speed-related illnesses as status devices, as a means of conferring authenticity, suggests a more recent and markedly more severe
disjuncture between hegemonic ideologies regarding health and power
and those within this subgroup. The position taken by the study, that
the Yorkville speed community was a distinct, separate, and otherwise
incomprehensible Other, is reflected in its conclusion that 'the drug-
using community, and the speed community in particular, is a world
apart.' It had become not simply a case of alienated, drug-addicted
youth who needed assistance; this phenomenon could be understood
only in terms of its circumscribed Otherness. '[This community] has its
own rules of conduct, sanctions, rewards and pressures ... The speed-
freak's investment in the community is frequently one of total depend-
ence. He needs the ritual of the life-style and the effect of the drug (in
that order) simply to provide a baseline identity and sense of purpose
for himself.'[97]

For many Villagers, the public impression of 'speed freaks' as suffering through their addiction was an attribute to be cultivated as an
attention-getting device. The realization that so much concern was
being lavished upon this particular fraction of the Yorkville scene perhaps invited many newcomers – more and more comprised of the long-

suffering refugees from unhappy and violent homes, destitute hitch-hikers from the small-town north, too-young runaways in no shape for the struggle of street life, and the clinically insane – to choose the mantle of 'speed freak' as a means of being recognized, of achieving a certain authentic status in the scene. Status, however, did not necessarily translate into respect or trust. Many Villagers saw little to be celebrated in the speed-freak performance. 'Speed-freaks are funny people,' explained one Villager in the summer of 1969. 'Like, they always think their kidneys are falling out or their livers are swollen and they are hypochondriacs. They really get into walking around going *oh-h, my kidneys!* They don't stop shooting speed; they just like complaining … They want you to say, *Oh, poor little speed-freak!*'[98] Longing for attention, pity, *help*, many of these neophytes were slipping into a vertiginous, and brutishly short, future of addiction, the deadly Sisyphean sport of shoot-cop-shoot.

Not all of the members of the study group in the 'high symptom' category perceived their illnesses to be enviable – both fear and insecurity played significant roles in keeping Villagers away from emergency rooms. The study put this problem succinctly, further entrenching the position that this group must be seen as an Other, with distinct and different ideologies, behaviours, identities: 'They often fear being reported to the police,' but, more important, 'they dislike being preached at over their appearance, way of life and behaviour.'[99] In this case as in most, the expression of community was as much a reflexive as an active exercise. While drug use was a badge of inclusion among Villagers, signifying a wide range of shared ideologies, even identities, in the simple practice of doing up, the external (mis)understanding of such ideologies and identities was equally important. For most Villagers, the belief that 'straight society' was unable to comprehend the scene was at least as important as the need for Village youth to understand one another.

But, in the emergency room, this artificial disjuncture between ideologies – straight doctors versus hip youth – played to the considerable disadvantage of the Villagers. Unwilling to be treated as a weird, unfortunate child – but simultaneously portraying himself in just so deliberately cultivated a fashion, based on his distaste for a society he hoped to subvert – the Villager who resorted to a downtown Toronto emergency room more than likely found the experience utterly alienating. Treated as an unfortunate, a disappointment, a failure, he would be asked to endure the horrific realization that his very *identity* as a Villager had brought him low. Still, if he were there to be treated in just this way – if he were interested primarily in the attention of others over his experience with drugs – he was sure to get exactly what he was looking for in the typical emergency room.

The importance of status and authenticity, given its most extreme articulation by those speed-addled Villagers who bragged about their illnesses, was also noted by the study in its assessment of the kinds of drugs taken (and championed) by Villagers. In the summer of 1969, the investigators analysed a variety of drugs they obtained in the Village, and came up with some disquieting results. 'Users are often not getting what they think they are getting,' they concluded. 'For example, LSD is frequently contaminated, cut, or inert or psychoactive in unexpected ways as a result of poor synthesis. Heroin is rarely heroin and is usually cut. Mescalin [sic] is often LSD and subject to the same provisos as above.' Still, the study concluded, this didn't seem to bother most of the Villagers they interviewed: 'It is important that young people *think* they have used a substance.'[100]

Of course, it shouldn't take too many experiences with drug addicts for medical professionals to realize that, even if the patient has come to the hospital seeking attention for her drug addiction, she may simply be seeking *attention*. In this case, after she has received the interest and concern she has sought, she will return to the street to look for another hit. Can it be surprising, then, that many health-care professionals became frustrated by the caricatures that came to them with track marks up and down their arms? When a 'speed freak' walked through the door, why wouldn't a nurse read her as a nuisance, rather than a patient? Or, more likely, as yet another nameless, faceless 'speed-freak,' undifferentiated in her symptoms, appearance, stock stories? And so, the study discovered, 'medical personnel often unintentionally reinforce the speed-freak's negative identity and behaviour by concentrating on his drug use.'[101]

The result was that an odd and treacherous paradox was born: 'The speed-freak can acquire status from the speed community by contracting hepatitis, and have the status perversely confirmed by the medical profession.'[102] Confirmed through external recognition, shock, and concern (feigned or real), the speed freak's status (as 'speed freak') then becomes the only real thing that can be perceived by either party. No longer necessarily visible as a young man or woman with a sickness – and no longer presented to the nurse as such – the person finds their status, identity, and behaviour reductively displayed, and superficially appreciated. For the young woman's disease is inevitably understood to be as much a result of her association with Yorkville as it is with the drugs that have wasted her body. As we have seen elsewhere, such a tangle of location/behaviour/identity ruled all interpretation: thus, for the medical profession in the late 1960s, Yorkville, drugs, and hippie meant the same thing.

A Complete Cycle: End Days at the Church Drop-In

As other humanitarian aid groups moved into the Yorkville scene, a curious kind of competition became evident. A new breed of distrust, previously barely apparent among the St Paul's regulars, had become evident in the wake of the allegations of drug pushing out of the Drop-In Centre.[103] As the Community Services Organization staff tried to downplay the accusation that they sanctioned drug use and dealing, they were also met with the even more dangerous allegation that bikers were using the church as a means to collect victims for their gang rapes. But the subsequent decision to ban the bikers from using the church at all was met with an angry reaction from the do-your-own-thing fraction of the scene, many of whom were caught up in an admiration of biker authenticity.[104]

That reaction, coupled with mounting fears that the CSO might be willing to turn in some users to offset the contention that they sanctioned drug use, prompted a boycott of the centre. The Reverend Smith explained the boycott in ambiguous terms: 'This political boycott was the work of underground activity groups that classed the CSO as "establishment." There was a difference in ideology which the CSO was powerless to change if it was to keep its financial support.'[105] Presumably, what Smith means by this is that, because the church was accepting its financial support from establishment sources, it could not be trusted by some Villagers. However, the 'underground activity groups' to which he refers remain shadowy.

Meanwhile, the Diggers, working to introduce Digger House as a comprehensive food bank and shelter for Yorkville youth, were finding their efforts emulated by the 49-ers, another aid group born out of the scene.[106] This new, youth-operated aid group came to St Paul's with the plan to organize a mass 'feed-in' for hundreds of Yorkville youth. Since the church was in the midst of the boycott, Smith and company decided (if only 'against our better judgment') to allow the Diggers/49-ers to take over the centre, hoping that this might rehabilitate the space in the eyes of the Village. 'They must be given an "A" for effort in their food program,' mused Smith, 'but they defied all city regulations and completely embarrassed their host.'[107] 'They called our volunteers the "bottle-picker-uppers" and made them feel irrelevant. After three days all cleaning stopped and the garbage was piling up mountain-high. Since they got their supplies from market leftovers the basement and kitchen were strewn with rotten vegetable leaves and peelings. There were quarrelling factions among the Hippies and some were fronting for a marijuana supplier. On the fifth day, we threw in the sponge.'[108] The centre recalled its volunteers and reopened as before, with the boycott still hanging over its head. Months went by before Villagers started to return, but Smith found this new cohort to be 'a dull and difficult clientele.' Apparently unorganizable, they were more violent (knifings were cited as one of the reasons young people no longer attended meetings at the centre) and took to swallowing harder drugs in larger quantities. 'Once [Mike] Waage could talk or threaten the teeny boppers out of taking street drugs,' lamented Smith, 'but the new crop ceased to respond.'[109]

A master's student in the School of Social Work at the University of Toronto wrote her thesis on Yorkville in the spring of 1968, using the Drop-In Centre as a base for her interviews and observations. The thirty-six Villagers in her focus group (all of whom were between the ages of sixteen and twenty-four) represented all but two Canadian provinces. Not only that, eight countries apart from Canada were listed as place of origin. None of them had enjoyed any form of university education, although four had tried technical schools. Moreover, all but five of the thirty-six had dropped out of high school before grade 13; four had dropped out as early as grade 8. Smith was, by 1968, working with a complex community; his flock – young, undereducated, often homeless – was hardly definable in the same terms as it might have been a few years earlier.[110]

Although the Drop-In ran along into 1971, it was no longer a primary party spot, no longer the jubilant dancehall it had been all those nights back in 1966. Now catering mostly to young people from the immediate area (rather than simply anyone who happened to want a place to hang out), the Drop-In entered 1970 at the tail end of what Smith dubbed 'a complete cycle.' 'A new crop of "little brothers and sisters"' had, just as had the 'young fry' before them, 'adopted the centre. They live in the Yorkville-Annex area and spend a great deal of their evening hours listening to CHUM and playing the table games. The presence of travelling Hippies is accepted nonchalantly by this group.'[111] Accepted, but not expected, hippies no longer defined the scene.

Rochdale College and the Rise of Hip Separatism

After 1968, many of the Villagers who would otherwise have been spending their days and nights very publicly on Yorkville's thin streets found a new home and hangout at Rochdale College.[112] Off the streets, effectively erased from the visage of the city, Rochdale's scene operated as a (mostly) self-contained, even self-reflexive, unit. Yorkville may have been metaphorically cut off from Toronto, tied to a map of meaning which treated it as a circumscribed island of difference within the wider cityscape; but Rochdale actually *was* cut off.[113] With its inhabitants seemingly cloistered (some rarely ever leaving the building!), contained under a kind of self-imposed exile from the wider community, Rochdale's inception marked the end of the Village scene.

Rochdale College was born of the post-baby boom movement in education towards accommodation and experimentation. Accommodation, that is, of youth and individuality, and experimentation with the form, function, and process of pedagogy. The innovation of Rochdale College – an eighteen-storey apartment complex at the corner of Bloor and Huron streets, not half a kilometre from the Village – was that it would be both a home to hundreds of students *and* a hyper-condensed campus.[114] This was to be a free school at which students would be encouraged to throw off the stultifying structures of the multiversity – at Rochdale there would be no structure to speak of (unless that's what you asked for), no traditional classrooms, no traditional homework, few traditional rules.[115] Rochdale opened (even though the building remained unfinished) in September 1968, just as the Yorkville hepatitis scare wound down, delivering a second, decisive, blow to an already struggling Village community.

From the very beginning, young people streamed into Rochdale, and they brought with them all of the problems that would keep the building from achieving many of the goals its founders had set for it. By 1969, as its most prominent supporters gave up on their creation in frustration and despair, Rochdale was collecting the accrual from an eroding Yorkville: 'crashers' and otherwise homeless teens, runaways and speed addicts, poets and radicals, hippies, bikers, and greasers looking for a new scene. Improving on Yorkville in a variety of ways (no cops, no parents, no politicians, no money, fewer – well, *different* – hassles) and re-creating, apart from live rock'n'roll, the best of what the Village had to offer (plentiful drugs, abundant sex, likeminded young people, a sense of community), Rochdale was the pushbroom that swept through the Village in the late 1960s, carrying most everyone away.

From 1968 to 1975, Rochdale served as an ongoing Happening fuelled by drugs, sex, politics, and the radical pursuit of freedom, a tumultuous and vibrant pedagogical experiment gone wrong (or right, depending on one's understanding of education) and a self-imposed concentration camp for the hip performance. Whereas Yorkville represented a 'cancer that is spreading through the city' to many frightened observers, Rochdale was self-contained and, as such, almost entirely non-threatening. These erstwhile Villagers *wanted* to stay inside; indeed, that was kind of the point. Toronto, however accidentally, had managed to find a way to rid its streets of hundreds of its most radical non-conformists. As Yorkville slipped into its desultory final period of rising rents, drug abuse, mental illness, and intense redevelopment, Rochdale called out to the curious and the desperate alike: *Yorkville is over, but we have only begun.*[116]

For those hundreds of committed Villagers to whom Rochdale's promise of high-octane zaniness, constant partying, experiential education, and revolving-door community wasn't appealing, there was always the back-to-the-land option. In the late 1960s and especially the early 1970s, rural communes were established across Canada, often run by ex-Villagers. Most famous of these was the series of communities founded near Killaloe, Ontario, in the late 1960s, including the Morning Glory Farm and, later, Rochdale Farm. Examples of a certain radical refusal of Canadian society, such communes also reflect (as did Rochdale) what is often referred to as the failure of the 'hippie revolution.' By removing themselves from the wider community – in some cases this removal was fairly substantial, since some farms were very nearly self-sufficient – these communities had, in effect, attempted to step out of the hegemonic process that Yorkville, as a highly visible battleground and symbol, was so much a part of. (Debates over the issue of engagement raged throughout the late 1960s and into the 1970s, and in some cases persist today.) With many of them still living according to the ideological credos which had led them to establish the community in the first place, the remaining 1960s-era rural communes represent a successful attempt to remake the scene in a new setting.[117]

The hippie diaspora, as represented by the emergence of communes and by the fortress of alternative identity that was Rochdale, was also, of course, present in the simple dispersion of Village performers into the wider population in the post-Yorkville era. The end of the Village may have meant the end of a scene where young people found a public stage on which to congregate (and, crucially, to confront the wider society), but anyone who lived through the early 1970s and beyond knows that the Villagers hardly disappeared when their space was finally given over to developers. Rather, they became, if anything, *more* visible, as longer hair, hippie fashions, and drug use bled into the mainstream, co-opted by major corporations and reflected in popular culture. As sociologist Sam Binkley and others have persuasively argued, the media, political, and consumerist obsession with youth culture in the 1960s led to the mainstreaming of what had been, during the Village heyday, distinctively hip aesthetics and performances.[118] In the 1970s, such Yorkville activities as 'soft' drug use, freer sexuality, and shaggier hair were no longer specifically tied to the hippie phenomenon.[119] In a sense, the spreading out of hippie identity and activity from prescribed centres such as Yorkville (or the Haight, or Kitsilano, or Greenwich Village) produced a wider cultural shift than had the more focused earlier phenomenon. Hippies were everywhere; although drop-out culture had been demystified, and radical student politics had lost much of their former coherence, their legacy was present, apparent, in most every aspect of Canadian (even *global*) society into the 1970s and beyond.[120]

Conclusion:

An Immense Accumulation of Spectacles

'In societies dominated by modern conditions of production,' argued Guy Debord in a landmark 1967 text, 'life is presented as an immense accumulation of *spectacles*. Everything that was directly lived has moved away into representation.'[1] Debord's famous criticism of the insubstantiality of modern life, of its repetitious, practised expressions, offers something of a frame through which we can view Yorkville in the 1960s.[2] Yorkville was the stage on which the Canadian counterculture gave its most celebrated, studied, and complex performance; and it was also a performance (often visually) consumed by millions as it was repeatedly represented in near-saturation coverage in newspapers and magazines, on television, and, eventually, in films. Indeed, Yorkville was a stage, its Villagers the performers in a spectacular expression of cultural rebellion and experimentation with alternative modes of dress, behaviour, belief, and practice.[3]

Outside the confines of the district by the mid-1960s, such unconventional activities as drug use and liberated sexuality, or aesthetics such as long hair and thrift-shop fashions, were being read by Torontonians as performances of *Yorkville*. As such, Yorkville played out for many Canadians (as thousands of young people crossed the country to take part in the scene), and for most Torontonian baby boomers curious enough to check it out, as a means to approach social rebellion merely by *being* someplace. Thus, Yorkville constituted a local-foreign space in and through which a disparate, diverse, and diffuse collection of people performed a protracted spectacle of social and cultural rebellion. But it must also be conceded that, for the vast majority of them, this was never more than a fleeting identity performance.

The political relevance of this space must not be dismissed. Although the spectacle of Yorkville was in some sense itself 'moving away into representation' virtually as soon as it emerged onto the public radar, and although such spectacles tend to obscure more pressing, more politically significant, issues, throughout the 1960s the Yorkville spectacular *did* constitute a meaningful site of social and cultural rebellion. For many, it was a site of amusement, a theatre in which to act out passing adolescent desires for community and identity, for fun and sex; but for many more, it constituted a site of politicized community, identity formation, and experimentation with living otherwise. Indeed, as Canada's foremost hip centre, visited by tens of thousands of people over a period of roughly ten years, Yorkville offered an incalculably influential example to a generation of Canadians.

That said, Yorkville also stands as a significant instance of the limitations of cultural experimentation in the 'Society of the Spectacle.' One hesitates to view the Village in terms of a winners-and-losers framework, but there is no question that this embrace of spectacle and performance allowed masses of people to engage with the scene while simultaneously setting up the space as a site of limited political potential. In general, New Left activists distanced themselves from the scene after 1965, and they were widely critical of the ethereality of Village performances. The sense was that, whatever these folks represented, they held no meaningful potential for real progressive change. In short, many (if not most) emerging political activists recognized, and disparaged, the spectacular nature of the Village.[4]

Throughout the 1960s, Yorkville was a contested territory. For some, it was a kind of sanctuary from the general common sense, a place in which you could 'do your own thing.' These Villagers shared a common uneasiness about (not to say disdain for) the wider public, and, although they acted in different ways, they all aimed to create in Yorkville a space in which hegemonic constructions of reality were rendered inconsistent. However, this sort of idealism failed to incorporate an appreciation of the political potential of their spectacle: in refusing these established norms of belief and propriety, and by revelling in deviant, even criminal, identity, many Villagers were simultaneously legitimating the very social norms they aimed to refuse. Their behaviours, their adopted identities, were not 'normal,' and they knew it – the very spectacle of their self-conscious performance of Otherness helped to define the Village against the 'normal' world. It was an unreal space – a representation, another version of the real world.[5]

In the 1998 film *The Big Lebowski*, perhaps the best Hollywood picture to deal with the legacy of the 1960s, the aging hippie played by Jeff Bridges finds himself in a darkened, fire-lit, book-lined study, discussing politics with a millionaire war veteran some thirty years his senior.[6] 'Your revolution is over,' counsels the conservative figure, as the bemused Bridges turns away. '[My] condolences. The bums lost. My advice is to do what your parents did: get a job, sir. The bums will *always* lose. Do you hear me?' But he doesn't. Do we?

Did the Villagers lose the culture war? If Yorkville was their Waterloo, then much of the evidence certainly suggests that they did. Yorkville, by 1970, was a fading memory. Where were those 'true hippies' who were supposed to have inhabited its streets, coffee houses, rock bars, and jam sessions? Not in Yorkville anymore, nor hanging around the Mont Blanc, Webster's, or the Drop-In Centre. Sure, you might find them at the Riverboat for a big show, at the Rockpile (Toronto's answer to Bill Graham's venerable Fillmore) to see the Doors, Kensington Market, the Grateful Dead, or Led Zeppelin. But, when the last notes rang out, even before that cerulean smoke cleared, they were gone, spreading into the night.

But we know that they weren't gone. The *Village* was gone, and its Villagers dispersed, but the reality of the early 1970s and beyond is that the number of young people performing at 'hippie,' espousing anti-establishment visions and opinions, taking mind drugs and practising a version of free love, clamouring for tickets to the next big rock festival, was *swelling*. This book has run up towards this final question, this apparently ambiguous ending. Most everyone who takes a moment to consider the story of the Village comes to the convenient conclusion that, since it *was*, and then *wasn't*, a 'hippie haven,' then the young people must have failed to win the day. *The bums lost*. But there are other, more apposite, ways of assessing this outcome, all tied to the themes we have explored above.

In Yorkville, throughout the 1960s, a series of competing heuristics saw the Village become an interpretive battleground. Its *maps of meaning* were based, all of them, on mutable concerns. Was Yorkville to be an oasis of beatnik youth or an enclave of carriage-trade sophistication? Was it to be the refuge for hippies or a rejuvenated shopping centre? A greaser and biker hangout, or a middle-class drop-out scene? In the end, but merely superficially, one side of this battle won the ground – Yorkville, by the end of 1970, was well on its way to becoming a shopping district with few remaining connections to youth. And because Yorkville was, throughout the 1960s, conflated with countercultural Toronto; because *performing* Yorkville was understood to be the same as *performing* counterculture; because Yorkville seemed to represent the *whole* scene, a synecdoche for the otherwise diffusive experimentations and convictions of 1960s youth; because of all of this, when Yorkville was refigured by developers and municipal initiatives, it was possible (at least metaphorically) to perceive this as the annihilation of the counterculture.

So the stuffy conservative character in *The Big Lebowski* was right (the 'bums' *had* lost the ground war), but he was just as hopelessly wrong. All of the emphasis on the battle for ground, for space, was misplaced, a misunderstanding of the real culture war. In the end, the pervasive influence of hip ideologies and performances is evident, even in this era of neo-liberal repression, in virtually every lighted corner of the global village. By the early 1990s, the Grateful Dead were the highest-grossing music act in the world, attracting lawyers, freaks and politicians, ageing hippies and the wistful young, all of them still acutely aware of the continued relevance of hip aesthetics and ideologies.[7] The Burning Man festival, which attracts tens of thousands of 'neo-hippies' to its carnivalesque proceedings each year, attests to the size and scope of the next generation of what, in 1965, was just a small collection of idealists and drop-outs.[8]

Ultimately, to reduce the Village to the simple equation of win/lose is to miss the plot. In the first place, it mistakenly assumes that there was something to win, something that could be gauged. But, more fundamentally, it fails to consider the reality that thousands upon thousands of people made the scene in those years, attracting and courting attention, confusion, and all of that electric noise. And so what Yorkville represented for that brief period remains as relevant today as it was to its participants at the time: in the most radical sense, and for all of its various collaborators, it was about performing emergent identity in new, exciting, and fundamentally *other* ways. It was about seeking an escape from the expectations of a world which seems fraught with conformity and boredom, absurdity and violence, apathy and repression. It was about repeatedly making and remaking an inspiring, extraordinary, invigorating scene, built on the twin principles of experimentation and freedom. And it is that scene, above all else, that stands as a point of reference, a signpost along the road to a transformed society.

Epilogue:

Where They Landed

Perhaps a measure of the significance of the noisy scene that was 1960s Yorkville can be taken by looking at the life trajectories of some of the influential people it helped to shape?

Gopala Alampur, today an insurance agent with Sun Life Financial, is the author of *Die Broke and Wealthy* (Toronto: Chestnut Publishing 2003).

Marilyn Brooks is one of Canada's most renowned fashion designers. Her achievements include the Order of Ontario and the Toronto's Designer Achievement Award. The mayor of Toronto declared 3 February 1988 to be 'Marilyn Brooks Day' in recognition of her contributions to the Canadian fashion industry. She retired from the spotlight in 2003 to focus attention on her painting.

June Callwood was among the best-loved and most active journalists of her generation, producing countless articles and books over her more than fifty years of professional writing. A tireless activist, she helped to create Nellie's (a women's shelter), the June Callwood Centre for Women and Families, and Casey House, Toronto's innovative hospice for people with HIV/AIDS. She passed away in 2007, not long after she agreed to be interviewed for this project. She will be missed.

W.R. (Bill) Clement is a Toronto-based author and fixture at the venerable Cameron House pub on Queen St West. His books include *Quantum Jump: A Survival Guide for the New Renaissance* (London, Ont.: Insomniac Press 1998) and *Reforming the Prophet: The Quest for Islamic Reformation* (London, Ont.: Insomniac Press 2002).

Clifford Collier, a former ballet dancer, volunteered with the Canadian Lesbian and Gay Archives in Toronto until quite recently when health concerns forced him to step back.

David DePoe is a proud grandfather, a retired elementary school teacher, and a long-time social activist in Toronto.

Suzanne DePoe is a successful film and television agent with Creative Technique and Westwood Creative Artists in Toronto.

James P. Felstiner retired from the bench in 2007 after an illustrious career.

Allan Lamport retired in the 1970s after a lengthy career in both provincial and municipal politics. Made a member of the Order of Canada in 1994, he passed away in 1999 at the age of ninety-six.

Dave Marden (Jack London) retired from professional music in the mid-1970s and became a successful real estate agent, eventually forming a company, Realty-Net, with his wife, Lynda, in the mid-1990s. He is based in Oshawa, Ontario.

Miguel Maropakis runs Miguel's Euro-Med Cuisine in Toronto, a favourite local restaurant and bar on Queen St East.

Judy Perly opened Toronto's venerable folk club The Free Times Café in 1980. Famous as the launching pad for a raft of successful folk musicians – Perly has been among the most significant supporters of acoustic music in Toronto for the past thirty years – it also offers one of the city's best brunches.

Judy Pocock is a PhD candidate in the Department of English at the University of Toronto. Her dissertation is entitled 'Genesis of a Discourse: *The Tempest* and the Emergence of Postcoloniality.'

Colleen Riley Roberts is a Toronto-based author and memoirist. Her books include *Loving a Legend: Memoirs of a Mistress* (Bloomington, Ind.: AuthorHouse 2001) and *The Life and Times of a Single Woman* (Bloomington, Ind.: AuthorHouse 2005).

Clayton Ruby is among Canada's most celebrated lawyers, specializing in criminal, constitutional, and civil rights law. He is an environmental activist, an advocate for freedom of expression, and the author of numerous legal texts and articles. In 2006 Ruby was made a member of the Order of Canada and awarded the doctor of laws degree by the Law Society of Upper Canada.

James (Smitty) Smith moved to Richmond Hill, north of Toronto, in the mid-1970s. He passed away in 2009 at the age of ninety-six, just four days before his wife of sixty-nine years, Jessie Smith.

Budd Sugarman would spend the better part of thirty years battling city hall in an effort to stop the construction of a parking lot on the south side of Cumberland St. When he finally won – with a little help from his friends – the result was the innovative and impressive urban park which occupies the space today. Upon his death in 2004 at the age of eighty-three, Sugarman was remembered and celebrated as the unofficial 'Mayor of Yorkville.'

Michael Valpy is a distinguished Toronto-based journalist and author. A long-time writer for the *Globe and Mail*, Valpy has been a fixture in the Canadian journalism scene since the 1960s. He ran for Parliament as an NDP candidate in the Toronto riding of Trinity-Spadina in 2000 but was defeated by the incumbent.

Mike Waage lives and works in Vancouver.

Myrna Wood has been a feminist activist, writer, and inspiration since the late 1960s. One of the key voices in the Canadian women's liberation movement, Wood has continued to campaign for women's rights and other causes. She lives in Picton, Ontario.

Notes

1. Remaking the Scene

1 Rainer Maria Rilke, 'Duino Elegies,' *Selected Poetry*, edited and translated by Stephen Mitchell (New York: Vintage 1989), 151–2.
2 A note regarding editorial practice. The terms 'greasers,' 'hippies,' and 'weekenders' are all cultural constructs and as such appear in quotation marks on first mention. However, I have chosen to employ the term *biker* (without quotation marks) as a stable category because identification with this category, unlike with other mutable and more subjectively conferred identity categories, relied upon membership in a motorcycle club. Whereas hippie, greaser, and weekender were only reluctantly accepted by most Villagers as descriptive labels, and thus fail to convey much agency on the part of the actor thus labelled, bikers were people who actively joined clubs in order to become bikers. My understanding of collective identity (in contrast to, and in collaboration with, individual identity) is indebted to Richard Jenkins's classic work in this area, *Social Identity*, 3rd ed. (London: Routledge 2008), where he notes: 'People must have something intersubjectively significant in common – no matter how vague, apparently unimportant or apparently illusory – before we can talk about their membership in a collectivity' (102).
3 In her recent study of transnational adoption, Karen Dubinsky considers the curious problem that 'self-reflection isn't foreign to historians, but it's not exactly popular. On the whole, historians are still more interested in the limitations, rather than the possibilities, of scholarly/personal combinations. We admit our full range of humanness only in the first few pages of our books, the acknowledgements pages.' *Babies without Borders: Adoption and Migration across the Americas* (Toronto: University of Toronto Press 2010), 4.

4 From Freud's definition of 'Race Memory.' Sigmund Freud, *Freud: Diction-ary of Psychoanalysis*, edited by Frank Gaynor (New York: Barnes and Noble Books 2003), 153. My emphasis.

5 Gramsci's framework offers a means of viewing society as a complex set of power relations, always in flux, which are affected by the twin forces of coercion and consent. Both coercion and consent are the tools of hegemo-ny, for it is in the broadening of popular consent (often, but not exclusively, through coercive measures) that the dominant classes strengthen their authority. It is in this way that, crucially, we recognize that hegemony is made (or done) by the dominant class and collaborated in by everyone else. It is very difficult (likely impossible) to act outside the hegemonic framework because the framework relies so much upon the fostering of ideologies which are in turn absorbed into a general common sense. Anto-nio Gramsci, *Selections from the Prison Notebooks*, edited and translated by Quintin Hoare et al. (New York: International Publishers 1971). See espe-cially pages 175–82 for the best discussion of power relations. My readings of Gramsci are much indebted to elaborations on his theories put forward by Ian McKay. See his recent distillation, 'Canada as a Long Liberal Revo-lution,' in Jean-François Constant and Michel Ducharme, eds., *Liberalism and Hegemony* (Toronto: University of Toronto Press 2009), 347–450. See also Stuart Hall, 'Culture, the Media, and the Ideological Effect,' in James Curran, ed., *Mass Communication and Society* (London: Edward Arnold / Open University Press 1977), 314–48; and especially Raymond Williams, *Marxism and Literature* (Oxford: Oxford University Press 1977), 55–71, for a discussion of *ideology* within Gramscian thought.

6 Incidentally, my parents are totally cool. But cool parents still have to suf-fer rebellious kids.

7 Neil Young, 'Ambulance Blues,' *On the Beach*, 1974.

8 Mary Louise Adams has made the crucial observation that 'in the postwar period, Toronto was the centre of English-language publishing, broadcast-ing, and cultural production, a position that contributed to the publiciz-ing of urban issues and Toronto-based perspectives across the country. In representing itself through national media, Toronto became entwined with the definition of the "national culture."' *The Trouble with Normal* (Toronto: University of Toronto Press 1997), 5.

9 Indeed, the propensity of scholars to rely on this term to describe the youth movements of the 1960s and early 1970s is by no means restricted to North America. Historians of Mexico, Brazil, Germany, and Great Britain (to name but a few) have employed 'counterculture' in recent years with-out much reflection on the term. See Eric Zolov, *Refried Elvis: The Rise of*

the Mexican Counterculture (Berkeley: University of California Press 2002); Christopher Dunn, *Brutality Garden: Tropicalia and the Emergence of a Brazilian Counterculture* (Chapel Hill: University of North Carolina Press 2000); Sabine Von Dirke, *All Power to the Imagination: The West German Counterculture from the Student Movement to the Greens* (Lincoln: University of Nebraska Press 1997); Ross Birrell and Eric Finlay, *Justified Sinners: An Archaeology of the Scottish Counterculture, 1960–2000* (Glasgow: Polygon Books 2002). In some cases, the term is used with no sense of its lack of established or agreed-upon coherence – Zolov, for example, never defines the term at all. In the index to his (very good) monograph, under *counterculture*, it reads: 'See *hippies*.'

10 See Paul Goodman's seminal *Growing up Absurd* (New York: Vintage New Edition 1962).

11 The Village of Yorkville was incorporated in 1853 and annexed to Toronto in 1883. Like other former villages incorporated into the wider city, it continues to be referred to as a 'village.'

12 Quoted in Pierre Berton, *1967: Canada's Turning Point* (Toronto: Seal Books 1997), 173.

13 David DePoe, interview with author, 20 December 2004.

14 In other words, it will not 'take as self-evident the identities of those whose experience is being documented and thus naturalize their difference.' Joan W. Scott, 'The Evidence of Experience,' *Critical Inquiry*, 17, no. 4 (1991): 773–97.

15 Culture is, admittedly, a difficult and complex word offering a variety of sometimes contradictory definitions. For our purposes, *culture* is the totality of learned behaviours of a people. But I appreciate that, since these behaviours are learned, not innate, there is nothing inevitable about culture. It is vast, but also mutable, performable, and escapable. When I speak of a youth culture (or, more specifically, a Village culture), I am referencing dominant behaviours contingent to a particular context. See Raymond Williams, *Keywords* (Oxford: Oxford University Press 1983), 87–93.

16 In contemporaneous reportage on Yorkville, such comparisons were ubiquitous.

17 The best available history of the Haight is Charles Perry's *The Haight-Ashbury: A History* (New York: Random House 1984). However, much of the deepest scholarship on the district has come in the form of chapters and incidental information in biographies of neighbourhood musicians. See especially Alice Echols, *Scars of Sweet Paradise: The Life and Times of Janis Joplin* (New York: Henry Holt 2000); Barney Hoskyns, *Beneath the Diamond Sky: Haight-Ashbury, 1965–1970* (New York: Simon and Schuster 1997);

Dennis McNally, *The Long Strange Trip: An Inside Story of the Grateful Dead* (New York: Broadway Books 2002); Blair Jackson, *Garcia: An American Life* (New York: Penguin USA 2000); Grace Slick, *Somebody to Love?: A Rock and Roll Memoir* (New York: Warner Books 1998). Of Greenwich Village, an earlier history is found in Ross Wetzsteon, *Republic of Dreams, Greenwich Village: The American Bohemia, 1915–1960* (New York: Simon and Schuster 2003). Also see the essays collected in Rick Beard et al., eds., *Greenwich Village: Culture and Counterculture* (New Brunswick, N.J.: Rutgers University Press 1997).

18 This point is made very clearly in many treatments of the Haight. See the lengthy discussions of racial politics in the Haight in Nicholas von Hoffman, *We Are the People Our Parents Warned Us Against* (New York: Elephant Books 1968), and Echols, *Scars of Sweet Paradise*.

19 See Perry, *The Haight-Ashbury*.

20 See, for example, William L. Partridge, *The Hippie Ghetto: The Natural History of a Subculture* (New York: Holt, Reinhart and Winston 1973).

21 Biographies (and, in some cases, autobiographies) of these Canadian musicians are available. All of these contain information on Yorkville: Scott Young, *Neil and Me* (Toronto: McClelland and Stewart 1997); Jimmy McDonough, *Shakey: Neil Young's Biography* (New York: Random House 2002); Karen O'Brien, *Joni Mitchell: Shadows and Light* (London: Virgin 2002); Ian Tyson, *I Never Sold My Saddle* (Calgary: Douglas and McIntyre 1997); Murray McLauchlan, *Getting out of Here Alive* (Toronto: Penguin Canada 1998).

22 This etymology is much debated and has been loudly criticized by at least one observer. See Jesse Sheidlower, 'Crying Wolof: Does the Word *Hip* Really Hail from a West African Language?' in *Slate*, posted 8 December 2004, http://www.slate.com/id/2110811/ (accessed 8 November 2010).

23 See David Dalby, 'Americanisms That May Once Have Been Africanisms,' in Alan Dundes, ed., *Mother Wit from the Laughing Barrel: Readings in the Interpretation of Afro-American Folklore* (Jackson: University Press of Mississippi 1990), 136–41. See also Clarence Major, *Juba to Jive: A Dictionary of African American Slang* (Harmondsworth, U.K.: Penguin 1994).

24 Major, *Juba to Jive*.

25 Norman Mailer, 'The White Negro: Superficial Reflections on the Hipster,' in *Advertisements for Myself* (Cambridge, Mass.: Harvard University Press 2005), 337–58.

26 See John Leland, *Hip: The History* (New York: Echo 2004).

27 See the highly influential 1956 critique of modern society in William H. Whyte, *Organization Man* (Philadelphia: University of Pennsylvania Press

2002). 'The fault is not in organization, in short; it is in our worship of it' (14).

28 Cannonball Adderley Sextet, *In New York* [1962], Riverside/OJN 2000.

29 There is an interesting parallel here with the similar (ideological) re-evaluation of youth performed at the turn of the century among bohemians in Greenwich Village. As Christine Stansell has distilled their view of generational politics, 'the idea of young/old as the axis of political struggle … also undercut the centrality of the class struggle to revolution and allowed an emerging intelligentsia to grant itself a greater imaginative role.' Christine Stansell, *American Moderns* (New York: Henry Holt 2000), 94. The obvious difference here relies, of course, on the question of scale – while the bohemians of the 1910s may have explored the connection between youth and radicalism, theirs was but a limited influence. The 'Young Generation' of 1966, on the other hand, was named 'Person of the Year' by *Time Magazine* on 7 January 1967.

30 Peter Braunstein, 'Forever Young: Insurgent Youth and the Sixties Culture of Rejuvenation,' in Peter Braunstein and Michael William Doyle, eds., *Imagine Nation* (New York: Routledge 2002), 243.

31 Theodore Roszak, *The Making of a Counterculture* (Garden City, N.Y.: Doubleday Anchor 1969), 1. Roszak was concerned, however, that young people might not be prepared to accept the weighty responsibility this entailed. 'It is indeed tragic that in a crisis that demands the tact and wisdom of maturity, everything that looks hopeful in our culture should be building from scratch – as must be the case with absolute beginners' (26).

32 Van Gosse, in his recent call for a more integrated study of the movement, and a recognition of its diversity, has emphasized that a vision of the New Left as explicitly a movement of the young is inaccurate. But it was the *symbolic* youthfulness of the movement that mattered – not the actual age of its supporters. Van Gosse, *Rethinking the New Left: An Interpretive History* (New York: Palgrave 2005), 24.

33 Doug Rossinow, *The Politics of Authenticity* (New York: Columbia University Press 1998), 2.

34 *Globe and Mail*, 14 January 1965.

35 Of course, affluence is another keyword one must relate to the baby boom generation in Canada. Widespread economic stability and something approaching full employment was available to most Canadians while their baby boomer offspring came of age. As François Ricard has put it, the baby boom generation was the first in history to 'experience, from early on, what we might call the normalization of riches.' Ricard, *The Lyric Generation: The Life and Times of the Baby Boomers* (Toronto: Stoddart 1994), 55.

36 Doug Owram, *Born at the Right Time* (Toronto: University of Toronto Press 1995), 5 and 31.
37 Martin Barber, interview with author, 29 March 2007.
38 Judith R. Walkowitz, *City of Dreadful Delight* (Chicago: University of Chicago Press 1992), 20.
39 Ibid.
40 See also Matt Houlbrook, *Queer London: Perils and Pleasures in the Sexual Metropolis, 1918–1957* (Chicago: University of Chicago Press 2005), 43–67.
41 Kay J. Anderson, *Vancouver's Chinatown: Racial Discourse in Canada, 1875–1980* (Montreal and Kingston: McGill-Queen's University Press 1995).
42 Jennifer Nelson, *Razing Africville: A Georgraphy of Racism* (Toronto: University of Toronto Press 2008).
43 Walkowitz refers to this as 'urban spectatorship'; I have chosen to redefine this category in order to emphasize the significance of *foreignness* in the case of Yorkville.
44 The role of young women in Yorkville as victims of hip sexual depravity was assumed, expected, and underlined in most every study of the district after 1965. The truth behind this position is debatable, largely because it relies on a simplistic view of sexual power and the conservative assumption that a young woman's sexual innocence is to be protected at all costs.
45 For a concise summary of the association between Yorkville and sexual violence/depravity, see *Globe and Mail*, 2 November 1967.
46 See, especially, Jacques Derrida, *The Ear of the Other*, translated by Peggy Kamuf et al. (Lincoln: University of Nebraska Press 1998).
47 Crucially, as Judith Butler has argued, '[the] name, as a convention, has a generality and a historicity that is in no sense radically singular, even though it is understood to exercise the power of conferring singularity.' In this way, appellation is a profoundly powerful act – it is both to endow a thing with a recognizable individuality and to establish its social and political (not to mention historical) context/meaning. It must be understood to have one and many meanings simultaneously, each politically and socially constructed, each bound to interpretations of common sense in a particular context. *Excitable Speech* (New York: Routledge 1997), 29.
48 Peter Jackson, *Maps of Meaning* (New York: Routledge 1993), 186.
49 Henri Lefebvre, quoted in Nelson, *Razing Africville*, 29.
50 Mary Gluck, *Popular Bohemia: Modernism and Urban Culture in Nineteenth-Century Paris* (Cambridge, Mass.: Harvard University Press 2005), 27–30. See also Seth Koven, *Slumming: Sexual and Social Politics in Victorian London* (Princeton, N.J.: Princeton University Press 2004).

51 Nan Enstad, *Ladies of Labor, Girls of Adventure* (New York: Columbia University Press 1999), 78.
52 Quoted in Robert O. Standish, 'A Reality Trip on the Freaks: A Historiography of the Counterculture of the 1960s,' MA thesis, Humbolt State University 2006, 8.
53 Michael Valpy, interview with author, 5 October 2006.
54 'No longer simply an age category, youth became a metaphor, an attitude toward life, a state of mind that even adults could access.' Braunstein, 'Forever Young,' 243.
55 *Toronto Daily Star*, 12 September 1967; *Satyrday*, 3, no. 5 (August 1968).
56 Jack Kerouac (from *On the Road* [New York: Penguin Books 1955]), quoted in Eldridge Cleaver, *Soul on Ice* (New York: Delta 1968), 72.
57 Cleaver recognized this particular trend very early on, while still in prison. Cleaver, *Soul on Ice*, 75.
58 Dudley Laws public presentation, 16 June 2007.
59 'Christopher's Movie Matinée,' Dir: Mort Ransen, National Film Board of Canada, 1968.
60 From post-Beat preoccupations with Hinduism to Timothy Leary's obsessions with the *Tibetan Book of the Dead*, from the Rolling Stones' use of the sitar to the popularization of Native American beadwork, it wasn't just the politicos who embraced and appropriated a romanticized version of the Third World. For a demonstration of the kinds of extremes taken by many young people in the period, and of the various ways such window dressings of orientalism tended to fail as tools of empowerment or solidarity, see Gita Mehta's classic *Karma Cola: Marketing the Mystic East* (New York: Vintage Books 1979; 1994). See also Edward W. Said, *Orientalism* (New York: Penguin Books 1978; 2003).
61 Stansell, *American Moderns*, 94.
62 Hunter S. Thompson, *Fear and Loathing in Las Vegas* (New York: Vintage Books 1971; 1998), 67.
63 Perry, *The Haight-Ashbury*. My emphasis.
64 Ten years prior to Roszak's hugely influential book, J. Milton Yinger's term 'contraculture' had been adopted by some sociologists to differentiate groups with political (i.e., transformative counter-hegemonic) aspirations from deviant subcultures. See Yinger, *Countercultures: The Promise and Peril of a World Turned Upside Down* (New York: The Free Press 1982).
65 Roszak, *The Making of a Counterculture*.
66 'If the resistance of the counterculture fails, I think there will be nothing in store for us but what anti-utopians like Huxley and Orwell have forecast –

though I have no doubt that these dismal despotisms will be far more stable and effective than their prophets have foreseen. For they will be equipped with techniques of inner-manipulation as unobtrusively fine as gossamer.' Ibid., xiii.

67 Historian Timothy Miller defined 'counterculture' in just such terms, using language so vague as to include most everyone under the age of twenty: 'The counterculture was a romantic social movement of the late 1960s and very early 1970s,' he wrote, 'mainly composed of teenagers and persons in their early twenties, who through their flamboyant lifestyle expressed their alienation from mainstream American life.' *The Hippies and American Values* (Knoxville: University of Tennessee Press 1991), 6.

68 We can refer to this as *common sense*. 'Ideology frequently takes the form of "commonsense" ideas that are sufficiently "taken for granted" as to be beyond the realm of rational debate.' Peter Jackson, *Maps of Meaning*, 51.

69 Raymond Williams, *Marxism and Literature*, 100.

70 The very word *psychedelic* – coined by Saskatchewan-based scientist Humphry Osmond in 1956, in a letter to his friend, celebrated author, and LSD guru Aldous Huxley – breaks down to *mind made visible*.

71 Todd Gitlin, *The Sixties: Years of Hope, Days of Rage* (New York: Bantam Books 1987), 10–11.

72 The *Toronto Daily Star* yielded 3,417 pages with a 'hit' for Yorkville; the *Globe and Mail* had 2,797. This total (6,214) included at least 1,000 advertisements or otherwise incidental information. Still, roughly 5,000 of these pages contained articles of some length on the district – needless to say, newspapers proved indispensable to this project.

73 As Frank Longstaff observed in 1965–6, 'while musicians aim to play the Village, in few cases are musicians Villagers. Even if they live in the Yorkville area, rehearsals and performances keep them out of Village circles.' 'Yorkville: An Observational Report' (unpublished report presented to the Interim Research Project on Unreached Youth, September 1966), 21.

74 The way that most people learned of my project and began to approach me was through reading an article I wrote on the hepatitis scare of 1968. The article (culled from the work-in-progress that eventually became this book) was published in the *Toronto Star* in the spring of 2006, and I was overwhelmed by e-mails and phone calls in the ensuing weeks. I have interviewed some of these former Villagers with varying degrees of success. Some of their stories made it into the body of this work; many did not. However, all of their words informed me, and most confirmed my theories about the multifarious nature of the Yorkville scene.

75 Kristin Ross, in an otherwise well-reasoned and deeply researched account

of the politics of competing memories of France's period of profound unrest in May 1968, refused to conduct her own interviews. 'Whom would I have interviewed,' she asked? 'What possible controls could govern my selection of the testimony of participants in a mass movement that extended throughout France, reaching virtually every town, professional sector, region, and age group?' Such a reluctance to engage with oral history – based, as it is, on the supposedly unscientific character ('*what possible controls*') of the pursuit – left a significant gap in her otherwise exemplary scholarship. Kristin Ross, *May '68 and Its Afterlives* (Chicago: University of Chicago Press 2002).

76 As numerous historians have pointed out, European disdain for oral history has complicated in a fundamental way the historical memory and construction of aboriginal pasts. For a brief discussion of this significant area of concern and inquiry, see Toby Morantz, 'Plunder or Harmony?: On Merging European and Native Views of Contact,' in Germain Warkentin and Carolyn Podruchny, eds., *Decentering the Renaissance: Canada and Europe in Multidisciplinary Perspective* (Toronto: University of Toronto Press 2001), 48–57.

77 Robert Perks and Alistair Thomson, 'Critical Developments,' in Perks and Thomson, eds., *The Oral History Reader* (New York: Routledge 2006), 1–13.

78 I have followed in the footsteps of a variety of extraordinary historians in this field, notably Franca Iacovetta, Ian McKay, Alice Echols, and Karen Dubinsky. Each of these historians has, in his or her own way, employed oral-history techniques to great effect. I have learned from them all, and have cherry-picked their most successful methods.

79 Gitlin, *The Sixties*. His allusion to the Weatherman action of 1969, while poetically effective, is a perfect example of this type of division between the good and bad 1960s. What began with hope ended with rage.

80 See Daniel Marcus for a fascinating examination of the ways the imagined 1950s and 1960s have functioned as devices in all presidential elections since 1972. While the conservative-led 1950s have been whitewashed as a period of comfort, security, and success, the liberal-led 1960s have been exaggerated into a period of darkness, confusion, and failure. Marcus, *Happy Days and Wonder Years* (New Brunswick, N.J.: Rutgers University Press 2004).

81 Kobena Mercer, '1968: Periodizing Politics and Identity,' in Lawrence Grossberg, Cary Nelson, and Paula Treichler, eds., *Cultural Studies* (New York: Routledge 1992), 425.

82 For the conservative angle, see Peter Collier and David Horowitz, *Destructive Generation: Second Thoughts about the Sixties* (New York: Summit Books

1989). For a worthy counterpoint to this treatment, see Philip Jenkins, *Decade of Nightmares: The End of the Sixties and the Making of Eighties America* (Oxford: Oxford University Press 2006).

83 Paul Ricoeur, *Time and Narrative*, vol. 1, translated by Kathleen McLaughlin and David Pellauer (Chicago: University of Chicago Press 1984), 41.

84 Jerry Garcia, in *The Quotable Musician: From Bach to Tupac*, edited by Sheila A. Anderson (New York: Alworth Press 2003), 137.

85 If, twenty years ago, geographer Charles Johnson could happily report that 'many of the original houses in the Village have retained their house form,' praising Toronto city planners for their successful 'preservation of Yorkville,' one certainly cannot do the same today. Charles Johnson, 'Preservation of Yorkville Village,' unpublished discussion paper, April 1984.

2. Getting to Yorkville

1 Williams, *Keywords*, 124.

2 *Toronto Daily Star*, 5 October 2002. My emphasis.

3 Generally attributed to an anonymous 'Montreal comedian.' See Bruce West, *Toronto* (Garden City, N.Y.: Doubleday 1967), 317.

4 Valerie Knowles, *Strangers at Our Gates: Canadian Immigration and Immigration Policy, 1540–2006*, rev. ed. (Toronto: Dundurn Press 2007), 170–1.

5 Michael Ornstein, 'Ethno-Racial Groups in Toronto, 1971–2001,' unpublished paper, York University, Institute for Social Research, 2006, http://www.isr.yorku.ca/download/Ornstein–Ethno-Racial_Groups_in_Toronto_1971-2001.pdf (accessed 22 November 2010).

6 Leland, *Hip: The History*. In fact, Leland would likely refuse my interpretation of the 1960s Yorkville scene as a site of 'hip,' given its paucity of cultural interchange. But, that's Toronto – it's a Torontonian hip, in its way as significant as the Haight or Greenwich.

7 See especially Franca Iacovetta, *Gatekeepers: Reshaping Immigrant Lives in Cold War Canada* (Toronto: Between the Lines 2006); Knowles, *Strangers at Our Gates*. Statistics and other information here are drawn from the very good website maintained by the City of Toronto: http://www.toronto.ca/culture/history/history-1951-onward.htm (accessed 22 November 2010).

8 Richard Harris meditates at length on this theme in his work on suburbanization in Canada, *Creeping Conformity* (Toronto: University of Toronto Press 2004).

9 Iacovetta, *Gatekeepers*; Harris, *Creeping Conformity*. Also see John Seeley

et al., *Crestwood Heights: A Study of the Culture of Suburban Life* (Toronto: University of Toronto Press 1956).

10 Clifford Collier, interview with author, 15 June 2006.

11 David Burnett, *Toronto Painting of the 1960s* (Toronto: Art Gallery of Ontario 1983), 10–11.

12 There is a wide literature on gentrification, but I am primarily influenced by Richard Lloyd's study of Wicker Park, Chicago's 1990s-era hip scene: *Neo-Bohemia: Art and Commerce in the Post-Industrial City* (New York: Routledge 2005). Lloyd's argument centres on the paradoxical belief held by many bohemians that their mere presence within a particular enclave sets them apart from mainstream culture, economy, and politics. The gentrification process, he argues, is tied to this blindness to the realities of class identity and politics frequently at work in the bohemian centre. For other (Marxist) readings of the gentrification process, see Neil Smith, *The New Urban Frontier: Gentrification and the Revanchist City* (New York: Routledge 1996); Neil Smith and Peter Williams, *Gentrification of the City* (Boston: Allen and Unwin 1986).

13 Judy Pocock, interview with author, 24 June 2006.

14 Johnson, 'Preservation of Yorkville Village,' 4.

15 Barbara Elizabeth Key, 'The Growth of Yorkville,' thesis, Department of Geography, York University, 1967, 31.

16 Ibid., 32.

17 Johnson, 'Preservation of Yorkville Village,' 4.

18 Judy Pocock, interview with author, 24 June 2006.

19 Key, 'The Growth of Yorkville,' 32.

20 Ibid.

21 Judy Pocock, interview with author, 24 June 2006.

22 This obituary ran in the *Richmond Hill Liberal*, 8 November 1962, Canadian Lesbian and Gay Archives (CLGA), Toronto.

23 *Toronto Daily Star*, 8 January 1962; *Globe and Mail*, 25 June 1963. Also, *Globe and Mail*, 14 January 1965.

24 Key, 'The Growth of Yorkville,' 33.

25 Ibid.

26 Ibid.

27 Ibid., 34.

28 Myrna Wood, interview with author, 19 April 2006.

29 John Sewell, *The Shape of the City* (Toronto: University of Toronto Press 1993).

30 Johnson, 'Preservation of Yorkville Village,' 7.

31 Miguel Maropakis, interview with author, 29 March 2007.

32 Myrna Wood, interview with author, 19 April 2006.

33 The Beat literary canon brims with homosocial (if not outright homo-erotic) situations, obsessions, and relationships. As Leerom Medovoi has shown, while there remained a certain ambivalence about the nature of homosexuality as an identity, Beat art was positively awash in homosexual imagery and desire. See *Rebels: Youth and the Cold War Origins of Identity* (Durham, N.C.: Duke University Press 2005), 225–8.

34 Nicholas Jennings, *Before the Gold Rush: Flashbacks to the Dawn of the Canadian Sound* (Toronto: Penguin Books 1997), 21.

35 Key, 'The Growth of Yorkville,' 34.

36 But, it must be noted, famous hangouts predated these Yorkville spots and weren't too far away. The Bohemian Embassy is certainly among the most significant of these, but the First Floor Club (on Asquith, at Yonge) was barely outside the Yorkville zone and was a key site for bohemian connections. See Jennings, *Before the Gold Rush*, 16–17.

37 Clifford Collier, interview with author, 15 June 2006.

38 *Macleans*, 23 March 1963.

39 Judy Perly, interview with author, 17 June 2006.

40 Dave Bidini, *On a Cold Road: Tales of Adventure in Canadian Rock* (Toronto: McClelland and Stewart 1998), 257.

41 Key, 'The Growth of Yorkville,' 35.

42 Ibid.

43 Judy Perly, interview with author, 27 June 2006.

44 For a sustained discussion of this connection, see Gillian Mitchell, *The North American Folk Music Revival: Nation and Identity in the United States and Canada, 1945–1980* (Burlington, Vt.: Ashgate 2007).

45 The *Toronto Daily Star* referred to this process as an experiment in 'how a declining old residential street can be reclaimed by sophisticated commercialism' on 18 March 1961.

46 See Key, 'The Growth of Yorkville,' appendix, 76–81. Key lists the principal occupants of each address on Yorkville, Cumberland, Hazelton, Scollard, and Avenue Rd in 1967.

47 Barbara Key's survey suggests that, since most of these shops and boutiques were operated by their owner and only a very small staff, a 'casual friendly atmosphere' predominated. Ibid., 40.

48 Ibid., 41.

49 Marilyn Brooks's 'The Unicorn [114 Cumberland St] is noted for its bizarre gifts which include such things as *papier maché* jewellery, decorative

matches, unusually shaped soaps, party decorations and a large collection of patterned mugs.' Ibid., 42.

50 Ibid.
51 Barbara Beckett, 'Yorkville: Study of a Neighbourhood,' *Globe and Mail*, Women's section, 14 January 1965.
52 Myrna Wood, interview with author, 19 April 2006.
53 Marilyn Brooks, interview with author, 29 March 2007.
54 Myrna Wood, interview with author, 19 April 2006.
55 *Globe and Mail*, Women's section, 14 January 1965.
56 Charles Reich, *The Greening of America* (New York: Bantam Books 1970), 2.
57 See Karl Marx, *Early Political Writings*, edited and translated by Joseph O'Malley with Richard A. Davis (Cambridge: Cambridge University Press 1994), 71–8.
58 Rossinow, *Politics of Authenticity*, 2.
59 Williams, *Keywords*, 36.
60 'I am. I am. I exist, I think, therefore I am; I am because I think that I don't want to be, I think that I ... because ... ugh! I flee. They will have to find something else to veil the enormous absurdity of their existence.' Jean-Paul Sartre, *Nausea*, translated by Lloyd Alexander (New York: New Directions Publishing 1964), 150.
61 'If you seek authenticity for authenticity's sake, you are no longer authentic.' Jean-Paul Sartre, *Notebooks for an Ethics*, translated by David Pellauer (Chicago: University of Chicago Press 1992), 4.
62 *Toronto Daily Star*, 3 March 1959.
63 Rossinow, *Politics of Authenticity*, 249.
64 Medovoi, *Rebels*, 19.
65 Ibid., 29.
66 For an overview of the ways the suburbs were affected by (and affected) gender roles and expectations, see Suzanne Morton, *Ideal Surroundings* (Toronto: University of Toronto Press 1995), 67–87. For examinations of the post-war family and the ways heterosexuality, conformity, and domesticity became normalized in the period, see Mona Gleason, *Normalizing the Ideal: Psychology, Schooling and the Family in Postwar Canada* (Toronto: University of Toronto Press 1999); Mary-Louise Adams, *The Trouble with Normal: Post-war Youth and the Making of Heterosexuality* (Toronto: University of Toronto Press 1997); Magda Fahrni, *Household Politics: Montreal Families and Postwar Reconstruction* (Toronto: University of Toronto Press 2005).
67 S.D. Clark, quoted in Harris, *Creeping Conformity*, 7.
68 Medovoi, *Rebels*, 30.

69 As Richard Harris has pointed out, many Canadian suburbs were not immediately so homogeneous as one might expect. Still, he found that during the same period they were written about as though they were sites of little diversity, interest, or value. Harris, *Creeping Conformity*, 6–15.

70 Tom Hayden, 'The Port Huron Statement,' in Alexander Bloom and Wini Breines, eds., *Takin' It to the Streets: A Sixties Reader* (New York: Oxford University Press 2003), 50.

71 In Maurice Isserman and Michael Kazin's history of social unrest in the 1960s, for example, the Port Huron Statement is referenced four times. Isserman and Kazin, *America Divided*, 2nd ed. (New York: Oxford University Press 2004).

72 Herbert Marcuse, *An Essay on Liberation* (Boston: Beacon Press 1969), vii.

73 As one Villager would write in 1968, 'there are two kinds of people who frequent the Village; those who belong there; and those who don't, but think they do.' *Satyrday*, 3, no. 5 (1968).

74 *Toronto Daily Star*, 3 March 1959.

75 The Voice of Women for Peace (VOW) was a significant feminist organization, a middle-class precursor to the more heterogeneous cultural feminists of the late 1970s, and a spur to the Royal Commission on the Status of Women in Canada's work in the late-1960s. Lotta Dempsey (with Jo Davis, Dorothy Henderson, Helen Tucker, Beth Touzel, and Maryon Pearson, wife of the soon-to-be prime minister) worked alongside activists such as Nancy Pocock (at whose home on Hazelton the women sometimes met) to propagate their anti-war message. See Judy Rebick, *Ten Thousand Roses* (New York: Penguin Books 2005), 3–13.

76 *Toronto Daily Star*, 3 March 1959.

77 See (for a rather more cynical view of this process) Joseph Heath and Andrew Potter, *The Rebel Sell: How the Counter Culture Became Consumer Culture* (West Sussex, U.K.: Capstone Publishing 2005).

78 *Toronto Daily Star*, 11 June 1960.

79 American photographer Fred McDarrah had, back in 1957, famously criticized the co-optation of Beat culture by running ads offering to rent out Beatnik poets. 'Rent a Genuine Beatnik. Fully Equipped. Eye-Shades, Beard, Dirty Shirt. With or Without Sandals. Special Discounts for No Beard or No Bath.' These ads were, contrary to all expectation, genuine. Ted Joans was among those honest-to-goodness poets who took part in the scheme, which brought in some much needed money. Leland, *Hip: A History*, 296.

80 See the essays collected in Jennie Skerl, ed., *Reconstructing the Beats* (New York: Palgrave Macmillan 2004); Brenda Knight, ed., *Women of the Beat Gen-*

eration: The Writers, Artists and Muses at the Heart of a Revolution (New York: Conari Press 1998).

81 Jennings, *Before the Gold Rush*, 15. The phrase in quotes is from *Howl*, Allen Ginsberg's remarkable poem, published in 1956. Ginsberg, *Howl and Other Poems* (San Francisco: City Lights Publishing 1991).

82 David DePoe, interview with author, 20 December 2004.

83 Jennings, *Before the Gold Rush*, 21.

84 Rosemary Sullivan, *The Red Shoes: Margaret Atwood Starting Out* (Toronto: Harper Collins 1998), 101–4.

85 Marilyn Brooks, interview with author, 29 March 2007.

86 Denise Leclerc and Pierre Dessureault, *The Sixties in Canada* (Ottawa: National Gallery of Canada 2005), 15.

87 The artistic community of Toronto in the 1950s and early 1960s has yet to receive the thoroughgoing treatment it deserves. However, a few biographies of its most prominent figures do exist and offer some colour to the sketches we have been handed down. See, for example, Iris Nowell, *Joyce Wieland: A Life in Art* (Toronto: ECW Press 2001); Dennis Reid and Matthew Teitelbaum, *Greg Curnoe: Life and Stuff* (Vancouver: Douglas and McIntyre 2001).

88 Leclerc and Dessureault establish these connections early and often in their study, *The Sixties in Canada*.

89 Dennis Reid, 'Marcel Duchamp in Canada,' *Canadian Art*, 4, no. 4 (1987).

90 Burnett, *Toronto Painting of the 1960s*, 10.

91 Ibid., 7.

92 *Globe and Mail*, 10 November 1962. There is a photo here of the Bohemian Embassy, a coffee house that doubled as an art gallery for local talent.

93 'Wild Bill,' interview with author, 11 March 2005. 'Wild Bill' is a pseudonym offered by the subject.

94 For brief mentions of the Village art scene, see Jane Lind, *Joyce Wieland: Artist on Fire* (Toronto: Lorimer 2001). See also Kristy Holmes-Moss, 'Negotiating the Nation: "Expanding" the Work of Joyce Wieland,' *Canadian Journal of Film Studies*, 15, no. 2 (2006).

95 'Between 1961 and 1964, the Isaacs Gallery was also the venue for Dada-derived mixed media concerts, lectures and film series.' Burnett, *Toronto Painting of the 1960s*, 15.

96 Judy Pocock, interview with author, 24 June 2006.

97 Leclerc and Dessureault, *The Sixties in Canada*, 21–3.

98 This arrangement broke down in 1962 when the Here and Now moved to Yonge St. *Globe and Mail*, 10 November 1962.

99 Ibid.

100 Immortalized in the news television spot now available in the CBC's online archives, the Embassy was situated at 7 St Nicholas St, one block north of Wellesley, roughly five minutes' walk south of the Village.

101 Leclerc and Dessureault, *The Sixties in Canada*, 167.

102 Burnett, *Toronto Painting of the 1960s*, 15.

103 Ibid. This is in stark contrast to the patently absurd claim made by CBC television in February 1963 that it was filming Canada's 'first Happening!' See http://archives.cbc.ca/IDCC-1-69-1587-3080/life_society/60s/ (accessed 22 November 2010).

104 That these spontaneous, disorienting Happenings were the antecedents to Ken Kesey and the Pranksters' Acid Tests is plain, and remains an exciting area of comparison for future studies.

105 Susan Sontag, 'Happenings: An Art of Radical Juxtaposition' (1962), *Against Interpretation and Other Essays* (New York: Picador Books 2001).

106 CBC Television, *Close-Up*, 'Toronto "Happening,"' 17 February 1963, http://archives.cbc.ca/IDC-1-69-580-3080/life_society/hippies/clip1 (accessed 22 November 2010).

107 For a sustained discussion of social spaces, music, and youth culture, see Sarah Thornton, *Club Cultures: Music, Media, and Subcultural Capital* (Lebanon, N.H.: Wesleyan University Press 1996).

108 The drinking age in Ontario was twenty-one before 1971 when it was lowered to eighteen.

109 There is some indication that the women were also subjected to impertinent (not to mention illegal) questioning about their sexual histories and preferences. *Globe and Mail*, 4 August 1961.

110 *Toronto Daily Star*, 1 May 1962.

111 The 'Metro Police Commission [made up of senior municipal authorities including Mayor Nathan Phillips and Metro Chairman Fred Gardner] suggested police use more restraint in handling house party raids ... [concluding] that police should have handled the [Yorkville] case with summonses rather than arrests.' *Toronto Daily Star*, 18 August 1961.

112 *Toronto Daily Star*, 25 September 1961.

113 *Toronto Daily Star*, 18 August 1961.

114 Graeber's 71 Club was a prototypical coffee house in Yorkville. When asked how he got started, the Riverboat's proprietor, Bernie Fiedler, explained in 1972 that while working as a coffee salesman in the early 1960s, one of his stops was the 71 Club. Graeber talked the young Fiedler into opening his own club. A short time later, Fiedler opened the Mousehole, and, in 1965, the Riverboat.

115 The odds of pot smoke *actually* filling the air of George's are exceedingly

slim. For his part, Clifford Collier describes the drug scene in the Yorkville coffee houses as fairly strictly monitored. 'There were no drugs in the Mousetrap,' he declared. 'Never.' Interview with author, 15 June 2006.

116 Moreover, 1959 saw the all-time high for heroin convictions (470) as well. Interestingly, if only incidentally, the story of the rapid, near exponential rise in marijuana convictions parallels a significant drop-off in heroin convictions. By 1972, there were 10,695 marijuana convictions in Canada, compared to merely 201 for heroin. See http://www.cfdp.ca/giffen.htm (accessed 22 November 2010).

117 A constable involved in the raid described the scene at 71 Club: '[I] found nine young men sitting around in the poorly lighted basement strumming guitars at the time of the raid.' A mellow scene, perhaps, but one apparently fraught with mystery and undertones of weirdness. Why else report it in the newspaper? *Globe and Mail*, 10 November 1961.

118 *Toronto Daily Star*, 1 May 1962. My emphasis.

119 His wife, Eva, however, had responded somewhat erratically. She refused to provide her name to the police and then escaped through a window after claiming to need a drink. She was caught and brought back. Very little is known to me of his wife – she rarely appears in the coverage, apart from in this article. *Globe and Mail*, 10 November 1961.

120 *Toronto Daily Star*, 1 May 1962.

121 There is a bizarre, if otherwise unrelated, conclusion to this story. On 20 February 1965 Graeber was arrested after he broke into a Willowdale home, armed with a 9-mm. semi-automatic pistol. The family living there managed to escape, and police were called to the scene. After an undisclosed period of time, during which one police officer who got inside and confronted Graeber found a gun aimed at his chest, the police opened fire with tear gas. They eventually subdued Graeber, whom they found standing in a shower, in his underwear, with a wet towel wrapped around his face to protect him from the gas. In the report of 4 March, the thirty-five-year-old Graeber is referred to as a 'Yorkville Avenue resident.' *Globe and Mail*, 4 March 1965 (front page).

122 *Toronto Daily Star*, 1 May 1962.

123 Ibid. My emphasis.

124 Recamier, a leisure-wear shop, opened on Old York Lane in November 1962; the One One Nine Shoppe, featuring marked-down runway fashions, opened at (you guessed it) 119 Yorkville Ave.

125 *Globe and Mail*, 7 September 1962. Decidedly upscale, Club Coiffure's hairdresser, Martina Eybe, 'likes her clients to think of her as a personal Fashion Consultant.'

126 An early (1961) note in the entertainment section of the *Toronto Daily Star* set up the dichotomous association between 'smart antique shops, interior decorators' salons, architect's offices and twenty-four-hour places offering "Teacup Readings."' *Toronto Daily Star*, 18 March 1961. Note the emphasis on *introduction* here – Yorkville was a new idea to many readers in 1961.

127 *Globe and Mail*, 10 May 1962. This line comes from an announcement for the opening of 'The Fashion Mine' at 105 Yorkville Ave.

128 In a year-end round-up of the best clubs for music, dancing, and night-time carousing in the city, *Toronto Daily Star* columnist Morris Duff referred to the Yorkville area a number of times without ever calling it *Yorkville*. Rather, he seemed to know it only as the 'Avenue Rd-Davenport area which is also the home of the folk song clubs.' *Toronto Daily Star*, 30 December 1961.

129 *Toronto Daily Star*, 25 April 1961.

130 *Toronto Daily Star*, 21 February 1963.

131 *Globe and Mail*, 12 June 1963.

132 *Globe and Mail*, 13 May 1963.

133 Clifford Collier, interview with author, 15 June 2006.

134 Not precisely *in* Yorkville proper, La Coterie Café was situated at 32 Avenue Rd, just two or three buildings up from Prince Arthur, on the west side. In other words, it was less than a thirty-second walk from Yorkville's boundaries – boundaries that were only vaguely formalized prior to about 1965.

135 Collier's description of the space continues: 'The house had been converted – it was a *house*, a big old Edwardian house. It had been converted so that the whole main floor just went right back. Because it was a coffee house and he specialized pretty well in pastries and light things, he didn't have a heavy kitchen. He just had storage refrigerators and so on. And, as for the coffee house part, all the machines were (like all coffee houses) in the front.' Interview with author, 15 June 2006.

136 Ibid.

137 Ibid.

138 Apart from the work of David Churchill and Stephen Maynard, the academic history of Toronto's post-war era gay communities remains largely unpublished, and certainly underexplored. See David Churchill, 'Mother Goose's Map: Tabloid Geographies and Gay Male Experience in 1950s Toronto,' *Journal of Urban History*, 30, no. 6 (2004): 826–52; David Churchill, 'Personal Ad/Politics: Race, Sexuality and Power at the Body Politic,' *Left History*, 8, no. 2 (2003): 114–34. For earlier histories of Toronto's gay

male scene, see Stephen Maynard's various works, but chiefly among them: 'Through a Hole in the Lavatory Wall: Homosexual Subcultures, Police Surveillance, and the Dialectics of Discovery, Toronto, 1890–1930,' in Joy Parr and Mark Rosenfeld, eds., *Gender and History in Canada* (Toronto: Copp Clark 1996), 165–84. For lesbian subcultures and their struggles for recognition, see Becki Ross, '"Down at the Whorehouse?": Reflections on Christian Community Service and Female Sex Deviance at Toronto's Street Haven, 1965–1969,' *Atlantis: A Women's Studies Journal*, 23, no. 1 (1998): 48–59.

139 Clifford Collier, interview with author, 15 June 2006.

140 Ibid.

141 Gay tea dances are a somewhat campy carryover from British tea-time dances (the original sense of the phrase). Since the 1950s, tea dances have come to refer to any late-afternoon or evening dance, especially at gay resorts. The 'tea trade' is also a euphemism in gay parlance for casual sex in washrooms.

142 'We never had any problems from the neighbours [because we were gay]. The only problem we ever had was noise! Not the noise from the coffee house, mind you, but the noise from all the people in line, waiting to get *into* the coffee house!' Clifford Collier, interview with author, 15 June 2006.

143 Ibid. One crowd that the Mousetrap *didn't* attract was the prostitutes. Collier stresses this point. 'These kids weren't hustlers. I mean you weren't getting hustlers coming in, or anything like that. They hung around certain locations, everyone knew where they were, so if you were interested in the hustle trade you went to those locations. They didn't come out to your areas. I would have been very much aware of it [if they had come to La Coterie].'

144 In a 1945 letter to Allen Ginsberg, Kerouac (who was known to be physical with both men and women) in some ways exemplified the deeply ambivalent attitude many Beats carried with respect to their various homosexual desires. He declared to his openly gay friend that 'the physical aspects of gay sex were disgusting; and though the desire for it might exist in his subconscious, there was no way of determining that for sure.' Gerald Nicosia, *Memory Babe: A Critical Biography of Jack Kerouac* (New York: Grove Press 1983), 142.

145 See Medovoi, *Rebels*, 215–35, for a stirring reading of *On the Road* from the perspective of homosocial (not to say homosexual) rebellion against conformity and alienation.

146 Marilyn Brooks, interview with author, 29 March 2007.

147 'I think it was when the dance clubs opened up on Yonge St. There was the Maison de Lis, there was the Melody Room, the 5–11 … When those dance clubs opened – and again, they were small clubs, they opened up early enough that you got the kids that couldn't go drinking, as long as they were over sixteen we didn't have a problem, and you got people that didn't want to drink that much, so they'd go dancing. There was no liquor at these clubs.' Clifford Collier, interview with author, 15 June 2006.

148 Ibid.

149 Ibid.

150 Formed in 1930 from former Methodist and Presbyterian congregations, St Paul's Avenue Road United was situated at 121 Avenue Rd and drew its congregation from the Annex, primarily. According to DePoe: '[The church] was torched by I believe a developer who wanted to build.' David DePoe, interview with author, 20 December 2004.

151 James E. Smith, 'I Wish I Was a Fish: A Search for Live Options in Yorkville' (unpublished chapbook, 1972), ii.

152 Judge James Felstiner, interview with author, 3 April 2006.

153 Smith, 'I Wish I Was a Fish,' 3.

154 See Ronald Takaki, *A Different Mirror: A History of Multicultural America* (London: Back Bay Books 1994), 166–90. In California the 1855 Greaser Act was explicitly designed to criminalize vagrancy, but it defined *vagrancy* along racial lines as 'all persons who are commonly known as Greasers or the issue of Spanish and Indian blood.' Ibid., 178.

155 For a more thorough discussion of the cultural legacy of the greaser identity and performance, see Daniel Marcus, *Happy Days and Wonder Years*, 2004.

156 Iacovetta, *Gatekeepers*, 199.

157 G. Reginald Smart and David Jackson, 'The Yorkville Subculture: A Study of the Life Styles and Interactions of Hippies and Non-Hippies, Prepared from the Field Notes of Gopala Alampur' (Toronto: Addiction Research Foundation 1969).

158 Iacovetta, *Gatekeepers*, 198.

159 Judge James Felstiner, interview with author, 3 April 2006.

160 Ibid.

161 Smith, 'I Wish I Was a Fish,' 4.

162 Ibid.

163 Crysdale went on to complete a PhD in sociology at the University of Toronto and then to become one of the central figures in the development of Atkinson College at York University, along with W.E. Mann, another sociologist interested in the plight of youth in the 1960s.

164 Smith, 'I Wish I Was a Fish,' 2.

165 Ibid., 3. This type of approach to troubled urban youth remains a popular alternative to traditional methods. The Pine River Institute, for example, runs a program in Creemore, Ontario, based on the principle of outdoor education and 'wilderness therapy.' See http://www.pineriverinstitute. com/ (accessed 22 November 2010).

166 The other competitors were not happy with the inclusion of such a team into their league, and in the first year they were banned from the league for misconduct. However, 'an inquiry was conducted in which it became apparent that all of the favoured clubs were baiting the St-Paul's team. They had started something which the gang members were quite prepared to finish.' They were reinstated, with illustrious results. Smith, 'I Wish I Was a Fish,' 8.

167 Ibid., 4.

168 Smith is vague about the date of his arrival on the scene. He mentions at one point that his first year as part-time director of the church program was 1962, but it appears that he actually came on the scene a few years prior to taking this job.

169 Smith, 'I Wish I Was a Fish,' 6.

170 Ibid., 7.

171 Curious that DePoe's visual description of the greasers is out of sync with those of Smith and Felstiner.

172 David DePoe, interview with author, 20 December 2004.

173 Mike Waage, interview with author, 3 March 2005.

174 The church basement was a kind of 'home' for the gang during the day as well: 'They often came at noon to eat their lunch and jive to the old record player and their favourite 45s.' Smith, 'I Wish I Was a Fish,' 7.

175 Ibid., 9.

176 Ibid.

177 Ibid.

178 Ibid.

3. Riots, Religion, and Rock'n'Roll

1 *Globe and Mail*, 13 August 1965.

2 In retrospect, the whole 'useless bastard' thing was probably a bad move.

3 Special, if only because Mikolasch was so much older than the curve. Most such situations, both prior to and after 1965, involved younger and younger people.

4 *Globe and Mail*, 13 August 1965.

5 *Toronto Daily Star*, 27 May 1965.

6 Judy Pocock, interview with author, 24 June 2006.

7 *Globe and Mail*, 15 May 1964. There is, tellingly, no mention of the festival in the 'Things to Do and See during the Weekend' section.

8 *Toronto Daily Star*, 15 May 1964.

9 *Toronto Daily Star*, 16 May 1964.

10 'I don't ever remember being afraid. I remember one, *sort* of riot, that we watched from home. But I had left home by that time, so it was after 1967! There was a kind of riot, I mean people running around, but I don't recall any windows broken, any damage.' Judy Pocock, interview with author, 24 June 2006.

11 *Toronto Daily Star*, 19 October 1964. See also *Globe and Mail*, same date.

12 'Police Say WATCH OUT to Yorkville Coffee House Rowdies,' *Toronto Daily Star*, 28 October 1964.

13 *Toronto Daily Star*, 23 January 1965.

14 I asked Judy Pocock just who these 'toughs' and 'rowdies' were, and she replied, simply: 'Oh, I just think they were kids. The place would just be thronging!' Interview with author, 24 June 2006.

15 'The Village of Yorkville Association ... staged a festival last May. Plagued by several days of poor weather, it was nonetheless a success, bringing thousands into the area. Unfortunately, it attracted some leather-jacketed toughs and the resultant publicity was considered so damaging to the prestige image [sic], the area is hoping the festival will not be repeated.' *Globe and Mail*, 14 January 1965.

16 *Globe and Mail*, 12 May 1965.

17 *Globe and Mail*, 10 April 1965.

18 *Globe and Mail*, 3 May 1965.

19 Ibid.

20 *Globe and Mail*, 27 May 1965.

21 Ibid.

22 *Globe and Mail*, 28 May 1965.

23 Ibid.

24 Ibid. Cooper cites a recent Central Neighbourhood House report which documented 'the forays of gangs of [downtown, low-rent housing project] Regent Park juveniles into Yorkville's crowded streets seeking – not coffee, but – liquor and "fights with the beatniks."' Again, we see coffee (associated with bohemian, middle-class youth cultures) pitted against liquor (associated with violent, lower-class youth activity).

25 *Globe and Mail*, 28 May 1965.

26 *Globe and Mail*, 31 May 1965.

27 'Wild Bill,' interview with author, 11 March 2005.
28 Ibid. This is, of course, somewhat of an exaggeration.
29 Smart and Jackson, 'The Yorkville Subculture.' The centrality of a certain construction of whiteness – what Daniel Coleman has termed 'White Civility' – underwrites such cultural alienation. Daniel Coleman, *White Civility* (Toronto: University of Toronto Press 2008). It is worth pointing out that DP was also sometimes defined as 'Dumb Polack.' Thanks to one of the publisher's anonymous readers for this tip.
30 *Globe and Mail*, 9 June 1965. See also the earlier article in the *Globe and Mail*, 10 April, where the Penny Farthing's Bryan Walker suggests that 'ineffectual' police are an issue.
31 *Globe and Mail*, 10 June 1965.
32 *Globe and Mail*, 9 June 1965.
33 *Globe and Mail*, 10 June 1965.
34 Ibid.
35 Ibid.
36 *Globe and Mail*, 11 June 1965. Scott Young's piece is tellingly entitled 'Shh! The Mayor Was There.'
37 *Globe and Mail*, 12 July 1965.
38 Greg Potter, *Hand Me Down World* (Toronto: Macmillan Canada 1999), 66.
39 The Free Times Café, on College St west of Spadina, is among the only bars in Toronto where an unknown, barebones folk act can be guaranteed a stage.
40 Judy Perly, interview with author, 27 June 2006. David DePoe, in a 1967 discussion with Allan Lamport, referred to the $2-cover charges at coffee houses as being too steep for most Villagers. http://archives.cbc.ca/IDCC-1-69-580-3217/life_society/hippies/ (accessed 22 November 2010).
41 David DePoe, interview with author, 20 December 2004.
42 Marcus has, for example, written an entire, full-length book on one single five-minute song. Greil Marcus, *Like a Rolling Stone: Bob Dylan at the Crossroads* (New York: Public Affairs 2005).
43 Dylan famously shocked the purists by taking the stage at the Newport Folk Festival in 1965 backed by a noisy and under-rehearsed rock'n'roll band.
44 Jennings, *Before the Gold Rush*, 39.
45 Ibid., 57.
46 Much of this ground has recently been covered in Ryan Edwardson's *Canuck Rock: A History of Canadian Popular Music* (Toronto: University of Toronto Press 2009).
47 Dave Bidini, *On a Cold Road: Tales of Adventure in Canadian Rock* (Toronto: McClelland and Stewart 1998), 258.

48 See Jimmy McDonough, *Shakey* (Toronto: Vintage Canada 2003); Karen O'Brien, *Shadows and Light: Joni Mitchell* (London: Virgin Books 2001).

49 John Einarson, *Neil Young: The Canadian Years* (Kingston, Ont.: Quarry Press 1992), 137.

50 McDonough, *Shakey*, 121.

51 Ibid., 134.

52 Ibid.

53 John Einarson, http://www.thrasherswheat.org/openbook/einarson.htm (accessed 1 May 2007).

54 See Einarson, *Neil Young*, 136–69. Also, see Scott Young, *Neil and Me* (Toronto: McClelland and Stewart 1984), 49–58.

55 Jennings, *Before the Gold Rush*, 35–53.

56 A telling example: Ian and Sylvia, Yorkville's biggest draws, went down to New York to get a record deal. However, when they were offered a huge, lucrative, major label deal, they turned it down. Instead, they accepted a deal on the smaller, but infinitely more 'authentic,' folk label, Vanguard.

57 Imagining the horror of the morning after, Dobson's stark dialogue takes place between the last two survivors, one innocent and searching, one cold and brazen: *Where have all the people gone my honey? / Where have all the people gone today? / There's no need for you to be worrying about all those people. / You never see those people anyway.* A staple of Grateful Dead concerts for nearly three decades, her version is available on *The Music Never Stopped: The Roots of the Grateful Dead*, Shanachie Records, 1995.

58 Jennings, *Before the Gold Rush*, 63.

59 Buffy Sainte-Marie, *It's My Way!* Vanguard Records, 1964.

60 David DePoe, interview with author, 20 December 2004.

61 Legend has it that another young Village folksinger was present that night. Gordon Lightfoot, soon to hit New York City to record his classic debut album, chose Ochs's aching love song for inclusion on *Lightfoot!* (1966). The record was recorded in 1964 but remained unreleased until January 1966. See the remarkably thorough fan site on Lightfoot, http://www.lightfoot.ca/lightrev.htm.

62 David DePoe, interview with author, 20 December 2004. American folksinger Phil Ochs, the tragic 1960s figure par excellence, was so disillusioned by the rock'n'roll turn, and the subsequent de-politicization of much of the hip music scene, coupled with the escalation of the Vietnam travesty, the events of Chicago '68, and the implosion of the SDS, that he seemed to pretty much fall apart. He hanged himself at his sister's home in 1976. Michael Schumacher, *There but for Fortune: The Life of Phil Ochs* (New York: Hyperion 1996).

63 For the record, I tend to believe DePoe's story, but I can't corroborate it.

64 See Jennings, *Before the Gold Rush*, 70.

65 Ibid., 71. 'We used to get letters addressed to Miss Penny Farthing,' laughs McHugh.

66 Ibid., 82.

67 One of the ways Fiedler managed to keep the venue intimate and cozy was to clear the room after every one-hour performance, and then charge fresh cover for the next set. This way, he could maximize sales, maximize space for customers, and maximize overall numbers of performances. Some nights the Riverboat offered five distinct sets of music, serving some 885 people. Ibid., 86.

68 Ibid., 116.

69 Ibid., 93.

70 Ibid., 99–100.

71 Brent Titcomb (Village musician) recalls that the north side of the street was folkier than the more acid-rock south side. *Where Have All the Flowers Gone?* Director: Karonne Lansel, Ryerson Student Film, 1988. Archives of Ontario, 4130–5245: T053623, T61693–T61696.

72 Colleen Riley Roberts, *The Life and Times of a Single Woman* (Bloomington, Ind.: AuthorHouse 2004), 82–3.

73 See Marcus, *Happy Days and Wonder Years*, 9–35, for a discussion of the ways this imagined wholesomeness was used in the 1970s and beyond as a tool of conservative memory.

74 The emergence of female sexual gratification as a political issue (catalysed by Anne Koedt's 1968 missive 'The Myth of the Vaginal Orgasm') began the slow process for many women of turning the focus of their sexual energy towards their own pleasure. As the myth of frigidity was ground down in the wake of such feminist articulations, sex became more pleasurable for the women (and men) who turned their minds to this line of thinking. Koedt, 'The Myth of the Vaginal Orgasm,' reprinted in Bloom and Breines, eds., *Taking It to the Streets* (New York: Oxford University Press 2003), 422–8.

75 Sullivan, *The Red Shoes*, 194.

76 Susan Swann, quoted in ibid.

77 Ibid.

78 Kerr had been thinking of employing topless dancers for years prior to the 1966 performance. When, fifteen months previously, he had asked his lawyer if it was a good idea, he had been advised that the time was not right. *Globe and Mail*, 11 August 1966.

79 Jennings, *Before the Gold Rush*, 104. See also Bidini, *On a Cold Road*, 260.

80 *Globe and Mail*, 11 August 1966.

81 Ibid.
82 Miguel Maropakis, interview with author, 29 March 2007.
83 As Sara Davidson observed, 'it [feminism] was resisted from top to bottom in society, by the straight world and just as vigorously and adamantly by the counterculture.' *Loose Change* (New York: Doubleday 1977).
84 Quoted in Susan Kuchinskas, 'That's Ms. Hippie Chick to You,' www. Salon.com, 17 November 1997 (accessed 3 May 2007).
85 Myrna Wood, interview with author, 19 April 2006.
86 Trina Robbins, an American writer and illustrator, neatly summarizes the way many women felt about their relationship to the male counterculture. 'In the '50s, it was, "Nice girls don't screw ... In the '60s, it was "Nice girls don't say no." If you said no, it meant you were frigid and, if the guy wasn't white, it meant you were prejudiced.' Quoted in Kuchinskas, 'That's Ms. Hippie Chick to You.'
87 In Gretchen Lemke-Santangelo's recently published monograph, *Daughters of Aquarius: Women of the Sixties Counterculture* (Lawrence: University Press of Kansas 2009), this dichotomy is continually referenced by her interview subjects.
88 Beth Bailey, 'Sex as a Weapon,' in Braunstein and Doyle, eds., *Imagine Nation*, 306.
89 Smart and Jackson, 'The Yorkville Subculture,' 71.
90 Clayton Ruby, interview with author, 3 March 2006.
91 Bidini, *On a Cold Road*, 260.
92 'Wild Bill,' interview with author, 11 March 2006.
93 Quoted in David Farber, 'Intoxicated State/Illegal Nation,' in Braunstein and Doyle, eds., *Imagine Nation*, 35.
94 Clayton Ruby, interview with author, 3 March 2006.
95 See Gary Miedema's monograph for the most comprehensive discussion of the role of Christianity in the Canadian 1960s. *For Canada's Sake: Public Religion, Centennial Celebrations, and the Re-Making of Canada in the 1960s* (Montreal and Kingston: McGill-Queen's University Press 2005).
96 Reginald Bibby, 'Who Says God Is Dead?' *Globe and Mail*, 17 April 2006.
97 The 1961 Canadian Census demonstrates an overwhelmingly Christian population. For example, in 1961 Christians (including Roman Catholics and United Church members, the two largest denominations) comprised 95.1 per cent of the population. Jews were listed at 1.5 per cent and 'Other' at 3.4 per cent. Among Villagers, Eastern religions were more than likely explored without the benefit of much personal contact with believers and adherents. Minister of Trade and Commerce, *Canada 1963: The Official*

Handbook of Present Conditions and Recent Progress (Ottawa: Dominion Bureau of Statistics 1963), 14.

98 Smart and Jackson, 'The Yorkville Subculture,' 31.

99 Tom Robbins, *Even Cowgirls Get the Blues* (New York: Houghton Mifflin 1976).

100 Smith, 'I Wish I Was a Fish,' ii.

101 Smart and Jackson, 'The Yorkville Subculture,' 13.

102 See Preston Shires, *The Hippies of the Religious Right* (Waco, Tex.: Baylor University Press 2007), for a useful study of the close connections between certain strains of countercultural thought and practice and developing faith-based communities of the United States.

103 Bruce Douville, presently a PhD candidate at York University, is actively pursuing these issues as part of his dissertation on hip religion in the early 1970s. '"And We've Got to Get Ourselves Back to the Garden": The Jesus People Movement in Toronto,' *Historical Papers: Canadian Society of Church History*, 19 (2006): 5–24.

104 As one of my interview subjects put it: 'We always held the hope that a significant number of people were having the real trip. I was involved in a community of people who, really, we regarded it as a sacrament. And for me, having been raised as a Roman Catholic, it was the closest thing to a religious experience I had ever had.' Anonymous LSD Dealer, interview with author, 13 October 2006.

105 Miller, *The Hippies and American Values*, 36.

106 See Erika Dyck, *Psychedelic Psychiatry: LSD from Clinic to Campus* (Baltimore, Md.: Johns Hopkins University Press 2008), for a thorough treatment of attempts to medicalize this odd substance.

107 Aldous Huxley, *The Doors of Perception and Heaven and Hell* (New York: Harper Collins 2004).

108 See Martin A. Lee and Bruce Shlain, *Acid Dreams: The Complete Social History of LSD* (New York: Grove Press 1992), 44–9.

109 See Tim Hardwick, 'On Being God: Transcendentalism and Romanticism, a Mystical Approach,' in *Lila: Journal of Cosmic Play*, http://www.lila.info/document_view.phtml?document_id=37 (accessed 1 May 2007).

110 *Playboy*, September 1966.

111 See Miller, *The Hippies and American Values*, 36–7. Continued associations between God, love, sex, and dope will be discussed in subsequent chapters.

112 Anonymous LSD Dealer, interview with author, 13 October 2006.

113 Ibid.

114 Longstaff, 'An Observational Report,' 18.

115 'The aim of the program in the Fish Net is to present a fundamentalist, literal religious philosophy to Villagers and to train church workers who will later work in other areas. It also aims to provide a haven of security and warmth. Because it is not very successful with its first two aims, it is very successful with the third.' Ibid., 17.

116 *Globe and Mail*, 4 July 1966. Deane (or Dean, it is unclear) was also a choir leader for the Avenue Rd Church. *Toronto Daily Star*, 29 September 1966.

117 The Avenue Rd Church, an evangelical mission founded by Charles B. Templeton, was largely behind the CMA and the Fish Net operation. The Reverend Opperman and many of his staff came from this congregation.

118 *Toronto Daily Star*, 29 September 1966.

119 Longstaff, 'An Observational Report,' 18.

120 Ibid., 18.

121 *Toronto Daily Star*, 28 September 1966.

122 Ibid., 18.

123 Phyllis McIntyre, for example, 'took a year off from a good job with the Encyclopaedia Britannica to run the Fish Net.' *Toronto Daily Star*, 29 September 1966.

124 *Globe and Mail*, 4 July 1966.

125 *Toronto Daily Star*, 28 September 1966.

126 Or Heite? He goes back and forth. *Toronto Daily Star*, 29 September 1966.

127 It was a kind of rental agreement. The Avenue Road Church paid out $650 per month to keep the Fish Net going: $265 for rent, a hundred or so for bills, and the rest for the coffee and snacks that they gave away every night. *Toronto Daily Star*, 29 September 1966.

128 Of course, not *all of them* were throwing bottles at the cops! The reality of the situation was hardly so cut and dried, and Haggart's own writings elsewhere on the sophistication of the Yorkville scene suggest that this was a deliberate exaggeration.

129 *Toronto Daily Star*, 29 September 1966.

130 See Gauri Viswanathan, *Outside the Fold: Conversion, Modernity, and Belief* (Princeton, N.J.: Princeton University Press 1998), for a detailed examination of the role of conversion in these processes (a subject that is far more complicated than I have suggested).

4. Are You Here to Watch Me Perform?

1 John Urry, *The Tourist Gaze* (London: Sage Publishing 1990; 2002), 3.

2 *Globe and Mail*, 14 May 1964.

3 Michael Valpy, interview with author, 5 October 2006.

4 Judy Pocock, interview with author, 24 June 2006.
5 Pocock: 'By the time I got home from Europe, the end of the summer, things had started to move across the Atlantic. I went to Britain just after the British Invasion, and it was so vital, so fun, there was so much going on.' Ibid.
6 Joel Lobenthal, *Radical Rags* (New York: Abbeville Books 2003), 217.
7 Smart and Jackson, 'The Yorkville Subculture,' 10. My emphasis. Or, in the words of an unnamed 'girl hippie': 'The Villagers wear clothes that are easy and comfortable. Women wear slacks and sweaters. Boys wear jeans.'
8 Clayton Ruby still equates hippie authenticity with the long-hair aesthetic: 'I never had long hair, never took part in the culture in the sense that you're thinking about. I was there for a lot of it, but I was never under the illusion that I was a hippie.' Interview with author, 3 March 2006.
9 *Toronto Daily Star*, 4 November 1964.
10 Ibid., 67. From Jack London and the Sparrows (1965) they became simply the Sparrows later that year, before reinventing, and then renaming, themselves as John Kay and Sparrow in 1966. Then, finally, they settled on the much snappier (and zeitgeist-fingering) Steppenwolf, in early 1968.
11 Judy Pocock, interview with author, 24 June 2006.
12 *Toronto Daily Star*, 4 January 1966.
13 In a classic scene in Alice Echols's biography of Janis Joplin (a Haight-Ashbury habitué and rock musician), she and her all-male band were pulled over by a highway patrolman. 'As the police in town searched the car, they kept taunting Sam, James, and Dave. "Are you guys or girls?" they asked. Janis wasn't having any of it and simply yelled, "Fuck you, man."' Joplin, never one to accept the gendered limitations placed upon her as a woman in a male world, was the only one to attack the bigoted officers. But was it about the mistreatment of her friends? Or was it because the patrolmen were leaving her *out* of the taunting, reminding her that the important subject here was the male? Echols, *Scars of Sweet Paradise*, 154.
14 Female expressions of Village identity were most commonly manifested in the donning of accoutrements. Baubles, beads, necklaces, bells, and flowers were worn by both sexes, but most often in exaggerated numbers by Village women. 'There are no limits to the number of necklaces and beads that are worn,' wrote Gopala Alampur. 'Some are made from animal teeth, bones, various nuts of beans, shells, chains, leather straps, and various talismans.' Smart and Jackson, 'The Yorkville Subculture,' 11.
15 Medovoi, *Rebels*, 21.
16 Medovoi demonstrates that the figure of the rebel can be read as a celebra-

tion of American individualism and agency in a Cold War era of pervasive vilification of Soviet conformism. Ibid.

17 Ibid. See especially chapter 5 for a discussion of the Oedipal paradigm.

18 Judy Perly, interview with author, 27 June 2006.

19 Ibid.

20 Lemke-Santangelo, in *Daughters of Aquarius*, 115, criticizes Didion for reinforcing 'the already prevalent stereotypes of female victim and spaced-out hippie chick' and introducing 'a new image: the negligent, drug-obsessed mother.'

21 Didion, quoted in Echols, *Shaky Ground*, 35.

22 Williams, *Keywords*, 87. Williams never offers any one overarching definition of this knotty word himself. For our purposes here, I have adopted a broad sociological view of culture, defining it as the combined set of behaviours, attitudes, and beliefs that are generally agreed upon at a particular moment (usually in a particular location) by an organization or group. Such a definition allows us to speak of *culture* in the most general sense (i.e., a North American culture) and the most specific (a Yorkville youth culture). Cultures, then, overlap, intertwine, and compete.

23 Stephen Yarbrough, *After Rhetoric* (Carbondale, Ill.: Southern Illinois University Press 1999), 108. This view is closely related to Benedict Anderson's famous declaration that a nation 'is imagined because the members of even the smallest nation will never know most of their fellow-members, meet them, or even hear of them, yet in the minds of each lives the image of their communion.' Culture operates much the same way as nationalism, although it tends towards a vastly more complicated politics in our increasingly multicultural nation-states. *Imagined Communities* (London: Verso 1983), 6. See also Said's equally seminal *Orientalism* for a discussion of the parallel concept of 'imagined geography.'

24 Reality is, therefore, experienced through people's interpretations of language and experience within systems of power (hegemony). This theory has been developed by diverse hands, but see especially Derrida, *The Ear of the Other*; Michel Foucault, *The History of Sexuality, Vol. I: An Introduction*, translated by Robert Hurley (New York: Pantheon 1978). See also Anthony Giddens, *Modernity and Self Identity* (Palo Alto, Calif.: Stanford University Press 1991).

25 Judith Butler, *Gender Trouble: Feminism and the Subversion of Identity* (London: Routledge 1990), 25. See also her elaboration on these themes in *Bodies That Matter* (New York: Routledge 1993).

26 See also Diana Fuss, *Essentially Speaking: Feminism, Nature and Difference* (New York: Routledge 1990); Denise Riley, *Am I That Name?: Feminism*

and the Category of 'Women' in History (Minneapolis: University of Minnesota Press 1988). Both of these works deconstruct categories of identity, establishing (respectively) the shiftiness of such apparently unquestionable categories as 'woman.'

27 See, for two ideal examples of such scholarship, both of which have greatly informed my understandings of class and race as performative categories, Matthew Frye Jacobson, *Whiteness of a Different Color* (Cambridge, Mass.: Harvard University Press 1998), and Nan Enstad, *Ladies of Labor, Girls of Adventure* (New York: Columbia University Press 1999).

28 Thus, as Joan Scott concludes: 'It is not individuals who have experience, but subjects who are constituted through experience.' Joan W. Scott, 'Experience,' *Critical Inquiry*, 17 (summer 1991): 773–97.

29 Enstad, *Ladies of Labor*, 205. I appreciate that Butler and Riley (among others) suggest moving beyond the social-construction theory in their approaches to identity – my view of performance does not allow for the radical notion that a subject might create him or herself from scratch. Instead, the performance of one's identity (although entirely prone to mutability and even whimsy in certain respects) is dialogically tied to hegemonic formulations of identity and behaviour.

30 Or, as K. Anthony Appiah has put it: 'These notions provide loose norms or models, which play a role in shaping the life plans of those who make these collective identities central to their individual identities.' See 'Identity, Authenticity, Survival: Multicultural Societies and Social Reproduction,' in Amy Gutmann, ed., *Multiculturalism* (Princeton, N.J.: Princeton University Press 1994), 159.

31 Ibid., 154.

32 Doug Rossinow neatly summarizes this emerging politics of authenticity: 'Amid the conditions of broad affluence, mass consumption, the bureaucratization of many areas of social life, and increasing disengagement from formal political participation, feelings of weightlessness migrated down the social scale, appearing among much broader strata of American society and leading to a widespread yearning for authenticity.' *The Politics of Authenticity*, 5.

33 Marshall McLuhan, *Playboy*, March 1969.

34 Letter from James Felstiner to Dr J.P. Harshman, 19 March 1966. Harshman Foundation Archives, Toronto.

35 Longstaff, 'Yorkville: An Observational Report,' 23.

36 *Globe and Mail*, 15 December 1965.

37 Ibid.

38 Judy Pocock, interview with author, 24 June 2006.

39 *Where Have All the Flowers Gone?* Director: Karonne Lansel, Ryerson Student Film, 1988. Archives of Ontario, 4130–5245: T053623, T61693–T61696.

40 *Globe and Mail*, 15 December 1965.

41 Judy Pocock, interview with author, 24 June 2006.

42 Michael Valpy, interview with author, 5 October 2006. Similarly, Charles Perry wrote of the San Francisco scene: 'The Haight was the perfect theatre, a large territory full of stoned people making the scene and vaguely waiting for something to happen.' Perry, *The Haight-Ashbury*, 243.

43 *Satyrday*, Second Issue, 1967. The 'Hip Parade' is likely a reference to the radio-cum-television program *Your Hit Parade*, a program showcasing popular music which ran from 1935 to 1959 on NBC.

44 Chris Jenks, 'The Centrality of the Eye in Western Culture,' in Jenks, ed., *Visual Culture* (New York: Routledge 1995), 2. See also Martin Jay, *Force Fields: Between Intellectual History and Cultural Critique* (New York: Routledge 1993), especially 114–34. See also the now classic work by John Berger, *Ways of Seeing* (London: Penguin Books 1972).

45 Urry, *The Tourist Gaze*, 1.

46 *Where Have All the Flowers Gone?*

47 Urry, *The Tourist Gaze*, 3. See also Dean MacCannell, *The Tourist: A New Theory of the Leisure Class* (Berkeley: University of California Press 1999); Urry makes great use of the work of Jonathan Culler, 'Semiotics of Tourism,' *American Journal of Semiotics*, 1 (1981): 127–40.

48 Don DeLillo, *White Noise* (New York: Penguin Books 1984), 12–13. 'We're not here to capture an image,' one character says to another as they gaze upon a tourist attraction. 'We're here to maintain one.'

49 Joergen Ole Baerenholdt et al., *Performing Tourist Places* (London: Ashgate 2004), 2.

50 Alderman Horace Brown's poetic description of the Village. *Toronto Daily Star*, 10 June 1965.

51 Clayton Ruby: 'In the beginning there was a small number of quote-hippie-unquote kids [in Yorkville]. Kids who were in some way committed, longer than a few weekends, to alternative ways of living, alternative lifestyles. And a lot more people came down on weekends. I think that remained the same forever, but the group that actually lived there was tiny in the beginning.' Interview with author, 3 March 2006.

52 *Where Have All the Flowers Gone?*

53 Judge James Felstiner, interview with author, 3 April 2006.

54 Mike Waage, interview with author, 3 March 2005.

55 'Wild Bill,' interview with author, 11 March 2005.

56 *Satan's Choice*, Directed by Donald Shebib, National Film Board of Canada, 1965.

57 Mike Waage, interview with author, 3 March 2005.

58 Longstaff, 'Yorkville: An Observational Report,' 6.

59 Perly, a pioneer in the whole-food movement in the 1970s, was highly attuned to such developments, learning from them ways to approach wholesome cooking at low prices. Interview with author, 27 June 2006.

60 Judy Pocock, interview with author, 24 June 2006.

61 Judy Perly, interview with author, 27 June 2006.

62 Michael Foley's recent study makes clear that the popular term 'draft dodger' is widely disliked by former draft resisters. 'One draft resistance leader has said on several occasions (only partly in jest) that when he dies, his epitaph should read, "I Didn't Dodge, I Resisted."' Foley, *Confronting the War Machine: Draft Resistance during the Vietnam War* (Chapel Hill: University of North Carolina Press 2003), 7.

63 David Churchill, 'When Home Became Away: American Expatriates and New Social Movements in Toronto, 1965–1977,' PhD thesis, University of Chicago, 2001, 158.

64 Ibid., 171.

65 CBC Television News, 10 May 1966, http://archives.cbc.ca/IDC-1-71-348-1925/conflict_war/draft_dodgers/ (accessed 22 November 2010).

66 However, sometimes both studies carry this too far. See John Hagan, *Northern Passage* (Cambridge, Mass.: Harvard University Press 2001), 82. David Churchill's study, while more interested in the vicissitudes of identity within the broadly generalized 'Draft Dodger and Deserter' category, still neatly avoids engaging with the Yorkville scene in a meaningful way. Rather, Churchill focuses on Rochdale as the more significant counterculture/ex-pat centre. But, since Rochdale opened its doors in September 1968, that leaves a few years off the ledger, so to speak.

67 'Most [draft resisters] remember Yorkville as a much more Toronto-based, Canadian scene than Baldwin Street, with its older, more politicized and American residents.' Hagan, *Northern Passage*, 82.

68 CBC Television News, 10 May 1966.

69 *Satyrday*, Fifth Issue, December 1966.

70 David DePoe, interview with author, 20 December 2004.

71 Norman 'Otis' Richmond, in conversation with author, 16 June 2007.

72 Judy Pocock: 'My parents were involved in the Toronto anti-draft program, and the Committee for a Sane Nuclear Policy [SANE], and the Ban-the-Bomb movement.' Interview with author, 24 June 2006.

73 Ibid.

74 Hagan's *Northern Passage* is focused on this vibrant scene.
75 Owram, *Born at the Right Time*, 198.
76 Martel's chapter on 'Measuring the Use of Illegal Drugs' establishes a variety of class, race, language, and gender gaps in the distribution of drug consumption. Throughout the 1960s, the chief grouping (at least with respect to the concerns of the general public, the mass media, and various governments) were white, middle-class males and females between the ages of thirteen and twenty-five. Marcel Martel, *Not This Time: Canadians, Public Policy, and the Marijuana Question, 1961–1975* (Toronto: University of Toronto Press 2006), 10–35.
77 Catherine Carstairs's study of narcotics laws in Canada establishes that marijuana was a minor player in the drug wars between the 1923 legislation (when pot was made illegal in Canada) and the early 1960s. Carstairs, *Jailed for Possession: Illegal Drug Use, Regulation, and Power in Canada, 1920–1961* (Toronto: University of Toronto Press 2006).
78 Owram, *Born at the Right Time*, 203.
79 For example, the first LSD arrest in Yorkville was not until very late 1966, and this came only following a three-month undercover operation. Although the drug was certainly more readily available by then than this arrest suggests, it was still clearly operating in the background. *Globe and Mail*, 16 December 1966.
80 Martin Barber, interview with author, 2007.
81 Miguel Maropakis, interview with author, 2007.
82 *Toronto Daily Star*, 2 July 1965.
83 In the case of LSD, for example, David Farber argues that 'criminalization made LSD both more dangerous … and more a clear sign of cultural rebellion.' Braunstein and Doyle, eds., *Imagine Nation*, 34.
84 Longstaff, 'Yorkville: An Observational Report,' 19.
85 *Globe and Mail*, 29 September 1965.
86 Anonymous LSD dealer, interview with author, 13 October 2006.
87 *Globe and Mail*, 29 September 1965.
88 Ibid. By way of comparison, an ounce of marijuana today will cost its buyer anywhere from $240 to $300, depending upon quality (both of the product, and of one's relationship with one's dealer!).
89 Ibid.
90 *Globe and Mail*, 16 December 1965.
91 *Globe and Mail*, 29 September 1965.
92 Jennings, *Before the Gold Rush*, 109. Maue, incidentally, would later marry John Kay of Sparrow and, eventually, Steppenwolf.
93 *Globe and Mail*, 16 December 1965.

94 Ibid. My emphasis.

95 Ibid.

96 *Globe and Mail*, 24 February 1965.

97 *Globe and Mail*, 12 August 1965.

98 *Globe and Mail*, 30 October, 25 November 1965.

99 *Globe and Mail*, 4 August 1966.

100 *Globe and Mail*, 1 July 1966.

101 *Globe and Mail*, 20 July 1966.

102 *Globe and Mail*, 28 September 1966.

103 *Globe and Mail*, 25 October 1966.

104 *Globe and Mail*, 4 July 1966.

105 Mike Waage, interview with author, 3 March 2005.

106 Smith, 'I Wish I Was a Fish,' 4.

107 W.R. Clement, interview with author, 5 March 2006.

108 Smith, 'I Wish I Was a Fish,' 10.

109 Mike Waage, interview with author, 3 March 2005.

110 Ibid.

111 Smith, 'I Wish I Was a Fish,' 14.

112 Ibid., 11.

113 Longstaff, 'Yorkville: An Observational Report,' 18–19.

114 Ibid., 19.

115 Smith, 'I Wish I Was a Fish,' 10–11.

116 *Toronto Daily Star*, 8 April 1967.

117 Anonymous LSD dealer, interview with author, 13 October 2006.

118 Smith, 'I Wish I Was a Fish,' 11.

119 Ibid.

120 David DePoe, interview with author, 20 December 2004.

121 Ibid.

122 *Toronto Daily Star*, 26 March 1965.

123 Ron (the Thud) Thody gets a byline in *Satyrday*, Fifth Issue, December 1966.

124 How well were such publications read? It is impossible to know for sure. But my interview subjects tended to make reference to the *Georgia Straight* (Vancouver), the *Oracle* (San Francisco), or the *East Village Other* (New York) before they mentioned the homegrown variety of underground paper.

125 'The reason for this oddity is that the publisher claims that the humorous and literary content is of permanent reading value, which is not to be discarded like an old newspaper.' *Satyrday*, Third Issue, 1966.

126 *Satyrday*, Fifth Issue, December, 1966.

127 David DePoe, interview with author, 20 December 2004.

128 Michael Valpy, interview with author, 5 October 2006.

129 Valerie Korinek's work on *Chatelaine* magazine has greatly informed my understanding of the ways letters to the editor can constitute a site of dialogue. *Roughing It in the Suburbs* (Toronto: University of Toronto Press 2000), 71–87.

130 *Satyrday*, vol. 3, no. 5 (August 1968).

131 *Satyrday*, Fifth Issue, December 1966.

132 *Satyrday*, Second Issue, 1967.

133 Michael Valpy, interview with author, 5 October 2006.

134 Martin Barber, interview with author, 29 March 2007.

135 *Satyrday*, Fifth Issue, December 1966.

136 According to Frank Longstaff: 'The Saturday night ruckus in May was caused by one of the few Villager-Greaser mix-ups. On the Friday night before, Greasers had found some Villagers alone in side alleys and had cut their hair. On the Saturday night, Villagers were ready for more trouble and around midnight, a scuffle broke out between two Villagers and two Greasers.' Longstaff, 'Yorkville: An Observational Report,' 12.

137 This, one of the rare instances in which black youth were connected to the Village scene, is maddeningly under-investigated in the press. Though the number of black people who moved into the Village scene may have been small, the casual way the media cover this event (suggesting no racial conflict, though this would have been a logical inference) demonstrates that it was by no means unexpected that black youth were hanging around. So, why the silence?

138 Longstaff, 'Yorkville: An Observational Report,' 12.

139 *Toronto Daily Star*, 30 May 1966. See also the article on the Wetzel case written by 'Crowbait,' *Satyrday*, Third Issue, 1966.

140 Ibid.

141 *Toronto Daily Star*, 22 July 1966.

142 *Satyrday*, Fifth Issue, December 1966.

143 *Toronto Daily Star*, 2 November 1966.

144 *Satyrday*, Second Issue, 1967.

145 *Toronto Daily Star*, 2 November 1966.

146 *Satyrday*, Fifth Issue, December 1966. Also *Toronto Daily Star*, 2 November 1966.

147 Ibid.

148 *Toronto Daily Star*, 3 November 1966.

149 *Satyrday*, Fifth Issue, December 1966.

5. Village Politics and the Summer of Love

1 Michael Valpy, interview with author, 5 October 2006.
2 'Recently, the police force has been sending a more mature, experienced group of police to patrol the village. We believe this is mainly a result of the Wetzel debauchle [sic].' *Satyrday*, Second Issue, 1967.
3 Gitlin, *The Sixties*; Echols, *Shaky Ground*; Thomas Frank, *Conquest of Cool* (Chicago: University of Chicago Press 1997). See also Kobena Mercer, '1968: Periodizing Politics and Identity,' in Lawrence Grossberg, Cary Nelson, and Paula Treichler, eds., *Cultural Studies* (New York: Routledge 1992), 424–49.
4 Thomas Frank takes pains to undo the widespread belief that advertisers merely co-opted hip attitudes, beliefs, and behaviours. Rather, he argues, advertisers in the late 1950s had already moved towards 'individualism' and 'youth' as primary figures of consumerism. 'Seeking a single metaphor by which to characterize the accelerated obsolescence and enhanced consumer friendliness to change which were their goals, leaders in [advertising] had already settled on "youth" and "youthfulness" several years before saturation TV and print coverage of the "Summer of Love" introduced middle America to the fabulous new lifestyles of the young generation.' Frank, *Conquest of Cool*, 27.
5 The complex interplay between consumption, identity, and politics has been explored in a variety of monographs in recent years. A few highlights: Nan Enstad, in her study of New York working women in the early part of the twentieth century, explores the 'imaginative value' these women placed on ladyhood, and the ways their consumptive practices challenged dominant meanings of 'public women' (Enstad, *Ladies of Labor*). Lizabeth Cohen's work on consumption in post-war U.S. politics demonstrates the centrality of shopping to discourses of patriotism and nationalism into the 1960s (Cohen, *A Consumer's Republic: The Politics of Mass Consumption in Postwar America* [New York: Vintage Books 2003]). Joy Parr's study of Canadian manufacturing in the suburbanized post-war years establishes the complexities of an expanding culture of consumption (Parr, *Domestic Goods: The Material, the Moral, and the Economic in the Postwar Years* [Toronto: University of Toronto Press 1999]).
6 Vance Packard, *Hidden Persuaders* (New York: Random House 1957).
7 Lizabeth Cohen has argued that the expansion of consumption in the postwar period both advanced and complicated the process of racial, class, and gender inequality in the United States. However, her arguments, while germane to our discussion, fail to consider the role of hip consumption in

any detailed way. As a result, one is left wondering where hip, rebellious youth fit into her formulation of the 'mass' and the 'segment.' *A Consumer's Republic*, 318–22.

8 How exactly do you 'break up' a district?

9 *Toronto Daily Star*, 23 March 1967. *Telegram* also, same date.

10 *Toronto Daily Star*, 5 April 1967. My emphasis.

11 Ibid.

12 Inspired by the American Peace Corps, the Company of Young Canadians was a Liberal government initiative, championed by Judy LaMarsh and others in Pearson's cabinet, which came into being in 1966. A political response to the popularity of campus activism in the mid-1960s, the CYC, an alternative, government-sponsored activist organization, can be read in a variety of ways and was indeed hotly debated by virtually everyone in the late 1960s. Decried by politicians as a state-supported Communist organization, attacked by New Left activists as a blatant tactic in a pervasive Liberal passive revolution, and cynically used by many of its own volunteers merely as a means for funding, the CYC was a failure for the Liberal government. Until 1970, when the government took up the reins and withdrew the CYC's autonomy, even its volunteers couldn't necessarily be counted among the supporters of the CYC and its mandate. The program limped along until 1977. For an excellent discussion, see Kevin Brushett, 'Making Shit Disturbers: The Selection and Training of the Company of Young Canadian Volunteers, 1965–1970,' in M. Athena Palaeologu, ed., *The Sixties in Canada: A Turbulent and Creative Decade* (Montreal: Black Rose Books 2009), 246–69.

13 Norman DePoe was arguably the most recognizable face on Canadian television in the 1960s, as principal correspondent on national (and occasionally) international affairs on the CBC.

14 John Diefenbaker was a vocal critic of the CYC and of DePoe and Curtis's role in the protest. In public, Pearson defended his volunteers, explaining that the two CYC volunteers had acted privately and 'as citizens of a free country.' Still, behind closed doors, Pearson was not pleased, and phone calls were made. Ian Hamilton, *The Children's Crusade: The Story of the Company of Young Canadians* (Toronto: Peter Martin Associates 1970), 47–50.

15 Ibid.

16 David DePoe, interview with author, 20 December 2004.

17 As Cyril Levitt pointed out in his seminal study on the New Left in the United States, Canada, and West Germany, such defections signalled the co-optation of the movement, 'the equivalent of committing a mortal sin in the New Left.' *Children of Privilege* (Toronto: University of Toronto Press 1984), 97.

18 David DePoe, interview with author, 20 December 2004.

19 'What did the CYC in was its own incompetence. And that incompetence was universal. Far more than David's project here – it caused embarrassment, unquestionably. But what really was the death knell was that it was funding the separatists in Quebec! You know, Gilles Duceppe was a CYC volunteer ... They were taking CYC money to fund separatist activities. But what David was doing was a totally legitimate project in terms of the CYC mandate, which was to build and empower community. Certainly, it was an uneven contest between the kids, city council, the cops, the property owners. So it was a totally legitimate project!' Michael Valpy, interview with author, 5 October 2006.

20 See Ian Hamilton's *Children's Crusade* for a critical chronicle of the CYC's first three years.

21 The Digger ideology was based upon the English Diggers (a.k.a. the Levellers), a proto-anarchist group active during the English Civil War, whose basic premise was an abolition of private property along with the entire profit-based economy. In its San Francisco incarnation, the Diggers was a profoundly contradictory and exciting political (or, perhaps apolitical) collective. In the words of one of the most famous collaborators, Peter Coyote, 'the Diggers was an anarchistic experiment dedicated to creating and clarifying distinctions between society's business-as-usual and our own imaginings of what-it-might-be, in the most potent way we could devise.' The Diggers' great pursuit of living otherwise was based around the realization that, in a profit-oriented economy, the only thing that cannot be co-opted is *doing things for free*. They established free food stalls, free medical clinics, free stores, and endorsed free entertainment, free love, free *everything*. See Peter Coyote, *Sleeping Where I Fall: A Chronicle* (Washington: Counterpoint Press 1998), 34–5.

22 Of the San Francisco Diggers: 'That's where the name came from. Occasionally you heard reports about what they were doing. We were interested, but there was no formal mechanism at all [connecting us] ... I've always been an anarchist, still am. Blues was interested in anarchist thought, and Dave was interested in anarchist thought.' Clayton Ruby, Interview with author, 3 March 2006.

23 David DePoe, interview with author, 20 December 2004.

24 I have tried, and failed, to contact both Don Riggan and Brian Chapman. I have not found Hans Wetzel, nor have I yet met anyone who knows how to contact him.

25 David DePoe, interview with author, 20 December 2004.

26 Hamilton, *The Children's Crusade*, 58.

27 June Callwood, interview with author, 11 March 2005.

28 Ibid.

29 David DePoe, interview with author, 20 December 2004.

30 Clayton Ruby, interview with author, 3 March 2006.

31 Ibid. Ruby leaves his name off the list because, as a law student, he was not as single-minded about the scene as his friends. 'Not me, I wasn't a hippie. I don't think I was an outsider, no. I was as much an insider as you could get. I had lots of friends, and people reacted very normally and openly to me, period. I don't think there was any discrimination at all, but it was also clear that I was a guy in law school. My priorities were not their priorities.'

32 Anonymous LSD dealer, interview with author, 13 October 2006.

33 *Satyrday*, Fifth Issue, December 1966.

34 Clayton Ruby recalls that, while 'a lot of our people went off to the CYC, I didn't ... It was slightly more mainstream than SUPA, which was a necessity when you've got government control. There was great debate about whether it was politically useful to [join CYC] ... It was just a real debate about whether or not working within a governmental structure you could make the fundamental social change we thought was needed, or whether it was always going to be superficial. But in the end the truth seems to be, in hindsight, that neither one worked.' Interview with author, 3 March 2006.

35 Such opportunism convinced many would-be SUPA stalwarts to bail out of the nascent student radical movement and move towards government-sponsored liberal activism. The big book on the relationship between these two organizations remains unwritten, but it is a hugely important story. I would certainly like to suggest that the advent of the CYC could be regarded as a highly effective passive revolutionary response which redefined the character of a student movement increasingly taking up radical politics.

36 Myrna Kostash, *Long Way From Home: The Story of the Sixties Generation in Canada* (Toronto: James Lorimer and Company 1980), 20.

37 Ibid.

38 Wood and Morton, along with Judy Bernstein and Linda Seese, were at work composing what would be the first major statement of the women's liberation movement in Canada. 'Sisters, Brothers, Lovers ... Listen ...,' although somewhat tame by today's standards, was indeed a powerful statement in its day, rattling SUPA male hegemony and precipitating the dissolution of the union by the end of the year. This foundational paper was republished in the early 1970s in Judy Bernstein et al., *Women Unite!: Up from the Kitchen, up from the Bedroom, up from Under* (Toronto: Canadian Women's Educational Press 1972).

39 Myrna Wood, interview with author, 19 April 2006.
40 David DePoe, interview with author, 20 December 2004.
41 Ibid.
42 Myrna Wood, interview with author, 19 April 2006.
43 Still, it is worth noting that in this same study Gosse separates the counterculture from the New Left in his analysis, leaving his discussion of their
   'links' to a six-page section at the end of a 210-page text. Gosse, *Rethinking
   the New Left*, 202–8.
44 Ibid.
45 Judy Pocock, interview with author, 24 June 2006.
46 David DePoe, interview with author, 20 December 2004.
47 Judy Perly, interview with author, 27 June 2006.
48 Ibid.
49 Echols, *Shaky Ground*, 34.
50 See Anne Koedt, 'The Myth of the Vaginal Orgasm,' in Bloom and Breines,
   eds., *Taking It to the Streets*, 422–8.
51 Bernstein et al., 'Sisters, Brothers, Lovers … Listen…,' 39.
52 Christine Stansell, *American Moderns* (New York: Owl Books 2001), 280.
   Stansell's work (especially in this eighth chapter to her book) underlines the
   politics of sex in the 1910s among the bohemians in ways that simply cannot
   be applied to the Village scene as I have understood it. For example, speaking of Emma Goldman and Neith Boyce, two sexual moderns par excellence,
   Stansell observes that they both looked to the politics of free love as 'opening up a space of reciprocity where jealousy, hurt, and humiliation could be
   banished to a bygone era of women's powerlessness' (297).
53 'The relationship between women's liberation and the larger Movement
   was at its core paradoxical. The Movement was a site of sexism, but it also
   provided women with a space in which they could develop political skills
   and self-confidence … Most important, it gave them no small part of the
   intellectual ammunition – the language and the ideas – with which to fight
   their own oppression.' Echols, *Shaky Ground*, 79.
54 Morgan's paper, originally printed in *Rat*, a New York-based underground
   paper, was reprinted all over the United States and in Canada before the
   end of 1970. It has recently been reprinted in Rosalyn Baxandall and Linda
   Gordon, eds., *Dear Sisters: Dispatches from the Women's Liberation Movement*
   (New York: Basic Books 2000), 53–7.
55 See Rebick, *Ten Thousand Roses*. 'The student movement,' recalls Canadian
   feminist Jean Rands, 'was dominated by articulate young men who were
   arrogant and full of themselves. Women were intimidated, and there was a
   lot of nasty, misogynist stuff that happened' (8–9).

56 There is virtually no mention of Yorkville, or of the hippies, for example, in either Becki Ross's overview of the emergence of lesbian separatism in Toronto in these years or Nancy Adamson, Linda Briskin, and Margaret McPhail's study of Canadian feminist history (which also emphasizes Toronto as a seedbed for the movement). See Becki L. Ross, *The House That Jill Built: The Emergence of Lesbian Feminist Discourse* (Toronto: University of Toronto Press 1995); Nancy Adamson, Linda Briskin, and Margaret McPhail, *Feminist Organizing for Change* (Oxford: Oxford University Press 1988). In a survey of the Toronto *Women's Liberation Newsletter* in the years 1970–1 (which fall, admittedly, at the tail end of our study), little mention is made of Yorkville or the Toronto counterculture. My thanks to Ian McKay for drawing this material to my attention.

57 Myrna Wood, interview with author, 19 April 2006.

58 For example, the famous girls-say-yes-to-boys-who-say-no campaign slogan designed for the U.S. draft resistance suggested that hipness was a free ride to free love, a veritable ticket to sex.

59 Moira Armour and Pat Staton, *Canadian Women in History: A Chronology* (Toronto: Green Dragon Press 1990), 82.

60 See 'Sisters, Brothers, Lovers … Listen …,' 31–9.

61 Nancy Adamson, 'Feminists, Libbers, Lefties, and Radicals: The Emergence of the Woman's Liberation Movement,' in Joy Parr, ed., *A Diversity of Women: Ontario, 1945–1980* (Toronto: University of Toronto Press 1996), 253–80.

62 See Rebick, *Ten Thousand Roses*, 9–12. Also see Canada, *Report of the Royal Commission on the Status of Women in Canada* (Ottawa: Information Canada 1970), 352.

63 See, especially, Alice Echols, *Daring to Be Bad* (Minneapolis: University of Minnesota Press 1989).

64 Ross, *The House That Jill Built*. See also Rebick, *Ten Thousand Roses*, 12.

65 Adamson, Briskin, and McPhail, *Feminist Organizing for Change*, 44.

66 See Bonnie Kreps's brief to the Royal Commission on the Status of Women in Canada for a concise, and pointed, discourse on this central premise. 'Radical Feminism 1,' in Bernstein et al., *Women Unite!* 71–5.

67 Adamson, Briskin, and McPhail, *Feminist Organizing for Change*, 45.

68 See Christabelle Sethna, 'The Evolution of the Birth Control Handbook: From Student Peer Education Manual to Feminist Self-Help Text, 1968–1975,' *Canadian Bulletin of Medical History / Bulletin canadien d'histoire de la medicine*, 23, no. 1 (2006): 89–117; 'The University of Toronto Health Service, Oral Contraception and Student Demand for Birth Control, 1960–1970,' *Historical Studies in Education / Revue d'histoire de l'éducation*, 17, no. 2 (2005):

265–92. See also Angus McLaren and Arlene Tigar McLaren, *The Bedroom and the State: The Changing Practices and Politics of Contraception and Abortion in Canada, 1880–1996* (New York: Oxford University Press 1986; 1998).
69 Smart and Jackson, 'The Yorkville Subculture,' 46.
70 *Satyrday*, Second Issue, 1967, 'a poem' by Lorne Jones.
71 Ibid., 47.
72 Colleen Riley, interview with author, 29 March 2007.
73 Ibid.
74 Marilyn Brooks, interview with author, 29 March 2007.
75 Judy Perly, interview with author, 27 June 2006.
76 *Toronto Daily Star*, 31 May 1967. My emphasis.
77 Anonymous LSD dealer, interview with author, 13 October 2006. Still, he continued, 'there were kinda orgy situations that did develop, with people taking MDA. I didn't attend, but they were described to me.'
78 Her name is also given as Kearns. *Toronto Daily Star*, 23 August 1967.
79 *Toronto Daily Star*, 23 August 1967.
80 Ibid.
81 David DePoe, interview with author, 20 December 2004.
82 *Toronto Daily Star*, 16 June 1967.
83 *Toronto Daily Star*, 30 June 1967.
84 *Toronto Daily Star*, 12 September 1967. One year hence, *Satyrday* went a step further, its cover proclaiming: 'The New Anti-Semitism ... Destroy the Hippies!' vol. 3, no. 5 (August 1968).
85 The *Globe and Mail*'s telling headline, 'Flowers between Toes, Hippies Enter the World of Lamport.' The clash-of-two-worlds frame writ large. *Globe and Mail*, 18 August 1967.
86 Lamport singled out DePoe at the talk-in as soon as the group entered. See *Christopher's Movie Matinee* (1968).
87 See Berton, *1967*, 173.
88 Towards the end of the meeting, Lamport tried to back away from this out-burst, admitting, 'There are obviously none of you who haven't washed,' by way of apology. *Globe and Mail*, 18 August 1967.
89 *Christopher's Movie Matinee* (1968).
90 *Toronto Daily Star*, 21 August 1967.
91 Clayton Ruby bristles at the overwrought language surrounding this event: 'It was not a riot! You've never been in a riot. I've been in Mississippi, I've been in Washington. I've been in riots. This was a quiet, peaceful demonstration.' *Where Have All the Flowers Gone?*
92 *Toronto Daily Star*, 25 August 1967.
93 Ibid.

94 This information was revealed in early November, as the protesters' trials got under way. *Globe and Mail*, 10 November 1967.

95 *Toronto Daily Star*, 30 August 1967.

96 *Globe and Mail*, 22 August 1967. The 23rd Psalm is a fixture in Christian funerals, and would seem to be inappropriate to the event. However, some Villagers might have found this line, its most famous, to be pertinent? 'Yea, though I walk through the valley of the shadow of death, I will fear no evil.'

97 David DePoe, interview with author, 20 December 2004.

98 Quoted in Jennings, *Before the Gold Rush*, 169.

99 *Toronto Daily Star*, 30 August 1967. Also *Globe and Mail*, 31 August 1967. Listen to the lengthy exchange at the CBC Internet archives: http://archives.cbc.ca/IDCC-1-69-580-3217/life_society/hippies/ (accessed 1 May 2007).

100 *Globe and Mail*, 31 August 1967. Also *Toronto Daily Star*, 31 August 1967.

101 David DePoe, interview with author, 20 December 2004.

102 *Toronto Daily Star*, 2 September 1967.

103 http://archives.cbc.ca/IDCC-1-69-580-3220/life_society/hippies/.

104 *Globe and Mail*, 1 September 1967.

105 *Globe and Mail*, 8 September 1967.

106 *Toronto Daily Star*, 1 September 1967.

107 *Star Weekly*, 23 September 1967.

108 'I was embarrassed because that isn't how I saw myself or felt about myself and I thought, "Oh man this is bad because now everybody's going to …" Oh, I got a lot of harassment! [Cameron] used me to get himself established as a magazine writer. So I felt exploited by Bill, big time. I mean, he'd probably admit it now! This was his breakthrough into magazine writing. His first big article. We were about the same age. For him, he would have been twenty-three, twenty-four.' David DePoe, interview with author, 20 December 2004. Bill Cameron passed away as I was researching this book.

109 Ibid.

110 Ibid.

111 *Satyrday*, vol. 3, no. 5 (August 1968).

112 *Where Have All the Flowers Gone?*

113 As *Christopher's Movie Matinee* so clearly demonstrates, the role of the media in the creation and exaggeration of the events of late August was pervasive. This film, alternately fascinating and boring to the point of stultification, moves between the interiors of city hall and coverage of the fractious 'talk-in' scenes of violence and disarray on the streets of

Yorkville Ave, and various sequences vaguely organized around the principle of Villagers expressing themselves.

114 *Globe and Mail*, 26 August 1967.

115 *Christopher's Movie Matinee*. See also *Flowers on a One-Way Street*, NFB, Dir: Robin Spry, 1967.

6. Authenticity among the *Fleurs du Mal*

1 CBC Newsmagazine, 4 September 1967, http://archives.cbc.ca/IDC-1-69-1587-10799/life_society/60s/clip11 (accessed 22 February 2007).

2 Gibson, widely credited with the invention of the cyberpunk genre in literature, is the author of many novels all concerned (in various, innovate ways) with the subversive, the countercultural, and the revolutionary potential of thinking otherwise. See especially *Neuromancer* (New York: Ace 1984) and *Pattern Recognition* (Berkeley, Calif.: Berkeley Books 2003). In short, this unwavering tension between the authentic and the plastic in a society of spectacle is his consistent intellectual premise.

3 See http://www.williamgibsonbooks.com/archive/2003_05_01_archive. asp (accessed 22 February 2007).

4 Charles Taylor has put this into clear terms. 'Being true to myself means being true to my own originality, and that is something only I can articulate and discover. In articulating it, I am also defining myself. I am realizing a potentiality that is properly my own. This is the background understanding to the modern ideal of authenticity, and to the goals of self-fulfillment or self-realization in which it is usually couched ... It is what gives sense to the idea of "doing your own thing" or "finding your own fulfillment."' Taylor, *The Malaise of Modernity* (Concord: Anansi 1991), 29.

5 See also Rossinow, *The Politics of Authenticity*, 53–68.

6 See Dyck, *Psychedelic Psychiatry*.

7 Perhaps the best sustained history of the drug can be found in Martin A. Lee and Bruce Shlain's *Acid Dreams: The Complete Social History of LSD* (New York: Grove Press 1985), 141–69. For a helpful discussion of the relationship between authenticity, alienation, and LSD, see David Farber, 'Intoxicated State/Illegal Nation: Drugs in the Sixties Counterculture,' in Braunstein and Doyle, eds., *Imagine Nation*, 17–40.

8 Anonymous LSD dealer, interview with author, 13 October 2006.

9 Martel, *Not This Time*, 16.

10 A writer at *Satyrday* claimed that this fact meant that 'pseudo-hip Toronto has at last caught up with New York, Chicago, and San Francisco.' *Satyrday*, Second Issue, 1967.

11 *Toronto Daily Star*, 20 March 1967.

12 Hayden had been a regular in the Village art scene since his first one-man show the previous year at the Gallery Moos. He is currently based out of Santa Rosa, California, and continues to create art. See samples of his work and a short biography at http://www.thinkinglightly.com/hayden/resume.html (accessed 22 February 2007).

13 Hayden wrote to me in an e-mail, received on 27 February 2007, about his role in the festival: 'I personally invited the participants from NYC = Allan [sic] Ginsberg, Tiger Morris, Ralph Metzner, Timothy Leary, The Fugs, (when I lived in New York, I was 1/2 block from where Tuli Kupferberg and Ed Sanders published *The East Village Other*) etc, as well as The City Muffin Boys, from Toronto, to perform.'

14 See also Martel, *Not This Time*, 41–2.

15 In the spring of 1967 *Satyrday*, always concerned about the effects of commercialization and co-optation of the Village scene, proclaimed regarding the advent of such drug-use-as-popular-entertainment enterprises: 'The Establishment is your corner dope peddler.' *Satyrday*, Second Issue, 1967.

16 *Toronto Daily Star*, 11 February 1967.

17 Judy Perly, interview with author, 27 June 2006.

18 Even his tape was seized by officials at the border. *Toronto Daily Star*, 13 February 1967.

19 Ibid.

20 Ibid.

21 Ibid.

22 Martel, *Not This Time*, 14–15.

23 This story was recounted in great detail in all three major papers. See, especially, *Toronto Daily Star*, 20 March 1967; *Toronto Telegram*, 20 March 1967; *Globe and Mail*, 21 March 1967.

24 A few days after the Toronto conference, Alpert made the scene at the inauguration of the League for Spiritual Discovery's headquarters in New York City. In an effort to get his audience to focus, he told the crowd about a particularly interesting breakfast date he had shared with Marshall McLuhan and Allen Ginsberg while at Perception '67. Don McNeill, *Moving through Here* (New York: Citadel Press 1990), 4.

25 *Toronto Daily Star*, 31 March 1967.

26 Anonymous LSD dealer, interview with author, 13 October 2006.

27 *Satyrday*, Second Issue, 1967.

28 Anonymous LSD dealer, interview with author, 13 October 2006.

29 'But I took many trips and on many occasions went through Yorkville. I was a kind of established character on the street, and I never was messed

with in that sort of way at all.' Anonymous LSD dealer, interview with author, 13 October 2006.

30 *Toronto Daily Star*, 31 March 1967.

31 W.R. Clement, interview with author, 5 March 2006.

32 According to Villager Suzanne DePoe, 'Queen Street [Mental Health] was the only place in the city that knew how to treat LSD. They knew how, and they *would*. Both, which was a jackpot. We didn't go anywhere else, there wasn't any point. Bill Clement did his work well. You know? He trained people how to treat bad trips at Queen Street and then he put the word out, that that was where to go. He was the only psycho-pharmacologist that I knew of who had any knowledge of psychotropic drugs!' Interview with author, 14 March 2006.

33 Thorazine (a.k.a. Chlorpromazine) is still regarded as a useful tool in LSD treatment, to Dr Clement's dismay. See Stanislav Grof, *LSD Psychotherapy: Exploring the Frontiers of the Human Mind* (Almeda: Hunter House Books 1994). For a discussion of the various ways to treat LSD, see especially the excerpt available at http://www.erowid.org/pharms/chlorpromazine/chlorpromazine_info1.shtml (accessed 22 February 2007).

34 W.R. Clement, interview with author, 5 March 2006.

35 Ibid.

36 'I've often wondered whether Bill oversold himself,' offers Valpy. 'But, I suspect he didn't. I mean, he probably saved a lot of kids' lives. You know, by pumping them full of Valium. He sure did love Valium ...' Michael Valpy, interview with author, 5 October 2006.

37 Smart and Jackson, 'The Yorkville Subculture,' 48.

38 *Satyrday*, Second Issue, 1967.

39 Ibid.

40 See Bryan D. Palmer, *Canada's 1960s* (Toronto: University of Toronto Press 2009), and specifically the chapter on 'riotous Victorianism.'

41 See McNeill, *Moving through Here*, 7–10. Of the New York Be-In, McNeill wrote: 'The password was "LOVE" and it was sung, chanted, painted on foreheads, and spelled out on costumes' (8).

42 *Toronto Daily Star*, 23 May 1967.

43 Kostash, *Long Way from Home*, 125.

44 Berton, *1967*, 174.

45 *Toronto Daily Star*, 23 May 1967.

46 *Toronto Daily Star*, 12 July 1967; *Globe and Mail*, 17 July 1967.

47 *Globe and Mail*, 17 July 1967.

48 Phil Lesh, *Searching for the Sound: My Life with the Grateful Dead* (New York: Little, Brown 2005), 109–11.

49 *Globe and Mail*, 29 July 1967.
50 See Echols, *Scars of Sweet Paradise*, 109. He and his friends would discover, however, that the 'good vibes' were more mythical than real, since 'what came to Toronto ... was an extremely unpleasant group of people known as the Jefferson Airplane and a very strange bunch of kind of hostile guys known as the Grateful Dead. And then there was the Headlights Light Show, which was two guys fighting with each other.'
51 *Globe and Mail*, 29 July 1967.
52 Ibid.
53 My emphasis.
54 Lesh, *Searching for the Sound*, 109–11.
55 Ibid.
56 *Globe and Mail*, 1 August 1967.
57 Kareda went on to become one of Toronto's most important dramatists after taking over, in 1982, as artistic director of the Tarragon Theatre. He passed away in 2001.
58 Ibid.
59 Judy Pocock, interview with author, 24 June 2006.
60 Quoted in Jennings, *Before the Gold Rush*, 164.
61 Ibid.
62 Ibid., 163–4. The band reformed in early 1970 and scored a hit with 'You Make Me High' before calling it quits a few months later.
63 *Toronto Daily Star*, 25 September 1967.
64 According to at least one account, however, this presence was sporadic and inconsequential. Miguel Maropakis claims that 'I don't remember bikers, OK? I lived here, and had so many places, and I don't remember bikers! Never remember fights. I don't know where these stories come from. I had the Bassetts [media moguls] in my place, I had the Eatons in my place ... If there were these fights, all these elements, they wouldn't have come around!' Miguel Maropakis, interview with author, 29 March 2007.
65 Longstaff, 'Yorkville: An Observational Report,' 12.
66 DePoe: 'No. There wasn't much involvement there with Choice. It was the Vagabonds that hung around Yorkville, not the Satan's Choice. We were, I think, *scared* of Satan's Choice.' Interview with author, 20 December 2004.
67 Anonymous LSD dealer, interview with author, 13 October 2006.
68 Ibid.
69 *Satan's Choice*, Dir: Donald Shebib, National Film Board of Canada, 1965.
70 Jennings, *Before the Gold Rush*, 170.
71 Quoted in Echols, *Shaky Ground*, 43.

72 Tom Wolfe, *The Electric Kool-Aid Acid Test* (New York: Bantam Books 1967; 1999), 178.

73 Haight-based artist Jack Jackson confided to Alice Echols that the Angels never lost their violent, frightening edge, even when on the supposedly pacifying dope. 'Biker guys [were] taking acid and smashing heads. It was like climbing in bed with Hitler.' Echols, *Shaky Ground*, 43.

74 'In fact,' argues John Wood, 'the Hell's Angels actually mimicked the mainstream American society that the counterculture fought so hard to eliminate.' Wood, 'Hell's Angels and the Illusion of the Counterculture,' *Journal of Popular Culture*, 37, no. 2 (2003): 336–51.

75 Perry, *The Haight-Ashbury*, 14–15.

76 David DePoe, interview with author, 20 December 2004.

77 Bob Brown, a Haight-based musician, tried to explain this apparent contradiction of peaceniks making connections with bikers: 'I can only believe it was the fascination the weak feel for the strong … Maybe there was some sense that the Establishment had their cops, their thugs, and now we had ours.' Echols, *Shaky Ground*, 43–4.

78 See J. Hoberman, *The Dream Life: Movies, Media and the Myth of the Sixties* (New York: New Books 2003), 176–7; also see Peter Biskind, *Easy Riders, Raging Bulls: How the Sex, Drugs and Rock'n'Roll Generation Saved Hollywood* (New York: Simon and Schuster 1998), 26–41; Braunstein, 'Forever Young,' in Braunstein and Doyle, eds., *Imagine Nation*, 261–5; and David E. James, 'The Movies Are a Revolution,' in Braunstein and Doyle, eds., *Imagine Nation*, 298–9.

79 Kael's review, originally published in the *New Yorker*, 21 October 1967, has been collected in the indispensable volume *For Keeps: 30 Years at the Movies* (New York: Plume Books 1996), 141–57.

80 Herbert Marcuse, fount of inspiration for many politicos, made a clear distinction between the violence 'of the oppressed and the oppressors.' As Jeremy Varon has pointed out, Marcuse 'distinguished between reactionary and emancipatory violence' and, in so doing, provided a framework for justifiable (i.e., authentic) violence. If violence is employed as a means to free oneself (or others) from their alienation from freedom, from the shackles of oppression, then it is (while morally unfortunate) acceptable, even perhaps laudable. Jeremy Varon, *Bringing the War Home* (Berkeley: University of California Press 2004), 188–9.

81 It should be noted that the glamorization of biker toughness dated to the 1950s, and persistent media attention to these 'rebels' had helped to foster unearned reputations and false images. As chronicler of the California Hell's Angels in the mid-1960s, Hunter S. Thompson was shocked by the

degree to which the bikers *acted* like bikers. 'The Hell's Angels as they exist today were virtually created by *Time, Newsweek,* and the *New York Times,*' he concluded. *Hell's Angels: A Strange and Terrible Saga* (New York: Random House 1967), 37.

82 *Satan's Choice,* 1965.
83 Ibid.
84 David DePoe, interview with author, 20 December 2004.
85 Alice Echols: 'The Angels, whatever their individual talents, acted as a group.' *Shaky Ground,* 43.
86 Jennings, *Before the Gold Rush,* 170–1.
87 'Wild Bill,' interview with author, 11 March 2005.
88 David DePoe, interview with author, 20 December 2004.
89 Clayton Ruby, interview with author, 3 March 2006.
90 Smart and Jackson, 'The Yorkville Subculture,' 19.
91 Ibid., 35.
92 'Wild Bill,' interview with author, 11 March 2005.
93 Smart and Jackson, 'The Yorkville Subculture,' 22.
94 *Voice of the Annex,* September 1968.
95 Smart and Jackson, 'The Yorkville Subculture,' 20–1.
96 June Callwood, interview with author, 3 March 2005.
97 Wolfe, *The Electric Kool-Aid Acid Test,* 177. Gretchen Lemke-Santangelo points out the ugly fact that Wolfe never uses the word 'rape' to describe this assault. Lemke-Santangelo, *Daughters of Aquarius,* 115.
98 *Toronto Daily Star,* 25 September 1967.
99 *Toronto Daily Star,* 5 September 1967.
100 *Toronto Daily Star,* 18 October 1967. In this particular example, 'Margaret,' a young woman, is said to be heading home to 'forgiving parents' after her run-in with the law.
101 *Toronto Daily Star,* 7 October 1967.
102 *Globe and Mail,* 2 November 1967.
103 *Toronto Daily Star,* 28 October 1967.
104 *Toronto Daily Star,* 11 May 1967, Front Page.
105 *Toronto Daily Star,* 12 May 1967. This much-maligned idea is weirdly reminiscent of R.B. Bennett's use of 'relief camps' in the early 1930s as a way to pacify unemployed workers.
106 The Sanskrit word *Kama* signifies *desire,* often sexual – this is a probable nom de guerre.
107 *Toronto Daily Star,* 26 May 1967.
108 Smart and Jackson, 'The Yorkville Subculture,' 24.
109 'Villagers are more likely to taunt the police than to avoid them, and

when they feel the police are intimidating them, they organize commit-
tees, stage protest marches, and inform the newspapers. In other words,
they use avenues of (middle-class) protest that lower class teenagers are
not aware of or would not employ.' Quoted in Haggart's column, *Toronto
Daily Star*, 17 May 1967.

110 Ibid.

111 His name is given differently in each publication. In the *Toronto Daily Star*
he is Zigmonde Nowoszynski, while in the *Globe and Mail* he is Zigmond
Nowosynski. I have chosen to go with the former spelling.

112 *Satyrday*, 3, no. 5 (August 1968).

113 *Toronto Daily Star*, 27 October 1967. Also, *Globe and Mail*, same date.

114 *Toronto Daily Star*, 2 October 1972. He is here listed as Zigmone Nowosynski.

115 Herbert Marcuse, *Eros and Civilization* (Boston: Beacon Press 1955; 1966), 50.

116 Recall Judith Walkowitz's work on the construction of Whitechapel as a
'labyrinth' in which young women become trapped, lose their agency,
and wind up destroyed. Walkowitz, *City of Dreadful Delight*, 100.

117 *Satyrday*, Second Issue, 1967.

118 Carstairs, *Jailed for Possession*, 21.

119 *Globe and Mail*, 2 November 1967.

120 Ibid.

121 This language is, of course, not new to the 1960s. Carolyn Strange, in her
study of women in Toronto around the turn of the century, uncovered
a variety of white-slavery narratives, all connected to anxiety over the
entrance of young women into the workforce. *Toronto's Girl Problem: The
Perils and Pleasures of the City, 1880–1930* (Toronto: University of Toronto
Press 1998). See especially pages 98–103, and compare the language of the
Reverend Shearer (a famous propagator of the white-slavery line) to what
we see on display in discussions of women in Yorkville. For example:
'Let women accept these jobs [and] the innocent lambs go blindly to the
slaughter' (99).

122 *Toronto Daily Star*, 3 November 1967.

123 In the United States, by way of comparison, the Federal Bureau of Investigation was searching for some 90,000 runaways in 1966. In Europe, some
10,000 were reportedly on the road, many of them apparently headed for
India. See Roszak, *The Making of a Counterculture*, 33–5.

124 *Globe and Mail*, 4 November 1967.

125 *Globe and Mail*, 2 November 1967. By contrast, in the much wider
and more complicated Haight-Ashbury scene, such fears were being
expressed from the inside as well as the outside.

126 *Satyrday*, 3, no. 5 (August 1968).
127 It must be noted that in none of my interviews was this point recollected, or even volunteered at all.
128 *Globe and Mail*, 3 November 1967.
129 Ibid.

7. Social Missions in the Teenage Jungle

1 Smart and Jackson, 'The Yorkville Subculture,' 82.
2 June Callwood, 'Hippies,' *Canadian Welfare*, 44 (September–October 1968): 17.
3 Ibid.
4 June Callwood, 'Digger House,' in W.E. Mann, ed., *The Underside of Toronto* (Toronto: McClelland and Stewart 1970), 128.
5 *Satyrday*, 3, no. 5 (August 1968).
6 *Harbinger*, 19 July–8 August 1968.
7 Michael Valpy, interview with author, 5 October 2006.
8 *Toronto Daily Star*, 3 November 1967.
9 Ibid.
10 Catherine Breslin, *Chatelaine*, October 1967.
11 *Toronto Telegram*, 22 July 1969.
12 Ibid.
13 See Frank, *The Conquest of Cool*.
14 Miguel Maropakis, interview with author, 29 March 2007.
15 Smart and Jackson, 'The Yorkville Subculture,' 2.
16 Alampur, having recently arrived in Canada from Hyderabad to work towards a graduate degree in anthropology at the University of Western Ontario, was a rather unlikely choice for an undercover field agent. Having done ethnographic field work with the Toda – the nature-worshipping tribe living in the Nilgiri mountains in southern India – Alampur was expected to have learned from his experience not to let 'new cultures' mystify him. However, there is a great difference between being confused or disoriented by ancient, primitive cultural experiences and the bewilderment many Torontonians shared when they heard tell of the Village.
17 Alampur explained to me that there was very little interpretation or artistic licence imposed upon his findings by Smart and Jackson's report. For all intents and purposes, the report reflects his work, not theirs. Therefore, all references to the report should be treated as the views of Gopala Alampur, and not the work of Smart and Jackson.
18 Smart and Jackson, 'The Yorkville Subculture,' 1.

19 Ibid.

20 Gopala Alampur, interview with author, 14 February 2005.

21 Yet, by refusing to consider Yorkville as anything but a deviant society standing in uneasy opposition to the 'straight society' – rather than working to complicate the functions of Yorkville within a hegemonic process – the study falls prey to its own conceptual trap. Yorkville winds up being treated by Alampur and, subsequently, the ARF as an ethnographic wonderland, a set of distinct and coherent categories of youth identity worthy of study and documentation. And, as such, youth cultures in Yorkville were given a highly subjective, largely distorted overview, one that emphasized the constructed differences between (and fractions within) pseudo-ethno-groupings rather than exploring the cosmopolitan realities of the Village.

22 Gopala Alampur, interview with author, 14 February 2005.

23 Smart and Jackson, 'The Yorkville Subculture,' 3.

24 Gopala Alampur, interview with author, 14 February 2005.

25 Smart and Jackson, 'The Yorkville Subculture,' 3.

26 Gopala Alampur, interview with author, 14 February 2005.

27 Ibid.

28 Ibid.

29 Alampur's status as outsider (as a non-native Torontonian, a non-Anglo, non-middle-class Canadian) was likely intended by the ARF to lend some legitimacy to claims of the impartiality of the study. Uninfluenced, or at least less influenced, by the cultural common sense of middle-class Toronto, Alampur was expected to be able to view the Yorkville scene without the baggage a locally raised observer might carry with her. But Alampur's double outsider status (both as an adult and as a non-Villager insinuating himself into the scene) was then further exaggerated by his Indian-ness, his visible minority status automatically differentiating him from the vast majority of the Villagers. In other words, to use a scientific allusion, Alampur's observations and conclusions were prone to the 'uncertainty principle.'

30 When I asked David DePoe if he remembered the ARF or Alampur, he responded without surprise: 'Well, I knew who Reg Smart was, and I thought he was sort of an exploiter and not a very nice person ... But, honestly, I never knew about *that!*' And yet, even if DePoe (along with many other Villagers) was unaware of the ARF project as it was ongoing, he was quick to place the name 'Krishna' when I asked him if he recalled an Indian man who lived in the Village at around the same time. 'I ... knew this guy Krishna, and I was really kind of suspicious of him,' he

explained. Interview with author, 20 December 2004. For his part, Alampur is surprised to hear this: 'David DePoe … was not even there when I was there. He wasn't a part of it at all. He wasn't there. He was gone. He had disappeared *completely.*' Interview with author, 14 February 2005.

31 Gopala Alampur, interview with author, 14 February 2005.
32 Smart and Jackson, 'The Yorkville Subculture,' 3.
33 Ibid., 48–9.
34 Ibid., 9.
35 Ibid., 10.
36 It should be noted that weekenders did not come to Yorkville only on weekends. Any day or night, any time, kids came down to the Village for a few hours to cop some pot, find a date, or simply sit and do their homework.
37 Smart and Jackson, 'The Yorkville Subculture,' 16.
38 Ibid.
39 Gopala Alampur, interview with author, 14 February 2005.
40 Smart and Jackson, 'The Yorkville Subculture,' 16.
41 Ibid.
42 'Most motorcycle gang members come from working-class families. Generally, their early experiences include violent or delinquent behaviour on the part of their parents … most members have done poorly in school, read few books, and appear to be primarily interested in machinery, sex and alcohol.' Ibid., 21.
43 'In fact, [greasers] are called "the paranoid people" because they fear that intimate relationships may cause them to divulge evidence of criminal activity to informers.' Ibid., 23.
44 Ibid., 22.
45 Some of my interview subjects agreed with this basic view. 'The sort of greaser, rounder, was sort of a downtown thug character. A bit more urban. A lot of them were into speed or whatever. They hadn't really engaged or bought into the hippie sensibility at all, so they were very kind of cynical about it all. They were a lot more likely to be into these other drugs than me and my friends. Although we experimented with them, we checked them out, they weren't for us.' Anonymous LSD dealer, interview with author, 13 October 2006.
46 Smart and Jackson, 'The Yorkville Subculture,' 23.
47 Ibid.
48 Ibid.
49 This is a dominant view. For example, in a master's of social work thesis from 1968, the author wrote that 'they are behind the drug racket, the

prostitution and the credit card rackets in Yorkville, and they force many of the youth in these other groups to work for them.' Ruth Patterson, 'An Exploratory Study of the Opinions of Local Religious Leaders towards Yorkville,' MSW thesis, University of Toronto, 1968.

50 Smart and Jackson, 'The Yorkville Subculture,' 24.

51 This is one of a very few direct mentions of people of West Indian or Caribbean descent moving through the Village scene. One of the few black men to frequent the district, Burnley 'Rocky' Jones, wrote to me in an e-mail, received 21 April 2006, about his recollections of a man named Len, who ran a bookstore. He was 'an old leftwinger [sic] who was passionate about the black struggle.' His only other immediate recollection of black presence in the Village was of the African trinkets sold at the Artisan, a Village store.

52 Smart and Jackson, 'The Yorkville Subculture,' 75.

53 Ibid., 60.

54 Ibid., 24.

55 Ibid., 25.

56 Alampur recalls this dichotomy today in much the same terms. 'One is gentle, kind, [unintelligible]; they are a minority. *That* is the true hippie. That is the true flower child: harmless. They left home, and just wanted to escape from the norm. And then the greasers, they're all kinds of these aggressive guys who say, "Hey, this is a great spot to be a part of all that stuff ..." The majority population were the greasers. Those were the criminal element. Those were the guys who were taking advantage of the situation. And moved in ... and then [it was] getting worse and worse because of drug pushing or, you know, conducting illegal businesses of a kind.' Gopala Alampur, interview with author, 14 February 2005.

57 Smart and Jackson, 'The Yorkville Subculture,' 21.

58 Ibid. The case study of 'Jay,' a biker, comes later in the report. This case study seems the basis for most of the generalizations made in the initial overview. Jay was born of a Polish mother and Hungarian father.

59 In his case study of Jay, Alampur makes reference to the 'swastika flag in his club room'; elsewhere, he refers to the Vagabond headquarters being adorned with 'pictures of motorcycles, hippies, Hitler and Mussolini, and a swastika flag' (ibid., 19). Still, the superficiality of the rest of the report suggests that he gained much of his understanding of the bikers through second-hand information.

60 Alampur also concedes that 'in his own dirty and bearded way he projects poise.' Ibid., 78.

61 Ibid., 19.

62 Ibid., 20.

63 Ibid., 21.

64 See *Toronto Daily Star*, 28 January 1969.

65 Why had such an apparently unrepresentative figure been used as a case study? Alampur recalls that he was likely chosen for superficial reasons. 'Maybe he was the most popular, that's why. I must have been fascinated with the guy, his looks probably. I don't know? There was no scientific base for my case studies … I should have probed into whole autobiographies before I picked one. My case study then must have been a poor representation of the population. Other than that, the guy was genuinely a hippie, and gentle.' Gopala Alampur, interview with author, 14 February 2005.

66 'One clear conclusion of this study is that Yorkville does not represent a monolithic cultural process. It is better termed a "culture area" than a subculture. The diversity in persons who frequent the area is very great as are the differences in their backgrounds, current behaviour, philosophy of life, and attitudes towards drugs and sex … The high degree of cultural diversity, of course, makes cultural change a difficult and complicated process if the larger society were to proceed against Yorkville by attempting to change the ethos.' Smart and Jackson, 'The Yorkville Subculture,' 81.

67 Mike Waage, interview with author, 3 March 2005.

68 *Globe and Mail*, 7 June 1968.

69 *Satyrday*, 3, no. 5 (August 1968).

70 John Kileeg, 'Village Service Unit for Alienated Youth: The "Trailer" in Yorkville,' report to the Social Planning Council of Metropolitan (Toronto 1968), 2.

71 Michael Valpy, interview with author, 5 October 2006.

72 Ibid.

73 Kileeg, 'Village Service Unit.'

74 *Globe and Mail*, 17 July 1970.

75 Globe and Mail, 7 June 1968.

76 Michael Valpy, interview with author, 5 October 2006.

77 *Toronto Daily Star*, 8 January 1970.

78 Kileeg, 'Village Service Unit.' 11.

79 Ibid.

80 Clayton Ruby, interview with author, 3 March 2006.

81 Ibid.

82 Paul Copeland and Clayton Ruby, *law law law* (Toronto: Anansi 1970).

83 'Paul Copeland and I wrote a little book called *law law law* which we published first as a pamphlet we gave away for free. Give people their rights. Then we expanded on it to do all kinds of stuff with the help of

other lawyers; Elaine King helped us, she was a judge who died recently. That got published by Anansi Press, and it financed the entire Anansi list for a few years because it made money on it at one dollar a booklet. It became a bestseller! It sold over 10,000 copies. Which in those days was a bestseller in Canada. We were thrilled to have Anansi, thrilled they printed it. It went through a lot of editions.' Clayton Ruby, interview with author, 3 March 2006.

84 Ibid.

85 *Toronto Daily Star*, 16 July 1970. Early in 1969 Johnson had already predicted the end of the Trailer and Yorkville. In a televised interview on the CBC in early 1969, she explained that 'we [Trailer staff] felt that there was some kind of a change.' 'Yorkville Upheaval,' CBC Television special, reporter Bill Casey, 29 January 1969, http://archives.cbc.ca/IDC-1-69-580-3203/life_society/hippies/clip10 (accessed 22 November 2010).

86 June Callwood, interview with author, 11 March 2005.

87 Ibid.

88 Ibid.

89 Callwood, 'Digger House, 125.

90 Michael Valpy, interview with author, 5 October 2006.

91 See Leland, *Hip*, 260–1.

92 John Donne, 'Death, Be Not Proud,' *The Complete Poetry and Selected Prose of John Donne*, ed. Charles M. Coffin (New York: Modern Library 2004), 250.

93 June Callwood, interview with author, 11 March 2005.

94 Ibid.

95 Michael Valpy, interview with author, 5 October 2006.

96 June Callwood, interview with author, 11 March 2005.

97 Ibid.

98 See http://archives.cbc.ca/society/youth/clips/8723/ (accessed 22 November 2010).

99 Sheila Pennington, 'For the First Time in My Life I Don't Feel That I Want to Run Away,' Toronto Archives, Series 100, box 46693–8, file 1245, n.d.

100 From a typical letter from Callwood to the Welfare and Housing Committee: 'As newspaper accounts are beginning to bear out, the hippie movement is no longer dominated by bemused intellectual dropouts but has become the refuge of young people whose personality, health and sanity have been damaged by a catastrophic family background.' Toronto Archives, Series 100, box 46693–8, file 1245, 17 June 1968.

101 Pennington, 'For the First Time in My Life.'

102 Callwood, Memo to all Members of Metro Welfare Committee in ref. to

Yorkville Diggers, 8 June 1968, Toronto Archives, Series 100, box 46693–8, file 1245. Her emphasis. The Toronto Archives contain a series of such requests, often written under the guise of humble pleas, not only from Callwood but also from her lawyers and other colleagues in the endeavour. All take up the shared view that Yorkville has become home to a truly distressing community of the disturbed; if Toronto continues to do nothing to help to save them from their alienation, they warn, only the worst can be expected.

103 Pennington, 'For the First Time in My Life.'
104 Ibid.
105 Ibid.
106 Surely Callwood knew that middle-class families were just as likely to produce unhappy children?
107 Ibid.
108 Callwood, 'Digger House,' 125.
109 Ibid.
110 Ibid.
111 Ibid., 124.

8. Toronto's Hippie Disease

 1 Emphasis added.
 2 Smith, 'I Wish I Was a Fish,' 30.
 3 Ibid., 11.
 4 See Rosengarten's spot-on review in *Canadian Literature*, 65 (summer 1975).
 5 John Reid, *The Faithless Mirror: An Historical Novel* (Toronto: Darkwood Press 1975).
 6 *Globe and Mail*, 3 October 1969.
 7 His character 'Steyl' (which, importantly, could be pronounced 'style' or 'stale') inhabits the novel as though it were a *bildungsroman* in reverse. Though he enters the scene brimming with intellectual inquisitiveness and naive optimism, he winds up somewhere south of broken, corrupt, and insane.
 8 Smart and Jackson, 'The Yorkville Subculture,' 51.
 9 Ibid., 52.
10 Ibid., 61–2.
11 Ibid., 66.
12 Ibid., 69.
13 *Harbinger*, August 1968.

14 Smart and Jackson, 'The Yorkville Subculture,' 61.

15 Portions of this section were previously published as 'Toronto's Hippie Disease: End Days in the Yorkville Scene, August 1968,' *Journal of the Canadian Historical Association*, 17, no. 1 (2006): 205–34.

16 E.W.R. Best, 'Introduction,' *Hepatitis in Yorkville, 1968: Report of the Co-ordinating Committee* (Ontario Department of Health, 15 September 1969), 1.

17 June Callwood, interview with author, 11 March 2005.

18 Best, 'Introduction,' 1.

19 Ibid.

20 Ibid., 2.

21 W.R. Clement, interview with author, 5 March 2006.

22 A subsequent study of the 'Health of Yorkville' lamented that hospital workers 'appear to have no motivation to adapt to the problems created by widespread drug use and have virtually atrophied to the point of consistent irrelevance.' Merrijoy Kelner et al., 'The Health of Yorkville,' unpublished report to the Ontario Department of Health (Toronto: Department of Behavioural Science, University of Toronto, 1970), 72.

23 W.R. Clement, interview with author, 5 March 2006.

24 Ibid. Clement, it should be stressed, still maintains that the exaggerated approach taken up by the medical authorities in their effort to contain the possible spread of hepatitis was the right move.

25 Nayan Shah, in his study of the ways race and disease were conflated in constructions of Chinese immigrants and residents in San Francisco, observes the way such discourses 'created nightmares of proximity between the diseased and the healthy.' *Contagious Divides: Epidemics and Race in San Francisco's Chinatown* (Berkeley: University of California Press 2001), 88.

26 *Toronto Daily Star*, 3 August 1968. Emphasis added.

27 *Globe and Mail*, 3 August 1968. Emphasis added.

28 W.R. Clement, interview with author, 5 March 2006.

29 See *Toronto Telegram*, 8 August 1968. Also, *Toronto Daily Star*, 8 August 1968.

30 W.R. Clement, interview with author, 5 March 2006.

31 The shopkeepers at the Grab Bag had taken to wearing surgical masks, a point that the *Toronto Daily Star* was quick to document. *Toronto Daily Star*, 8 August 1968.

32 *Toronto Daily Star*, 6 August 1968.

33 *Globe and Mail*, 5 August 1968.

34 According to Callwood: 'Everybody had to get immunized. And it was a nasty shot – my son Casey who was six or seven years old at the time had to be immunized because he was with me all the time at Digger House.' Interview with author, 11 March 2005.

35 Ibid. Emphasis added. It had been observed at the meeting of 2 August, to which Clement referred, that 'the number of cases of infectious hepatitis reported in Toronto in July 1968, although greater than in July 1967, was still less than half the number reported in July 1966.' Best, 'Introduction,' 1.

36 *Globe and Mail*, 7 August 1968.

37 *Globe and Mail*, 8 August 1968. This story appeared on the front page.

38 Suzanne DePoe, interview with author, 14 March 2006.

39 Ibid.

40 'Needless to say, Norman DePoe was decidedly pissed off. He was the chief CBC news announcer!' W.R. Clement, interview with author, 5 March 2006.

41 *Toronto Daily Star*, 7 August 1968. Emphasis added.

42 *Toronto Daily Star*, 10 August 1968.

43 Ibid.

44 *Toronto Daily Star*, 8 August 1968.

45 *Toronto Daily Star*, 9 August 1968.

46 Ibid.

47 *Toronto Daily Star*, 12 August 1968.

48 *Toronto Daily Star*, 13 August 1968.

49 Ibid.

50 *Toronto Daily Star*, 13 August 1968.

51 *Globe and Mail*, 10 August 1968.

52 *Globe and Mail*, 13 August 1968.

53 *Toronto Daily Star*, 14 August 1968. Elsewhere in this edition, a headline ran: 'Nail Her Death Certificate All over Yorkville.' It seems that a man whose wife had died of hepatitis four years previously was anxious to do anything he could to alert people to the dangers of the disease. Neither he nor his wife, it should be noted, had ever even been to Yorkville.

54 *Globe and Mail*, 15 August 1968.

55 J.C. Sinclair, 'Clinical Aspects, Section II: Review,' *Hepatitis in Yorkville, 1968*, 10.

56 Caroline Hetenyi and F.M. Hill, 'Clinical Aspects, Section I: Clinical Report,' ibid., 7–8.

57 Callwood maintains that Anne Keyl did the right thing by raising the spectre of epidemic, because we'll never know if she stopped it in its tracks by acting so deliberately. 'She got all the shots, she did it in the Trailer, set up a little clinic there, and everyone thought she was overreacting. But there *wasn't* an epidemic. So did she nail it, or was she overreacting? We'll never know, but there wasn't an epidemic.' Interview with author, 11 March 2005.

58 The immediate fallout from the 'epidemic' on Yorkville businesses and

hangouts was, as was pointed out above, dire, but it was its combination with the more organic result of the end of summer vacation which served to devastate Yorkville merchants in the following months. Clement: 'It was the end of August; it was a natural event. Go home, have baths, get haircuts, go to school. I mean, these are middle-class kids!' Interview with author, 5 March 2006.

59 *Toronto Daily Star*, 4 July 1969.

60 'There was *never* violence. I have lived here for years!' maintains Marilyn Brooks. Interview with author, 29 March 2007.

61 A common complaint at Rochdale College (which would open in September 1968 – see below) was that the influx of too many Villagers spoiled the brew. The film *Dream Tower*, Dir: Ron Mann, National Film Board of Canada, 1994, effectively blames Rochdale's failings on Yorkville.

62 *Toronto Daily Star*, 31 May 1969.

63 Quoted in Marcel Martel, 'They Smell Bad, Have Diseases, and Are Lazy: RCMP Officers Reporting on Hippies in the Late Sixties,' *Canadian Historical Review*, 90, no. 2 (2009): 215–45.

64 *Toronto Daily Star*, 21 June 1969.

65 *Toronto Daily Star*, 28 July 1969. Also 17 and 18 November 1969.

66 *Toronto Daily Star*, 25 August 1969.

67 *Globe and Mail*, 13 September 1969.

68 *Toronto Daily Star*, 18 August 1969.

69 *Globe and Mail*, 5 March 1969.

70 *Toronto Daily Star*, 27 August 1969.

71 *Toronto Daily Star*, 17 September 1969.

72 *Globe and Mail*, 22 November 1969.

73 *Toronto Daily Star*, 13 December 1969.

74 *Toronto Daily Star*, 12 August 1969.

75 *Toronto Daily Star*, 27 September 1969.

76 In the *Toronto Daily Star* of 18 January 1969, Richard Wookey lays out his plans for the post-Villager era. Also, see *Toronto Daily Star* of 24 January for Harry Jordan's similar vision of the future.

77 *Toronto Daily Star*, 29 January 1969.

78 *Globe and Mail*, 21 May 1969. For a brief history of the (racially motivated) neglect of the South Bronx (and Powell's role in the ugly affair), see Jeff Chang, *Can't Stop Won't Stop: A History of the Hip Hop Generation* (New York: Picador Press 2005), 7–19.

79 David E. Smith, John Luce, and Ernest A. Dernburg, 'The Health of Haight-Ashbury,' in Howard S. Becker, ed., *Culture and Civility in San Francisco* (San Francisco: Transaction 1971), 77.

80 Ibid., 83.

81 Ibid., 93.

82 Kelner et al., 'The Health of Yorkville.'

83 Ibid., i.

84 For example, the 'study population' employed for the 'Survey of Young People's Behaviour in Relation to Health Care' included some 515 young people, but only 103 who were designated as 'Yorkville' residents. The other subjects were found throughout the Metro Toronto area, including at Rochdale College (124 subjects), roughly three blocks away from the Yorkville district. Hence the claim: 'Essentially, we have done a group survey in which the study population is continuously redefined by the participants themselves.' Ibid., 17.

85 Ibid., 2.

86 Ibid., 9.

87 Apart, as we have seen, from Women's College Hospital and Dr Anne Keyl, both of whom could generally be counted upon.

88 Kelner et al., 'The Health of Yorkville,' 68.

89 Ibid., 69.

90 The categorization process broke down thusly: one to five check marks meant a 'low symptom' subject; six to twenty-five symptoms meant a subject belonged to the 'high symptom' category. If a respondent failed to check any boxes, she was placed in the 'healthy' category.

91 Even casual, or occasional, speed use can lead to increased muscle tension, backaches, chest pain, shortness of breath, and dizziness. Kelner et al., 'The Health of Yorkville,' 37.

92 A telling piece of evidence: by the time of the 'Health of Yorkville' study, cannabis use had become expected behaviour for the Yorkville district to the extent that it was considered mere 'Simple Drug Use'; even more significantly, 'Soft Drugs' now were comprised of the psychedelics, which until only recently had been considered 'Hard Drugs' (LSD, Mescaline, Psilocybin, Opium, STP, and MDM [a forerunner of MDMA, the present-day 'Ecstasy' drug]). 'Hard Drugs,' then, had become nearly exclusively comprised of needle and addicting drugs: Speed/Methedrine, other Amphetamines, Heroin, Morphine, Cocaine, Barbiturates, Belladonna, Stramonium, and Glue rounded out this list. What is immediately striking about these categories, from a medical point of view, is that the 'Soft Drugs' category is comprised of a series of drugs which are by no means any safer than those in the 'Hard Drugs' category. Kelner et al., 'The Health of Yorkville,' 45.

93 'So we started seeing more of these guys we called rounders, those kind of downtown thugs, and pimps … And then of course, because of the

prohibition, you really had to deal with [these] criminal networks. And so, in order to go and buy your bag of pot or your hit of acid, at the street level you were often being offered other things as well. This is the situation that still goes on – it's one of the fundamental fucked things about these stupid, unjustifiable laws.' Anonymous LSD dealer, interview with author, 13 October 2006.

94 'I'd blame suppression for a lot of that because it muddied the lines between … drug experiences. It muddied the line between [psychedelic] substances (which in my opinion are reasonable interests of reasonable people) and these other noxious substances like PCP and STP and TMA and fucking *cocaine* and all this other crap!' Anonymous LSD dealer, interview with author, 13 October 2006.

95 Kellner et al., 'The Health of Yorkville,' 37–8.

96 Ibid.

97 Ibid., 48–9.

98 Ibid., 40.

99 Ibid.

100 Ibid., 160.

101 Ibid.

102 Ibid., 41.

103 Smith, 'I Wish I Was a Fish,' 10–11.

104 Ibid., 12.

105 Ibid.

106 The story of the 49-ers is rickety at best – theirs was a short-lived, restless organization – but after they joined forces with the Diggers in 1968 they began to have a greater impact on the scene. Frustratingly, no one I asked could tell me why they were named the 49-ers. Perhaps this was a show of connectedness with the San Francisco scene (the 49-ers were, historically, the miners who filed into the Bay Area in 1849 in search of gold)?

107 Smith, 'I Wish I Was a Fish,' 13.

108 Ibid.

109 Ibid., 14.

110 Carol Ann Graham, 'Yorkville: An Exploratory Study of the Attitudes of Yorkville Youth towards the Educational System,' MSW thesis, University of Toronto, 1968, 38–45.

111 Smith, 'I Wish I Was a Fish,' 26.

112 I am currently at work on a monograph on Rochdale College and hip separatism in the 1970s. Two histories of the college have been produced, both worthy in their respective ways: David Sharpe, *Rochdale: The Runaway College* (Toronto: Anansi 1987); and Henry Mietkiewicz and Bob

Mackowycz, *Dream Tower: The Life and Legacy of Rochdale College* (Toronto: Ryerson 1988).

113 See, for example, Ralph Osborne's lively memoir of his time as the general manager of the college. He barely goes outside. For years! Osborne, *From Someplace Else: A Memoir* (Toronto: ECW Press 2003).

114 See Dennis Lee's record of the frustrating experience of university politics in the 1960s, and his list of reasons for founding the college. 'Getting to Rochdale,' *This Magazine Is about Schools*, winter 1968.

115 Ibid.

116 See *Dream Tower*, Dir: Ron Mann, National Film Board of Canada, 1994.

117 See the *Mother Earth News*, 8 (March/April 1971), for a lively and informative overview of the Killaloe/Barry's Bay intentional community scene in the early 1970s. Available at http://www.motherearthnews.com/Livestock_and_Farming/1971_March_April/Visit_To_The_Canadian_Hog_Farm (accessed 22 November 2010). See also the *Toronto Star* article 'Living Green before Their Time,' 20 May 2007, a recognition that the residents of the Morning Glory farm (and, by implication, other such intentional communities) made an early turn to environmentalism, adopting 'green' values. The article reminds us that many of these communities still exist, even thrive, and maintain many of the most exciting, significant, and radical hip beliefs, practices, and aesthetics.

118 Sam Binkley, *Getting Loose: Lifestyle Consumption in the 1970s* (Durham, N.C.: Duke University Press 2007).

119 Frank, *The Conquest of Cool*.

120 For a tantalizing cross-section of recent scholarship on the global 1960s, see Karen Dubinsky et al., *New World Coming: The Sixties and the Shaping of a Global Consciousness* (Toronto: Between the Lines Press 2009).

Conclusion: An Immense Accumulation of Spectacles

1 Guy Debord, *The Society of the Spectacle*, translated by Ken Knabb, http://www.bopsecrets.org/SI/debord/ (accessed 2 May 2007). Emphasis added. My use of Debord is indebted to the work done by Caroline Evans in her recent study of deathliness and fashion in the 1990s. See *Fashion at the Edge: Spectacle, Modernity and Deathliness* (New Haven, Conn.: Yale University Press 2003).

2 Martin Jay, in his discussion of the 'Society of the Spectacle' (which he called the 'deathgrip of desiccated images'), emphasizes the relationship between the spectacle and a certain desert (even death) of the spirit. *Downcast Eyes: The Denigration of Vision in Twentieth-Century French*

Thought (Berkeley: University of California Press 1993), 425. His emphasis on the primacy of visuality in modern society has informed my treatments of tourism.

3 There was a real self-consciousness to the performances on display in all the major hip centres, led, in part, by actual theatre groups such as the San Francisco Mime Troupe and the Living Theatre (in New York) which took their theatre 'to the streets.' Tellingly, the Diggers in San Francisco referred to the experience of living as 'life acting'; alternatively, it was said that 'the Living Theatre actor merely plays himself on stage.' See Michael William Doyle, 'Staging the Revolution,' in Braunstein and Doyle, eds., *Imagine Nation*, 71–98; Peter Biner, 'The Living Theatre,' in Bloom and Breines, eds., *Takin' It to the Streets* (New York: Oxford University Press 2003), 234–7. Also see Bradford D. Martin, *The Theater Is in the Street* (Boston: University of Massachusetts Press 2004).

4 It is often maintained that, while they were not necessarily unrelated, the New Left and the counterculture were different animals and needn't be discussed in tandem. To take a recent example, sociologist John Cleveland conducted a survey of some 471 'leading 1960s activists in Quebec and English Canada' to discover the answer to a series of questions regarding political beliefs and affiliations during the period. No countercultural figures (leaders or otherwise) were consulted, even though Cleveland points out that a defining feature of all New Left organizations was the presence of 'a large and influential counterculture [which] developed in the periphery of the movements.' John W. Cleveland, 'New Left, Not New Liberal: 1960s Movements in English Canada and Quebec,' *Canadian Review of Sociology and Anthropology / Review canadienne de sociologie et anthropologie*, 41, no. 1 (2004): 67–84.

5 Or, as Jean Baudrillard argued, following Debord, a simulacrum is not a replica of the real but becomes real (or truth) in its own right. 'The territory no longer precedes the map, nor does it survive it. It is nevertheless the map that precedes the territory – precession of simulacra – that engenders the territory.' *Simulacra and Simulation*, translated by Sheila Faria Glaser (Ann Arbor: University of Michigan Press 1994), 1.

6 *The Big Lebowski*, Dir: Joel Cohen, 1998.

7 See http://encarta.msn.com/encyclopedia_761555135/the_grateful_dead. html (accessed 22 November 2010).

8 http://www.burningman.com/ (accessed 10 November 2010).

Works Cited

Primary Sources

Archival Collections

Archives of Ontario, 4130–5245: T053623, T61693–T61696.
Canadian Lesbian and Gay Archives, Toronto.
Canadian Women's Movement Archives, Ottawa, Toronto Women's Libera-
tion fonds.
James Harshman Foundation Collections and Archive, Toronto.
Toronto Archives, Digger House fonds, Series 100, box 46693–8, file 1245.
Toronto Archives, Metropolitan Police fonds, Series 11, box 47859–11, file 858.

Government Documents

Canada. *Report of the Royal Commission on the Status of Women in Canada.*
Ottawa: Information Canada 1970.
– Minister of Trade and Commerce. *Canada 1963: The Official Handbook of Present
Conditions and Recent Progress.* Ottawa: Dominion Bureau of Statistics 1963.
Canadian Welfare Council. *Transient Youth (Three Parts).* Ste-Adèle, Que.: Tran-
sient Youth Inquiry, Canadian Welfare Council, 1969–71.
Commission of Inquiry into the Non-Medical Use of Drugs. *The Non-Medical
Use of Drugs: Interim Report of the Canadian Government's Commission of
Inquiry.* Harmondsworth, U.K.: Penguin 1971.
Toronto Planning Board. 'Plan for Yorkville' (unpublished, Toronto, 1968).

Theses and Unpublished Papers

Churchill, David. 'When Home Became Away: American Expatriates and

New Social Movements in Toronto, 1965–1977.' PhD thesis, University of Chicago, 2001.

Graham, Carol Ann. 'Yorkville: An Exploratory Study of the Attitudes of Yorkville Youth towards the Educational System.' MSW thesis, University of Toronto, 1968.

Henderson, Stuart. 'Taking Pictures of Taking Pictures: Reading Weekend Magazine in the 1960s.' MA thesis, McGill University, 2001.

Johnson, Charles. 'The Preservation of Yorkville Village.' Discussion Paper no. 28, York University, Department of Geography, April 1984.

Key, Barbara Elizabeth. 'The Growth of Yorkville.' BA thesis, York University, 1967.

Marquis, Greg. 'The Hippie as a Public Health Threat/Opportunity: Canada 1968–73.' Unpublished Paper, 2006.

Patterson, Ruth. 'An Exploratory Study of the Opinions of Local Religious Leaders towards Yorkville.' MSW thesis, University of Toronto, 1968.

Standish, Robert O. 'A Reality Trip on the Freaks: A Historiography of the Counterculture of the 1960s.' MA thesis, Humbolt State University, 2006.

Other Printed Primary Sources

Best, E.W.R. 'Introduction.' In *Hepatitis in Yorkville, 1968: Report of the Coordinating Committee*. Ontario Department of Health, 15 September 1969.

Byles, John A. 'Alienation, Deviance and Social Control: A Study of Adolescents in Metropolitan Toronto.' Toronto: Interim Research Project on Unreached Youth 1969.

Hetenyi, Caroline, and F.M. Hill. 'Clinical Aspects, Section I: Clinical Report.' In *Hepatitis in Yorkville, 1968: Report of the Co-ordinating Committee*. Ontario Department of Health, 15 September 1969.

Johnstone, John W.C. 'Young People's Images of Canadian Society: An Opinion Survey of Canadian Youth, 13 to 20.' Chicago: National Opinion Research Center, University of Chicago, 1966.

Kelner, Merrijoy, et al. 'The Health of Yorkville.' Unpublished Report to the Ontario Department of Health. Toronto: Department of Behavioural Science, University of Toronto, 1970.

Kileeg, John. 'Village Service Unit for Alienated Youth: The "Trailer" in Yorkville.' Report to the Social Planning Council of Metropolitan Toronto, 1968.

Longstaff, Frank. 'Yorkville: An Observational Report.' Unpublished report presented to the Interim Research Project on Unreached Youth, September 1966.

Mann, W.E. 'Canadian Trends in Premarital Behaviour.' Toronto: Anglican
   Church of Canada 1967.
Pennington, Sheila. 'For the First Time in My Life I Don't Feel That I Want
   to Run Away.' Unpublished document, Toronto Archives, Series 100, box
   46693–8, file 1245, n.d.
Smart, Reginald G., and David Jackson. 'The Yorkville Subculture: A Study of
   the Life Styles and Interactions of Hippies and Non-Hippies, Prepared from
   the Field Notes of Gopala Alampur.' Toronto: Addiction Research Foundation 1969.
Smith, James E. 'I Wish I Was A Fish: A Search for Live Options in Yorkville.'
   Unpublished, 1972.

Interviews and Correspondence

Alampur, Gopala. Interview with author, 4 February 2005.
Anonymous beat cop. Interview with author, October 2003.
Anonymous LSD dealer. Interview with author, 13 October 2006.
Banack, Alan. Interview with author, 26 June 2006.
Barber, Martin. Interview with author, 29 March 2007.
Brooks, Marilyn. Interview with author, 29 March 2007.
Callwood, June. Interview with author, 11 March 2005.
Clement, W.R. Interview with author, 5 March 2006.
Collier, Clifford. Interview with author, 15 June 2006.
DePoe, David. Interview with author, 20 December 2004.
DePoe, Suzanne. Interview with author, 14 March 2006.
Felstiner, James. Interview with author, 3 April 2006.
Ferri, Paul. Interview with author, 29 March 2007.
Gerstein, Reva. Interview with author, 25 April 2006.
Hayden, Michael. E-mail received 27 February 2007.
Jones, Burnley 'Rocky.' E-mail received 21 April 2006.
Laws, Dudley. Public presentation, 16 June 2007.
Maropakis, Miguel. Interview with author, 29 March 2007.
McLuhan, Eric. Interview with author, 11 April 2006.
Perly, Judy. Interview with author, 27 June 2006.
Pocock, Judy. Interview with author, 24 June 2006.
Richmond, Norman 'Otis.' Public presentation, 16 June 2007.
Riley Roberts, Colleen. Interview with author, 29 March 2007.
Ruby, Clayton. Interview with author, 3 March 2006.
Valpy, Michael. Interview with author, 5 October 2006.
Waage, Mike. Interview with author, 3 March 2005.

'Wild Bill.' Interview with author, 11 March 2005.
Wood, Myrna. Interview with author, 19 April 2006.

Magazines, Newspapers, and Periodicals

Canadian Literature, 65 (summer 1975).
Canadian Welfare, 1969.
Chatelaine, October 1967.
Globe and Mail, 1958–72.
Harbinger, 1968–70.
Maclean's, 23 March 1963.
New Yorker, 21 October 1967.
Playboy, September 1966.
Playboy, March 1969.
Satyrday, 1966–8.
Star Weekly Magazine, 23 September 1967.
This Magazine Is About Schools, winter 1968.
Toronto Daily Star, 1958–72.
Toronto Telegram, 1960–70.
Toronto Women's Liberation Newsletter, 1970–1.
Voice of the Annex, September 1968.

Websites and Online Materials (All Accessed 22 November 2010)

CBC Television, *Close-Up*, 'Toronto "Happening,"' 17 February 1963, http://archives.cbc.ca/IDC-1-69-580-3080/life_society/hippies/clip1.
– *News*, 10 May 1966, http://archives.cbc.ca/IDC-1-71-348-1925/conflict_war/draft_dodgers/.
– *Newsmagazine*, 4 September 1967, http://archives.cbc.ca/IDC-1-69-1587-10799/life_society/60s/clip11.
– *Special*: *Yorkville Upheaval*, 29 January 1969, http://archives.cbc.ca/IDC-1-69-580-3203/life_society/hippies/clip10.
City of Toronto. *The Modern Metropolis, 1951–*, http://www.toronto.ca/culture/history/history-1951-onward.htm.
Debord, Guy. *The Society of the Spectacle*. Translated by Ken Knabb. http://www.bopsecrets.org/SI/debord/.
Diggers Project. www.diggers.org.
Francis, Wayne. 'Lightfoot!' http://www.lightfoot.ca/lightrev.htm.
Gibson, William. http://www.williamgibsonbooks.com/archive/2003_05_01_archive.asp.

Grateful Dead Resources. http://www.celticguitarmusic.com/grateful_dead_
links.htm.

Hardwick, Tim. 'On Being God: Transcendentalism and Romanticism, a
Mystical Approach.' In 'Lila: Journal of Cosmic Play,' http://www.lila.info/
document_view.phtml?document_id=37.

Hayden, Michael. http://www.thinkinglightly.com/hayden/resume.html.

Jackson, Bruce. 'The Myth of Newport: It Wasn't Dylan They Were Booing,'
http://buffaloreport.com/020826dylan.html.

Kuchinskas, Susan. 'That's Ms. Hippie Chick to You.' *Salon.com*, 17 November
1997.

Mother Earth News, 8 (March/April 1971), http://www.motherearthnews.com/
Livestock_and_Farming/1971_March_April/Visit_To_The_Canadian_Hog_
Farm.

Recordings

Adderley, Julian 'Cannonball.' *In New York* [1962] Riverside/OJN 2000.

Lightfoot, Gordon. *Lightfoot!* United Artist Records 1966.

Sainte-Marie, Buffy. *It's My Way!* Vanguard Records 1964.

Various Artists. *Made in Canada, Volume One: The Early Years*. BMG Music 1990.

Various Artists. *Made in Canada, Volume Three: Eclectic Avenue*. BMG Music
1990.

Various Artists. *The Music Never Stopped: The Roots of the Grateful Dead*, Shanachie Records 1995.

Young, Neil. *On the Beach*. Reprise 1974.

Films

The Big Lebowski. Dir: Joel Coen, Polygram Filmed Entertainment 1998.

Christopher's Movie Matinee. Dir: Mort Ransen, National Film Board of Canada
1968.

Dream Tower. Dir: Ron Mann, National Film Board of Canada 1994.

Flowers on a One-Way Street. Dir: Robin Spry, National Film Board of Canada
1967.

Prologue. Dir: Robin Spry, National Film Board of Canada 1969.

Satan's Choice. Dir: Donald Shebib, National Film Board of Canada 1965.

The Summer of '67. Dir: Albert Kish and Donald Winkler, National Film Board
of Canada 1994.

Where Have All the Flowers Gone? Dir: Karonne Lansel, Ryerson Student Film
1988.

Wild in the Streets. Dir: Barry Shear, American International Pictures 1968.
Woodstock: Three Days of Peace and Music. Dir: Michael Wadleigh, Warner
    Brothers Pictures 1969.

Secondary Sources

Adams, Mary Louise. *The Trouble with Normal: Postwar Youth and the Making of
    Heterosexuality*. Toronto: University of Toronto Press 1997.
Adamson, Nancy. 'Feminists, Libbers, Lefties, and Radicals: The Emergence
    of the Woman's Liberation Movement.' In *A Diversity of Women: Ontario,
    1945–1980*. Toronto: University of Toronto Press 1996. 253–80.
Adamson, Nancy, Linda Briskin, and Margaret McPhail. *Feminist Organizing
    for Change*. Oxford: Oxford University Press 1988.
Allyn, David. *Make Love Not War*. Boston: Little, Brown 2000.
Anderson, Benedict. *Imagined Communities*. London: Verso 1991.
Appiah, K. Anthony. 'Identity, Authenticity, Survival: Multicultural Societies
    and Social Reproduction.' In Amy Gutmann, ed., *Multiculturalism*. Princ-
    eton, N.J.: Princeton University Press 1994.
Armour, Moira, and Pat Staton. *Canadian Women in History: A Chronology*.
    Toronto: Green Dragon Press 1990.
Baerenholdt, Joergen Ole, et al. *Performing Tourist Places*. London: Ashgate 2004.
Bailey, Beth. 'Sex as a Weapon.' In Peter Braunstein and Michael William
    Doyle, eds., *Imagine Nation: The American Counterculture of the 1960s and 70s*.
    New York: Routledge 2002.
Baudrillard, Jean. *Simulacra and Simulation*. Translated by Sheila Faria Glaser.
    Ann Arbor: University of Michigan Press 1994.
Baxandall, Rosalyn, and Linda Gordon. *Dear Sisters: Dispatches from the
    Women's Liberation Movement*. New York: Basic Books 2000.
Beard, Rick, and Leslie Cohen, eds. *Greenwich Village: Culture and Countercul-
    ture*. New Brunswick, N.J.: Rutgers University Press 1993.
Berger, John. *Ways of Seeing*. London: Penguin Books 1972.
Bernstein, Judy, et al. 'Sisters, Brothers, Lovers … Listen …' In *Women Unite!:
    Up from the Kitchen, up from the Bedroom, up from Under*. Toronto: Canadian
    Women's Educational Press 1972.
Berton, Pierre. *1967: Canada's Turning Point*. Toronto: Seal Books 1997.
Bidini, Dave. *On a Cold Road: Tales of Adventure in Canadian Rock*. Toronto:
    McClelland and Stewart 1998.
Biner, Pierre. 'The Living Theatre.' In Alexander Bloom and Wini Breines, eds.,
    Takin' It to the Streets. New York: Oxford University Press 2003. 234–7.
Binkley, Sam. *Getting Loose: Lifestyle Consumption in the 1970s*. Durham, N.C.:
    Duke University Press 2007.

Birrell, Ross, and Eric Finlay. *Justified Sinners: An Archaeology of the Scottish Counterculture, 1960–2000*. Glasgow: Polygon Books 2002.

Biskind, Peter. *Easy Riders, Raging Bulls: How the Sex-Drugs-and-Rock'n'Roll Generation Saved Hollywood*. New York: Simon and Schuster 1999.

Braunstein, Peter, and Michael William Doyle. 'Introduction.' In Braunstein and Doyle, eds., *Imagine Nation: The American Counterculture of the 1960s and 70s*. New York: Routledge 2002.

Breines, Wini. *Community Organization in the New Left, 1962–1968: The Great Refusal*. New Brunswick, N.J.: Rutgers University Press 1989.

Bronstein, Ruth. *The Hippy's Handbook*. New York: Canyon Book 1967.

Brushett, Kevin. 'Making Shit Disturbers: The Selection and Training of the Company of Young Canadian Volunteers, 1965–1970.' In M. Athena Palaeologu, ed., *The Sixties in Canada: A Turbulent and Creative Decade* (Montreal: Black Rose Books 2009), 246–69.

Burnett, David. *Toronto Painting of the 1960s*. Toronto: Art Gallery of Ontario 1983.

Butler, Judith. *Gender Trouble: Feminism and the Subversion of Identity*. London: Routledge 1990.

– *Bodies That Matter*. New York: Routledge 1993.

– *Excitable Speech*. New York: Routledge 1997.

Byles, John. 'Alienated Youth.' In W.E. Mann, ed., *The Underside of Toronto*. Toronto: McClelland and Stewart 1970.

Callwood, June. 'Digger House.' In W.E. Mann, ed., *The Underside of Toronto*. Toronto: McClelland and Stewart 1970.

Carstairs, Catherine. *Jailed for Possession: Illegal Drug Use, Regulation, and Power in Canada, 1920–1961*. Toronto: University of Toronto Press 2006.

Cavan, Sherri. *Hippies of the Haight*. St Louis, Mo.: New Critics Press 1972.

Chang, Jeff. *Can't Stop Won't Stop: A History of the Hip Hop Generation*. New York: Picador Press 2005.

Chauncey, George. *Gay New York: Gender, Urban Culture, and the Making of the Gay Male World, 1890–1940*. New York: Basic Books 1995.

Chenier, Elise. *Strangers in Our Midst: Sexual Deviancy in Postwar Ontario*. Toronto: University of Toronto Press 2008.

Churchill, David. 'Personal Ad/Politics: Race, Sexuality and Power at the Body Politic.' *Left History*, 8, no. 2 (2003): 114–34.

– 'Mother Goose's Map: Tabloid Geographies and Gay Male Experience in 1950s Toronto.' *Journal of Urban History*, 30, no. 6 (2004): 826–52.

Cleaver, Eldridge. *Soul on Ice*. New York: Delta 1968.

Cleveland, John W. 'New Left, Not New Liberal: 1960s Movements in English Canada and Quebec.' *Canadian Review of Sociology and Anthropology / Review canadienne de sociologie et anthropologie*, 41, no. 1 (2004): 67–84.

Cohen, Lizabeth. *A Consumer's Republic: The Politics of Mass Consumption in Postwar America*. New York: Vintage Books 2003.

Cohen, Stanley. *Folk Devils and Moral Panics*. London: MacGibbon and Kee 1972.

Colby, Paul, et al. *The Bitter End: Hanging out at America's Nightclub*. New York: Rowman and Littlefield 2002.

Collier, Peter, and David Horowitz. *Destructive Generation: Second Thoughts about the Sixties*. New York: Summit Books 1989.

Cowl, Nathaniel. *Sex, Drugs and Henry Thoreau: A Diary from the Canadian Woods*. Maynouth, Ont.: Snow Flea 1994.

Coyote, Peter. *Sleeping Where I Fall*. New York: Basic Books 1999.

Cruz, Jon, and Justin Lewis, eds. *Viewing, Reading, Listening: Audiences and Cultural Reception*. Boulder, Colo.: Westview Presss 1994.

Culler, Jonathan. 'Semiotics of Tourism.' *American Journal of Semiotics*, 1 (1981): 127–40.

Daly, Margaret. *The Revolution Game: The Short, Unhappy Life of the Company of Young Canadians*. Toronto: New Press 1970.

Davidson, Sara. *Loose Change*. New York: Doubleday 1977.

DeLillo, Don. *White Noise*. New York: Penguin Books 1984.

Derrida, Jacques. *The Ear of the Other*. Translated by Peggy Kamuf et al. Lincoln: University of Nebraska Press 1998.

Dickerson, James. *North to Canada: Men and Women against the Vietnam War*. Westport, Conn.: Praeger 1999.

Dickstein, Morris. *Gates of Eden: American Culture in the Sixties*. New York: Basic Books 1977.

Didion, Joan. *Slouching towards Bethleham*. New York: Farrar, Straus and Giroux 1990.

Donne, John. *The Complete Poetry and Selected Prose of John Donne*. Edited by Charles M. Coffin. New York: Modern Library 2004.

Doyle, Michael William. 'Staging the Revolution.' In Peter Braunstein and Michael William Doyle, eds., *Imagine Nation: The American Counterculture of the 1960s and 70s*. New York: Routledge 2002. 71–98.

Dubinsky, Karen. *The Second Greatest Disappointment: Honeymooners, Heterosexuality and the Tourist Industry at Niagara Falls*. New Brunswick, N.J.: Rutgers University Press 1999.

– *Babies without Borders: Adoption and Migration across the Americas*. Toronto: University of Toronto Press 2010.

Dunn, Christopher. *Brutality Garden: Tropicalia and the Emergence of a Brazilian Counterculture*. Chapel Hill: University of North Carolina Press 2000.

Dyck, Erika. *Psychedelic Psychiatry: LSD from Clinic to Campus*. Baltimore: Johns Hopkins University Press 2008.

Dyer, Gillian. *Advertising as Communication*. London: Methuen Books 1982.

Early, Gerald L. *This Is Where I Came In: Black America in the 1960s*. Lincoln: University of Nebraska Press 2003.

Echols, Alice. *Daring to be Bad: Radical Feminism in America, 1967–1975*. Minneapolis: University of Minnesota Press 1989.

– *Scars of Sweet Paradise: The Life and Times of Janis Joplin*. New York: Henry Holt 2000.

– *Shaky Ground: The Sixties and Its Aftershocks*. New York: Columbia University Press 2002.

Einarson, John. *Don't Be Denied: Neil Young: The Canadian Years*. Kingston, Ont.: Quarry Press 1992.

Emberley, Peter C., ed. *By Loving Our Own: George Grant and the Legacy of Lament for a Nation*. Ottawa: Carleton University Press 1990.

Enstad, Nan. *Ladies of Labor, Girls of Adventure*. New York: Columbia University Press 1999.

Evans, Caroline. *Fashion at the Edge: Spectacle, Modernity and Deathliness*. New Haven, Conn.: Yale University Press 2003.

Ewen, Stuart. *All Consuming Images: The Politics of Style in Contemporary Culture*. New York: Basic Books 1988.

Fahrni, Magda. *Household Politics: Montreal Families and Postwar Reconstruction*. Toronto: University of Toronto Press 2005.

Fetherling, Douglas. *Way Down Deep in the Belly of the Beast: A Memoir of the Seventies*. Toronto: Lester 1996.

– *Travels by Night: A Memoir of the Sixties*. Toronto: McArthur 2000.

Foucault, Michel. *The History of Sexuality, Vol. I: An Introduction*. Translated by Robert Hurley. New York: Pantheon 1978.

– 'The Birth of the Asylum.' In Paul Rabinow, ed., *The Foucault Reader*. New York: Pantheon 1984.

– 'Truth and Power.' In Paul Rabinow, ed., *The Foucault Reader*. New York: Pantheon Books 1984.

Frank, Thomas. *The Conquest of Cool: Business Culture, Counterculture, and the Rise of Hip Consumerism*. Chicago: University of Chicago Press 1997.

Freud, Sigmund. *Freud: Dictionary of Psychoanalysis*. Edited by Frank Gaynor. New York: Barnes and Noble Books 2003.

Friedan, Betty. *The Feminine Mystique*. Toronto: George G. McLeod Books 1963.

Frost, Jennifer. *An Interracial Movement of the Poor: Community Organizing and the New Left in the 1960s*. New York: New York University Press 2001.

Fuss, Diana. *Essentially Speaking: Feminism, Nature and Difference*. New York: Routledge 1990.

Gaskin, Stephen. *Haight-Ashbury Flashbacks: Amazing Dope Tales of the Sixties*. Berkeley, Calif.: Ronin 1998.

Giddens, Anthony. *Modernity and Self Identity*. Palo Alto, Calif.: Stanford University Press 1991.

Giffen, P.J., et al. *Panic and Indifference: The Politics of Canada's Drug Laws*. Ottawa: Canadian Centre on Substance Abuse 1991.

Ginsberg, Allen. *Howl and Other Poems*. San Francisco: City Lights Publishing 1991.

Gitlin, Todd. *The Sixties: Years of Hope, Days of Rage*. Toronto: Bantam Books 1987.

– *The Whole World Is Watching: Mass Media in the Making and Unmaking of the New Left*. 2nd ed. Berkeley: University of California Press 2003.

Gleason, Mona. *Normalizing the Ideal: Psychology, Schooling, and the Family in Postwar Canada*. Toronto: University of Toronto Press 1999.

Goffman, Ken (a.k.a. R.U. Sirius), and Dan Joy. *Counterculture through the Ages*. New York: Vintage 2004.

Gosse, Van. *Rethinking the New Left: An Interpretive History*. New York: Palgrave Macmillan 2005.

Gramsci, Antonio. *Selections from the Prison Notebooks*. Edited and translated by Quintin Hoare et al. New York: International Publishers 1971.

Grant, George. *Lament for a Nation: The Defeat of Canadian Nationalism*. Toronto: McClelland and Stewart 1965.

Grof, Stanislav. *LSD Psychotherapy: Exploring the Frontiers of the Human Mind*. Almeda, Calif.: Hunter House Books 1994.

Hagan, John. *Northern Passage: American Vietnam War Resisters in Canada*. Cambridge, Mass.: Harvard University Press 2001.

Hajdu, David. *Positively Fourth Street: The Lives and Times of Joan Baez, Bob Dylan, Mimi Baez Fariña and Richard Fariña*. New York: North Point Press 2002.

Halbwachs, Maurice. *The Collective Memory*. New York: Harper Colophon 1980.

Hall, Stuart. 'Culture, the Media, and the Ideological Effect.' In James Curran et al., *Mass Communication and Society*. London: Edward Arnold 1977.

Hall, Tim. *Urban Geography*. New York: Routledge 2001.

Hamilton, Ian. *The Children's Crusade: The Story of the Company of Young Canadians*. Toronto: Peter Martin Associates 1970.

Harris, Richard. *Creeping Conformity*. Toronto: University of Toronto Press 2004.

Havens, Ritchie. *They Can't Hide Us Anymore*. New York: William Morrow 2000.

Heath, Joseph, and Andrew Potter. *The Rebel Sell: How the Counter Culture Became Consumer Culture*. West Sussex, U.K.: Capstone Publishing 2005.

Henderson, Stuart. 'Toronto's Hippie Disease: End Days in the Yorkville Scene, August 1968.' *Journal of the Canadian Historical Association*, 17, no. 1 (2006): 205–34.

Hoberman, J. *The Dream Life: Movies, Media and the Mythology of the Sixties*. New York: New Press 2005.

Holmes-Moss, Kristy. 'Negotiating the Nation: "Expanding" the Work of Joyce Wieland.' *Canadian Journal of Film Studies*, 15, no. 2 (fall 2006): 20–43.

Hoskyns, Barney. *Across the Great Divide: The Band and America*. London: Viking 1993.

Houlbrook, Matt. *Queer London: Perils and Pleasures in the Sexual Metropolis, 1918–1957*. Chicago: University of Chicago Press 2005.

Huxley, Aldous. *The Doors of Perception and Heaven and Hell*. New York: Harper Collins 2004.

Iacovetta, Franca. *Gatekeepers: Reshaping Immigrant Lives in Cold War Canada*. Toronto: Between the Lines 2006.

Innis, Harold. *The Bias of Communication*. 2nd ed. Toronto: University of Toronto Press 971.

Isserman, Maurice. *If I Had a Hammer: The Death of the Old Left and the Birth of the New Left*. Chicago: University of Illinois Press 1993.

Isserman, Maurice, and Michael Kazin. *America Divided: The Civil War of the 1960s*. Oxford: Oxford University Press 2000.

Jackson, Blair. *Garcia: An American Life*. New York: Penguin 2000.

Jackson, Peter. *Maps of Meaning*. New York: Routledge 1989; 1993.

Jacobs, Jane M. *Edge of Empire: Postcolonialism and the City*. New York: Routledge 1996.

Jacobson, Matthew Frye. *Whiteness of a Different Color: European Immigrants and the Alchemy of Race*. Cambridge, Mass.: Harvard University Press 1998.

Jay, Martin. *Downcast Eyes: The Denigration of Vision in Twentieth-Century French Thought*. Berkeley: University of California Press 1993.

– *Force Fields: Between Intellectual History and Cultural Critique*. New York: Routledge 1993.

Jenkins, Philip. *Decade of Nightmares: The End of the Sixties and the Making of Eighties America*. Oxford: Oxford University Press 2006.

Jenks, Chris. 'The Centrality of the Eye in Western Culture.' In Jenks, ed., *Visual Culture*. New York: Routledge 1995.

Jennings, Nicholas. *Before the Gold Rush: Flashbacks to the Dawn of the Canadian-Sound*. Toronto: Penguin Books 1997.

Kerouac, Jack. *On the Road*. New York: Penguin Books 1955.

Kimball, Roger. *The Long March: How the Cultural Revolution of the 1960s Changed America*. New York: Encounter Books 2000.

Klatch, Rebecca. *Generation Divided: The New Left, the New Right and the 1960s.* Berkeley: University of California Press 1999.

Knight, Brenda. *Women of the Beat Generation: The Writers, Artists and Muses at the Heart of a Revolution.* New York: Conari Press 1998.

Knowles, Valerie. *Strangers at Our Gates: Canadian Immigration and Immigration Policy, 1540–2006.* Rev. ed. Toronto: Dundurn Press 2007.

Koedt, Anne. 'The Myth of the Vaginal Orgasm.' In Alexander Bloom and Wini Breines, eds., *Takin' It to the Streets.* New York: Oxford University Press 2003. 422–8.

Koestenbaum, Wayne. *Andy Warhol.* New York: Viking Books 2001.

Korinek, Valerie. *Roughing It in the Suburbs: Reading Chatelaine Magazine in the Fifties and Sixties.* Toronto: University of Toronto Press 2000.

Kornbluth, Jesse. *Notes from the New Underground.* New York: Viking 1968.

Kostash, Myrna. *Long Way from Home: The Story of the Sixties Generation in Canada.* Toronto: James Lorimer 1980.

Kreps, Bonnie. 'Radical Feminism 1.' In *Women Unite!: Up from the Kitchen, up from the Bedroom, up from Under.* Toronto: Canadian Women's Educational Press 1972.

Leclerc, Denise, and Pierre Dessureault. *The Sixties in Canada.* Ottawa: National Gallery of Canada 2005.

Leland, John. *Hip: The History.* New York: Echo 2004.

Lemke-Santangelo, Gretchen. *Daughters of Aquarius: Women of the Sixties Counterculture.* Lawrence: University Press of Kansas 2009.

Lesh, Phil. *Searching for the Sound: My Life with the Grateful Dead.* New York: Little, Brown 2005.

Levitt, Cyril. *Children of Privilege: Student Revolt in the Sixties.* Toronto: University of Toronto Press 1984.

Lind, Jane. *Joyce Wieland: Artist on Fire.* Toronto: Lorimer 2001.

Lloyd, Richard. *Neo-Bohemia: Art and Commerce in the Post-Industrial City.* New York: Routledge 2005.

Lobenthal, Joel. *Radical Rags.* New York: Abbeville Books 2003.

Loo, Tina. 'Flower Children in Lotusland.' *The Beaver* (February/March 1998), 36–7.

Lyotard, Jean-François. *The Postmodern Condition: A Report on Knowledge.* Translated by Geoff B. Bennington and Brian M. Massumi. Minneapolis: University of Minnesota Press 1993.

MacCannell, Dean. *The Tourist: A New Theory of the Leisure Class.* Berkeley: University of California Press 1999.

Mackowycz, Henry, and Bob Mietkiewicz. *Dream Tower: The Life and Legacy of Rochdale College.* Toronto: Ryerson 1988.

Mailer, Norman. 'The White Negro: Superficial Reflections on the Hipster.' In *Advertisements for Myself*. Cambridge, Mass.: Harvard University Press 2005. 337–58.

Major, Clarence. *Juba to Jive: A Dictionary of African American Slang*. Harmondsworth, U.K.: Penguin 1994.

Mann, W.E., ed. *The Underside of Toronto*. Toronto: McClelland and Stewart 1970.

Marcus, Daniel. *Happy Days and Wonder Years: The Fifties and Sixties in Contemporary Politics*. New Brunswick, N.J.: Rutgers University Press 2004.

Marcus, Greil. *Like a Rolling Stone: Bob Dylan at the Crossroads*. New York: Public Affairs 2005.

Marcuse, Herbert. *Eros and Civilization*. Boston: Beacon Press 1955; 1966.

– *An Essay on Liberation*. Boston: Beacon Press 1969.

Martel, Marcel. *Not This Time: Canadians, Public Policy and the Marijuana Question, 1961–1975*. Toronto: University of Toronto Press 2006.

– 'They Smell Bad, Have Diseases, and Are Lazy: RCMP Officers Reporting on Hippies in the Late Sixties.' *Canadian Historical Review*, 90, no. 2 (2009): 215–45.

Martin, Bradford D. *The Theater Is in the Street*. Boston: University of Massachusetts Press 2004.

Marx, Karl. *Early Political Writings*. Edited and translated by Joseph O'Malley with Richard A. Davis. Cambridge: Cambridge University Press 1994.

Maynard, Stephen. 'Through a Hole in the Lavatory Wall: Homosexual Subcultures, Police Surveillance, and the Dialectics of Discovery, Toronto, 1890–1930.' In Joy Parr and Mark Rosenfeld, eds., *Gender and History in Canada*. Toronto: Copp Clark 1996. 165–84.

McDonough, Jimmy. *Shakey: Neil Young's Biography*. New York: Random House 2002.

McLaren, Angus, and Arlene Tigar McLaren. *The Bedroom and the State: The Changing Practices and Politics of Contraception and Abortion in Canada, 1880–1996*. New York: Oxford University Press 1986; 1998.

McLauchlan, Murray. *Getting out of Here Alive*. Toronto: Penguin Canada 1998.

McLuhan, Marshall. *Understanding Media: The Extensions of Man*. Toronto: Signet Books 1964.

– *Essential McLuhan*. Edited by Eric McLuhan and Frank Zingrone. Concord, Ont.: House of Anansi Press 1995.

McNally, Dennis. *The Long Strange Trip: An Inside Story of the Grateful Dead*. New York: Broadway Books 2002.

McNeill, Don. *Moving through Here*. New York: Citadel 1990.

Medovoi, Leerom. *Rebels: Youth and the Cold War Origins of Identity*. Durham, N.C.: Duke University Press, 2005.

Mehta, Gita. *Karma Cola: Marketing the Mystic East*. New York: Vintage Books 1979; 1994.

Mercer, Kobena. '1968: Periodizing Politics and Identity.' In Lawrence Grossberg, Cary Nelson, and Paula Treichler, eds., *Cultural Studies*. New York: Routledge 1992.

Michals, Debra. 'From Consciousness Expansion to Consciousness Raising: Feminism and the Countercultural Politics of the Self.' In Peter Braunstein and Michael William Doyle, eds., *Imagine Nation: The American Counterculture of the 1960s and 1970s*. New York: Routledge 2002.

Miedema, Gary. *For Canada's Sake: Public Religion, Centennial Celebrations, and the Re-Making of Canada in the 1960s*. Montreal and Kingston: McGill-Queen's University Press 2005.

Miller, Daniel, et al. *Shopping, Place and Identity*. London: Routledge 1998.

Miller, Timothy. *The Hippies and American Values*. Knoxville: University of Tennessee Press 1991.

Mills, Sean. *The Empire Within: Postcolonial Thought and Political Activism in Sixties Montreal*. Montreal and Kingston: McGill-Queen's University Press 2010.

Morton, Suzanne. *Ideal Surroundings*. Toronto: University of Toronto Press 1995.

Nicholson, Virginia. *Among the Bohemians*. New York: Harper Perennials 2004.

Nicosia, Gerald. *Memory Babe: A Critical Biography of Jack Kerouac*. New York: Grove Press 1983.

Nietzsche, Friedrich. *The Will to Power*. Translated by Walter Kaufmann. New York: Vintage 1968.

Nowell, Iris. *Joyce Wieland: A Life in Art*. Toronto: ECW Press 2001.

O'Brien, Karen. *Shadows and Light: Joni Mitchell*. London: Virgin Books 2001.

Osborne, Ralph. *From Someplace Else: A Memoir*. Toronto: ECW Press 2003.

Owram, Doug. *Born at the Right Time: A History of the Baby Boom Generation*. Toronto: University of Toronto Press 1996.

Packard, Vance. *The Hidden Persuaders*. New York: Random House 1957.

Palmer, Bryan D. *Canada's 1960s: The Ironies of Identity in a Rebellious Era*. Toronto: University of Toronto Press 2009.

Parr, Joy. *Domestic Goods: The Material, the Moral, and the Economic in the Postwar Years*. Toronto: University of Toronto Press 1999.

Partridge, William L. *The Hippie Ghetto: The Natural History of a Subculture*. New York: Holt, Reinhart and Winston 1973.

Perks, Robert, and Alistair Thomson. 'Critical Developments.' In Perks and Thomson, eds., *The Oral History Reader*. New York: Routledge 2006.

Perry, Charles. *The Haight-Ashbury: A History*. New York: Random House 1984.

– 'The Port Huron Statement.' In Alexander Bloom and Wini Breines, eds.,

Takin' It to the Streets: A Sixties Reader. New York: Oxford University Press 2003.

Potter, Greg. *Hand Me Down World*. Toronto: Macmillan 1999.

Powe, B.W. *The Solitary Outlaw*. Toronto: Lester and Orpen Dennys 1987.

Rappaport, Amos. *The Meaning of the Built Environment*. Tuscon: University of Arizona Press 1990.

Rebick, Judy. *Ten Thousand Roses*. New York: Penguin Books 2005.

Reich, Charles. *The Greening of America*. New York: Bantam Books 1970.

Reid, Dennis. 'Marcel Duchamp in Canada.' *Canadian Art*, 4, no. 4 (winter 1987): 52–4.

Reid, Dennis, and Matthew Teitelbaum. *Greg Curnoe: Life and Stuff*. Vancouver: Douglas and McIntyre 2001.

Reid, John. *The Faithless Mirror: An Historical Novel*. Toronto: Darkwood Press 1975.

Ricard, François. *The Lyric Generation: The Life and Times of Baby Boomers*. Translated by Donald Winkler. Toronto: Stoddart 1994.

Riley, Denise. *Am I That Name?: Feminism and the Category of 'Women' in History*. Minneapolis: University of Minnesota Press 1988.

Riley Roberts, Colleen. *The Life and Times of a Single Woman*. Bloomington, Ind.: Author House 2004.

Rilke, Rainer Maria. *Selected Poetry*. Edited and translated by Stephen Mitchell. New York: Vintage 1989.

Robbins, Tom. *Even Cowgirls Get the Blues*. New York: Houghton Mifflin 1976.

Roediger, David R. *The Wages of Whiteness: Race and the Making of the American Working-Class*. London: Verso 1999.

Ross, Becki L. *The House That Jill Built: A Lesbian Nation in Formation*. Toronto: University of Toronto Press 1995.

– '"Down at the Whorehouse?": Reflections on Christian Community Service and Female Sex Deviance at Toronto's Street Haven, 1965–1969.' *Atlantis: A Women's Studies Journal*, 23, no. 1 (1998): 48–59.

Ross, Kristin. *May '68 and Its Afterlives*. Chicago: University of Chicago Press 2002.

Rossinow, Doug. *The Politics of Authenticity: Liberalism, Christianity and the New Left in America*. New York: Columbia University Press 1998.

Roszak, Theodore. *The Making of a Counterculture*. Garden City, N.Y.: Doubleday Anchor 1969.

Rotenberg, Robert. 'Introduction.' In Rotenberg et al., *The Cultural Meaning of Urban Space*. Westport, Conn.: Bergin and Garvey 1993.

Roussopoulos, Dimitrios J. *The New Left in Canada*. Montreal: Black Rose Books 1970.

Ruby, Clayton, and Paul Copeland. *law law law*. Toronto: Anansi 1970.

Said, Edward. *Orientalism*. New York: Pantheon Books 1978.

Sartre, Jean-Paul. *Nausea*. Translated by Lloyd Alexander. New York: New Directions Publishing 1964.

– *Notebooks for an Ethics*. Translated by David Pellauer. Chicago: University of Chicago Press 1992.

Schumacher, Michael. *There but for Fortune: The Life of Phil Ochs*. New York: Hyperion 1996.

Scott, Joan W. 'Experience.' *Critical Inquiry*, 17 (summer 1991): 773–97.

Seeley, John, et al. *Crestwood Heights: A Study of the Culture of Suburban Life*. Toronto: University of Toronto Press 1956.

Sendak, Maurice. *Where the Wild Things Are*. Toronto: Harper Collins Canada 1963; 1988.

Sethna, Christabelle. 'The University of Toronto Health Service, Oral Contraception and Student Demand for Birth Control, 1960–1970.' *Historical Studies in Education / Revue d'histoire de l'éducation*, 17, no. 2 (2005): 265–92.

– 'The Evolution of the Birth Control Handbook: From Student Peer Education Manual to Feminist Self-Help Text, 1968–1975.' *Canadian Bulletin of Medical History / Bulletin canadien d'histoire de la medicine*, 23, no. 1 (2006): 89–117.

Sewell, John. *The Shape of the City*. Toronto: University of Toronto Press 1993.

Shah, Nayan. *Contagious Divides: Epidemics and Race in San Francisco's Chinatown*. Berkeley: University of California Press 2001.

Sharpe, David. *Rochdale: The Runaway College*. Toronto: Anansi Press 1987.

Shires, Preston. *Hippies of the Religious Right*. Waco, Tex.: Baylor University Press 2007.

Skerl, Jennie. *Reconstructing the Beats*. New York: Palgrave Macmillan 2004.

Slick, Grace. *Somebody to Love?: A Rock and Roll Memoir*. New York: Warner Books 1998.

Smith, David E., et al. 'The Health of Haight-Ashbury.' In Howard S. Becker, ed., *Culture and Civility in San Francisco*. San Francisco: Transaction 1971.

Smith, Neil. *The New Urban Frontier: Gentrification and the Revanchist City*. New York: Routledge 1996.

Smith, Neil, and Peter Williams. *Gentrification of the City*. Boston: Allen and Unwin 1986.

Sontag, Susan. 'Happenings: An Art of Radical Juxtaposition.' In *Against Interpretation and Other Essays*. New York: Picador Books 2001.

Stansell, Christine. *American Moderns*. New York: Owl Books 2001.

Strange, Carolyn. *Toronto's Girl Problem: The Perils and Pleasures of the City, 1880–1930*. Toronto: University of Toronto Press 1998.

Takaki, Ronald. *A Different Mirror: A History of Multicultural America*. London: Back Bay Books 1994.

Taylor, Charles. *The Malaise of Modernity*. Concord, Ont.: House of Anansi 1991.

Thompson, Hunter S. *Hell's Angels: A Strange and Terrible Saga*. New York: Random House 1967.

– *Fear and Loathing in Las Vegas*. New York: Vintage Books, 1971; 1998.

Turner, Peter. *There Can Be No Light without Shadow*. Toronto: Rochdale College Publications 1971.

Twitchell, James B. *Carnival Culture: The Trashing of Taste in America*. New York: Columbia University Press 1992.

Urry, John. *The Tourist Gaze*. London: Sage Publishing 1990; 2002.

Varon, Jeremy. *Bringing the War Home*. Berkeley: University of California Press 2004.

Verzuh, Ron. *Underground Times: Canada's Flower-Child Revolutionaries*. Ottawa: Deneau 1989.

Viswanathan, Gauri. *Outside the Fold: Conversion, Modernity, and Belief*. Princeton, N.J.: Princeton University Press 1998.

Von Dirke, Sabine. *All Power to the Imagination: The West German Counterculture from the Student Movement to the Greens*. Lincoln: University of Nebraska Press 1997.

Von Hoffman, Nicholas. *We Are the People Our Parents Warned Us Against*. Chicago: Elephant Paperbacks 1968.

Vonnegut, Kurt. *Slaughterhouse-Five: Or the Children's Crusade, a Duty Dance with Death*. New York: Laurel Books 1969; 1991.

Walkowitz, Judith R. *City of Dreadful Delight*. Chicago: University of Chicago Press 1992.

West, Bruce. *Toronto*. Garden City, N.Y.: Doubleday 1967.

Westhues, Kenneth. *Society's Shadow: Studies in the Sociologies of Countercultures*. Toronto: McGraw-Hill Ryerson 1972.

Wetzsteon, Ross. *Republic of Dreams, Greenwich Village: The American Bohemia, 1915–1960*. New York: Simon and Schuster 2003.

Williams, Paul. *Neil Young: Love to Burn: 30 Years of Speaking Out*. London: Omnibus Press 1997.

Williams, Raymond. 'Base and Superstructure in Marxist Cultural Theory.' *New Left Review*, 82 (1973): 3–16.

– *Marxism and Literature*. Oxford: Oxford University Press 1977.

– *Keywords: A Vocabulary of Culture and Society*. Rev. ed. Oxford: Oxford University Press 1990.

Witcover, Jules. *The Year the Dream Died: Revisiting 1968 in America*. New York: Warner Books 1997.

Wolfe, Tom. *The Electric Kool-Aid Acid Test*. New York: Farrar, Straus and Giroux 1969.

Wood, John. 'Hell's Angels and the Illusion of the Counterculture.' *Journal of Popular Culture*, 37, no. 2 (2003): 336–51.

Yablonsky, Lewis. *The Hippie Trip*. New York: Pegasus 1968.

Yarbrough, Stephen. *After Rhetoric*. Carbondale, Ill.: University of Southern Illinois Press 1999.

Yinger, J. Milton. *Countercultures: The Promise and Peril of a World Turned Upside Down*. New York: The Free Press 1982.

Yorke, Ritchie. *Axes, Chops and Hot Licks*. Edmonton: M.G. Hurtig 1971.

Young, Scott. *Neil and Me*. Toronto: McClelland and Stewart 1984.

Yow, Valerie. '"Do I Like Them Too Much?": Effects of the Oral History Interview on the Interviewer and Vice Versa.' In Robert Perks and Alistair Thomson, eds., *The Oral History Reader*. New York: Routledge 2006.

Zolov, Eric. *Refried Elvis: The Rise of the Mexican Counterculture*. Berkeley: University of California Press 2002.

Illustration Credits

Author's collection: *Satyrday* endorses Trudeau (sort of) (May 1968); 'The Futility of Dropping Out' (April 1968); Penny Farthing Coffee House menu (summer 1968); The Trailer's calling card (circa 1969).

GetStock.com: 'A little bit of Europe' (2085200086, 25 July 1963, Photographer: Harold Whyte); Making the scene by day (2085200026, 18 April 1966, Photographer: Reg Innell); June Callwood (2084200552, summer 1968, Photographer: Frank Lennon); The 'Yorkville Hip Parade' (2085200001, June 1968, Photographer: Reg Innell); 'Hippie Hepatitis' (2085200080, 7 August 1968, Photographer: Barry Philp).

York University, Clara Thomas Archives, Toronto Telegram fonds: The Dirty Shames (Image 580, 21 December 1965, Photographer: McFadden); The city fathers tour Yorkville (ASC Image 601, 29 May 1965, Photographer: Sale); The Sparrows at Chez Monique (ASC Image 612, 3 January 1966, Photographer: Sale); Critical mass at the traffic protest (ASC Image 616, 22 August 1967, Photographer: Terry Hancey); 'The Crawl' (ASC Image 614, 17 July 1967, Photographer: Russell); The generation gap personified? (ASC Image 621, 17–18 August 1967, Photographer: Julian Hayashi); A trio of bikers (ASC Image 638, 22 June 1968, Photographer: Loek).

Index